History as Literature

by Orville Prescott

History as Literature

Princes of the Renaissance

A Father Reads to His Children:
An Anthology of Prose and Poetry

The Undying Past

Mid-Century: An Anthology of Distinguished
Contemporary Short Stories

The Five-Dollar Gold Piece:
The Development of a Point of View

In My Opinion: An Inquiry into
the Contemporary Novel

History as

Literature

Edited and with an Introduction by

ORVILLE PRESCOTT

HARPER & ROW, PUBLISHERS

NEW YORK AND EVANSTON

FIRST EDITION

LIBRARY OF CONGRESS CATALOG CARD NUMBER: 72-123959

ACKNOWLEDGMENTS

"The Downfall of Croesus" from *The Persian Wars* by Herodotus. Translated by George Rawlinson.

"Melos and the Politics of Power" from *The History of the War Fought Between Athens and Sparta* by Thucydides. Translated by Rex Warner. Copyright 1954 by Rex Warner. Published by Penguin Books Ltd. Reprinted by permission.

"Woe to the Vanquished" from *The Early History of Rome* by Livy. Translated by Aubrey de Selincourt. Copyright © 1960 by Aubrey de Selincourt. Reprinted by permission of Penguin Books Ltd.

"The Ides of March" from *The Greatness and Decline of Rome* by Guglielmo Ferrero. Translated by Alfred E. Zimmern. Copyright 1907 by G. P. Putnam's Sons. Reprinted by permission of the publisher.

"Antony and Cleopatra" from *The Lives of the Noble Grecians and Romans* by Plutarch. Translated by Thomas North, edited and revised by Roland Baughman. From The Heritage Press edition, copyright 1941, 1969 by The George Macy Companies, Inc. Reprinted by permission of the publisher.

"Imperial Matricide" from *The Annals of Imperial Rome* by Tacitus. Translated by Michael Grant. Copyright © 1956 by Michael Grant. Reprinted by permission of Penguin Books Ltd.

"Imperial Suicide" from *The Twelve Caesars* by Suetonius. Translated by Robert Graves. Copyright © 1957 by Robert Graves. Published by Penguin Books Ltd. Reprinted by permission of Robert Graves and Collins-Knowlton-Wing, Inc.

"The Emperor Septimus Severus" from *The Decline and Fall of the Roman Empire* by Edward Gibbon.

"Two Holy Men" from *History of the Franks* by Gregory of Tours. Translated by Ernest Brehaut. Copyright 1916 by Ernest Brehaut. Reprinted by permission of the Columbia University Press.

"What Counsel Edwin Took with His Nobles About Embracing the Faith of Christ; and How His High Priest Profaned His Own Altars" from *The Ecclesiastical History of the English People* by Bede. Translated by J. A. Giles. Copyright © 1968 by Simon & Schuster, Inc. Reprinted by permission of Simon & Schuster, Inc.

"Death of the Conqueror" from *William the Conqueror* by George Slocombe. Copyright © 1959 by George Slocombe. Reprinted by permission of Harold Ober Associates Incorporated and David Higham Associates, Ltd.

"Jerusalem Delivered" from *The Crusades* by Zoé Oldenbourg. Translated by

Anne Carter. Copyright © 1966 by Random House, Inc. Reprinted by permission of Pantheon Books, a division of Random House, Inc.

"The Burghers of Calais" from *Chronicles* by Jean Froissart. Translated by Geoffrey Brereton. Copyright © 1968 by Geoffrey Brereton. Published by Penguin Books Ltd. Reprinted by permission of the publisher.

"The Black Death" from *The Age of Chivalry: The Atlantic Saga* by Sir Arthur Bryant. Copyright © 1963 by Arthur Bryant. Reprinted by permission of Doubleday & Company, Inc.

"The Violent Tenor of Life" from *The Waning of the Middle Ages* by J. Huizinga. Reprinted by permission of St. Martin's Press and Edward Arnold, Ltd.

"The Last Days of Louis XI" from *The Memoirs of Philip de Commines.* Edited by Andrew R. Scoble.

"The Princes in the Tower" from *History of King Richard III* by Sir Thomas More.

"The Character of Henry VII" from *History of the Reign of Henry VII* by Francis Bacon.

"The Personality of Erasmus" from *The English Spirit: Essays in Literature and History* by A. L. Rowse. Copyright © 1966 by A. L. Rowse. Reprinted by permission of the publisher, Funk & Wagnalls, New York, and Curtis Brown, Ltd.

"The Golden Age of Spain" from *Great River* by Paul Horgan. Copyright 1954 by Paul Horgan. Reprinted by permission of Holt, Rinehart and Winston, Inc.

"The Great Montezuma" from *The Discovery and Conquest of Mexico* by Bernal Diaz del Castillo. Translated by A. P. Maudslay. Copyright © 1956 by Farrar, Straus & Cudahy. Reprinted by permission of Farrar, Straus & Giroux, Inc.

"The 'Noche Triste' " from *History of the Conquest of Mexico* by William H. Prescott.

"The Terrible Duke of Alva" from *The Rise of the Dutch Republic* by John Lothrop Motley.

"A Queen Possessed by a Hundred Thousand Devils" from *A History of the English People* by John Richard Green.

"The Execution at Fotheringhay Castle" from *History of England from the Fall of Wolsey to the Defeat of the Armada* by James Anthony Froude.

"San Lorenzo de Escorial" from *The Armada* by Garrett Mattingly. Copyright © 1959 by Garrett Mattingly. Reprinted by permission of the publisher, Houghton Mifflin Company.

"The Tragic Folly of the Earl of Essex" from *History of England* by David Hume.

"Sir John Harington" from *Portraits in Miniature* by Lytton Strachey. Copyright 1931 by Lytton Strachey; copyright © 1959 by James Strachey. Reprinted by permission of Harcourt Brace Jovanovich, Inc.

"John Hampden" from *The True Historical Narrative of the Rebellion and Civil Wars in England* by Edward Hyde, First Earl of Clarendon.

Acknowledgments

"The Thirtieth of January" from *Oliver Cromwell* by John Buchan. Copyright 1934 by John Buchan. Reprinted by permission of the Trustees of the Tweedsmuir Estate and Hodder & Stoughton.

"The Persecution of the Protestants by Louis XIV" from *The Age of Louis XIV* by Voltaire. Translated by J. H. Brumfit. Copyright © 1963 by Washington Square Press, Inc. Reprinted by permission of Washington Square Press division of Simon & Schuster, Inc.

"Justice Jeffreys and the Bloody Assizes" from *History of England* by Thomas Babington Macaulay.

"The Duke of Marlborough" from *England Under Queen Anne*, Volume I by George M. Trevelyan. Reprinted by permission of the Longman Group Limited.

"The King's Selfishness" from *The Memoirs of Louis de Rouvroy Duc de Saint-Simon Covering the Years 1691-1723* by Saint-Simon. Translated by Desmond Flower and Ralph Wright in The Heritage Press edition. Copyright © 1959 by The George Macy Companies, Inc. Reprinted by permission of the publisher.

"The World" from *The Young Melbourne*, by David Cecil. Copyright 1939 by David Cecil. Reprinted by permission of the publishers, The Bobbs-Merrill Company, Inc., and David Higham Associates, Ltd.

"Major-General James Wolfe" from *Montcalm and Wolfe* by Francis Parkman.

"The Heights of Abraham" from *Montcalm and Wolfe* by Francis Parkman.

"Benjamin Franklin" from *The American Revolution* by George Otto Trevelyan. Copyright 1914 by Longmans, Green & Co. Copyright renewed 1941 by Charles Philip Trevelyan, George Macaulay Trevelyan and Robert Calverley Trevelyan. Copyright © 1964 by Richard B. Morris. Reprinted by permission of David McKay Company, Inc.

"Thomas Jefferson: A Portrait" from *Jefferson and Hamilton* by Claude G. Bowers. Copyright © 1953 by Claude G. Bowers. Reprinted by permission of the publisher, Houghton Mifflin Company.

"Treason Most Foul" from *George Washington in the American Revolution 1775-1783* by James Thomas Flexner. Copyright © 1967, 1968 by James Thomas Flexner. Reprinted by permission of Little, Brown and Co.

"Maillard, the Consumptive" from *The Turbulent City: Paris 1783-1871* by André Castelot. Translated by Denise Folliot. Copyright © 1962 by André Storms. Reprinted by permission of Harper & Row, Publishers, Inc.

"The Ohio Frontier" from *Wilderness for Sale* by Walter Havighurst. Copyright © 1956 by Walter Havighurst. Reprinted by permission of Hastings House, Publishers, Inc.

"Women and General Bonaparte" from *Bonaparte in Egypt* by J. Christopher Herold. Copyright © 1962 by J. Christopher Herold. Reprinted by permission of Harper & Row, Publishers, Inc.

"Women and the Emperor Napoleon" from *In Search of Two Characters* by Dormer Creston. Copyright 1946 by Charles Scribner's Sons. Reprinted by permission of Charles Scribner's Sons and Macmillan & Co. Ltd.

"The Last of the *Tonquin*" from *Astoria* by Washington Irving.

"Waterloo" from *Wellington* by Philip Guedalla. Copyright 1931 by Philip Guedalla; copyright renewed 1959 by Nellie Guedalla. Reprinted by permission of Mrs. Guedalla.

"Mountain Men" from *The Final Challenge* by Dale Van Every. Copyright © 1964 by Dale Van Every. Reprinted by permission of William Morrow and Company, Inc.

"The Young Disraeli: Social, Political, and Amorous" from *Dizzy: The Life and Personality of Benjamin Disraeli* by Hesketh Pearson. Copyright © 1951 by Hesketh Pearson. Reprinted by permission of Mrs. Hesketh Pearson.

"Profile of a President" from *Abraham Lincoln: A Biography* by Benjamin P. Thomas. Copyright 1952 by Benjamin P. Thomas. Reprinted by permission of Alfred A. Knopf, Inc.

"Valley of Dry Bones" from *Glory Road* by Bruce Catton. Copyright 1952 by Bruce Catton. Reprinted by permission of Doubleday & Company, Inc.

Contents

Contents

CONTENTS

xi

Introduction

History is as difficult to define as poetry or love. It has been clear for centuries that history isn't just "past politics." It concerns everything in the past which is part of the story of the human race. So we have not only political and military history (the commonest and most popular varieties), but also scores of other kinds, among them social, economic, constitutional, religious, scientific, artistic, and local history.

Journalists provide some of the raw material for history when they write about what happened yesterday, last week, or last year. Historians write about a more distant past, only when they have time to consider it carefully and usually when they have made strenuous efforts to find out about it in many sources: written, oral, archaeological, and so on. Most history, as I prefer to define it, is a record and an interpretation of the past as seen through the distorting lens of an individual mind. The historian must choose much of his data from partial and partisan sources. His selections and his interpretations reflect his own personality, prejudices, and preconceived ideas. And these prejudices and ideas are profoundly influenced by the era in which he lives. Consequently, every generation needs must rewrite the history of the past in the light of the present and its currently fashionable shibboleths and its currently crucial events.

Just what is the proper purpose of history is almost as hard to put into precise words as to define history itself. Francis Bacon once wrote: "It is the true office of history to represent the events themselves, together with the counsels; and to leave the observations and conclusions thereupon to the liberty and faculty of every man's judgment." This is an argument for objective narration and the withholding of personal opinion. Numerous historians have aspired to this ideal, which is much in vogue today, but it is an unobtainable goal because no writer can ignore his personal views.

But some historians have come close to Bacon's precept. More, however, who wrote well enough to achieve the heights of literature have filled their pages with their fiercely held opinions, their emotions, and the flavorsome impact of their personalities. Such great historians as Thucydides, author of the *History of the Peloponnesian War*, and William H. Prescott, author of the *History of the Conquest of Mexico*, resolutely excluded personal opinions and moral judgments from their pages. But they are outnumbered by the great historians who delighted to express their righteous convictions as eloquently as possible, among them Tacitus, Plutarch, Gibbon, Voltaire, and Macaulay.

xiii

Introduction

"The business of history is to recover the past," wrote Philip Guedalla. So it is. But the past can be approached from many directions. Many learned historians have written massive and indigestible works in which they had assembled thousands of facts which they had unearthed through decades of patient labor. Their pride was in their accurateness and thoroughness. But they deliberately chose to ignore the crucial fact that history is not just scholarship. It is a branch of literature. The historian who presents information unadorned by art has done only half his job. The other half is to write well. "The first duty of a great historian is to be an artist," wrote Lytton Strachey, who was not a great historian but who was an artist.

Nevertheless, the historical scholars who labor mightily with neither the inclination nor the ability to write well still perform an indispensable service and deserve humble respect. They provide the raw ore which others may polish to a bright sheen. Those who mine much of their own ore and also present it bright and gleaming with narrative pace, selectivity and compression, dramatic power, insight into character, humor, and sympathetic understanding of the thought and customs of a vanished era are the great men of history. They know that the purpose of history is not only to recover the past and to inform; it is also to stimulate thought, to delight, and to entertain.

The study of history can be both a sobering and an encouraging business. While we are entertained by the excitement and pageantry of the past, while we brood on the perennially tragic drama of human affairs, and while we are horrified by the immense suffering of mankind, we are intellectually depressed to learn about the rulers men have suffered to direct their destinies—so sorry a lot were most of them. But then when we consider the incompetence, greed, and corruption of rulers and politicians, perhaps we should be encouraged. With all their shortcomings, the men in power in the nontotalitarian governments of the present are immeasurably superior to most of their predecessors, except to those few who aspired to more than personal and national power and glory. Compared to those of any previous century, most modern statesmen are wonderfully honest and diligent. The exceptional man of genius may be no more often at the helm of state today. But the witless fool and the scheming knave are less often in control than formerly.

One of the principal reasons why the reading of history can be an emotionally rewarding experience was expressed eloquently by the distinguished English historian George M. Trevelyan in his *Autobiography and Other Essays*:

"I take delight in history, even in its most prosaic details, because they become poetical as they recede into the past. The poetry of history lies in the quasi-miraculous fact that once, on this earth, once, on this familiar spot of ground, walked other men and women, as actual as we are today, thinking their own thoughts, swayed by their own passions, but now all gone, one generation vanishing after another, gone as utterly as we ourselves shall shortly be gone like ghosts at cock-crow. This is the most familiar and certain fact about life, but it is also the most poetical; and the knowledge of it has never ceased to entrance me, and to throw a halo of poetry round the dustiest record that Dryasdust can bring to light."

This anthology is intended to provide samples of the joys of history when it is written sufficiently well to achieve the stature of literature. Many of its selections were written by the acknowledged masters of history, men whose names ring grandly down the corridors of time. Others of the authors represented here are distinguished contemporary writers whom I greatly admire. Some are insufficiently well known in my opinion, but deserve wide recognition.

To make a manageable volume, much had to be excluded. I have ignored all works of technical scholarship and all books of embattled controversy. To provide some kind of unity, I have concentrated on narratives of dramatic events, portrait sketches of great personages, and descriptions of ways of life and thought (social history). Such kinds of historical writing abound from the eighteenth century onward, although social history has only come into its own within comparatively recent years. The Greek and Roman historians were the great pioneers and produced immortal masterpieces. But some of them took legendary stories more seriously than we do today. Still, since these stories reflected the thought of the time and demonstrated it, too, I have not scrupled to include two examples: Herodotus's story of Croesus and Livy's account of the sack of Rome by the Gauls.

In the Middle Ages, historians were not as well educated or as sophisticated as their classical predecessors. Monks, or bishops, or poets, or courtiers, they recorded what they knew, often with simple-minded credulity. But they told grand tales and revealed much about their times. Perhaps only chroniclers rather than true historians, nevertheless they did achieve literary stature and several are represented here: Gregory of Tours, the Venerable Bede, and Jean Froissart.

Another kind of historian I thought absolutely essential to include is the writer of historical memoirs. Such a man either played a part in great events or was an eyewitness of them and in his leisure or old age wrote, often exceedingly well, an account based upon his personal experience. From their distinguished ranks, I have chosen Philippe de Commines, Bernal Díaz del Castillo, the Earl of Clarendon, and Saint-Simon.

Another kind of historian is the writer of historical biography. Although his interest is focused upon one man, he is as obviously a true historian as the writer who discusses many men over a considerable period of time. So I have decided that for the purposes of this volume any biography which is concerned with a man who participated in, or who profoundly influenced, great events in his own time is genuine history. But it seems reasonable to me to exclude biographies of persons whose lives were largely private as not works of history.

To edit an anthology is to exercise a series of personal choices. Some celebrated historians are not represented in this one, not because I fail to appreciate their merits but because I could not find appropriate selections from their works. Some great historians scatter their best paragraphs over many pages with less effective or less interesting material between them. Or they do not write episodes with an independent unity of their own which can stand alone. Or they refer so often to people and circumstances previously mentioned that a selection would be bewildering when carved from its parent work. I don't think that many of the world's supreme historians are omitted from these pages. But I know well that many fine historians, particularly contemporary ones, are missing.

My first goal was to find writers who wrote history so well that I wanted to include them. A secondary goal was to have as many of the great historical periods and great men represented as possible. But limits of space walled me in. For practical purposes, I have ignored the history of Asia, Africa, South America, and Eastern Europe. And there are, of course, great gaps in Western history in this volume. Nevertheless, what is here is representative of the art of history at its best, when it is literature.

Among the historians conspicuous by their absence, one is so famous and in his own time was regarded with such extravagant admiration that I would not like any reader to think that I have overlooked him. Thomas Carlyle is not here because I firmly believe that his style is atrocious, a badly botched mass of exclamatory remarks, invocations, and clumsy pretensions. I also deplore his ideas and consider his worship of force a sinister contribution to the ideas which helped foster the growth of twentieth-century Fascism.

Although Carlyle was a hero to many in the nineteenth century, the verdict was not unanimous. William H. Prescott wrote of Carlyle's *The French Revolution*: "A shower of twaddle . . . new-fangled words . . . ridiculous affectations . . . perfectly contemptible."

Among those who helped me find my way through hundreds of historical works, my chief thanks go to my wife, Lilias, who read every selection as I made it and listened to my sometimes prolonged deliberations with unfailing patience. I also wish to thank four historians, two of them included in these pages, for suggestions on which I have acted with enthusiasm: A. L. Rowse, James Thomas Flexner, Edward Grierson, and Serge Hughes. Recommendations for which I am grateful were also given me by Harry W. Baehr and my son Peter S. Prescott.

History as Literature

The Downfall of Croesus

HERODOTUS

546 B.C. The defeat of Croesus, the mighty king of Lydia, by the Persian emperor Cyrus seemed to Herodotus still another example of divine retribution, the punishment certain to fall upon the presumptuous, proud, and arrogant. Herodotus's The Persian Wars, the first prose work written in Greek and the first history, is an enduring masterpiece, a rich storehouse of facts, and a marvelous collection of entertaining stories. Although discursive, scrappy, full of tall tales and of inadequate accounts of great events, The Persian Wars is the noble ancestor of every history written after it. Herodotus's curiosity, diligence in research, and literary skill will always deserve the emulation of historians.

The messengers who had the charge of conveying these treasures to the shrines, received instructions to ask the oracles whether Croesus should go to war with the Persians, and if so, whether he should strengthen himself by the forces of an ally. Accordingly, when they had reached their destinations and presented the gifts, they proceeded to consult the oracles in the following terms, "Croesus, king of Lydia and other countries, believing that these are the only real oracles in all the world, has sent you such presents as your discoveries deserved, and now inquires of you whether he shall go to war with the Persians, and if so, whether he shall strengthen himself by the forces of a confederate." Both the oracles agreed in the tenor of their

1

reply, which was in each case a prophecy that if Croesus attacked the Persians, he would destroy a mighty empire, and a recommendation to him to look and see who were the most powerful of the Greeks, and to make alliance with them.

At the receipt of these oracular replies Croesus was overjoyed, and feeling sure that he would destroy the empire of the Persians, he sent once more to Pytho, and presented to the Delphians, the number of whom he had ascertained, two gold staters apiece. In return for this the Delphians granted to Croesus and the Lydians the privilege of precedency in consulting the oracle, exemption from all charges, the most honorable seat at the festivals, and the perpetual right of becoming at pleasure citizens of the town.

After sending these presents to the Delphians, Croesus a third time consulted the oracle, for having once proved its truthfulness, he wished to make constant use of it. The question whereto he now desired an answer was, "Whether his kingdom would be of long duration?" The following was the reply of the priestess:

> "Wait till the time shall come when a mule is monarch of Media;
> Then, thou delicate Lydian, away to the pebbles of Hermus;
> Haste, oh! haste thee away, nor blush to behave like a coward."

Of all the answers that had reached him, this pleased him best, for it seemed incredible that a mule should ever come to be king of the Medes, and so he concluded that the sovereignty would never depart from himself or his seed after him.

* * *

Meanwhile Croesus, taking the oracle in the wrong sense, led his forces into Cappadocia, fully expecting to defeat Cyrus and destroy the empire of the Persians. While he was still engaged in making preparations for his attack, a Lydian named Sandanis, who had always been looked upon as a wise man, but who after this obtained a very great name indeed among his countrymen, came forward and counseled the king in these words, "You are about, king, to make war against men who wear leathern trousers, and have all their other garments of leather; who feed not on what they like, but on what they can get from a soil that is sterile and unkindly; who do not indulge in wine, but drink water; who possess no figs nor anything else that is good to eat. If, then, you conquer them, what can you get from them, seeing that they have nothing at all? But if they conquer you, consider how much that is precious you will lose: if they once get a taste of our pleasant things, they will keep such hold of them that we shall never be able to make them loose their grasp. For my part, I am thankful to the gods, that they have not put it into the hearts of the Persians to invade Lydia."

Croesus was not persuaded by this speech, though it was true enough; for before the conquest of Lydia, the Persians possessed none of the luxuries or delights of life.

* * *

There were two motives which led Croesus to attack Cappadocia: firstly, he coveted the land, which he wished to add to his own dominions; but the chief reason was, that he wanted to revenge on Cyrus the wrongs of Astyages, and was made confident by the oracle of being able to do so: for the Astyages, son of Cyaxares and king of the Medes, who had been dethroned by Cyrus, son of Cambyses, was Croesus' brother by marriage.

* * *

Having passed the Halys with the forces under his command, Croesus entered the district of Cappadocia which is called Pteria. It lies in the neighborhood of the city of Sinope upon the Euxine, and is the strongest position in the whole country thereabouts. Here Croesus pitched his camp, and began to ravage the fields of the Syrians. He besieged and took the chief city of the Pterians, and reduced the inhabitants to slavery: he likewise made himself master of the surrounding villages. Thus he brought ruin on the Syrians, who were guilty of no offense towards him. Meanwhile, Cyrus had levied an army and marched against Croesus, increasing his numbers at every step by the forces of the nations that lay in his way. Before beginning his march he had sent heralds to the Ionians, with an invitation to them to revolt from the Lydian king: they, however, had refused compliance. Cyrus, notwithstanding, marched against the enemy, and encamped opposite them in the district of Pteria, where the trial of strength took place between the contending powers. The combat was hot and bloody, and upon both sides the number of the slain was great; nor had victory declared in favor of either party, when night came down upon the battle field. Thus both armies fought valiantly.

Croesus laid the blame for his ill success on the number of his troops, which fell very short of the enemy; and as on the next day Cyrus did not repeat the attack, he set off on his return to Sardis, intending to collect his allies and renew the contest in the spring. He meant to call on the Egyptians to send him aid, according to the terms of the alliance which he had concluded with Amasis, previous to his league with the Lacedaemonians. He intended also to summon to his assistance the Babylonians, under their king Labynetus, for they too were bound to

3

him by treaty: and further, he meant to send word to Sparta, and to appoint a day for the coming of their succours. Having got together these forces in addition to his own, he would, as soon as the winter was past and springtime come, march once more against the Persians. With these intentions Croesus, immediately on his return, dispatched heralds to his various allies, with a request that they would join him at Sardis in the course of the fifth month from the time of the departure of his messengers. He then disbanded the army—consisting of mercenary troops—which had been engaged with the Persians and had since accompanied him to the capital, and let them depart to their homes, never imagining that Cyrus, after a battle in which victory has been so evenly balanced, would venture to march upon Sardis.

* * *

Cyrus, however, when Croesus broke up so suddenly from his quarters after the battle at Pteria, conceiving that he had marched away with the intention of disbanding his army, considered a little, and soon saw that it was advisable for him to advance upon Sardis with all haste, before the Lydians could get their forces together a second time. Having thus determined, he lost no time in carrying out his plan. He marched forward with such speed that he was himself the first to announce his coming to the Lydian king. That monarch, placed in the utmost difficulty by the turn of events which had gone so entirely against all his calculations, nevertheless led out the Lydians to battle. In all Asia there was not at that time a braver or more warlike people. Their manner of fighting was on horseback; they carried long lances, and were clever in the management of their steeds.

The two armies met in the plain before Sardis. It is a vast flat, bare of trees, watered by the Hyllus and a number of other streams, which all flow into one larger than the rest, called the Hermus. This river rises in the sacred mountain of the Dindymenian Mother, and falls into the sea near the town of Phocaea.

When Cyrus beheld the Lydians arranging themselves in order of battle on this plain, fearful of the strength of their cavalry, he adopted a device which Harpagus, one of the Medes, suggested to him. He collected together all the camels that had come in the train of his army to carry the provisions and the baggage, and taking off their loads, he mounted riders upon them accoutred as horsemen. These he commanded to advance in front of his other troops against the Lydian horse; behind them were to follow the foot soldiers, and last of all the cavalry. When his arrangements were complete, he gave his troops orders to slay all the other Lydians who came in their way without mercy, but to spare Croesus and not kill him, even if he should be seized and offer resistance. The reason that Cyrus opposed his camels to the enemy's horse was because the horse has a natural dread of the camel, and cannot abide either the sight or the smell of that animal. By this stratagem he hoped to make Croesus' horse useless to him, the horse being what he chiefly depended upon for victory. The two armies then joined battle, and immediately the Lydian war-horses, seeing and smelling the camels, turned round and galloped off; and so it came to pass that all Croesus' hopes withered away. The Lydians, however, behaved manfully. As soon as they understood what was happening, they leaped off their horses, and engaged with the Persians on foot. The combat was long; but at last, after a great slaughter on both sides, the Lydians turned and fled. They were driven within the walls and the Persians laid siege to Sardis.

* * *

The following is the way in which Sardis was taken. On the fourteenth day of the siege Cyrus bade some horsemen ride about his lines, and make proclamation to the whole army that he would give a reward to the man who should first mount the wall. After this he made an assault, but without success. His troops retired, but a certain Mardian, Hyroeades by name, resolved to approach the citadel and attempt it at a place where no guards were ever set. On this side the rock was so precipitous, and the citadel (as it seemed) so impregnable, that no fear was entertained of its being carried in this place. Here was the only portion of the circuit round which their old king Meles did not carry the lion which his concubine bore him. For when the Telmessians had declared that if a lion were taken round the defenses, Sardis would be impregnable, and Meles, in consequence, carried it round the rest of the fortress where the citadel seemed open to attack, he scorned to take it round this side, which he looked on as a sheer precipice, and therefore absolutely secure. It is on that side of the city which faces Mount Tmolus. Hyroeades, however, having the day before observed a Lydian soldier descend the rock after a helmet that had rolled down from the top, and having seen him pick it up and carry it back, thought over what he had witnessed, and formed his plan. He climbed the rock himself, and other Persians followed in his track, until a large number had mounted to the top. Thus was Sardis taken, and given up entirely to pillage.

* * *

And Croesus himself fell into their hands, after having reigned fourteen years, and been besieged in his capital fourteen days; thus too did Croesus fulfill the oracle, which said that he should destroy a mighty empire, by destroying his own. Then the Persians who had made Croesus prisoner brought him before Cyrus. Now a vast pile had been raised by his orders, and Croesus, laden with fetters, was placed upon it, and with him twice seven of the sons of the Lydians. I know not whether Cyrus was minded to make an offering of the first-fruits to some god or other, or whether he had vowed a vow and was performing it, or whether, as may well be, he had heard that Croesus was a holy man, and so wished to see if any of the heavenly powers would appear to save him from being burnt alive. However it might be, Cyrus was thus engaged, and Croesus was already on the pile, when it entered his mind in the depth of his woe that there was a divine warning in the words which had come to him from the lips of Solon, "No one while he lives is happy." When this thought smote him he fetched a long breath, and breaking his deep silence, groaned aloud, thrice uttering the name of Solon. Cyrus caught the sounds, and bade the interpreters inquire of Croesus who it was he called on. They drew near and asked him, but he held his peace, and for a long time made no answer to their questionings, until at length, forced to say something, he exclaimed, "One I would give much to see converse with every monarch." Not knowing what he meant by this reply, the interpreters begged him to explain himself; and as they pressed for an answer, and grew to be troublesome, he told them how, a long time before, Solon, an Athenian, had come and seen all his splendor, and made light of it; and how whatever he had said to him had fallen out exactly as he foreshowed, although it was nothing that especially concerned him, but applied to all mankind alike, and most to those who seemed to themselves happy. Meanwhile, as he thus spoke, the pile was lighted, and the outer portion began to blaze. Then Cyrus, hearing from the interpreters what Croesus had said, relented, bethinking himself that he too was a man, and that it was a fellow man, and one who had once been as blessed by fortune as himself, that he was burning alive; afraid, moreover, of retribution, and full of the thought that whatever is human is insecure. So he bade them quench the blazing fire as quickly as they could, and take down Croesus and the other Lydians, which they tried to do, but the flames were not to be mastered.

Then, the Lydians say that Croesus, perceiving by the efforts made to quench the fire that Cyrus had relented, and seeing also that all was in vain, and that the men could not get the fire under, called with a loud voice upon the god Apollo, and prayed him, if he had ever received at his hands any acceptable gift, to come to his aid, and deliver him from his present danger. As thus with tears he besought the god, suddenly, though up to that time the sky had been clear and the day without a breath of wind, dark clouds gathered, and the storm burst over their heads with rain of such violence, that the flames were speedily extinguished. Cyrus, convinced by this that Croesus was a good man and a favorite of heaven, asked him after he was taken off the pile, "Who

6

it was that had persuaded him to lead an army into his country, and so become his foe rather than continue his friend?" To which Croesus made answer as follows, "What I did, O King, was to thy advantage and to my own loss. If there be blame, it rests with the god of the Greeks, who encouraged me to begin the war. No one is so foolish as to prefer to peace war, in which, instead of sons burying their fathers, fathers bury their sons. But the gods willed it so."

Thus did Croesus speak. Cyrus then ordered his fetters to be taken off, and made him sit down near himself, and paid him much respect, looking upon him, as did also the courtiers, with a sort of wonder. Croesus, wrapped in thought, uttered no word. After a while, happening to turn and perceive the Persian soldiers plundering the town, he said to Cyrus, "May I now tell you, O King, what I have in my mind, or is silence best?" Cyrus bade him speak his mind boldly. Then he put this question, "What is it, Cyrus, which those men yonder are doing so busily?" "Plundering your city," Cyrus answered, "and carrying off your riches." "Not my city," rejoined the other, "nor my riches. They are not mine any more. It is your wealth which they are pillaging."

Cyrus, struck by what Croesus had said, bade all the court to withdraw, and then asked Croesus what he thought it best for him to do as regarded the plundering. Croesus answered, "Now that the gods have made me your slave, Cyrus, it seems to me that it is my part, if I see anything to your advantage, to show it to you. Your subjects, the Persians, are a poor people with a proud spirit. If then you let them pillage and possess themselves of great wealth, I will tell you what you may expect at their hands. The man who gets the most, look to having him rebel against you. Now then, if my words please you, do thus: Let some of thy body-guards be placed as sentinels at each of the city gates, and let them take their booty from the soldiers as they leave the town, and tell them that they do so because the tenths are due to Zeus. So you will escape the hatred they would feel if the plunder were taken away from them by force; and they, seeing that what is proposed is just, will do it willingly."

Cyrus was beyond measure pleased with this advice, so excellent did it seem to him. He praised Croesus highly, and gave orders to his body-guard to do as he had suggested. Then, turning to Croesus, he said, "Croesus, I see that you are resolved both in speech and act to show yourself a virtuous prince: ask me, therefore, whatever you wish as a gift at this moment." Croesus replied, "My lord, if you will suffer me to send these fetters to the god of the Greeks, whom I once honored above all other gods, and ask him if it is his wont to deceive his benefactors; that will be the highest favor you can confer on me."

Cyrus upon this inquired what charge he had to make against the god. Then Croesus gave him a full account of all his projects, and of the answers of the oracle, and of the offerings which he had sent, on which he dwelt especially, and told him how it was the encouragement given him by the oracle which had led him to make war upon Persia. All this he related, and at the end again besought permission to reproach the god with his behavior. Cyrus answered with a laugh, "This I readily grant you, and whatever else you shall at any time ask at my hands." Croesus, finding his request allowed, sent certain Lydians to Delphi, enjoining them to lay his fetters upon the threshold of the temple, and ask the god, "If he were not ashamed of having encouraged him, as the destined destroyer of the empire of Cyrus, to begin a war with Persia, of which such were the first-fruits?" As they said this they were to point to the fetters; and further they were to inquire, "If it was the wont of the Greek gods to be ungrateful?"

The Lydians went to Delphi and delivered their message, on which the priestess is said to have replied, "It is not possible even for a god to escape the decree of destiny. Croesus has been punished for the sin of his fifth ancestor, who, when he was one of the body-guard of the Heraclidae, joined in a woman's fraud, and, slaying his master, wrongfully seized the throne. Apollo was anxious that the fall of Sardis should not happen in the lifetime of Croesus, but be delayed to his son's days; he could not, however, persuade the Fates. All that they were willing to allow he took and gave to Croesus. Let Croesus know that Apollo delayed the taking of Sardis three full years, and that he is thus a prisoner three full years later than was his destiny. Moreover it was Apollo who saved him from the burning pile. Nor has Croesus any right to complain with respect to the oracular answer which he received. For when the god told him that, if he attacked the Persians, he would destroy a mighty empire, he ought, if he had been wise, to have sent again and inquired which empire was meant, that of Cyrus or his own; but if he neither understood what was said, nor took the trouble to seek for enlightenment, he has only himself to blame for the result. Besides, he had misunderstood the last answer which had been given him about the mule. Cyrus was that mule. For the parents of Cyrus were of different races, and of different conditions, his mother a Median princess, daughter of King Astyages, and his father a Persian and a subject, who, though so far beneath her in all respects, had married his royal mistress."

Such was the answer of the priestess. The Lydians returned to Sardis and communicated it to Croesus, who confessed, on hearing it, that the fault was his, not the god's. Such was the way in which Ionia was first conquered, and so was the empire of Croesus brought to a close.

8

Melos and the Politics of Power

THUCYDIDES

*416 B.C. In the sixteenth year of the Peloponnesian War, the great struggle
between Athens and Sparta, the Athenians attacked the small island of Melos.
The brutally cynical arguments used by the Athenians to persuade the islanders
to surrender were recorded by Thucydides in his history of the war, one of the
first and one of the greatest works of history ever written. Thucydides made no
comment; but it is plain that similar reasoning still disgraces the conduct of men
and states. Explaining his use of speeches, Thucydides wrote: "My method
has been, while keeping as closely as possible to the general sense of the words
that were actually used, to make the speakers say what, in my opinion, was
called for by each situation."*

The Athenians also made an expedition against the island of Melos.
They had thirty of their own ships, six from Chios, and two from
Lesbos; 1,200 hoplites, 300 archers, and twenty mounted archers, all from
Athens; and about 1,500 hoplites from the allies and the islanders.

The Melians are a colony of Sparta. They had refused to join the
Athenian empire like the other islanders, and at first had remained
neutral without helping either side; but afterwards, when the Athenians
had brought force to bear on them by laying waste their land, they had
become open enemies of Athens.

Now the generals Cleomedes, the son of Lycomodes, and Tisias, the son of Tisimachus, encamped with the above force in Melian territory and, before doing any harm to the land, first of all sent representatives to negotiate. The Melians did not invite these representatives to speak before the people, but asked them to make the statement for which they had come in front of the governing body and the few. The Athenian representatives then spoke as follows:

Athenians: So we are not to speak before the people, no doubt in case the mass of the people should hear once and for all and without interruption an argument from us which is both persuasive and incontrovertible, and should so be led astray. This, we realize, is your motive in bringing us here to speak before the few. Now suppose that you who sit here should make assurance doubly sure. Suppose that you, too, should refrain from dealing with every point in detail in a set speech, and should instead interrupt us whenever we say something controversial and deal with that before going on to the next point? Tell us first whether you approve of this suggestion of ours.

The Council of the Melians replied as follows:

Melians: No one can object to each of us putting forward our own views in a calm atmosphere. That is perfectly reasonable. What is scarcely consistent with such a proposal is the present threat, indeed the certainty, of your making war on us. We see that you have come prepared to judge the arguments yourselves, and that the likely end of it all will be either war, if we prove that we are in the right, and so refuse to surrender, or else slavery.

Athenians: If you are going to spend the time enumerating your suspicions about the future, or if you have met here for any other reason except to look the facts in the face and on the basis of these facts to consider how you can save your city from destruction, there is no point in our going on with this discussion. If, however, you will do as we suggest, then we will speak on.

Melians: It is natural and understandable that people who are placed as we are should have recourse to all kinds of arguments and different points of view. However, you are right in saying that we are met together here to discuss the safety of our country on the lines that you have laid down.

Athenians: Then we on our side will use no fine phrases saying, for example, that we have a right to our empire because we defeated the Persians, or that we have come against you now because of the injuries you have done us—a great mass of words that nobody would believe. And we ask you on your side not to imagine that you will influence us by saying that you, though a colony of Sparta, have not joined Sparta in the war, or that you have never done us any harm. Instead we recommend that you try to get what it is possible for you to get, taking into consideration what we both really do think; since you know as well as we do that, when these matters are discussed by practical people, the standard of justice depends on the quality of power to compel and that in fact the strong do what they have the power to do and the weak accept what they have to accept.

Melians: Then in our view (since you force us to leave justice out of account and to confine ourselves to self-interest)—in our view it is at any rate useful that you should not destroy a principle that is to the general good of all men—namely, that in the case of all who fall into danger there should be such a thing as fair play and just dealing, and that such people should be allowed to use and to profit by arguments that fall short of a mathematical accuracy. And this is a principle which affects you as much as anybody else, since your own fall would be visited by the most terrible vengeance and would be an example to the world.

Athenians: As for us, even assuming that our empire does come to an end, we are not despondent about what would happen next. One is not so much frightened of being conquered by a power which rules over others, as Sparta does (not that we are concerned with Sparta now), as of what would happen if a ruling power is attacked and defeated by its own subjects. So far as this point is concerned, you can leave it to us to face the risks involved. What we shall do now is to show you that it is for the good of our own empire that we are here and that it is for the preservation of your city that we shall say what we are going to say. We do not want any trouble in bringing you into our empire, and we want you to be spared for the good both of yourselves and of ourselves.

Melians: And how could it be just as good for us to be the slaves as for you to be the masters?

Athenians: You, by giving in, would save yourselves from disaster; we, by not destroying you, would be able to profit from you.

Melians: So you would not agree to our being neutral, friends instead of enemies, but allies of neither side?

Athenians: No, because it is not so much your hostility that injures us; it is rather the case that, if we were on friendly terms with you, our subjects would regard that as a sign of weakness in us, whereas your hatred is evidence of our power.

Melians: Is that your subjects' idea of fair play—that no distinction should be made between people who are quite unconnected with you and people who are mostly your own colonists or else rebels whom you have conquered?

Athenians: So far as right and wrong are concerned they think that there is no difference between the two, that those who still preserve their independence do so because they are strong, and that if we fail to attack them it is because we are afraid. So that by conquering you we shall increase not only the size but the security of our empire. We rule the sea and you are islanders, and weaker islanders, too, than the others; it is therefore particularly important that you should not escape.

Melians: But do you think that there is no security for you in what we suggest? For here again, since you will not let us mention justice, but tell us to give in to your interests, we, too, must tell you what our interests are and, if yours and ours happen to coincide, we must try to persuade you of the fact. Is it not certain that you will make enemies of all states who are at present neutral, when they see what is happening here and naturally conclude that in course of time you will attack them, too? Does not this mean that you are strengthening the enemies you have already and are forcing others to become your enemies even against their intentions and their inclinations?

Athenians: As a matter of fact we are not so much frightened of states on the continent. They have their liberty, and this means that it will be a long time before they begin to take precautions against us. We are more concerned about islanders like yourselves, who are still unsubdued, or subjects who have already become embittered by the constraint which our empire imposes on them. These are the people who are most likely to act in a reckless manner and to bring themselves and us, too, into the most obvious danger.

Melians: Then surely, if such hazards are taken by you to keep your empire and by your subjects to escape from it, we who still are free would show ourselves great cowards and weaklings if we failed to face everything that comes rather than submit to slavery.

Athenians: No, not if you are sensible. This is no fair fight, with honor on one side and shame on the other. It is rather a question of saving your lives and not resisting those who are far too strong for you.

Melians: Yet we know that in war fortune sometimes makes the odds more level than could be expected from the difference in numbers of the two sides. And if we surrender, then all our hope is lost at once, whereas, so long as we remain in action, there is still a hope that we may yet stand upright.

Athenians: Hope, that comfort in danger! If one already has solid advantages to fall back upon, one can indulge in hope. It may do harm, but will not destroy one. But hope is by nature an expensive commodity, and those who are risking their all on one cast find out what it means only when they are already ruined; it never fails them in the period when such a knowledge would enable them to take precautions. Do not let this happen to you, you who are weak and whose fate depends upon a single movement of the scale. And do not be like those people who, as so commonly happens, miss the chance of saving themselves in a human and practical way, and, when every clear and distinct hope has left them in their adversity, turn to what is blind and vague, to prophecies and oracles and such things which by encouraging hope lead men to ruin.

Melians: It is difficult, and you may be sure that we know it, for us to oppose your power and fortune, unless the terms be equal. Nevertheless we trust that the gods will give us fortune as good as yours, because we are standing for what is right against what is wrong; and as for what we lack in power, we trust that it will be made up for by our alliance with the Spartans, who are bound, if for no other reason, than for honor's sake, and because we are their kinsmen, to come to our help. Our confidence, therefore, is not so entirely irrational as you think.

Athenians: So far as the favor of the gods is concerned, we think we have as much right to that as you have. Our aims and our actions are perfectly consistent with the beliefs men hold about the gods and with the principles which govern their own conduct. Our opinion of the gods and our knowledge of men lead us to conclude that it is a general and necessary law of nature to rule wherever one can. This is not a law that we made ourselves, nor were we the first to act upon it when it was made. We found it already in existence, and we shall leave it to exist for ever among those who come after us. We are merely acting in accordance with it, and we know that you or anybody else with the same power as ours would be acting in precisely the same way. And therefore, so far as the gods are concerned, we see no good reason why we should fear to be at a disadvantage. But with regard to your views about Sparta and your confidence that she, out of a sense of honor, will come to your aid, we must say that we congratulate you on your simplicity but do not envy you your folly. In matters that concern themselves or their own constitution, the Spartans are quite remarkably good; as for their relations with others, that is a long story, but it can be expressed shortly and clearly by saying that of all people we know the Spartans are the most conspicuous for believing that what they like doing is honorable and what suits their interests is just. And this kind of attitude is not going to be of much help to you in your absurd quest for safety at the moment.

Melians: But this is the very point where we can feel most sure. Their own self-interest will make them refuse to betray their own colonists, the Melians, for that would mean losing the confidence of their friends among the Hellenes and doing good to their enemies.

Athenians: You seem to forget that if one follows one's self-interest one wants to be safe, whereas the path of justice and honor involves one in danger. And, where danger is concerned, the Spartans are not, as a rule, very venturesome.

Melians: But we think that they would even endanger themselves for our sake and count the risk more worth taking than in the case of others, because we are so close to the Peloponnese that they could operate more easily, and because they can depend on us more than on others, since we are of the same race and share the same feelings.

Athenians: Goodwill shown by the party that is asking for help does not mean security for the prospective ally. What is looked for is a positive preponderance of power in action. And the Spartans pay attention to this point even more than others do. Certainly they distrust their own native resources so much that when they attack a neighbor they bring a great army of allies with them. It is hardly likely therefore that, while we are in control of the sea, they will cross over to an island.

Melians: But they still might send others. The Cretan sea is a wide one, and it is harder for those who control it to intercept others than for those who want to slip through to do so safely. And even if they were to fail us, they would turn against your own land and against those of your allies left unvisited by Brasidas. So, instead of troubling about a country which has nothing to do with you, you will find trouble nearer home, among your allies, and in your own country.

Athenians: It is a possibility, something that has in fact happened before. It may happen in your case, but you are well aware that the Athenians have never yet relinquished a single siege operation through fear of others. But we are somewhat shocked to find that, though you announced your intention of discussing how you could preserve yourselves, in all this task you have said absolutely nothing which could justify a man in thinking that he could be preserved. Your chief points are concerned with what you hope may happen in the future, while your actual resources are too scanty to give you a chance of survival against the forces that are opposed to you at this moment. You will therefore be showing an extraordinary lack of common sense if, after you have asked us to retire from this meeting, you still fail to reach a conclusion wiser than anything you have mentioned so far. Do not be led astray by a false sense of honor—a thing which often brings men to ruin when they are faced with an obvious danger that somehow affects their pride. For in many cases men have still been able to see the dangers ahead of them, but this thing called dishonor, this word, by its own force of seduction, has drawn them into a state where they have surrendered to an idea, while in fact they have fallen voluntarily into irrevocable disaster, in dishonor that is all the more dishonorable because it has come to them from their own folly rather than their misfortune. You, if you take the right view, will be careful to avoid this. You will see that there is nothing

14

disgraceful in giving way to the greatest city in Hellas when she is offering you such reasonable terms—alliance on a tribute-paying basis and liberty to enjoy your own property. And, when you are allowed to choose between war and safety, you will not be so insensitively arrogant as to make the wrong choice. This is the safe rule—to stand up to one's equals, to behave with deference towards one's superiors, and to treat one's inferiors with moderation. Think it over again, then, when we have withdrawn from the meeting, and let this be a point that constantly recurs to your minds —that you are discussing the fate of your country, that you have only one country, and that its future for good or ill depends on this one single decision which you are going to make.

The Athenians then withdrew from the discussion. The Melians, left to themselves, reached a conclusion which was much the same as they indicated in their previous replies. Their answer was as follows:

Melians: Our decision, Athenians, is just the same as it was at first. We are not prepared to give up in a short moment the liberty which our city has enjoyed from its foundation for 700 years. We put our trust in the fortune that the gods will send and which has saved us up till now, and in the help of men—that is, of the Spartans; and so we shall try to save ourselves. But we invite you to allow us to be friends of yours and enemies to neither side, to make a treaty which shall be agreeable to both you and us, and so to leave our country.

The Melians made this reply, and the Athenians, just as they were breaking off the discussion, said:

Well, at any rate, judging from this decision of yours, you seem to us quite unique in your ability to consider the future as something more certain than what is before your eyes, and to see uncertainties as realities, simply because you would like them to be so. As you have staked most on and trusted most in Spartans, luck, and hopes, so in all these you will find yourselves most completely deluded.

The Athenian representatives then went back to the army, and the Athenian generals, finding that the Melians would not submit, immediately commenced hostilities and built a wall completely round the city of Melos, dividing the work out among the various states. Later they left behind a garrison of some of their own and some allied troops to blockade the place by land and sea, and with the greatest part of their army returned home. The force left behind stayed on and continued the siege.

* * *

Meanwhile the Melians made a night attack and captured the part of the Athenian lines opposite the market-place. They killed some of the troops, and then, after bringing in corn and everything else useful that they could lay their hands on, retired again and made no further move, while the Athenians took measures to make their blockade more effective in future. So the summer came to an end.

* * *

About this time the Melians again captured another part of the Athenian lines where there were only a few of the garrison on guard. As a result of this, another force came out afterwards from Athens under the command of Philocrates, the son of Demeas. Siege operations were now carried on vigorously and, as there was also some treachery from inside, the Melians surrendered unconditionally to the Athenians, who put to death all men of military age whom they took, and sold the women and children as slaves. Melos itself they took over for themselves, sending out later a colony of 500 men.

Woe to the Vanquished

LIVY

390 B.C. Rome had recently captured the Etruscan city of Veii after a ten-year siege, but it was still only a small city on the banks of the Tiber. And Rome's great general, Camillus, was a political exile in the neighboring city of Ardea and so ineligible to take command of the city's defense against attack by barbarian Gauls. The result was total defeat in a battle fought just eight miles from the city, and the first sack of Rome. Livy's The History of Rome from Its Foundation, *from which this excerpt is taken, credulously retells many ancient legends and contains much moralizing to glorify Roman courage and virtue; but its narrative power and literary quality have enthralled readers for 2,000 years.*

About this time a plebeian named Caedicius told the tribunes that in the New Road where the shrine now stands above the temple of Vesta, he had heard, in the silence of the night, a voice. The voice was something more than human, and "Tell the magistrates," it said, "that the Gauls are coming." The tale was more or less laughed off, partly because Caedicius, who told it, was a person of no consequence, and partly because the Gauls lived a long way off and were therefore little known. Nevertheless the voice was a warning from heaven—doom was drawing near, but the warning was ignored.

* * *

17

The Gauls could hardly believe their eyes, so easy, so miraculously swift their victory had been. For a while they stood rooted to the spot, hardly realizing what had happened; then after a moment of fear lest the whole thing was a trap, they began to collect the arms and equipment of the dead and to pile them, as their manner is, in heaps. Finally, when no sign of an enemy was anywhere to be seen, they marched, and shortly before sunset reached the vicinity of Rome. Mounted men were sent forward to reconnoitre: the gates stood open, not a sentry was on guard; no soldiers manned the walls. Once more the astonishing truth held them spellbound. Yet still the night might have hidden terrors—and the city was totally unknown; so after a further reconnaissance of the walls and the other gates to discover, if it were possible, their enemy's intention in his desperate plight, they encamped somewhere between the city and the Anio.

As more than half the Roman army had taken refuge in Veii, it was universally believed in Rome itself that the rest, who had made their way home, were the only survivors. Rome was indeed a city of lamentation—of mourning for the living and the dead alike. Then news came that the Gauls were at the gates; the anguish of personal bereavement was forgotten in a wave of panic, and all too soon cries like the howling of wolves and barbaric songs could be heard, as the Gallic squadrons rode hither and thither close outside the walls. All the time between then and the following day was filled with unbearable suspense. When would the assault come? Again and again they believed it to be imminent: they expected it on the first appearance of the Gauls—for why had they marched on the city, and not stayed at the Allia, unless this had been their intention? They expected it at sunset—because there was little daylight left, and surely it would come before dark. Then, when darkness had fallen, they thought it had been deliberately postponed in order to multiply its terrors. But the night passed, and dawn, when it drew near, made them almost desperate; and then at last, hard upon this long-drawn-out and insupportable anxiety, came the thing itself, and the enemy entered the gates.

During that night and the following day Rome showed little resemblance to the fugitive army on the Allia. As there was no hope of defending the city with the handful of available troops, the decision was taken to withdraw all men capable of bearing arms together with the women and children and able-bodied senators into the fortress on the Capitol; from that stronghold, properly armed and provisioned, it was their intention to make a last stand for themselves, for their gods, and for the Roman name. The priest and priestesses of Vesta were ordered to remove their sacred emblems to some spot far away from bloodshed and burning, and their cult was not to be abandoned till there were none left alive to observe its rites. It was felt that if the Citadel, home of the city's tutelary gods, could survive the impending ruin—if the few men still able to fight, if the Senate, fountain-head of true government, could escape the general disaster, it would be tolerable to leave in the city below the aged and useless, who had not, in any case, much longer to live. It was a stern decision, and to make it easier for the commons to bear, the old aristocrats who long before had served as consuls or celebrated their Triumphs said that they would die side by side with their humble compatriots, and never consent to burden the inadequate stores of the fighting few with bodies which could no longer bear arms in the country's defense. To tell each other of this noble resolve was the only consolation of the doomed men, who then turned to address words of encouragement to the young and vigorous whom they were seeing on their way to the Capitol, and to commend to the valor of their youth whatever good fortune might yet remain for a city which for three hundred and sixty years had never been defeated.

The time came to part—these to the Capitol with the future in their hands, those to the death to which their own resolve not to survive the city's fall had condemned them. It was a cruel separation, but even more heart-rending was the plight of the women, who weeping and torn by love and loyalty did not know which way to go, but followed now husbands, now sons, in grief and bewilderment at the terrible choice they had had imposed upon them, as it would have been inhuman to reduce deliberately the number of non-combatants in the Citadel, as purely military considerations required. Thousands more—mostly plebeians—who could neither have been lodged nor fed on the small and inadequately provisioned hill, streamed in an unbroken line from the city towards the Janiculum, whence some scattered over the countryside while others made for neighboring towns—a rabble without leader or common aim. For them, Rome was already dead; each was his own counsellor and followed where his hopes led him. Meanwhile the priest of Quirinus and the Vestal Virgins, careless of their personal belongings, were discussing the fate of the sacred objects in their care—what to take and what to leave, as they had not the means to carry all away, and where what they could not take might safely be deposited. The best course, they thought, would be to store them in jars and bury them in the shrine near the priest's house (at the spot where spitting is now considered sacrilegious); the rest they managed between them to carry along the road which leads over the pile-bridge to the Janiculum. On the slope of the hill they were noticed by a man of humble birth named Albinius, who was driving his wife and family in a cart, amongst the rabble of other non-combatants escaping from the city. Even at such a moment Albinius could remember the difference between what was due to God and what to man, and feeling it to be an impious thing that he and his family should be seen driving while priestesses of the state toiled along on foot carrying the nation's sacred emblems, he told his wife to get out of the cart with her little boys, took up the Vestals and their burdens instead, and drove them to their destination in Caere.

In Rome everything possible in the circumstances had now been done to prepare for the defense of the Citadel, and the grey-haired senators had gone home to await, unflinching, the coming of the enemy. It was the wish of those who had held the highest offices of state to dress for death in the outward signs of such rank as they had enjoyed or service they had rendered in the days of their former fortune; so putting on the ceremonial robes of the dignitaries who at the Circensian Games escort the chariots of the gods, or of generals who enter the City in triumph, they took their seats, each in the courtyard of his house, on the ivory-inlaid chairs of the curule magistrates, having first—we are told —repeated after Marcus Folius the Pontifex Maximus a solemn vow to offer themselves as a sacrifice for their country and the Roman people.

A night having passed without action, the Gauls found their lust for fighting much abated. At no time had they met with any serious resistance, and there was no need now to take the city by assault. When therefore they entered on the following day, it was coolly and calmly enough. The Colline Gate was open, and they made their way to the Forum, looking with curiosity at the temples and at the Citadel, the only place to give the impression of a city at war. They left a reasonably strong guard in case of attack from the fortified heights and then dispersed in search of plunder; finding the streets empty, crowds of them broke into the first houses they came to; others went further afield, presumably supposing that buildings more remote from the Forum would offer richer prizes, but there the very silence and solitude made them uneasy, separated as they were from their companions, and suggested the possibility of a trap, so that they soon returned, keeping close together, to the neighborhood of the Forum. Here they found the humbler houses locked and barred but the mansions of the nobility open; the former they were ready enough to break into, but it was a long time before they could bring themselves to enter the latter: something akin to awe held them back at what met their gaze—those figures seated in the open courtyards, the robes and decorations august beyond reckoning, the majesty expressed in those grave, calm eyes like the majesty of gods. They might have been statues in some holy place, and for a while the Gallic warriors stood entranced; then, on an impulse, one of them touched the beard of a certain Marcus Papirius—it was long, as was the fashion of those days—and the Roman struck him on the head with his ivory staff. That was the beginning: the barbarian flamed into anger and killed him, and the others were butchered where they sat. From that moment no mercy was shown; houses were ransacked and the empty shells set on fire.

The extent of the conflagration was, however, unexpectedly limited. Some of the Gauls may have been against the indiscriminate destruction of the city; or possibly it was their leaders' policy, first, to start a few fires in the hope that the besieged in the Citadel might be driven to surrender by the fear of losing their beloved homes, and, secondly, to leave a portion of the city intact and to use it as a sort of pledge or security—or lever—to induce the Romans to accept their terms. In any case the havoc wrought by the fire was on the first day by no means universal—or even widespread—and much less than might have been expected in the circumstances.

For the Romans beleaguered in the Citadel the full horror was almost too great to realize; they could hardly believe their eyes or ears as they looked down on the barbaric foe roaming in hordes through the familiar streets, while at every moment, everywhere and anywhere, some new terror was enacted: fear gripped them in a thousand shapes; now here, now there, the yells of triumph, women's screams or the crying of children, the roar of flames or the long rumbling crash of masonry forced them to turn unwilling eyes upon some fresh calamity, as if fate had made them spectators of the nightmare stage-scene of their country's ruin, helpless to save anything they possessed but their own useless bodies. Never before had beleaguered men been in a plight so pitiful—not shut within their city, but excluded from it, they saw all that they loved in the power of their enemies.

The night which followed was as bad as the day. Another dawn came, and brought with each succeeding moment the sight of some new disaster; yet nothing could break the determination of the little garrison, under its almost intolerable weight of anguish, to hold out to the end: even if the whole city were burnt to dust before their eyes, they were resolved to play the man and defend the one spot which still was free—the hill where they stood, however small, however ill-provided. Thus day after day the tale of disaster went on, until sheer familiarity with suffering dulled the sense of what they had lost. Their one remaining hope was in their shields and swords.

The Gauls by this time had become aware that a final effort was necessary if they were to achieve their object. For several days they had been directing their fury only against bricks and mortar. Rome was a heap of smouldering ruins, but something remained—the armed men in the Citadel; and when the Gauls saw that, in spite of everything, they remained unshaken and would never yield to anything but force, they resolved to attempt an assault. At dawn, therefore, on a given signal the whole vast horde assembled in the Forum; then, roaring out their challenge, they locked shields and moved up the slope of the Citadel.

The Romans remained calm. Guards were strengthened at every possible point of approach; where the thrust seemed to be coming, the best troops were stationed to meet it. Then they waited, letting the enemy climb, and confident that the steeper the slope he reached the more easily they could hurl them back. About half way up the attackers paused, and the Romans, from the heights above them, charged; the steepness of the descent itself made the weight of their impact irresistible, and the Gallic masses were flung back and down with such severe losses that a similar attempt, with either a part or the whole of their forces, was never made again. Disappointed, therefore, of their hopes of a direct assault, they prepared for a siege. For them the decision was an unfortunate one, for, not having thought of it before, they had destroyed in the fires all the city's store of grain, while what had not yet been brought in had been smuggled during the past few days into Veii; their solution to the difficulty was to employ a part of their force to invest the Citadel, while the remainder supplied it by raiding the territory of neighboring peoples.

* * *

While the siege continued, the heroic exile Camillus raised an army in Ardea and Veii and marched to the relief of the Roman citadel.

During these transactions in Veii the Citadel in Rome passed through a brief period of extreme danger from an attempted surprise. It may be that the messenger from Veii had left footprints, and the Gauls had noticed them, or possibly they had observed, in the ordinary course of their duties, that the rocky ascent near the shrine of Carmenta was easily practicable. In any case, one starlit night, they made the attempt. Having first sent an unarmed man to reconnoitre the route, they began the climb. It was something of a scramble: at the awkward spots a man would get a purchase for his feet on a comrade below him, then haul him up in his turn—weapons were passed up from hand to hand as the lie of the rocks allowed—until by pushing and pulling one another they reached the top. What is more, they accomplished the climb so quietly that the Romans on guard never heard a sound, and even the dogs—who are normally aroused by the least noise in the night—noticed nothing. It was the geese that saved them—Juno's sacred geese, which in spite of the dearth of provisions had not been killed. The cackling of the birds and the clapping of their wings awoke Marcus Manlius—a distinguished officer who had been consul three years before—and he, seizing his sword and giving the alarm, hurried, without waiting for the support of his bewildered comrades, straight to the point of danger. One Gaul was already up, but Manlius with a blow from the boss of his shield toppled him headlong down the cliff. The falling body carried others with it; panic spread; many more who dropped their weapons to get a better grip of the rocks were killed by Manlius, and soon more Roman troops were on the scene, tumbling the climbers down with javelins and stones, until every man of them was dislodged and sent hurtling to the bottom of the cliff.

When the excitement had died down, the garrison was undisturbed for the remainder of the night—so far as the phrase can be used of men in such a situation, unable, as they were, to think even of the past peril without a shudder. At dawn next morning the bugle summoned all ranks to parade before the military tribunes, to be rewarded—or punished— for the events of the night before. Manlius, having been commended for his brave conduct, was given presents not only by the commanding officers but by the troops as well, every one of them agreeing to take to his house in the Citadel half a pound of flour and a gill of wine. That may sound a small thing, but in the light of the general scarcity the fact the men in order to show their appreciation of a comrade were willing to go short of necessary supplies, was a signal proof of their affectionate regard. The sentries who had been on guard and had failed to observe the enemy's ascent were then called. It was the intention of Sulpicius, one of the officers in command, to punish all of them with death, in the "military manner"; but he was induced to change his mind by the unanimous protest of the troops, who insisted that one man only had been to blame. The rest were accordingly spared, and the single culprit, whose guilt was beyond doubt, was flung from the rock. Both verdict and punishment were universally approved. The memory of that night of peril led the Romans to keep a stricter watch; the Gauls, too, began to tighten their precautions, as it was common knowledge that messages were passing between Veii and Rome.

In both armies it was hunger that now caused more distress than anything else. The Gauls had disease as well to contend with, as the position they occupied on low ground between hills was an unhealthy one, and rendered more so by the parched condition of the earth after the conflagrations, and the heat, and the choking clouds of ashes and dust whenever the wind blew. Such conditions were intolerable to a people accustomed to a wet, cold climate; the heat stifled them, infection spread, and they were soon dying like cattle. Before long the survivors had not the energy to bury the dead separately, but piled the corpses in heaps and burned them. The spot where they burnt them came afterwards to be known as the Gallic Pyres.

About this time an armistice was agreed to and the commanders allowed the troops to communicate with each other. Gallic soldiers used frequently in talking to tell the Romans that they knew they were starving and ought therefore to surrender, and the story goes that the Romans, to make them believe that that they were not, threw loaves of bread from various points in their lines down into the Gallic outposts. None the less the time soon came when hunger could no longer be either concealed or endured. Camillus was raising troops at Ardea, where after instructing his Master of Horse, Lucius Valerius, to bring up his men from Veii, he was busy training a force fit to deal with the Gauls on equal terms—while the beleaguered army on the Capitol waited and hoped. It was a terrible time: ordinary military duties were by now beyond their strength; they had survived all other ills that flesh is heir to, but one enemy—famine—which nature herself has made invincible, remained. Day after day they looked to see if help from Camillus was near; but at last when hope as well as food began to fail, and they were too weak to carry the weight of their equipment when they went on duty, they admitted that they must either surrender, or buy the enemy off on the best terms they could get—for the Gauls were already letting it be known pretty clearly that they would accept no very great sum to abandon the siege. The Senate accordingly met, and the military tribunes were authorized to arrange the terms; Quintus Sulpicius conferred with the Gallic chieftain Brennus and together they agreed upon the price, one thousand pounds' weight of gold—the price of a nation soon to rule the world. Insult was added to what was already sufficiently disgraceful, for the weights which the Gauls brought for weighing the metal were heavier than standard, and when the Roman commander objected the insolent barbarian flung his sword into the scale, saying "Woe to the vanquished!"—words intolerable to Roman ears.

Nevertheless it was neither God's purpose nor man's that the Romans—of all people—should owe their lives to a cash payment. The argument about the weights had unduly protracted the weighing-out of the gold, and it so happened that before it was finished and the infamous bargain completed, Camillus himself appeared upon the scene. He ordered the gold to be removed and the Gauls to leave, and answered their indignant remonstrances by denying the existence of any valid agreement; such an agreement as there was had, he pointed out, been entered into after his appointment as Dictator and by an inferior magistrate acting without his instructions. The Gauls, therefore, must prepare to fight. He then ordered his troops to pile their baggage and get ready for action. "It is your duty," he said, "to recover your country not by gold but by the sword. You will be fighting with all you love before your eyes: the temples of the gods, your wives and children, the soil of your native land scarred with the ravages of war, and everything which honor and truth call upon you to defend, or recover, or avenge."

It was no place for military manoeuvre: the city was half in ruins and the ground, in any case, uneven and rough; but Camillus in his dispositions made the best of his opportunities, such as they were, and used all his experience to give the initial advantage to his own men. The Gauls were taken by surprise; arming themselves hurriedly, they attacked, but with more fire than judgement. Luck had turned at last; human skill, aided by the powers of heaven, was fighting on the side of Rome, and the invaders were scattered at the first encounter with as little effort as had gone to their victory on the Allia. A second, and more regular, engagement was fought later eight miles on the road to Gabii, where the Gauls had reorganized, and resulted in another victory for Camillus. This time it was bloody and complete: the Gallic camp was taken, and the army annihilated. Camillus returned in triumph to Rome, his victorious troops roaring out their bawdy songs and saluting their commander by the well-merited titles of another Romulus, father of his country and second founder of Rome.

The Ides of March

GUGLIELMO FERRERO

44 B.C. Was Julius Caesar a sincere political reformer bent on reorganizing a corrupt and inefficient government, or only an ambitious opportunist? Historians have expressed boldly personal opinions about the greatest Roman, but they are not yet agreed. Ferrero, who delighted in controversial theories, wrote his The Greatness and Decline of Rome *in five volumes, which were published between 1907 and 1909. He opposed Mussolini and was exiled in 1930. He refers to the "Roman democracy," which was not a democracy as the word is now used, but an oligarchic republic.*

Modern historians almost all express surprise at the ease with which the conspiracy was arranged; in their very justifiable admiration for the man who was seeking to reorganize the Roman world they have been unsparing in their judgments upon the treachery, the obstinacy, the short-sightedness of his murderers. Had they tried to form an estimate of the actual situation, as it must have appeared to men at the time, they might have found reason to modify both their surprise and their condemnation. Great man as Caesar was, it was impossible that his contemporaries should anticipate the child-like hero-worship of posterity or see in him a demi-god whose very blunders and self-deceptions were material for adoration! Many of the conspirators

26

may indeed have been actuated by paltry and personal considerations. But these after all were not the real dynamic forces at work. Neither the conspiracy itself nor Caesar's work as a whole can be judged good or bad by a simple inquiry into the private motives of the actors concerned. We must realize, in all its dramatic intensity, the unique situation which impelled them to action.

Caesar was a genius—a man whose powers have seldom or never been equalled in history. He was at once student, artist and man of action: and in every sphere of his activity he left the imprint of greatness. His soaring yet intensely practical imagination, his wonderfully clear-cut and well-balanced intelligence, his untiring energy and lightning quickness of decision, his marvellous elasticity of temper and iron power of self-control, his indifference even at moments of the greatest strain to anything of the nature of sentiment or mysticism would have made him, at any time in the world's history, one of the giants of his age. Under twentieth-century conditions he might have become a captain of industry in the United States or a great pioneer or mine-owner in South Africa, or a scientist or man of letters in Europe with a world-wide influence over his contemporaries. In the Rome of his day both family tradition and personal inclination forced him into politics. Political life is always perilous to a man of genius. There is no sphere of activity which is so much at the mercy of unforeseen accidents or where the effort put out is so incommensurable with the result obtained. In the field of Roman politics Caesar succeeded in becoming a great general, a great writer, a great character. He failed to become a great statesman.*

There were three great political objects for which he fought during his career: the reconstruction of the Constitutional Democratic party in 59, a bold adoption and extension of the imperialism of Lucullus in 56, and the regeneration of the Roman world by the conquest of Parthia after the death of Pompey. The first and second of these ideas were taken up too late: the third was inherently impossible. The first ended in the revolutionary Radicalism of his Consulship, the second in the field of Carrhae and the horrors of the death struggle with Vercingetorix, the third in the Ides of March. It would be unjust to lay the blame for these failures at Caesar's door. If he was not a statesman, it was because the times forbade him to become one. In a democracy bitten with the mad passion for power, riches and self-indulgence, a man who stands aloof from these temptations may live very happily in retirement and write books upon philosophy; but he must not stray into the hazardous paths of politics. An inexorable destiny

---

* This opinion is directly contrary to that of Mommsen. "No doubt," he says, "Caesar was a great orator, a great writer, and a great general, but he became all these because he was an incomparable statesman."

seems to dog Caesar all his days. It was events which drove him to the revolutionary measures of his Consulship. Again it was the necessity under which he lay to save himself, his party and his work from the results of that revolution which drove him to the boldest step in his life, the annexation of Gaul. Annexation once proclaimed, it was no longer in his power to turn back; he was pushed on to those sanguinary acts of repression which form the darkest page in his history. The civil war arose so inevitably out of the policy which he adopted in Gaul that all his efforts to avert it were doomed to failure. His success in the civil war proved even greater than he had hoped—so great, in fact, as to defeat his own object. Victory left him an unexpected and painfully difficult position. Ostensibly master of the Roman world, he was in reality suspended between two equally impossible alternatives—either to abandon the position he had just triumphantly captured, or, almost single-handed, with the help of a few personal adherents, to administer a huge and disorganized Empire. He dreamt of escaping from this dilemma by the conquest of Parthia, an enterprise which was to be the beginning of a new era in Roman history. With the experience of twenty centuries to guide us, it is easy to understand how he entertained such an idea: but easy also to understand that it was a fantastic illusion.

Caesar was not a great statesman; but he was a great destroyer. In him were personified all the revolutionary forces, the magnificent but devastating forces, of a mercantile age in conflict with the traditions of an old-world society—its religious scepticism, its indifference to morality, its insensibility to family affection, its opportunist and undisciplined politics, its contempt for precedent and tradition, its Eastern luxury, its grasping militarism, its passion for the baser forms of commerce and speculation, its first tentative efforts towards intellectual refinement, its naïve enthusiasm for art and science. There is hardly a stranger irony in history than that the rulers of Germany and Russia should have assumed the title of this prince of revolutionaries. For we fail to grasp the true significance of Caesar's career till we discern that, like Pompey and Crassus and the other great figures of his day, his mission was primarily destructive—to complete the disorganization and dissolution of the old world, both in Italy and the provinces, and thus make way for a stabler and juster system.

But when he imagined that he could apply his unrivalled powers of mind and will to all the intellectual and social influences of his time, and direct them to his own purposes, he displeased all parties and was removed from the scene. It matters little that in the latter part of his life he displayed more wisdom and moderation than in the earlier; that he attempted in part, though with many inconsistencies, to repair as a reformer the mistakes he had committed as a demagogue; that he had at last come to see that a discontented society, blind and breathless in the race for riches and self-indulgence, had set its selfish course, beyond all turning, for the Abyss.

To avert this collapse was beyond any single man's powers. Too many foes were struggling for mastery in the Roman society of his day—from the truceless conflict between riches and poverty or capital and debt, to the antagonism between the spirit of revolution and the spirit of authority, Asiatic profusion and Latin frugality, the new Hellenistic culture and the traditions of Roman life. No doubt Caesar had displayed a marvellous vigor and elasticity, far beyond that of any contemporary, in his prolonged resistance against the rolling and tossing of the Roman democracy, adrift as it was, like a derelict in a stormy ocean, amid the blasts of a perverse and excitable public opinion. But how could he compose or control these far-reaching conflicts in the whole of society when he could not even dominate those within the ranks of his own party? Until the struggle had reached its climax in the great crisis which began at Caesar's death and raged without intermission through the whole of the next decade, it was impossible for a new generation to build a sounder and more sheltered society out of the *débris* left by its predecessors—a busy, fortunate, Titanic breed of builders, but too worn and weary, too arrogant, too much embittered by war and hatred, too prone to licence in morals and politics and in their general philosophy of life, to be dowered with lasting happiness. The times called for a quieter, a more cautious, a more patient race of workers. Caesar's hour had come and gone. He must pass, as Crassus, Pompey, Cato, had passed before him, as Cicero was to follow after a few more months, together with the flower of the aristocracy that had lived through the greatest and most stirring age of Roman history.

It is in this role of Titanic destroyer therefore that we must admire him, a role which demanded almost superhuman qualities of conception and achievement. We find him, it is true, at the close of his career, busy with the reorganization of a world whose disorder he had done so much to promote, attempting to build on the field which he and his contemporaries had piled with wreckage. But for the success of this work two conditions were necessary. First, Caesar must retain sufficient vigor and elasticity to adapt himself to the needs of an altered policy; second, the great solvents that had been at work for the last century, loosening the fabric of Italian society, must have finished their work with the civil war. To the former condition fate forbids us the reply. Perhaps the Archdestroyer had still strength enough left him to turn that Protean genius to the work of reconstruction. As to the second, we have the evidence of the next twenty-five years. The forces of dissolution were indeed very far from exhausted. So far were they from being arrested at the time of Caesar's death, that they went on to provoke what was perhaps one of the most tremendous crises in world-history.

Moreover the fact that Caesar did not succeed in healing or even allaying the dissensions within his own party is in itself significant. It does not suggest that he would have been more successful in controlling the similar but far more violent antagonism in the wider field of society. We need not be surprised that Caesar, who could not see into the future, had little sense of the realities of the situation: that he naïvely looked forward to the conquest of Parthia as the prelude to an easy reorganization of the Republic. But the modern observer, viewing the centuries behind him in their right perspective, has a clearer vision of his dilemma. He has no excuse for regarding the plot to which Caesar fell a victim as an unlucky misadventure, due to the weakness or the wickedness of a few isolated individuals. The very opposite is the truth. The conspiracy was the first outcome of an important movement, inevitable both for practical and sentimental reasons. It marks a genuine alliance between the surviving Conservatives and the right wing of Caesar's party. Its object was to hinder the Parthian expedition. The conspirators were in fact less concerned with the actual situation than with that which would face them when Caesar returned victorious from the East. Not all his most emphatic denials could convince them that he was not intending an open kingship. As the representatives of the old Latin and Conservative Republic, the defenders of property and class interest, they banded themselves together against the Asiatic and revolutionary monarchy which they saw looming in the East, between the folds of Caesar's conquering banners.

The plot was so well taken up that by the 1st of March it comprised according to one account sixty, according to another, no less than eighty Senators. One of the last to join was Decimus Brutus, Caesar's favorite friend, who had returned to Rome from Gaul towards the end of February. Cicero on the other hand was not admitted into the secret; they were unwilling to expose the veteran writer and speaker to the dangers of conspiracy. The large number of plotters is astonishing in view of the fact that the risk of indiscretions is always necessarily increased with the number of accomplices. But there was probably good reason for their action. The loyalty of the army to their general was regarded as unassailable; while the proletariat, among whom the excitement was rising daily higher, seemed, rightly or wrongly, to be wholly on Caesar's side. It was therefore absolutely necessary that Caesar should be struck down not by a few personal enemies but by a practically unanimous Senate. It was the only way in which the coalition of Pompeians and moderate Caesarians could hope, after his death, to maintain control over the legions, the populace and the Provinces. This is no doubt also the reason why, after lengthy discussion, it was decided that Antony should not meet the same fate as his leader. It was not Brutus, with his scruples against the shedding of Roman blood, that saved him, but more probably the reflection that the simultaneous disappearance of the two Consuls would have prevented the immediate restoration of the old constitution. No doubt they also hoped that so recent a convert to the party of tyranny would return to his old allies on the death of the Dictator.

The place and the method of the assassination are clear evidence of the real intentions of its authors. These details opened up a very difficult question, and a number of alternative plans were discussed during the visits which the conspirators paid to one another in their houses; for to avoid suspicion no common meeting was held. But the days were passing and immediate action was imperative. Caesar would be shortly starting for Parthia. His veterans, who were to escort him out of the city, were already streaming in from all parts of Italy, finding quarters as best they could in the temples. Several different proposals were made, but no one seemed satisfactory. The conspirators began to lose heart; several already repented having joined. There was one moment of awful suspense when the weaker section threatened to break off the whole enterprise. But the force of events and the danger in which they were already involved came to strengthen their sinking resolution.

Caesar was moving on from illegality to illegality. He had gone so far as to pass through the Senate a law providing that before his departure magistrates should be chosen to cover the whole of the next three years, the probable duration of his campaign. Early in March Hirtius and Pansa were nominated Consuls for 43, together with a new batch of Tribunes. According to one report, a Sibylline oracle had declared that only a king could conquer the Parthians, and Lucius Aurelius Cotta, the Consul of 65, against whom Caesar had conspired in 66, was about to propose his proclamation as king of the whole Roman Empire outside of Italy. When at last it was known that Caesar intended to convoke the Senate on the 15th in the Curia of Pompey to settle the question of Dolabella's Consulship and other outstanding business, and that he was to leave Rome on the 17th, all agreed that this last opportunity must not be allowed to go by. Cut down in the Senate-house by a band of eighty influential Senators Caesar would seem to fall like Romulus at the hands of his country.

There was no more drawing back. On the Ides of March the blow must be struck, cost what it might. The last days before the sitting began slowly to run their course. Every evening in eighty of the richest houses of Rome men who had often and often faced death on the battlefield went trembling to their beds, not knowing whether Caesar would let them live till morning. At dawn they would recommence the wearisome round of visits to friends' houses, avoiding the curious eyes of passers-by in the streets, baffling the listening ears of the slaves in the houses, with the pretended indifference of a ceremonious visitor. Brutus suffered especially from these torments of doubt and anxiety. If he bore himself in the streets with all the outward marks of serenity, within doors he would plunge into long and melancholy reveries; he would toss and sigh in his sleep, with a trouble that Portia was unable to divine. Fear, gratitude and affection were fighting a hard battle within him against his obstinate ambition to play the hero's part. Meanwhile the days were passing; nothing stirred in Rome; the secret was well kept.*

Neither Caesar not his intimates seemed to dream of danger. Only Portia, by constant questioning, had wrung the truth from her husband.

Bit by bit at private meetings all the details of the assassination were arranged. The conspirators were to conceal daggers under their togas; Trebonius was to detain Antony in conversation. In the theatre of Pompey, just outside the Curia, Decimus Brutus was to station a troop of gladiators that he had hired for the Games, who would defend the conspirators in case of need. Immediately after the murder Brutus was to deliver a speech to the Senate explaining the reasons of their action and proposing the reconstruction of the Republic. The 14th of March came and passed without a hint of trouble. Caesar had arranged to spend that evening with Lepidus, and would return home late—a clear sign that he had no suspicions. How many eyes must have been turned that night towards the sky, to watch for the setting of the stars and the rising of the sun that was to see Caesar dead and the Republic restored! Only Caesar, home late from his friend, slept innocent of his doom—the broken sleep of a sick and weary man.

On the morning of the 15th the conspirators were early at their rendezvous, at the colonnade of Pompey, near the present Campo dei Fiori. Brutus, who was Praetor, mounted the judgment-seat and began quietly to attend to his day's litigation, controlling his inward excitement. The rest of the conspirators awaited the opening of the sitting, walking up and down the colonnade talking to their friends and trying to conceal their agitation. In the neighboring theatre of Pompey a performance was going on. There was the usual bustle and traffic in the streets. Caesar might arrive at any moment.

But Caesar delayed to come, detained, it seems, by a slight indisposition, which had almost induced him for a moment to postpone the sitting. The conspirators, already excited, began to grow anxious, to start up at every passing noise. A friend approached Casca, one of the conspirators, and said to him, laughing, "You know how to keep a secret, but Brutus has told

---

* I believe that there is a great deal of exaggeration in the ancient stories of warnings given to Caesar. If the conspiracy had been so well known it would have come to the ears of Antony, Lepidus and other faithful friends, which would have been enough to stop it. It was not necessary that Caesar himself should be warned. It is probable that during these days he received imaginary revelations of a conspiracy such as he had often received before, like all heads of a government.

me everything." Casca, dumfounded, was about to reveal the whole plot, when his friend's next words showed that he was alluding to Casca's intention of standing for the Aedileship. One of the Senators, Popilius Lena, came up to Brutus and Cassius and whispered into their ear, "Success is possible, but whatever you do do quickly." Still Caesar did not come. It was perhaps about ten in the morning and the sun was already high in the heavens. They spoke of treachery and their nerve began to fail. At last Cassius resolved to send Decimus Brutus to Caesar's house, to see what was detaining him and to bring him to the Curia. Decimus hurriedly threaded the back streets by Campus Martius, descended into the Forum, and found his way into the *domus publica*, where Caesar had his official dwelling as Pontifex Maximus. He found him just on the point of postponing the sitting. It was the crucial moment. But Decimus had the nerve, or the ferocity, to drag to the slaughter-house the friend who trusted blindly to his guidance. He engaged him in pleasant conversation, and persuaded him to come.

At last Caesar's litter hove in sight. Just outside the Curia the Dictator descended, and the conspirators, who were already collected in the hall, observed Popilius Lena go up to him and address him in low tones. It was a cruel instant of suspense for Brutus and Cassius. Cassius very nearly lost his self-control; but Brutus, calmer than his colleague, had the courage to look Caesar in the face. That stern, emaciated, careworn countenance, with the marks of his work lined upon it, was listening unmoved. Brutus beckoned Cassius that all was well. But there was another delay. Caesar stopped outside the Senate-house to make the sacrifices ordained by the State ritual. At last he entered and took his seat, while Trebonius was detained in conversation outside. Tullius Cimber approached the Dictator to demand pardon for an exiled brother. The others gathered round him, as though to join their prayers to Cimber's, till Caesar, feeling that they were pressing him too close, stood up and bade them move farther away. Then Tullius seized him by the toga, which slipped down to his feet, leaving the body covered only with a light tunic. It was the appointed signal. Casca aimed the first blow, but missed in his fright, hitting him in the shoulder. Caesar turned sharply on him with a cry, seizing his *stilus* in self-defence. Casca called for help to his brother, who plunged his dagger in Caesar's side. Cassius struck him in the face, Decimus in the groin. In an instant the whole band was upon him, so excited that they hit one another, while Caesar fought like a wild beast at bay, and the rest of the Senators, after a moment's stupor, fled panic-stricken from the hall, shouting and pushing and stumbling over one another in their haste, Caesar's own supporters, even Antony, amongst them. Only two rushed forward to rescue Caesar. Their loyalty was in vain. Still madly beating off his enemies Caesar had fought his way to the foot of Pompey's statue, where he had fallen at last in a sea of blood.*

The murder over, Brutus turned to deliver his speech to the Senate. But the Curia was empty. The conspirators had not reflected that a childish panic might upset their elaborate plan for at once decreeing the restoration of the Republic. What was to be done? In the excitement of the moment they held a brief consultation. Fearing trouble from the veterans and the people they resolved to summon the gladiators of Decimus and take them up to a fortified position on the Capitol, where they could deliberate in greater calm. Then they emerged from the Curia, with their togas twisted round their left arms for shields, brandishing their bloody daggers in their right hands, bearing aloft on a stick the cap, the symbol of Liberty, and shouting to Liberty, to the Republic, and to Cicero, the philosopher of Republicanism. But outside they found all was noise and confusion. In the colonnade and the neighboring streets people had taken fright at the sudden emergence of the Senators and the appearance of the armed gladiators. The alarm was raised in an instant and the public took to their heels. The noise of the shouting reached the spectators in the theatre of Pompey, who rushed out to join the fugitives, while pickpockets laid hands on the baskets and carts of the strolling costers round the theatre. There was a general rush for refuge into houses and shops, which their owners as promptly closed. The sudden appearance of a crowd of armed men, reeking with blood, increased the disorder in the streets they traversed. It was in vain that, led by Brutus, they shouted and gesticulated to quiet the crowd. Men were far too frightened to listen. Meanwhile the news was spreading rapidly to the farthest corners of Rome, and everywhere people were flying panic-stricken for shelter. Before long Antony was safely shut up in his house, the conspirators were entrenched in the Capitol, the frightened public had retired expectant to their homes, and Rome was wrapped in funereal silence, like a city of the dead. All parties were afraid of one another.

Parthia was saved. The Archdestroyer had himself been cut down at the moment when he was setting out to conquer the Empire of Parthia and set Rome on the road trodden by Alexander. For this was the dream which had absorbed all his energies during the last months of his life, while the rumors as to his monarchical ambitions were probably nothing more than inventions or at least exaggerations on the part of his enemies. How he

---

* I have only given the details of the beginning of the assassination, as they alone are probable. It is natural enough that the conspirators should have remembered the first acts in the mêlée and retained no clear memory of the rest. Caesar's words to Brutus as he wrapped himself in his toga are certainly a myth. How could he wrap himself in his toga with his assassins striking at him from all sides?

would have acted on his return, supposing he returned victorious, no one can say. Perhaps he did not know himself. After all, he had been an opportunist all his life. Thrown into politics in an age of unexampled confusion, he had learnt, by thirty years' experience, to adapt himself to the most widely divergent conditions. Always entirely engrossed in the question of the hour, he was at this moment only considering how he could use the Dictatorship that he had won in the civil war to become a second Alexander and bring home from Parthia the secret of social reorganization.

But for once the incomparable opportunist had mistaken his reckoning. Caesar had already, without knowing it, contributed more than all his contemporaries to the future of the world. His greatest work for posterity was the conquest of Gaul, to which he himself attributed so little importance. But to the men of his own day he had no remedy to offer. Before the great regeneration of her society could come about Rome needed, not feats of arms on her distant frontiers, but a great crisis at home in which the forces of dissolution, now at work for a century, could at last run their course. Twenty more long years of storm and tragedy. Then, when all the foremost figures of the age had gone to their deaths by violence and their bones lay scattered through the lands of the Empire they had done so much to extend, an ordered and peaceful world would reap the tardy fruits of their labors. Then at last it would be plain how the conspirators had in part been right; that the hour of military autocracy was still far off; that as yet no citizen could raise an Eastern palace in the capital of the old Latin Republic; that death, the far-seeing liberator, had rescued Caesar from an entanglement which not even he could have unravelled; that not through absolutism, however inspired, but by the free, patient and often halting development of infinite small social forces, the stormy morning of the Roman Empire would broaden into a clear and tranquil noon.

Antony and Cleopatra

PLUTARCH

41–30 B.C. The most celebrated love affair in history lasted for eleven years, from Cleopatra's visit to Antony at Tarsus until their suicides in Alexandria after Antony's defeat by Octavius Caesar, great-nephew of Julius Caesar and the future Emperor Augustus. These glimpses of their love story provided the source of Shakespeare's play. They are taken from Plutarch's biography of Antony in his collection of forty-six biographies of Greeks and Romans called The Parallel Lives. *Plutarch was a historian almost by accident. His primary interest was in character analysis and moral conclusions. Plutarch was a prolific Greek writer and a priest of Apollo. He died about A.D. 120. The Elizabethan translation by Sir Thomas North was edited and revised in 1941 by Roland Baughman.*

The manner how he fell in love with her was this.

Antonius, going to make war with the Parthians, sent to command Cleopatra to appear personally before him when he came into Cilicia, to answer unto such accusations as were laid against her, being this: that she had aided Cassius and Brutus in their war against him. The messenger sent unto Cleopatra to make this summons unto her was called Dellius, who when he had thoroughly considered her beauty, the excellent grace and sweetness of her tongue, he nothing mistrusted that Antonius would do any hurt to so noble a lady, but rather assured himself that within a few days she would be in great favor with him. Thereupon he did her great honor and persuaded her to come into Cilicia as honorably furnished as she could possible, and bade her not to be afraid at all of Antonius, for he was a more courteous lord than any she had ever seen. Cleopatra, on the other side, believing Dellius' words, and guessing by the former access and credit she had with Julius Caesar and Cneus Pompey (the son of Pompey the Great) only for her beauty, she began to have good hope that she might more easily win Antonius. For Caesar and Pompey knew her when she was but a young thing, and knew not then what the world meant; but now she went to Antonius at the age when a woman's beauty is at the prime, and she also of best judgment. So she furnished herself with a world of gifts, store of gold and silver, and of riches and other sumptuous ornaments, as is credible enough she might bring from so great a house and from so wealthy and rich a realm as Egypt was. But yet she carried nothing with her wherein she trusted more than in herself, and in the charms and enchantment of her passing beauty and grace.

Therefore, when she was sent unto by diverse letters, both from Antonius himself and also from his friends, she made so light of it and mocked Antonius so much, that she disdained to set forward otherwise but to take her barge in the river of Cydnus, the poop whereof was of gold, the sails of purple, and the oars of silver; which kept stroke in rowing after the sound of the music of flutes, hautboys, citherns, viols, and such other instruments as they played upon in the barge. And now for the person of herself: she was laid under a pavilion of cloth of gold tissue, apparelled and attired like the goddess Venus commonly drawn in picture; and hard by her, on either hand of her, pretty fair boys, apparelled as painters do set forth god Cupid, with little fans in their hands, with the which they fanned wind upon her. Her ladies and gentlewomen also, the fairest of them were apparelled like the nymphs Nereides (which are the mermaids of the waters) and like the Graces, some steering the helm, others tending the tackle and robes of the barge, out of which there came a wonderful passing sweet savor of perfume, that perfumed the wharf's side, pestered with innumerable multitudes of people. Some of them followed the barge all alongst the river's side; others also ran out of the city to see her coming in. So that in th'end there ran such multitudes of people one after another to see her, that Antonius was left post alone in the market place, in his imperial seat to give audience; and there went a rumor in the people's mouths that the goddess Venus was come to play with the god Bacchus for the general good of all Asia.

When Cleopatra landed, Antonius sent to invite her to supper to him. But she sent him word again he should do better rather to come and sup with her. Antonius therefore to show himself courteous unto her at her arrival, was contented to obey her, and went to supper to her; where he found such passing sumptuous fare that no tongue can express it. But amongst all other things, he most wondered at the infinite number of lights and torches hanged on the top of the house, giving light in every place, so artificially set and ordered by devices—some round, some square— that it was the rarest thing to behold that eye could discern or that ever books could mention. The next night, Antonius feasting her, contended to pass her in magnificence and fineness, but she overcame him in both. So that he himself began to scorn the gross service of his house, in respect of Cleopatra's sumptuousness and fineness. And when Cleopatra found Antonius' jests and slents to be but gross and soldierlike in plain manner, she gave it him finely and without fear taunted him thoroughly.

Now her beauty (as it is reported) was not so passing, as unmatchable of other women, nor yet such as upon present view did enamor men with her; but so sweet was her company and conversation that a man could not possibly but be taken. And besides her beauty, the good grace she had to talk and discourse, her courteous nature that tempered her words and deeds, was a spur that pricked to the quick. Furthermore, besides all these, her voice and words were marvellous pleasant; for her tongue was an instrument of music to divers sports and pastimes, the which she easily turned to any language that pleased her. She spake unto few barbarous people by interpreter, but made them answer herself, or at the least the most part of them; as the Ethiopians, the Arabians, the Troglodytes, the Hebrews, the Syrians, the Medes, and the Parthians, and to many others also, whose languages she had learned. Whereas divers of her progenitors, the kings of Egypt, could scarce learn the Egyptian tongue only, and many of them forgot to speak the Macedonian.

Now Antonius was so ravished with the love of Cleopatra that, though his wife Fulvia had great wars and much ado with Caesar for his affairs, and that the army of the Parthians (the which the king's lieutenants had given to the only leading of Labienus) was now assembled in Mesopotamia ready to invade Syria, yet, as though all this had nothing touched him, he yielded himself to go with Cleopatra into Alexandria, where he spent and lost in childish sports (as a man might say) and idle pastimes, the most precious thing a man can spend, as Antiphon saith; and that is, time. For they made an order between them, which they called *Amimetobion* (as much to say, no life comparable and matchable with it), one feasting each other by turns. . . .

* * *

But now again to Cleopatra. Plato writeth that there are four kinds of flattery, but Cleopatra divided it into many kinds. For she, were it in sport, or in matter of earnest, still devised sundry new delights to have Antonius at commandment, never leaving him night or day, nor once letting him go out of her sight. For she would play at dice with him, drink with him, and hunt commonly with him, and also be with him when he went to any exercise or activity of body. And sometime also, when he would go up and down the city disguised like a slave in the night, and would peer into poormen's windows and their shops, and scold and brawl with them within the house, Cleopatra would also be in a chambermaid's array, and amble up and down the streets with him, so that oftentimes Antonius bore away both mocks and blows. Now, though most men misliked this manner, yet the Alexandrians were commonly glad of this jollity and liked it well, saying very gallantly and wisely that Antonius showed them a comical face, to wit, a merry countenance, and the Romans a tragical face, to say, a grim look.

But to reckon up all the foolish sports they made, revelling in this sort, it were too fond a part of me, and therefore I will only tell you one among the rest. On a time he went to angle for fish, and when he could take none, he was as angry as he could be, because Cleopatra stood by. Wherefore he secretly commanded the fishermen that, when he cast in his line, they should straight dive under the water and put a fish on his hook which they had taken before; and so snatched up his angling rod and brought up a fish twice or thrice. Cleopatra found it straight, yet she seemed not to see it but wondered at his excellent fishing; but when she was alone by herself among her own people, she told them how it was, and bade them the next morning to be on the water to see the fishing. A number of people came to the haven and got into the fisher boats to see this fishing. Antonius then threw in his line and Cleopatra straight commanded one of her men to dive under the water before Antonius' men, and to put some old salt fish upon his bait, like unto those that are brought out of the country of Pontus. When he had hung the fish on his hook, Antonius thinking he had taken a fish indeed, snatched up his line presently. Then they all fell a-laughing. Cleopatra laughing also, said unto him, "Leave us (my lord) Egyptians (which dwell in the country of Pharus and Canobus) your angling rod: this is not thy profession; thou must hunt after conquering realms and countries."

* * *

Cleopatra in the meantime was very careful in gathering all sorts of poisons together to destroy men. Now, to make proof of these poisons which made men die with the least pain, she tried it upon condemned men in prison. For when she saw the poisons that were sudden and vehement, and brought speedy death with grievous torments, and, in contrary manner, that such as were more mild and gentle had not that quick speed and force to make one die suddenly, she afterwards went about to prove the stinging of snakes and adders, and made some to be applied to men in her sight, some in one sort and some in another. So when she had daily made divers and sundry proofs, she found none of all of them she had proved so fit as the biting of an aspic; the which only causeth a heaviness of the head, without swounding or complaining, and bringeth a great desire also to sleep, with a little sweat in the face, and so by little and little taketh away the senses and vital powers, no living creature perceiving that the patients feel any pain. For they are so sorry when anybody waketh them up, as those that being taken out of a sound sleep are very heavy and desirous to sleep.

This notwithstanding, they sent ambassadors unto Octavius Caesar in Asia, Cleopatra requesting the realm of Egypt for her children, and Antonius praying that he might be suffered to live at Athens like a private man, if Caesar would not let him remain in Egypt.

* * *

When Antonius saw that his men did forsake him and yielded unto Caesar, and that his footmen were broken and overthrown, he then fled into the city, crying out that Cleopatra had betrayed him unto them, with whom he had made war for her sake.

Then she, being afraid of his fury, fled into the tomb which she had caused to be made, and there locked the doors unto her, and shut all the springs of the locks with great bolts; and in the meantime sent unto Antonius to tell him that she was dead. Antonius believing it said unto himself: "What dost thou look for further, Antonius, sith spiteful fortune hath taken from thee the only joy thou hadst, for whom thou yet reservedst thy life?" When he had said these words, he went into a chamber and unarmed himself, and being naked said thus: "O Cleopatra, it grieveth me not that I have lost thy company, for I will not be long from thee; but I am sorry that having been so great a captain and Emperor, I am indeed condemned to be judged of less courage and noble mind than a woman."

Now he had a man of his called Eros, whom he loved and trusted much, and whom he had long before caused to swear unto him that he should kill him when he did command him; and then he willed him to keep his promise. His man drawing his sword lift it up as though he had meant to have stricken his master; but turning his head at one side he thrust his sword into himself, and fell down dead at his master's foot. Then said Antonius, "O noble Eros, I thank thee for this, and it is valiantly done of thee, to show me what I should do to myself, which thou couldst not do for me." Therewith he took his sword and thrust it into his belly, and so fell down upon a little bed. The wound he had killed him not presently, for the blood stinted a little when he was laid, and when he came somewhat to himself again, he prayed them that were about him to dispatch him. But they all fled out of the chamber and left him crying out and tormenting himself; until at last there came a secretary unto him called Diomedes, who was commanded to bring him into the tomb or monument where Cleopatra was.

When he heard that she was alive, he very earnestly prayed his men to carry his body thither, and so he was carried in his men's arms into the entry of the monument. Notwithstanding, Cleopatra would not open the gates, but came to the high windows and cast out certain chains and ropes, in the which Antonius was trussed, and Cleopatra her own self, with two women only which she had suffered to come with her into these monuments, triced Antonius up. They who were present to behold it said they never saw so pitiful a sight. For they plucked up poor Antonius, all bloody as he was, and drawing on with pangs of death, who holding up his hands to Cleopatra raised up himself as well as he could. It was a hard thing for these women to do, to lift him up, but Cleopatra stooping down with her head, putting to all her strength to her uttermost power, did lift him up with much ado, and never let go her hold, with the help of the women beneath that bade her be of good courage, and were as sorry to see her labor so, as she herself.

So, when she had gotten him in after that sort, and laid him on a bed, she rent her garments upon him, clapping her breast, and scratching her face and stomach. Then she dried up his blood that had berayed his face, and called him her lord, her husband, and Emperor, forgetting her own misery and calamity for the pity and compassion she took of him. Antonius made her cease her lamenting and called for wine, either because he was athirst, or else for that he thought to hasten his death. When he had drunk, he earnestly prayed her and persuaded her that she would seek to save her life, if she could possible, without reproach and dishonor; and that chiefly she should trust Proculeius above any man else about Caesar. And, as for himself, that she should not lament or sorrow for the miserable change of his fortune at the end of his days, but rather that she should think him the more fortunate for the former triumphs and honors he had received; considering that while he lived he was the noblest and greatest prince of the world, and that now he was overcome not cowardly but valiantly, a Roman by another Roman.

As Antonius gave the last gasp, Proculeius came that was sent from Caesar. For after Antonius had thrust his sword in himself, as they carried him into the tombs and monuments of Cleopatra, one of his guard called Dercataeus took his sword with the which he had stricken himself, and hid it; then he secretly stale away and brought Octavius Caesar the first news of his death and showed him his sword that was bloodied. Caesar hearing these news straight withdrew himself into secret place of his tent, and there burst out with tears, lamenting his hard and miserable fortune that had been his friend and brother-in-law, his equal in the empire, and companion with him in sundry great exploits and battles. Then he called for all his friends and showed them the letters Antonius had written to him, and his answers also sent him again, during their quarrel and strife, and how fiercely and proudly the other answered him to all just and reasonable matters he wrote unto him.

After this, he sent Proculeius, and commanded him to do what he could possible to get Cleopatra alive, fearing lest otherwise all the treasure would be lost; and furthermore, he thought that if he could take Cleopatra and bring her alive to Rome, she would marvellously beautify him and set out his triumph. But Cleopatra would never put herself into Proculeius' hands, although they spake together. For Proculeius came to the gates that were very thick and strong and surely barred, but yet there were some cranews through the which her voice might be heard; and so they without understood that Cleopatra demanded the kingdom of Egypt for her sons, and that Proculeius answered her that she should be of good cheer and not be afraid to refer all unto Caesar. After he had viewed the place very well, he came and reported her answer unto Caesar. Who immediately sent Gallus to speak once again with her, and bade him purposely hold her with talk, whilst Proculeius did set up a ladder against that high window by the which Antonius was triced up, and came down into the monument with two of his men, hard by the gate where Cleopatra stood to hear what Gallus said unto her.

One of her women which was shut in her monument with her saw Proculeius by chance as he came down, and shrieked out, "O, poor Cleopatra, thou art taken." Then, when she saw Proculeius behind her as she came from the gate, she thought to have stabbed herself in with a short dagger she ware of purpose by her side. But Proculeius came suddenly upon her, and taking her by both the hands said unto her, "Cleopatra, first thou shalt do thyself great wrong, and secondly unto Caesar, to deprive him of the occasion and opportunity openly to show his bounty and mercy, and to give his enemies cause to accuse the most courteous and noble prince that ever was, and to appeach him as though he were a cruel and merciless man that were not to be trusted." So even as he spoke the word, he took her dagger from her, and shook her clothes for fear of any poison hidden about her. Afterwards Caesar sent one of his enfranchised men called Epaphroditus, whom he straitly charged to look well unto her, and to beware in any case that she made not herself away; and for the rest, to use her with all the courtesy possible.

* * *

Many princes, great kings, and captains did crave Antonius' body of Octavius Caesar, to give him honorable burial; but Caesar would never

42

take it from Cleopatra, who did sumptuously and royally bury him with her own hands, whom Caesar suffered to take as much as she would to bestow upon his funerals. Now was she altogether overcome with sorrow and passion of mind, for she had knocked her breast so pitifully that she had martyred it, and in divers places had raised ulcers and inflammations, so that she fell into a fever withal; whereof she was very glad, hoping thereby to have good color to abstain from meat, and that so she might have died easily, without any trouble. She had a physician called Olympus, whom she made privy of her intent, to th'end he should help her to rid her out of her life, as Olympus writeth himself, who wrote a book of all these things. But Caesar mistrusted the matter by many conjectures he had, and therefore did put her in fear and threatened her to put her children to shameful death. With these threats, Cleopatra for fear yielded straight as she would have yielded unto strokes, and afterwards suffered herself to be cured and dieted as they listed.

Shortly after, Caesar came himself in person to see her and to comfort her. Cleopatra being laid upon a little low bed in poor estate, when she saw Caesar come into her chamber, she suddenly rose up, naked in her smock, and fell down at his feet marvellously disfigured, both for that she had plucked her hair from her head, as also for that she had martyred all her face with her nails; and besides her voice was small and trembling, her eyes sunk into her head with continual blubbering, and moreover they might see the most part of her stomach torn in sunder. To be short, her body was not much better than her mind; yet her good grace and comeliness and the force of her beauty was not altogether defaced. But notwithstanding this ugly and pitiful state of hers, yet she showed herself within by her outward looks and countenance. When Caesar had made her lie down again, and sate by her bed's side, Cleopatra began to clear and excuse herself for that she had done, laying all to the fear she had of Antonius. Caesar, in contrary manner, reproved her in every point. Then she suddenly altered her speech and prayed him to pardon her, as though she were afraid to die, and desirous to live.

At length, she gave him a brief and memorial of all the ready money and treasure she had. But by chance there stood Seleucus by, one of her treasurers, who to seem a good servant came straight to Caesar to disprove Cleopatra—that she had not set in all, but kept many things back of purpose. Cleopatra was in such a rage with him that she flew upon him, and took him by the hair of the head, and boxed him well favoredly. Caesar fell a-laughing, and parted the fray. "Alas," said she, "O Caesar, is not this a great shame and reproach, that thou having vouchsafed to take the pains to come unto me, and hast done me this honor—poor wretch and caitiff creature, brought into this pitiful and miserable estate—and that mine own servants should come now to accuse me; though it may be I have reserved some jewels and trifles meet for women, but not for me (poor soul) to set out myself withal, but meaning to give some pretty presents and gifts unto Octavia and Livia, that they making means and intercession for me to thee, thou mightest yet extend thy favor and mercy upon me?" Caesar was glad to hear her say so, persuading himself thereby that she had yet a desire to save her life. So he made her answer that he did not only give her that to dispose of at her pleasure, which she had kept back, but further promised to use her more honorably and bountifully than she would think for, and he so took his leave of her, supposing he had deceived her; but indeed he was deceived himself.

There was a young gentleman, Cornelius Dolabella, that was one of Caesar's very great familiars, and besides did bear no evil will unto Cleopatra. He sent her word secretly, as she had requested him, that Caesar determined to take his journey through Syria, and that within three days he would send her away before with her children. When this was told Cleopatra, she requested Caesar that it would please him to suffer her to offer the last oblations of the dead unto the soul of Antonius. This being granted her, she was carried to the place where his tomb was, and there falling down on her knees, embracing the tomb with her women, the tears running down her cheeks, she began to speak in this sort: "O, my dear lord Antonius, not long sithence I buried thee here, being a free woman; and now I offer unto thee the funeral sprinklings and oblations, being a captive and prisoner; and yet I am forbidden and kept from tearing and murdering this captive body of mine with blows, which they carefully guard and keep only to triumph of thee; look therefore henceforth for no other honors, offerings, nor sacrifices from me, for these are the last which Cleopatra can give thee, sith now they carry her away. Whilst we lived together, nothing could sever our companies, but now at our death I fear me they will make us change our countries. For as thou being a Roman has been buried in Egypt, even so, wretched creature, I an Egyptian shall be buried in Italy, which shall be all the good that I have received by thy country. If therefore the gods where thou art now have any power and authority—sith our gods here have forsaken us—suffer not thy true friend and lover to be carried away alive, that in me they triumph of thee; but receive me with thee and let me be buried in one self tomb with thee. For though my griefs and miseries be infinite, yet none hath grieved me more, nor that I could less bear withal, than this small time which I have been driven to live alone without thee."

Then having ended these doleful plaints and crowned the tomb with garlands and sundry nosegays and marvellous lovingly embraced the same she commanded they should prepare her bath, and when she had bathed and washed herself, she fell to her meat and was sumptuously served. Now whilst she was at dinner there came a country man and brought her a basket. The soldiers that warded at the gates asked him straight what he had in his basket. He opened the basket and took out the leaves that covered the figs and showed them that they were figs he brought. They all of them marvelled to see so goodly figs. The country man laughed to hear them, and bade them take some if they would. They believed he told them truely, and so bade him carry them in. After Cleopatra had dined, she sent a certain table written and sealed unto Caesar, and commanded them all to go out of the tombs where she was, but the two women; then she shut the doors to her. Caesar, when he received this table and began to read her lamentation and petition, requesting him that he would let her be buried with Antonius, found straight what she meant and thought to have gone thither himself; howbeit he sent one before in all haste that might be, to see what it was.

Her death was very sudden. For those whom Caesar sent unto her ran thither in all haste possible and found the soldiers standing at the gate, mistrusting nothing, nor understanding of her death. But when they had opened the doors, they found Cleopatra stark dead, laid upon a bed of gold, attired and arrayed in her royal robes, and one of her two women, which was called Iras, dead at her feet; and her other woman called Charmion, half dead, and trembling, trimming the diadem which Cleopatra ware upon her head. One of the soldiers, seeing her, angrily said unto her, "Is that well done, Charmion?" "Very well," said she again, "and meet for a princess descended from the race of so many noble kings." She said no more, but fell down dead hard by the bed.

Some report that this aspic was brought unto her in the basket with figs, and that she had commanded them to hide it under the fig leaves, that when she should think to take out the figs the aspic should bite her before she should see her; howbeit, that when she would have taken away the leaves for the figs, she perceived it, and said, "Art thou here then?" And so, her arm being naked, she put it to the aspic to be bitten. Others say again, she kept it in a box and that she did prick and thrust it with a spindle of gold, so that the aspic being angered withal leapt out with great fury and bit her in the arm. Howbeit few can tell the troth. For they report also that she had hidden poison in a hollow razor which she carried in the hair of her head; and yet was there no mark seen of her body, or any sign discerned that she was poisoned, neither also did they find this serpent in her tomb. But it was reported only that there were seen certain fresh steps or tracks where it had gone, on the tomb side toward the sea, and specially by the door's side. Some say also that they found two little pretty bitings on her arm, scant to be discerned; the which it seemeth Caesar himself gave credit unto, because in his triumph he carried Cleopatra's image with an aspic biting her arm. And thus goeth the report of her death.

Now Caesar, though he was marvellous sorry for the death of Cleopatra, yet he wondered at her noble mind and courage, and therefore commanded she should be nobly buried and laid by Antonius; and willed also that her two women should have honorable burial. Cleopatra died being eight and thirty years old, after she had reigned two and twenty years, and governed above fourteen of them with Antonius. And for Antonius, some say that he lived three and fifty years; and others say, six and fifty. All his statues, images, and metals were plucked down and overthrown, saving those of Cleopatra, which stood still in their places by means of Archibius, one of her friends, who gave Caesar a thousand talents that they should not be handled as those of Antonius were.

Imperial Matricide

TACITUS

A.D. 59. Nero became Emperor of Rome in A.D. *54 at the age of sixteen. His terrible mother, Agrippina, arranged his succession to the throne by poisoning her uncle and husband, the Emperor Claudius. Agrippina was so avid in her lust for power that when her teen-age son thwarted her desire to rule she threatened to make Claudius's son Britannicus emperor in his stead. So Nero poisoned Britannicus. Four years later, he arranged the murder of his interfering mother. Tacitus, a senator, consul, and imperial governor, wrote his* The Annals of Imperial Rome *at the end of the first century. It is widely considered the most brilliant history written in Latin.*

When the new year came, Nero ceased delaying his long-meditated crime. As his reign became longer, he grew bolder. Besides, he loved Poppaea more every day. While Agrippina lived, Poppaea saw no hope of his divorcing Octavia and marrying her. So Poppaea nagged and mocked him incessantly. He was an emperor under orders, she said—master neither of the empire nor of himself. "Otherwise," she said, "why do you postpone marrying me? I suppose my looks and victorious ancestors are not good enough. Or do you distrust my capacity to bear children? Or the sincerity of my love?

"No! I think you are afraid that, if we were married, I might tell you

47

frankly how the senate is downtrodden and the public enraged by your mother's arrogance and greed. If Agrippina can only tolerate daughters-in-law who hate her son, let me be Otho's wife again! I will go anywhere in the world where I can only hear the emperor's humiliations rather than see them—and see you in danger, like myself!" The appeal was reinforced by tears and all a lover's tricks. Nero was won. Nor was there any opposition. Everyone longed for the mother's domination to end. But no one believed that the son's hatred would go as far as murder.

According to one author, Agrippina's passion to retain power carried her so fast that at midday, the time when food and drink were beginning to raise Nero's temperature, she several times appeared before her inebriated son all decked out and ready for incest. Their companions observed sensual kisses and evilly suggestive caresses. Seneca, supposing that the answer to a woman's enticements was a woman, called in the ex-slave Acte. She feared for Nero's reputation—and for her own safety. Now she was instructed to warn Nero that Agrippina was boasting of her intimacy with her son, that her boasts had received wide publicity, and that the army would never tolerate a sacrilegious emperor.

Another writer agrees in attributing successful intervention to Acte's wiles, but states that the desires were not Agrippina's but Nero's. But the other authorities support the contrary version. So does the tradition. That may be because Agrippina really did intend this monstrosity. Or perhaps it is because no sexual novelty seemed incredible in such a woman. In her earliest years she had employed immorality as a means to power. Through the same ambition she had sunk to be Pallas' mistress. So Nero avoided being alone with her. When she left for her gardens or country mansions, he praised her intention of taking a holiday.

Finally, however, he concluded that wherever Agrippina was she was intolerable. He decided to kill her. His only doubt was whether to employ poison, or the dagger, or violence of some other kind. Poison was the first choice. But a death at the emperor's table would not look fortuitous after Britannicus had died there. Yet her criminal conscience kept her so alert for plots that it seemed impractical to corrupt her household. Moreover, she had strengthened her physical resistance by a preventive course of antidotes. No one could think of a way of stabbing her without detection. And there was another danger: that the selected assassin might shrink from carrying out his dreadful orders.

However, a scheme was put forward by Anicetus, an ex-slave who commanded the fleet at Misenum. In Nero's boyhood Anicetus had been his tutor; he and Agrippina had hated each other. A ship could be made, he now said, with a section which would come loose at sea and hurl Agrippina into the water without warning. Nothing is so productive of surprises as the sea, remarked Anicetus; if a shipwreck did away with her, who could be so unreasonable as to blame a human agency instead of wind and water? Besides, when she was dead the emperor could allot her a temple and altars and the other public tokens of filial duty.

This ingenious plan found favor. The time of year, too, was suitable, since Nero habitually attended the festival of Minerva at Baiae. Now he enticed his mother there. "Parents' tempers must be borne!" he kept announcing. "One must humor their feelings." This was to create the general impression that they were friends again, and to produce the same effect on Agrippina. For women are naturally inclined to believe welcome news.

As she arrived from Antium, Nero met her on the shore. After welcoming her with outstretched hands and embraces, he conducted her to Bauli, a mansion on the bay between Cape Misenum and the waters of Baiae. Some ships were standing there. One, more sumptuous than the rest, was evidently another compliment to his mother, who had formerly been accustomed to travel in warships manned by the imperial navy. Then she was invited to dinner. The crime was to take place on the ship under cover of darkness. But an informer, it was said, gave the plot away; Agrippina could not decide whether to believe the story, and preferred a sedan chair as her conveyance to Baiae.

There her alarm was relieved by Nero's attentions. He received her kindly, and gave her the place of honor next himself. The party went on for a long time. They talked about various things; Nero was boyish and intimate—or confidentially serious. When she left, he saw her off, gazing into her eyes and clinging to her. This may have been a final piece of shamming—or perhaps even Nero's brutal heart was affected by his last sight of his mother, going to her death.

But heaven seemed determined to reveal his crime. For it was a quiet, star-lit night and the sea was calm. The ship began to go on its way. Agrippina was attended by two of her friends. One of them, Crepereius Gallus, stood near the tiller. The other, Acerronia, leant over the feet of her resting mistress, happily talking about Nero's remorseful behavior and his mother's re-established influence. Then came the signal. Under the pressure of heavy lead weights, the roof fell in. Crepereius was crushed, and died instantly. Agrippina and Acerronia were saved by the raised sides of their couch, which happened to be strong enough to resist the pressure. Moreover, the ship held together.

In the general confusion, those in the conspiracy were hampered by the many who were not. But then some of the oarsmen had the idea of throwing their weight on one side, to capsize the ship. However, they took too long to concert this improvised plan, and meanwhile others brought weight to bear in the opposite direction. This provided the opportunity to make a gentler descent into the water. Acerronia ill-advisedly started crying out, "I am Agrippina! Help, help the emperor's mother!" She was struck dead by blows from poles and oars and whatever ship's gear happened to be available. Agrippina herself kept quiet and avoided recognition. Though she was hurt—she had a wound in the shoulder—she swam until she came to some sailing boats. They brought her to the Lucrine lake, from which she was taken home.

There she realized that the invitation and special compliment had been treacherous, and the collapse of her ship planned. The collapse had started at the top, like a stage-contrivance. The shore was close by, there had been no wind, no rock to collide with. Acerronia's death and her own wound also invited reflection. Agrippina decided that the only escape from the plot was to profess ignorance of it. She sent an ex-slave Agerinus to tell her son that by divine mercy and his lucky star she had survived a serious accident. The messenger was to add, however, that despite anxiety about his mother's dangerous experience Nero must not yet trouble to visit her—at present rest was what she needed. Meanwhile, pretending unconcern, she cared for her wound and physical condition generally. She also ordered Acerronia's will to be found and her property to be sealed. Here alone no pretence was needed.

To Nero, awaiting news that the crime was done, came word that she had escaped with a slight wound—after hazards which left no doubt of their instigator's identity. Half-dead with fear, he insisted she might arrive at any moment. "She may arm her slaves! She may whip up the army, or gain access to the senate or assembly, and incriminate me for wrecking and wounding her and killing her friends! What can I do to save myself?" Could Burrus and Seneca help? Whether they were in the plot is uncertain. But they were immediately awakened and summoned.

For a long time neither spoke. They did not want to dissuade and be rejected. They may have felt matters had gone so far that Nero had to strike before Agrippina, or die. Finally Seneca ventured so far as to turn to Burrus and ask if the troops should be ordered to kill her. He replied that the Guard was devoted to the whole imperial house and to Germanicus' memory; they would commit no violence against his offspring. Anicetus, he said, must make good his promise. Anicetus unhesitatingly claimed the direction of the crime. Hearing him Nero cried that this was the first day of his reign—and the magnificent gift came from a former slave! "Go quickly!" he said. "And take men who obey orders scrupulously."

Agrippina's messenger arrived. When Nero was told, he took the initiative, and staged a fictitious incrimination. While Agerinus delivered his message, Nero dropped a sword at the man's feet and had him arrested as if caught red-handed. Then he could pretend that his mother had plotted against the emperor's life, been detected, and—in shame—committed suicide.

Meanwhile Agrippina's perilous adventure had become known. It was believed to be accidental. As soon as people heard of it they ran to the beach, and climbed onto the embankment, or fishing-boats nearby. Others waded out as far as they could, or waved their arms. The whole shore echoed with wails and prayers and the din of all manner of inquiries and ignorant answers. Huge crowds gathered with lights. When she was known to be safe, they prepared to make a show of rejoicing.

But a menacing armed column arrived and dispersed them. Anicetus surrounded her house and broke in. Arresting every slave in his path, he came to her bedroom door. Here stood a few servants—the rest had been frightened away by the invasion. In her dimly lit room a single maid waited with her. Agrippina's alarm had increased as nobody, not even Agerinus, came from her son. If things had been well there would not be this terribly ominous isolation, then this sudden uproar. Her maid vanished. "Are you leaving me, too?" called Agrippina. Then she saw Anicetus. Behind him were a naval captain and lieutenant. "If you have come to visit me," she said, "you can report that I am better. But if you are assassins, I know my son is not responsible. He did not order his mother's death." The murderers closed round her bed. First the captain hit her head with a truncheon. Then as the lieutenant was drawing his sword to finish her off, she cried out: "Strike here!" pointing to her womb. Blow after blow fell, and she died.

So far accounts agree. Some add that Nero inspected his mother's corpse and praised her figure; but that is contested. She was cremated that night, on a dining couch, with meagre ceremony. While Nero reigned, her grave was not covered with earth or enclosed, though later her household gave her a modest tomb beside the road to Misenum, on the heights where Julius Caesar's mansion overlooks the bay beneath. During the cremation one of her former slaves stabbed himself to death. Either he loved his patroness, or he feared assassination.

This was the end which Agrippina had anticipated for years. The prospect had not daunted her. When she asked astrologers about Nero, they had answered that he would become emperor but kill his mother. Her reply was, "Let him kill me—provided he becomes emperor!" But Nero only understood the horror of his crime when it was done. For the rest of the night, witless and speechless, he alternately lay paralyzed and leapt to his feet in terror—waiting for the dawn which he thought would be his last. Hope began to return to him when at Burrus' suggestion the colonels and captains of the Guard came and cringed to him, with congratulatory handclasps for his escape from the unexpected menace of his mother's evil activities. Nero's friends crowded to the temples. Campanian towns nearby followed their lead and displayed joy by sacrifices and deputations.

Nero's insincerity took a different form. He adopted a gloomy demeanor, as though sorry to be safe and mourning for his parent's death. But the features of the countryside are less adaptable than those of men; and Nero's gaze could not escape the dreadful view of that sea and shore. Besides, the coast echoed (it was said) with trumpet blasts from the neighboring hills —and wails from his mother's grave. So Nero departed to Neapolis.

Imperial Suicide

SUETONIUS

A.D. 68. Nero, a monster of sexual depravity, was also a monster of murderous ferocity. His murders were so many and so capricious it is reasonable to think that Nero was insane. When revolts against his tyranny broke out in Gaul and Spain, he took no rational steps to suppress them and so hastened his death. Suetonius, chief secretary to the Emperor Hadrian, wrote many books which have not survived. His celebrated The Twelve Caesars *is full of scandalous gossip, but it was based on extensive research in contemporary memoirs and public documents. Suetonius was personally acquainted with many of Nero's contemporaries.*

At the first news of revolt Nero is said to have formed several appalling, though characteristic, schemes for dealing with the situation. Thus, he intended to recall all army commanders and provincial governors, and execute them on a charge of conspiracy; and to dispatch all exiles everywhere, for fear they might join the rebels; and all Gallic residents at Rome, because they might be implicated in the rising. He further considered giving the army free permission to pillage Gaul; poisoning the entire Senate at a banquet; and setting fire to the city again, but first letting wild beasts loose in the streets to hinder the citizens from coping with the blaze. However, he had to abandon these schemes, not because he scrupled to carry

53

them out, but because he realized their impracticability in view of the military campaign soon to be forced on him. So he dismissed the Consuls from office before their term ended, and took over both consulships himself, declaring: "It stands to reason: only a Consul can subdue Gaul." But one day, soon after assuming the consular insignia, he left the dining room with his arms around two friends' shoulders, and remarked that when he reached Gaul he would at once step unarmed in front of the embattled enemy and weep, and weep. This would soften their hearts and win them back to loyalty; and on the next day he would stroll among his joyful troops singing paeans of victory, which he really ought to be composing now.

In his military preparations he was mainly concerned with finding enough wagons to carry his stage equipment and arranging for the concubines who would accompany him to have male haircuts and be issued with Amazonian shields and axes. When this was settled, Nero called the Roman commons to arms; but no eligible recruit came forward, so he forcibly enlisted a number of slaves, choosing the best from each household and refusing exemption even to stewards or secretaries. All classes had to pay an income-tax, and every tenant of a private house or flat was told that he owed a year's rent to the Privy Purse. Nero insisted on being paid in none but newly-minted coins, or in silver and gold of high standard; hence many people would not contribute anything, protesting that he would do much better if he reclaimed his fees from his informers.

He aggravated popular resentment by profiteering in grain, which was already priced far too high. And unluckily for him, word went around, during the general shortage of food, that a ship from Alexandria had just unloaded a cargo of sand for the Imperial wrestlers.

Nero was now so universally loathed that no bad enough abuse could be found for him. Someone tied a tress of hair to the head of one of his statues, with a note attached in Greek: "This is a real contest for once, and you are going to lose!" A sack was draped around the neck of another statue, with a similar note reading: "I have done what I could, but you preserve the sack"—presumably the sack reserved for parricides. Insults were scrawled on columns about his crowing having aroused even the cocks—for *Galli* means both "cocks" and Gauls—and several people played the same trick, pretending to have trouble with their slaves at night, and shouting out: "Vengeance is coming!"—a reference to Vindex's name.

The implications of auspices, of omens old and new, and of his own dreams, began to terrify Nero. In the past he had never known what it was to dream, but after killing his mother he dreamed that he was steering a ship and that someone tore the tiller from his hands. Next, his wife Octavia pulled him down into thick darkness, where hordes of winged ants swarmed over him. Then, the statues of the nations, which had been dedicated in the

Theatre of Pompey, began to hem him in and prevent him from getting away; while his favorite Asturian horse turned into an ape, or all except the head, which whinnied a tune. Finally, the doors of the Mausoleum opened by themselves and a voice from inside called: "Enter, Nero!"

On 1 January the Household-gods, which had just been decorated, tumbled to the ground during preparations for the New Year sacrifice, and as Nero was taking the auspices Sporus gave him a ring engraved with Proserpine's descent to the Underworld. Then a great crowd gathered to pay their annual vows to Nero, but the keys to the Capitol were mislaid. Again, while his speech against Vindex was being read in the Senate, a passage running: ". . . the criminals will soon incur the punishment, and die the death which they so thoroughly deserve," was hailed on all sides with cries of: "Augustus, you will do so!" People also noticed that Nero, at his latest public appearance, sang the part of Oedipus in Exile and ended with the line:

"Wife, mother, father, do my death compel!"

When a dispatch bringing the news that the other armies, too, had revolted was brought him at dinner, he tore it up, pushed over the table, and sent smashing to the ground two of his "Homeric" drinking cups— so called because they were engraved with scenes from Homer. He made Locusta give him some poison, which he put in a golden box; then crossed to the Servilian Gardens, where he tried to persuade the Guards officers to flee with him—because his most faithful freedman had gone ahead to equip a fleet at Ostia. Some answered evasively, others flatly refused. One even shouted out the Virgilian tag: "Is it so terrible a thing to die?"

Nero had no idea what to do. A number of alternatives offered—for example, throwing himself on the mercy of the Parthians, or of Galba; or appearing pathetically on the Rostra to beg the people's pardon for his sins —they might at least make him prefect of Egypt, he thought, if they could not find it in their hearts to forgive him altogether. A speech to this effect was later found among the papers in his bureau, and the usual view is that only fear of being torn to pieces before he reached the Forum prevented him from delivering it.

Nero suspended his deliberations until the following day, but woke at midnight to find that his bodyguard had deserted him. He leaped out of bed and summoned his friends who were staying in the Palace. When they did not appear he went with a few members of his staff to knock at their doors. But nobody either opened or answered. He returned to his room. By now even the valets had absconded with the bed linen and the box of poison. He shouted for Spiculus the gladiator or any other trained executioner, to end his misery at one blow. No one came. "What? Have I then neither friends nor enemies left?" he cried, and dashed out of the Palace. Apparently he intended to hurl himself into the Tiber.

Changing his mind once more, however, he said that all he wanted was some secluded spot where he could collect his thoughts at leisure. Phaon, an Imperial freedman, suggested his own suburban villa, four miles away, between the Nomentanan and the Salarian Ways. Nero jumped at the offer. He was in undershirt and slippers; but simply pulled on a faded cloak and hat, took horse and trotted off, holding a handkerchief over his face. Four servants went with him, including Sporus. Suddenly a slight earth-tremor was felt and lightning flashed in their eyes, which terrified Nero. Then, from the near-by camp soldiers began shouting about the defeat which Galba would inflict on him. He heard one man exclaim as they passed: "Those fellows are in pursuit of the Emperor," and another: "What's the latest news of him in town?" Then Nero's horse took fright at the smell of a dead body lying by the roadside; which made him expose his face. He was immediately recognized and saluted by a Guards veteran. They reached a lane leading to Phaon's villa and, abandoning their horses, followed a path which ran through a briar patch and a plantation of reeds to the rear wall of the house. Because the going was difficult Nero made them spread a cloak for him to walk on. When begged by Phaon to lie low for a while in a gravel pit, he answered: "No, I refuse to go underground before I die." While the servants tunnelled through the wall he scooped up some water in his hands from a neighboring pool and drank it, saying: "This is Nero's own special brew." Then he pulled out all the thorns from his ragged cloak and crawled into the villa by way of the tunnel. Finding himself in a slave's bedroom, beside a couch with a poor mattress over which an old cape had been thrown, he sank down on it and, although hungry, refused some coarse bread; but confessed himself still thirsty and sipped a little warm water.

Finally, when his companions unanimously insisted on his trying to escape from the miserable fate threatening him, he ordered them to dig a grave at once, of the right size, and then collect any pieces of marble that they could find and fetch wood and water for the disposal of the corpse. As they bustled about obediently he muttered through his tears: "Dead! And so great an artist!"

A runner brought him a letter from Phaon. Nero tore it from the man's hands and read that, having been declared a public enemy by the Senate, he would be punished "in ancient style" when arrested. He asked what "ancient style" meant, and learned that the executioners stripped their victim naked, thrust his head into a wooden fork, and then flogged him to death with sticks. In terror he snatched up the two daggers which he had brought along and tried their points; but threw them down again, protesting that the fatal hour had not yet come. Then he begged Sporus to weep and mourn for him, but also begged one of the other three to set him an example by committing suicide first. He kept moaning about his cowardice, and muttering: "How ugly and vulgar my life has become!" And then in Greek: "This certainly is no credit to Nero, no credit at all," and: "Come, pull yourself together, man!" By this time the troop of cavalry who had orders to take him alive were coming up the road. Nero gasped:

"Hark to the sound I hear! It is hooves of galloping horses." Then, with the help of his scribe, Epaphroditus, he stabbed himself in the throat and was already half dead when a cavalry officer entered, pretending to have rushed to his rescue, and staunched the wound with his cloak. Nero muttered: "Too late! But, ah, what fidelity!" He died, with eyes glazed and bulging from their sockets, a sight which horrified everybody present. He had made his companions promise, whatever happened, not to let his head be cut off, but to have him buried all in one piece. Galba's freedman Icelus, who had been imprisoned when the first news came of the revolt and was now at liberty again, granted this indulgence.

They laid Nero on his pyre, dressed in the gold-embroidered white robes which he had worn on 1 January. The funeral cost 2,000 gold pieces. Ecloge and Alexandria, his old nurses, helped Acte, his mistress, to carry the remains to the Pincian Hill, which can be seen from the Campus Martius. His coffin, of white porphyry, stands there in the Domitian family tomb behind a rail of Thasian stone and overshadowed by an altar of Luna marble.

The Emperor Septimus Severus

EDWARD GIBBON

A.D. 193–211. After their murder of the Emperor Pertinax, the members of the Praetorian Guard auctioned the throne of the Roman Empire to the highest bidder. In the turmoil which followed, three popular generals contended for power. One was Septimus Severus. No selection from Gibbon can adequately display the wit and irony which gleam throughout The History of the Decline and Fall of the Roman Empire. *But Gibbon's account of the reign of Severus, which he considered a crucial turn for the worse in the general decline, is typical of his skeptical, eighteenth-century point of view and admirably displays his formal, elegant, elaborate style.*

The Pannonian army was at this time commanded by Septimus Severus, a native of Africa, who, in the gradual ascent of private honors, had concealed his daring ambition, which was never diverted from its steady course by the allurements of pleasure, the apprehension of danger, or the feelings of humanity. On the first news of the murder of Pertinax, he assembled his troops, painted in the most lively colors the crime, the insolence, and the weakness of the Praetorian guards, and animated the legions to arms and to revenge. He concluded (and the peroration was thought extremely eloquent) with promising every soldier about four hundred pounds; an honorable donative, double in value to the infamous bribe with which

Julian had purchased the empire. The acclamations of the army immediately saluted Severus with the names of Augustus, Pertinax, and Emperor; and he thus attained the lofty station to which he was invited by conscious merit and a long train of dreams and omens, the fruitful offspring of his superstition or policy.

The new candidate for empire saw and improved the peculiar advantage of his situation. His province extended to the Julian Alps, which gave an easy access into Italy; and he remembered the saying of Augustus, that a Pannonian army might in ten days appear in sight of Rome. By a celerity proportioned to the greatness of the occasion, he might reasonably hope to avenge Pertinax, punish Julian, and receive the homage of the senate and people, as their lawful emperor, before his competitors, separated from Italy by an immense tract of sea and land, were apprized of his success, or even of his election. During the whole expedition, he scarcely allowed himself any moments for sleep or food; marching on foot, and in complete armor, at the head of his columns, he insinuated himself into the confidence and affection of his troops, pressed their diligence, revived their spirits, animated their hopes, and was well satisfied to share the hardships of the meanest soldier, whilst he kept in view the infinite superiority of his reward.

The wretched Julian had expected, and thought himself prepared, to dispute the empire with the governor of Syria; but in the invincible and rapid approach of the Pannonian legions, he saw his inevitable ruin. The hasty arrival of every messenger increased his just apprehensions. He was successively informed that Severus had passed the Alps; that the Italian cities, unwilling or unable to oppose his progress, had received him with the warmest professions of joy and duty; that the important place of Ravenna had surrendered without resistance, and that the Hadriatic fleet was in the hands of the conqueror. The enemy was now within two hundred and fifty miles of Rome; and every moment diminished the narrow span of life and empire allotted to Julian.

He attempted, however, to prevent, or at least to protract, his ruin. He implored the venal faith of the Praetorians, filled the city with unavailing preparations for war, drew lines round the suburbs, and even strengthened the fortifications of the palace; as if those last intrenchments could be defended, without hope of relief, against a victorious invader. Fear and shame prevented the guards from deserting his standard; but they trembled at the name of the Pannonian legions, commanded by an experienced general, and accustomed to vanquish the barbarians on the frozen Danube. They quitted, with a sigh, the pleasures of the baths and theatres, to put on arms, whose use they had almost forgotten, and beneath the weight of which they were oppressed. The unpractised elephants, whose uncouth appearance, it was hoped, would strike terror into the army of the North, threw their unskilful riders; and the awkward evolutions of the marines, drawn from the fleet of Misenum, were an object of ridicule to the populace; whilst the senate enjoyed, with secret pleasure, the distress and weakness of the usurper.

Every motion of Julian betrayed his trembling perplexity. He insisted that Severus should be declared a public enemy by the senate. He entreated that the Pannonian general might be associated to the empire. He sent public ambassadors of consular rank to negotiate with his rival; he dispatched private assassins to take away his life. He designed that the Vestal virgins, and all the colleges of priests, in their sacerdotal habits, and bearing before them the sacred pledges of the Roman religion, should advance, in solemn procession, to meet the Pannonian legions; and, at the same time, he vainly tried to interrogate, or to appease, the fates, by magic ceremonies, and unlawful sacrifices.

Severus, who dreaded neither his arms nor his enchantments, guarded himself from the only danger of secret conspiracy by the faithful attendance of six hundred chosen men, who never quitted his person nor their cuirasses, either by night or by day, during the whole march. Advancing with a steady and rapid course, he passed, without difficulty, the defiles of the Apennine, received into his party the troops and ambassadors sent to retard his progress, and made a short halt at Interamna, about seventy miles from Rome. His victory was already secure; but the despair of the Praetorians might have rendered it bloody; and Severus had the laudable ambition of ascending the throne without drawing the sword. His emissaries, dispersed in the capital, assured the guards that, provided they would abandon their worthless prince, and the perpetrators of the murder of Pertinax, to the justice of the conqueror, he would no longer consider that melancholy event as the act of the whole body. The faithless Praetorians, whose resistance was supported only by sullen obstinacy, gladly complied with the easy conditions, seized the greatest part of the assassins, and signified to the senate that they no longer defended the cause of Julian. That assembly, convoked by the consul, unanimously acknowledged Severus as lawful emperor, decreed divine honors to Pertinax, and pronounced a sentence of deposition against his unfortunate successor. Julian was conducted into a private apartment of the baths of the palace, and beheaded as a common criminal, after having purchased, with an immense treasure, an anxious and precarious reign of only sixty-six days. The almost incredible expedition of Severus, who, in so short a space of time, conducted a numerous army from the banks of the Danube to those of the Tiber, proves at once the plenty of provisions produced by agriculture and commerce, the goodness of the roads, the discipline of the legions, and the indolent subdued temper of the provinces.

The first cares of Severus were bestowed on two measures, the one dictated by policy, the other by decency; the revenge, and the honors due to the memory of Pertinax. Before the new emperor entered Rome, he issued his commands to the Praetorian guards, directing them to wait his arrival on a large plain near the city, without arms, but in the habits of ceremony in which they were accustomed to attend their sovereign. He was obeyed by those haughty troops, whose contrition was the effect of their just terrors. A chosen part of the Illyrian army encompassed them with levelled spears. Incapable of flight or resistance, they expected their fate in silent consternation. Severus mounted the tribunal, sternly reproached them with perfidy and cowardice, dismissed them with ignominy from the trust which they had betrayed, despoiled them of their splendid ornaments, and banished them, on pain of death, to the distance of an hundred miles from the capital. During the transaction, another detachment had been sent to seize their arms, occupy their camp, and prevent the hasty consequences of their despair.

The funeral and consecration of Pertinax was next solemnized with every circumstance of sad magnificence. The senate, with a melancholy pleasure, performed the last rites to that excellent prince, whom they had loved and still regretted. The concern of his successor was probably less sincere. He esteemed the virtues of Pertinax, but those virtues would for ever have confined his ambition to a private station. Severus pronounced his funeral oration with studied eloquence, inward satisfaction, and well-acted sorrow; and by this pious regard to his memory, convinced the credulous multitude that *he alone* was worthy to supply his place. Sensible, however, that arms, not ceremonies, must assert his claim to the empire, he left Rome at the end of thirty days, and, without suffering himself to be elated by this easy victory, prepared to encounter his more formidable rivals.

The uncommon abilities and fortune of Severus have induced an elegant historian to compare him with the first and greatest of the Caesars. The parallel is, at least, imperfect. Where shall we find, in the character of Severus, the commanding superiority of soul, the generous clemency, and the various genius, which could reconcile and unite the love of pleasure, the thirst of knowledge, and the fire of ambition? In one instance only, they may be compared, with some degree of propriety, in the celerity of their motion, and their civil victories. In less than four years, Severus subdued the riches of the East, and the valor of the West. He vanquished two competitors of reputation and ability, and defeated numerous armies, provided with weapons and discipline equal to his own. In that age, the art of fortification and the principles of tactics, were well understood by all the Roman generals; and the constant superiority of Severus was that of an artist, who uses the same instruments with more skill and industry than

61

his rivals. I shall not, however, enter into a minute narrative of these military operations; but as the two civil wars against Niger and against Albinus were almost the same in their conduct, event, and consequences, I shall collect into one point of view the most striking circumstances, tending to develop the character of the conqueror, and the state of the empire.

Falsehood and insincerity, unsuitable as they seem to the dignity of public transactions, offend us with a less degrading idea of meanness than when they are found in the intercourse of private life. In the latter, they discover a want of courage; in the other, only a defect of power; and, as it is impossible for the most able statesman to subdue millions of followers and enemies by their own personal strength, the world, under the name of policy, seems to have granted them a very liberal indulgence of craft and dissimilation. Yet the arts of Severus cannot be justified by the most ample privileges of state-reason. He promised only to betray, he flattered only to ruin; and however he might occasionally bind himself by oaths and treaties, his conscience, obsequious to his interest, always released him from the inconvenient obligation.

If his two competitors, reconciled by their common danger, had advanced upon him without delay, perhaps Severus would have sunk under their united effort. Had they even attacked him at the same time, with separate views and separate armies, the contest might have been long and doubtful. But they fell, singly and successively, an easy prey to the arts as well as arms of their subtle enemy, lulled into security by the moderation of his professions, and overwhelmed by the rapidity of his action. He first marched against Niger, whose reputation and power he the most dreaded: but he declined any hostile declarations, suppressed the name of his antagonist, and only signified to the senate and people his intention of regulating the eastern provinces. In private he spoke of Niger, his old friend and intended successor, with the most affectionate regard, and highly applauded his generous design of revenging the murder of Pertinax. To punish the vile usurper of the throne was the duty of every Roman general. To persevere in arms, and to resist a lawful emperor, acknowledged by the Senate, would alone render him criminal. The sons of Niger had fallen into his hands among the children of the provincial governors, detained at Rome as pledges for the loyalty of their parents. As long as the power of Niger inspired terror, or even respect, they were educated with the most tender care, with the children of Severus himself; but they were soon involved in their father's ruin, and removed, first by exile, and afterwards by death, from the eye of public compassion.

Whilst Severus was engaged in his eastern war, he had reason to apprehend that the governor of Britain might pass the sea and the Alps, occupy the vacant seat of empire, and oppose his return with the authority of the senate and the forces of the West. The ambiguous conduct of Albinus, in not assuming the Imperial title, left room for negotiation. Forgetting at once his professions of patriotism and the jealousy of sovereign power, he accepted the precarious rank of Caesar, as a reward for his fatal neutrality. Till the first contest was decided, Severus treated the man whom he had doomed to destruction with every mark of esteem and regard. Even in the letter in which he announced his victory over Niger he styles Albinus the brother of his soul and empire, sends him the affectionate salutations of his wife Julia, and his young family, and entreats him to preserve the armies and the republic faithful to their common interest. The messengers charged with this letter were instructed to accost the Caesar with respect, to desire a private audience, and to plunge their daggers into his heart. The conspiracy was discovered, and the too credulous Albinus at length passed over to the continent, and prepared for an unequal contest with his rival, who rushed upon him at the head of a veteran and victorious army.

The military labors of Severus seem inadequate to the importance of his conquests. Two engagements, the one near the Hellespont, the other in the narrow defiles of Cilicia, decided the fate of his Syrian competitor; and the troops of Europe asserted their usual ascendant over the effeminate natives of Asia. The battle of Lyons, where one hundred and fifty thousand Romans were engaged, was equally fatal to Albinus. The valor of the British army maintained, indeed, a sharp and doubtful contest with the hardy discipline of the Illyrian legions. The fame and person of Severus appeared, during a few moments, irrevocably lost, till that warlike prince rallied his fainting troops, and led them on to a decisive victory. The war was finished by that memorable day.

The civil wars of modern Europe have been distinguished, not only by the fierce animosity, but likewise by the obstinate perseverance, of the contending factions. They have generally been justified by some principle, or, at least, colored by some pretext, of religion, freedom, or loyalty. The leaders were nobles of independent property and hereditary influence. The troops fought like men interested in the decision of the quarrel; and as military spirit and party zeal were strongly diffused throughout the whole community, a vanquished chief was immediately supplied with new adherents, eager to shed their blood in the same cause. But the Romans, after the fall of the republic, combatted only for the choice of masters. Under the standard of a popular candidate for empire, a few enlisted from affection, some from fear, many from interest, none from principle. The legions, uninflamed by party zeal, were allured into civil war by liberal donatives, and still more liberal promises. A defeat, by disabling the chief from the performance of his engagements, dissolved the mercenary allegiance of his followers, and left them to consult their own safety by a timely desertion of an unsuccessful cause. It was of little moment to the provinces under whose name they were oppressed or governed; they were driven by the impulsion of the present power, and as soon as that power yielded to a superior force, they hastened to implore the clemency of the conqueror, who, as he had an immense debt to discharge, was obliged to sacrifice the most guilty countries to the avarice of his soldiers. In the vast extent of the Roman empire there were few fortified cities capable of protecting a routed army; nor was there any person, or family, or order of men, whose natural interest, unsupported by the powers of government, was capable of restoring a sinking party.

Yet, in the contest between Niger and Severus, a single city deserves an honorable exception. As Byzantium was one of the greatest passages from Europe into Asia, it had been provided with a strong garrison, and a fleet of five hundred vessels was anchored in the harbor. The impetuosity of Severus disappointed this prudent scheme of defence; he left to his generals the siege of Byzantium, forced the less guarded passage of the Hellespont, and, impatient of a meaner enemy, pressed forward to encounter his rival. Byzantium, attacked by a numerous and increasing army, and afterwards by the whole naval power of the empire, sustained a siege of three years, and remained faithful to the name and memory of Niger. The citizens and soldiers (we know not from what cause) were animated with equal fury; several of the principal officers of Niger, who despaired of, or who disdained a pardon, had thrown themselves into this last refuge; the fortifications were esteemed impregnable, and, in the defence of the place, a celebrated engineer displayed all the mechanic powers known to the ancients. Byzantium, at length, surrendered to famine. The magistrates and soldiers were put to the sword, the walls demolished, the privileges suppressed, and the destined capital of the East subsisted only as an open village, subject to the insulting jurisdiction of Perinthus. The historian Dion, who had admired the flourishing, and lamented the desolate, state of Byzantium, accused the revenge of Severus for depriving the Roman people of the strongest bulwark against the barbarians of Pontus and Asia. The truth of this observation was but too well justified in the succeeding age, when the Gothic fleets covered the Euxine, and passed through the undefended Bosphorus into the centre of the Mediterranean.

Both Niger and Albinus were discovered and put to death in their flight from the field of battle. Their fate excited neither surprise nor compassion. They had staked their lives against the chance of empire, and suffered what they would have inflicted; nor did Severus claim the arrogant superiority of suffering his rivals to live in a private station. But his unforgiving temper, stimulated by avarice, indulged a spirit of revenge, where there was no room for apprehension. The most considerable of the provincials, who, without any dislike to the fortunate candidate, had obeyed the governor under whose authority they were accidentally placed, were punished by death, exile, and especially by the confiscation of their estates. Many cities of the East were stript of their ancient honors, and obliged to pay, into the treasury of Severus, four times the amount of the sums which had been contributed by them for the service of Niger.

Till the final decision of the war, the cruelty of Severus was, in some measure, restrained by the uncertainty of the event and his pretended reverence for the senate. The head of Albinus, accompanied with a menacing letter, announced to the Romans that he was resolved to spare none of the adherents of his unfortunate competitors. He was irritated by the just suspicion that he had never possessed the affections of the senate, and he concealed his old malevolence under the recent discovery of some treasonable correspondencies. Thirty-five senators, however, accused of having favored the party of Albinus, he freely pardoned; and, by his subsequent behavior, endeavored to convince them that he had forgotten, as well as forgiven, their supposed offences. But, at the same time, he condemned forty-one other senators, whose names history has recorded; their wives, children, and clients, attended them in death, and the noblest of provincials of Spain and Gaul were involved in the same ruin. Such rigid justice, for so he termed it, was, in the opinion of Severus, the only conduct capable of ensuring peace to the people, or stability to the prince; and he condescended slightly to lament that, to be mild, it was necessary that he should first be cruel.

The true interest of an absolute monarch generally coincides with that of his people. Their numbers, their wealth, their order, and their security, are the best and only foundations of his real greatness; and, were he totally devoid of virtue, prudence might supply its place, and would dictate the same rule of conduct. Severus considered the Roman empire as his property, and had no sooner secured the possession, than he bestowed his care on the cultivation and improvement of so valuable an acquisition. Salutary laws, executed with inflexible firmness, soon corrected most of the abuses with which, since the death of Marcus, every part of the government had been infected. In the administration of justice, the judgments of the emperor were characterized by attention, discernment, and impartiality; and, whenever he deviated from the strict line of equity, it was generally in favor of the poor and oppressed; not so much indeed from any sense of humanity, as from the natural propensity of a despot to humble the pride of greatness, and to sink all his subjects to the same common level of absolute dependence. His expensive taste for building, magnificent shows, and, above all, a constant and liberal distribution of corn and provisions, were the surest means of captivating the affection of the Roman people. The misfortunes of civil discord were obliterated. The calm of peace and prosperity was once more experienced in the provinces, and many cities, restored by the munificence of Severus, assumed the title of his colonies, and attested by public monuments their gratitude and felicity. The fame of the Roman arms was revived by that warlike and successful emperor, and he boasted, with a just pride, that, having received the empire oppressed with foreign and domestic wars, he left it established in profound, universal, and honorable peace.

Although the wounds of civil war appeared completely healed, its mortal poison still lurked in the vitals of the constitution. Severus possessed a considerable share of vigor and ability; but the daring soul of the first Caesar, or the deep policy of Augustus, were scarcely equal to the task of curbing the insolence of the victorious legions. By gratitude, by misguided policy, by seeming necessity, Severus was induced to relax the nerves of discipline. The vanity of his soldiers was flattered with the honor of wearing gold rings; their ease was indulged in the permission of living with their wives in the idleness of quarters. He increased their pay beyond the example of former times, and taught them to expect, and soon to claim, extraordinary donatives on every public occasion of danger or festivity. Elated by success, enervated by luxury, and raised above the level of subjects by their dangerous privileges, they soon became incapable of military fatigue, oppressive to the country, and impatient of a just subordination. Their officers asserted the superiority of rank by a more profuse and elegant luxury. There is still extant a letter of Severus, lamenting the licentious state of the army, and exhorting one of his generals to begin the necessary reformation from the tribunes themselves; since, as he justly observes, the officer who has forfeited the esteem will never command the obedience of his soldiers. Had the emperor pursued the train of reflection, he would have discovered that the primary cause of this general corruption might be ascribed, not indeed to the example, but to the pernicious indulgence, however, of the commander-in-chief.

The Praetorians, who murdered their emperor and sold the empire, had received the just punishment of their treason; but the necessary, though dangerous, institution of guards was soon restored on a new model by Severus, and increased to four times the ancient number. Formerly these troops had been recruited in Italy; and, as the adjacent provinces gradually imbibed the softer manners of Rome, the levies were extended to Macedonia, Noricum, and Spain. In the room of these elegant troops, better adapted to the pomp of courts than to the uses of war, it was established by Severus, that, from all the legions of the frontiers, the soldiers most distinguished for strength, valor, and fidelity, should be occasionally draughted, and promoted, as an honor and reward, into the more eligible service of the guards. By this new institution, the Italian youth were diverted from the exercise of arms, and the capital was terrified by the strange aspect and manners of a multitude of barbarians. But Severus flattered himself that the legions would consider these chosen Praetorians as the representatives of the whole military order; and that the present aid of fifty thousand men, superior in arms and appointments to any force that could be brought into the field against them, would for ever crush the hopes of rebellion, and secure the empire to himself and his posterity.

The command of these favored and formidable troops soon became the first office of the empire. As the government degenerated into military despotism, the Praetorian praefect, who in his origin had been a simple captain of the guards, was placed, not only at the head of the army, but of the finances, and even of the law. In every department of administration, he represented the person, and exercised the authority, of the emperor. The first praefect who enjoyed and abused this immense power was Plautianus, the favorite minister of Severus. His reign lasted above ten years, till the marriage of his daughter with the eldest son of the emperor, which seemed to assure his fortune, proved the occasion of his ruin. The animosities of the palace, by irritating the ambition and alarming the fears of Plautianus, threatened to produce a revolution, and obliged the emperor, who still loved him, to consent with reluctance to his death. After the fall of Plautianus, an eminent lawyer, the celebrated Papinian, was appointed to execute the motley office of Praetorian praefect.

Till the reign of Severus, the virtue, and even the good sense, of the emperors had been distinguished by their zeal or affected reverence for the senate, and by a tender regard to the nice frame of civil policy instituted by Augustus. But the youth of Severus had been trained in the implicit obedience of camps, and his riper years were spent in the despotism of military command. His haughty and inflexible spirit could not discover, or would not acknowledge, the advantage of preserving an intermediate power, however imaginary, between the emperor and the army. He disdained to profess himself the servant of an assembly that detested his person and trembled at his frown; he issued his commands, where his request would have proved as effectual; assumed the conduct and the style of a sovereign and a conqueror, and exercised, without disguise, the whole legislative as well as the executive power.

The victory over the senate was easy and inglorious. Every eye and every passion were directed to the supreme magistrate, who possessed the arms and treasure of the state; whilst the senate, neither elected by the people, nor guarded by the military force, nor animated by public spirit, rested its declining authority on the frail and crumbling basis of ancient opinion. The fine theory of a republic insensibly vanished, and made way for the more natural and substantial feelings of monarchy. As the freedom and honors of Rome were successfully communicated to the provinces, in which the old government had been either unknown, or was remembered with abhorrence, the tradition of republican maxims was gradually obliterated. The Greek historians of the age of the Antonines observed, with a malicious pleasure, that, although the sovereign of Rome, in compliance with an obsolete prejudice, abstained from the name of a king, he possessed the full measure of regal power. In the reign of Severus, the senate was filled with polished and eloquent slaves from the eastern provinces, who justified personal flattery by speculative principles of servitude. These new advocates of prerogative were heard with pleasure by the court, and with patience by the people, when they inculcated the duty of passive obedience, and descanted on the inevitable mischiefs of freedom. The lawyers and the historians concurred in teaching that the Imperial authority was held, not by the delegated commission, but by the irrevocable resignation, of the senate; that the emperor was freed from the restraint of civil laws, could command by his arbitrary will the lives and fortunes of his subjects, and might dispose of the empire as of his private patrimony. The most eminent of the civil lawyers, and particularly Papinian, Paulus, and Ulpian, flourished under the house of Severus; and the Roman jurisprudence, having closely united itself with the system of monarchy, was supposed to have attained its full maturity and perfection.

The contemporaries of Severus, in the enjoyment of the peace and glory of his reign, forgave the cruelties by which it had been introduced. Posterity, who experienced the fatal effect of his maxims and example, justly considered him as the principal author of the decline of the Roman empire.

The ascent to greatness, however steep and dangerous, may entertain an active spirit with the consciousness and exercise of its own powers: but the possession of a throne could never yet afford a lasting satisfaction to an ambitious mind. This melancholy truth was felt and acknowledged by Severus. Fortune and merit had, from an humble station, elevated him to the first place among mankind. He had been "all things," as he said himself, "and all was of little value." Distracted with the care, not of acquiring, but of preserving, an empire, oppressed with age and infirmities, careless of fame, and satiated with power, all his prospects of life were closed. The desire of perpetuating the greatness of his family was the only remaining wish of his ambition and paternal tenderness.

Like most of the Africans, Severus was passionately addicted to the vain studies of magic and divination, deeply versed in the interpretation of dreams and omens, and perfectly acquainted with the science of judicial astrology; which, in almost every age except the present, has maintained its dominion over the mind of man. He had lost his first wife whilst he was governor of the Lyonese Gaul. In the choice of a second, he sought only to connect himself with some favorite of fortune; and, as soon as he had discovered that a young lady of Emesa in Syria had *a royal nativity,* he solicited and obtained her hand. Julia Domna (for that was her name) deserved all that the stars could promise her. She possessed, even in an advanced age, the attractions of beauty, and united to a lively imagination a firmness of mind, and strength of judgment, seldom bestowed on her sex. Her amiable qualities never made any deep impression on the dark and jealous temper of her husband; but, in her son's reign, she administered the principal affairs of the empire with a prudence that supported his authority; and with a moderation that sometimes corrected his wild extravagancies. Julia applied herself to letters and philosophy with some success, and with the most splendid reputation. She was the patroness of every art, and the friend of every man of genius. The grateful flattery of the learned has celebrated her virtues; but, if we may credit the scandal of ancient history, chastity was very far from being the most conspicuous virtue of the Empress Julia.

Two sons, Caracalla and Geta, were the fruit of this marriage, and the destined heirs of the empire. The fond hopes of the father, and of the Roman world, were soon disappointed by these vain youths, who displayed the indolent security of hereditary princes, and a presumption that fortune would supply the place of merit and application. Without any emulation of virtue or talents, they discovered, almost from their infancy, a fixed and implacable antipathy for each other. Their aversion, confirmed by years, and fomented by the arts of their interested favorites, broke out in childish, and gradually in more serious, competitions; and at length divided the theatre, the circus, and the court, into two factions, actuated by the hopes and fears of their respective leaders. The prudent emperor endeavored, by every expedient of advice and authority, to allay this growing animosity. The unhappy discord of his sons clouded all his prospects, and threatened to overturn a throne raised with so much labor, cemented with so much blood, and guarded with every defence of arms and treasure. With an impartial hand he maintained between them an exact balance of favor, conferred on both the rank of Augustus, with the revered name of Antoninus; and for the first time the Roman world beheld three emperors. Yet even this equal conduct served only to inflame the contest, whilst the fierce Caracalla asserted the right of primogeniture, and the milder Geta courted the affections of the people and the soldiers. In the anguish of a disappointed father, Severus foretold that the weaker of his sons would fall a sacrifice to the stronger; who, in his turn, would be ruined by his own vices.

In these circumstances the intelligence of a war in Britain, and of an invasion of the province by the barbarians of the North, was received with pleasure by Severus. Though the vigilance of his lieutenants might have been sufficient to repel the distant enemy, he resolved to embrace the honorable pretext of withdrawing his sons from the luxury of Rome, which enervated their minds and irritated their passions, and of inuring their youth to the toils of war and government. Notwithstanding his advanced age (for he was above threescore), and his gout, which obliged him to be carried in a litter, he transported himself in person into that remote island, attended by two sons, his whole court, and a formidable army. He immediately passed the walls of Hadrian and Antoninus, and entered the enemy's country, with the design of completing the long-attempted conquest of Britain. He penetrated to the northern extremity of the island without meeting an enemy. But the concealed ambuscades of the Caledonians, who hung unseen on the rear and flanks of his army, the coldness of the climate, and the severity of a winter march across the hills and morasses of Scotland, are reported to have cost the Romans above fifty thousand men. The Caledonians at length yielded to the powerful and obstinate attack, sued for peace, and surrendered a part of their arms, and a large tract of territory. But their apparent submission lasted no longer than the present terror. As soon as the Roman legions had retired, they resumed their hostile independence. Their restless spirit provoked Severus to send a new army into Caledonia, with the most bloody orders, not to subdue, but to extirpate the natives. They were saved by the death of their haughty enemy.

This Caledonian war, neither marked by decisive events, nor attended with any important consequences, would ill deserve our attention; but it is supposed, not without a considerable degree of probability, that the invasion of Severus is connected with the most shining period of the British history of fable. Fingal, whose fame, with that of his heroes and bards, has been revived in our language by a recent publication, is said to have commanded the Caledonians in that memorable juncture, to have eluded the power of Severus, and to have obtained a signal victory on the banks of the Carun, in which the son of *the King of the World*, Caracul, fled from his arms along the fields of his pride.

Something of a doubtful mist still hangs over these Highland traditions; nor can it be entirely dispelled by the most ingenious researches of modern criticism: but if we could, with safety, indulge the pleasing supposition that Fingal lived, and that Ossian sung, the striking contrast of the situation and manners of the contending nations might amuse a philosophic mind. The parallel would be little to the advantage of the more civilized people, if we compared the unrelenting revenge of Severus with the generous clemency of Fingal; the timid and brutal cruelty of Caracalla, with the bravery, the tenderness, the elegant genius of Ossian; the mercenary chiefs who, from motives of fear or interest, served under the Imperial standard, with the freeborn warriors who started to arms at the voice of the King of Morven; if, in a word, we contemplated the untutored Caledonians, glowing with the warm virtues of nature, and the degenerate Romans, polluted with the mean vices of wealth and slavery.

The declining health and last illness of Severus inflamed the wild ambition and black passions of Caracalla's soul. Impatient of any delay or division of empire, he attempted, more than once, to shorten the small remainder of his father's days, and endeavored, but without success, to excite a mutiny among the troops. The old emperor had often censured the misguided lenity of Marcus, who, by a single act of justice, might have saved the Romans from the tyranny of his worthless son. Placed in the same situation, he experienced how easily the rigor of a judge dissolves away in the tenderness of a parent. He deliberated, he threatened, but he could not punish; and this last and only instance of mercy was more fatal to the empire than a long series of cruelty. The disorder of his mind irritated the pains of his body; he wished impatiently for death, and hastened the instant by his impatience. He expired at York in the sixty-fifth year of his life, and in the eighteenth of a glorious and successful reign. In his last moments he recommended concord to his sons, and his sons to the army. The salutary advice never reached the heart, or even the understanding, of the impetuous youths; but the more obedient troops, mindful of their oath of allegiance, and of the authority of their deceased master, resisted the solicitations of Caracalla, and proclaimed both brothers emperors of Rome. The new princes soon left the Caledonians in peace, returned to the capital, celebrated their father's funeral with divine honors, and were cheerfully acknowledged as lawful sovereigns by the senate, the people, and the provinces. Some pre-eminence of rank seems to have been allowed to the elder brother; but they both administered the empire with equal and independent power.

Two Holy Men

GREGORY OF TOURS

Circa A.D. 550–590. In the depths of the Dark Ages at the end of the sixth century, Gregory, Bishop of Tours, a Romanized Gaul, wrote his celebrated History of the Franks. *He admired the Franks because they were Catholic converts and fought heretics and pagans. His confused chronicle of perpetual violence and cheerful slaughter takes appalling anarchy for granted and piously records scores of edifying miracles performed by numerous saints. His book provides an intimate glimpse of ways of life and of thought which seem infinitely remote today.*

HOSPICIUS, THE RECLUSE OF NICE

There was at this time in the city of Nice a recluse, Hospicius, who was very abstemious. He wore iron chains next his body and over these a hair shirt and ate nothing but plain bread with a few dates. And during Lent he lived on roots of Egyptian herbs such as the hermits use, which were brought to him by traders. First he would drink the soup in which they were cooked and eat the roots next day. The Lord did not disdain to work great miracles through him. For at one time the Holy Spirit revealed to him the coming of the Lombards into the Gauls and he foretold it as follows: "The Lombards," said he, "will come into the Gauls and will lay waste seven cities because their wicked-

72

ness has grown in the sight of God, since no one understands, no one seeks God, no one does good to appease the anger of God. For all the people are unfaithful, given up to perjury, addicted to thievery, ready to kill, and from them comes no fruit of justice at all. Tithes are not paid, the poor are not fed, the naked are not clothed, strangers are not received with hospitality or satisfied with food. Therefore this affliction has come. And now I say to you: 'Gather all your substance within the inclosure of the walls that the Lombards may not take it, and fortify yourselves in the strongest places.' "

At these words all stood gaping and they said good-bye and returned home with great admiration. He also said to the monks: "You, too, depart from the place and take with you what you have. For behold, the people I have named draw near." But when they replied: "We will not leave you, most holy father," he said to them: "Don't fear for me; for they will offer me insults but they will not harm me unto death."

The monks went away and that people came and laying waste all they found, they came to the place where the holy recluse of God was. And he showed himself to them at the window of the tower. They went all round the tower but could find no entrance by which they could come to him. Then two climbed up and pulled the roof off, and seeing him bound with chains and clad in a hair shirt they said: "Here is a malefactor who has killed a man and therefore is kept bound in these fetters." They called an interpreter and asked him what crime he had committed to be so confined in punishment. And he confessed that he was a homicide and guilty of all crime.

Then one of them drew his sword to strike at his head, but his lifted right arm stiffened in the very act of striking and he could not draw it back to him. He let go the sword and let it fall on the ground. Seeing this, his comrades raised a shout to heaven begging the saint to declare to them kindly what they were to do. And he made the sign of salvation and restored the arm to health. The man was converted on the spot and received the tonsure and is now reckoned a most faithful monk.

And two dukes who listened to him returned safe to their native place but those who despised his command perished wretchedly in the province. Many of them were seized with demons and cried: "Why, holy and blessed one, do you torture and burn us?" And he laid his hand on them and cured them. After this there was a man of Angers who in a severe fever had lost both speech and hearing, and when he got better of the fever he continued deaf and dumb. Now a deacon was sent from that province to Rome to obtain relics of the blessed apostles and other saints who protect that city. And when he came to

73

this infirm person's relatives they begged him to take him as a companion on the journey, believing that if he reached the tombs of the blessed apostles he would forthwith be cured.

They went on their way and came to the place where the blessed Hospicius lived. After greeting and kissing him, the deacon told the purpose of his journey and said he was starting for Rome and asked the holy man to recommend him to ship-captains who were friends of his. And while he was still staying there the blessed man felt that power was in him through the spirit of the Lord. And he said to the deacon: "I beg you to bring to my sight the infirm person who is the companion of your journey."

The deacon made no delay but went swiftly to his lodging and found the infirm person full of fever, and he indicated by signs that there was a humming in his ears. The deacon seized him and led him to the saint of God. The holy man took hold of his hair and drew his head into the window, and taking oil that had been blessed, he took hold of his tongue with his left hand and poured the oil in his mouth and on top of his head, saying: "In the name of my lord Jesus Christ let your ears be opened and let that power which once drove a wicked demon from a deaf and dumb man open your lips." Having said this, he asked him his name, and he answered in a clear voice: "I am called so-and-so." When the deacon saw this he said: "I give thee endless thanks, Jesus Christ, who deignest to work such miracles by thy servant. I was seeking Peter, I was seeking Paul and Laurence and the others who made Rome glorious with their blood; here I have found them all, I have discovered every one."

As he was saying this with loud weeping and great admiration the man of God, wholly intent on avoiding vanity, said: "Be silent, beloved brother, it is not I who do this, but he who created the universe out of nothing, who took on man for our sake, and gave sight to the blind, hearing to the deaf, speech to the dumb; who bestowed on lepers the skin they had before, on the dead life, and on all the infirm abundant healing." Then the deacon said farewell and departed rejoicing with his comrades.

When they had gone a certain Dominic—this was the man's name—who had been blind from birth, came to prove his miraculous power, and when he had dwelt in the monastery two or three months praying and fasting, at length the man of God called him to him and said: "Do you wish to recover your sight?" And he replied: "I wish to know a thing unknown. For I do not know what the light is. Only one thing I know, that it is praised by all men. But I have not deserved to see from the beginning of my life until now." Then he made the holy cross over his eyes with oil that had been blessed and said: "In the name of Jesus Christ our redeemer let your eyes be opened." And at once his eyes were opened and he wondered and contemplated the great works of God which he saw in this world.

Then a certain woman who, as she herself asserted, had three demons, was brought to him. And he blessed her with a sacred touch and made the cross in holy oil on her forehead and the demons were driven out and she departed cleansed. Moreover he cured by his blessing a girl who was vexed with an unclean spirit. And when the day of his death was drawing nigh he summoned the prior of the monastery and said: "Bring iron tools to open the wall and send messengers to the bishop of the city to come and bury me. For on the third day I shall depart from this world and go to the appointed rest which the Lord has promised me." Upon this the prior sent messengers to the bishop of Nice to carry this word.

After this one Crescens went to his window and seeing him bound with chains and full of worms he said: "O my master, how can you bear such tortures so bravely?" And he replied: "He comforts me in whose name I suffer this. For I tell you that I am now freed from these bonds and am going to my rest." When the third day came he laid aside the chains by which he was bound and prostrated himself in prayer, and after he had prayed and wept a long time he lay down on a bench and stretched out his feet and raised his hands to heaven and thanked God and died. And immediately all the worms that were boring through his holy limbs disappeared. And bishop Austadius came and most carefully placed the blessed body in the grave. All these things I learned from the lips of the very deaf and dumb man who as I related above was healed by him. He told me many other miracles of his but I have been kept from describing them by the fact that I have been told that his life has been written by many persons.

VULFILAIC, THE ASCETIC OF TRÈVES

We started on the journey and came to the town of Yvois and there were met by deacon Vulfilaic and taken to his monastery, where we received a very kind welcome. This monastery is situated on a mountain top about eight miles from the town I have mentioned. On this mountain Vulfilaic built a great church and made it famous for its relics of the blessed Martin and other saints. While staying there I began to ask him to tell me something of the blessing of his conversion and how he had entered the clergy, for he was a Lombard by race. But he would not speak of these matters since he was quite determined to avoid vain-glory. But I urged him with terrible oaths, first promising that I would disclose to no one what he told me and I began to ask him to conceal from me none of the matters of which I would ask.

After resisting a long time he was overcome at length by my entreaties and protestations and told the following tale: "When I was a small boy," said he, "I heard the name of the blessed Martin, though I did not know yet whether he was a martyr or confessor or what good he had done in the world, or what region had the merit of receiving his blessed limbs in the tomb; and I was already keeping vigils in his honor, and if any money came into my hands I would give alms. As I grew older I was eager to learn and I was able to write before I knew the order of the written letters [before I could read]. Then I joined the abbot Aridius and was taught by him and visited the church of Saint Martin. Returning with him he took a little of the dust of the holy tomb for a blessing. This he placed in a little case and hung it on my neck. Coming to his monastery in the territory of Limoges he took the little case to place it in his oratory and the dust had increased so much that it not only filled the whole case but burst out at the joints wherever it could find an exit. In the light of this miracle my mind was the more on fire to place all my hope in his power.

"Then I came to the territory of Trèves and on the mountain where you are now built with my own hands the dwelling you see. I found here an image of Diana which the unbelieving people worshiped as a god. I also built a column on which I stood in my bare feet with great pain. And when the winter had come as usual I was so nipped by the icy cold that the power of the cold often caused my toe-nails to fall off and frozen moisture hung from my beard like candles. For this country is said to have a very cold winter."

And when I asked him urgently what food or drink he had and how he destroyed the images on the mountain, he said: "My food and drink were a little bread and vegetables and a small quantity of water. And when a multitude began to flock to me from the neighboring villages I preached always that Diana was nothing, that her images and the worship which they thought it well to observe were nothing; and that the songs which they sang at their cups and wild debauches were disgraceful; but it was right to offer the sacrifice of praise to all-powerful God who made heaven and earth. I often prayed that the Lord would deign to hurl down the image and free the people from this error. And the Lord's mercy turned the rustic mind to listen to my words and to follow the Lord, abandoning their idols. Then I gathered some of them together so that by their help I could hurl down the huge image which I could not budge with my own strength, for I had already broken the rest of the small images, which was an easier task.

"When many had gathered at this statue of Diana ropes were fastened and they began to pull but their toil could accomplish nothing. Then I hastened to the church and threw myself on the ground and weeping begged the divine mercy that the power of God should destroy that which human

76

energy could not overturn. After praying I went out to the workmen and took hold of the rope, and as soon as I began to pull at once the image fell to the ground where I broke it with iron hammers and reduced it to dust. But at this very hour when I was going to take food my whole body was so covered with malignant pimples from sole to crown that no space could be found that a single finger might touch.

"I went alone into the church and stripped myself before the holy altar. Now I had there a jar full of oil which I had brought from Saint Martin's church. With this I oiled all my body with my own hands and soon lay down to sleep. I awoke about midnight and rose to perform the service and found my whole body cured as if no sore had appeared on me. And I perceived that these sores were sent not otherwise than by the hate of the enemy. And inasmuch as he enviously seeks to injure those who seek God, the bishops, who should have urged me the more to continue wisely the work I had begun, came and said: "This way which you follow is not the right one, and a base-born man like you cannot be compared with Simon of Antioch who lived on a column. Moreover the situation of the place does not allow you to endure the hardship. Come down rather and dwell with the brethren you have gathered." At their words I came down, since not to obey the bishops is called a crime. And I walked and ate with them. And one day the bishop summoned me to a village at a distance and sent workmen with crowbars and hammers and axes and destroyed the column I was accustomed to stand on. I returned the next day and found it all gone. I wept bitterly but could not build again what they had torn down for fear of being called disobedient to the bishop's order. And since then I am content to dwell with the brothers just as I do now."

What Counsel Edwin Took with His Nobles About Embracing the Faith of Christ; and How His High Priest Profaned His Own Altars

BEDE

A.D. 627. *A learned and pious Benedictine monk named Bede, usually called "the Venerable," was the first Englishman to write a work of history. His* The Ecclesiastical History of the English People *was written in Latin and completed in* A.D. 731. *Although full of tall tales about heroic bishops and holy miracles, it is the chief source for early Saxon times and has justly earned its author the title of Father of English History. Many of its stories reveal much about the lives and thoughts of the Anglo-Saxon conquerors who established rival kingdoms in England, fought the British, and fought among themselves. The Edwin of this episode was king of Northumbria. Paulinus was a Christian bishop and missionary.*

When he had heard these things, the king replied that he was indeed both willing and obliged to embrace the faith which Paulinus taught. But he said that he would still confer about it with his friends, nobles, and councilors so that if they would be of his opinion, they might all be dedicated to Christ in the font of life together. With Paulinus's assent he did as he had said. For he held a council with wise men and asked each of them individually what view he took of this hitherto unheard-of doctrine and of the worship of the new God, which was being preached.

Coifi, the chief of his priests, answered at once, "O King, look into the nature of this which is now preached to us. For I most truely avow to you what I have learned for certain, that that religion which we have observed until now has no kind of power and no use. None of your people has devoted himself to the worship of our gods more zealously than I. Nevertheless there are many who receive greater favors and higher honors from you than I do, and who prosper better in all they undertake to do or to gain. But if the gods were good for anything, they would rather wish to help me who have taken pains to do them richer service. So we may conclude that, if upon examination you find these new doctrines which are now preached to us to be better and more efficacious, we ought to hasten to accept them without any delay."

Another of the king's nobles expressed agreement with Coifi's advice and with his prudent words, and immediately added, "O King, the time of man's life here on earth compared to that time which is unknown to us seems to me such as this. When you are sitting at dinner with your nobles and thegns in wintertime, with the hall warmed by a fire lit in its midst, and storms of wintry rain and snow are raging everywhere outside, a single sparrow comes and flies very quickly through the house. It comes in through one door and soon goes out by the other. During just the time in which it is indoors, it is not touched by the wintry storm, yet the little space of calm is passed in a moment and soon, from winter to winter returning, it is lost to your sight. So does this life of man appear here for a short space, but of what follows and what went before, we know nothing at all. If therefore this new doctrine brings any greater certainty, it seems justly to deserve to be followed." The other elders and councilors of the king, by Divine inspiration, continued to the same effect.

But Coifi added that he wished to listen more attentively to Paulinus speaking about the God Whom he preached. Paulinus, at the king's command, did as he was asked. Coifi heard his words and cried out, saying, "I realized long ago that there was nothing in what we worshiped, for indeed the more carefully I sought truth in that worship, the less did I find it. Now, however, I openly acknowledge that in this preaching there shines out that truth which can bestow on us the gifts of life, of salvation, and of eternal happiness. Therefore, O King, I advise that we at once consign to anathema and to fire the temples and altars which we have consecrated without reaping any benefit."

What more is there to say? The king openly gave assent to Paulinus's missionary work, renounced idolatry, and professed his acceptance of the Christian faith. And when he asked the aforesaid high priest of his rites who should be the first to profane the altars and temples of the idols and the enclosures which surrounded them, the priest replied, "I will. For who more fittingly can, as an example to others, and through the wisdom given to me by the true God, now destroy those things which I worshiped through foolishness?" Then, in contempt of vain superstition, he at once asked the king to give him arms and a stallion, which he might mount, and so go to destroy the idols. For it had not been lawful for a priest of those rites either to bear arms or to ride on other than a mare. So, girt with a sword, he took a spear in his hand, mounted the king's stallion, and went to the idols. When the multitude saw him, they thought he was mad. But he did not hesitate, and as soon as he drew near to the temple, he desecrated it by throwing into it the lance he held in his hand. Rejoicing greatly in knowledge of the worship of the true God, he ordered his companions to pull down the temple and all its enclosures and to set them on fire. This place where the idols once were is to be seen not far to the east of York, beyond the river Derwent, and is today called Goodmanham. It was there that the high priest, by the inspiration of the true God, profaned and destroyed the altars which he had himself consecrated.

Death of the Conqueror

GEORGE SLOCOMBE

1087. Twenty-one years after the battle of Hastings, William of Normandy, grown old and fat but still a mighty warrior, went to war once more. Whether he intended only to conquer the district between Normandy and Paris called the Vexin or to conquer Paris itself is not known. In any case, while triumphantly superintending the sack of Mantes William was mortally wounded in an accident. This vivid account of the bizarre circumstances of the Conqueror's death comes from George Slocombe's excellent biography, William the Conqueror, *which was published in 1959.*

The Conqueror was then lying in his palace at Rouen, undergoing medical treatment and submitting to a strict diet to reduce his corpulence. When he heard of the French raids he burst into a furious fit of rage. Uttering terrible threats of vengeance if his ultimatum were not accepted, he sent a message to Paris complaining of the acts of Philip's commanders and demanding the immediate cession to Normandy of the French Vexin, including the towns of Pontoise, Chaumont and Mantes. In theory William was still Philip's vassal as Duke of Normandy, although he was in fact, as King of England, independent of Philip and far more powerful. By his demand for the French Vexin and his threat of reprisals if it were not granted, he had clearly meant to imply that henceforth Normandy renounced her allegiance, however formal, to France.

Philip's reaction to the message was naturally to refuse. But he accompanied his refusal with a stupid and vulgar jest. The King of the English, he said to the Norman envoys, was lying-in at Rouen, and there would doubtless be a great show of candles at his churching. Philip's allusion to his swollen body provoked William to an outburst of his habitual energy. He struggled from his bed in a great rage and swore one of his most magnificent oaths. "By the Resurrection and the Splendor of God," he threatened, "I will go for my churching to Notre Dame in Paris, and I will bring ten thousand lances for candles."

In the last days of July 1087 he ordered his men to march on Mantes, on the road which follows the Seine from Rouen to Paris. The corn was in the fields, the grapes were in the vineyards and the apples in the orchards. The Normans blazed a trail of destruction as they advanced. Before they reached Mantes they found that the French garrison had left the safety of their walls to gaze upon their ruined vines and crops. When the advance guard of William's army reached the town, defenders and besiegers crowded through the gates together. Mantes, now called Mantes-la-Jolie, must have been even lovelier then, with its great church profiled against the sky and mirrored in the river, its bridge over the Seine, its stone and timber buildings and its many abbeys. At William's command the candles were lighted in the French King's border fortress. Fire swept through the churches and abbeys, burnt out the wooden buildings, the roof-timbers of the stone houses and filled the streets with burning debris.

Riding triumphantly amid the flames and the confusion, the cries, the smoke of the burning city, the Conqueror must have presented a fearful and wonderful spectacle to his knights and his victims. His vast bulk, his majestic bearing, his fierce brooding look, revived in French memories the tales of the terrible Vikings who had invaded Mantes and all the valley of the Seine nearly two centuries before, on their way to besiege Paris. William had gone berserk with the lust for battle and the desire for vengeance. He rode through the city urging on his followers to burn and destroy.

And then retribution fell. His great war-stallion, treading on a burning ember outside a church, stumbled. William was thrown violently against the heavy iron pommel of his saddle. He kept his seat, but he had received a mortal injury. In consternation the men of his escort helped him to dismount, unlaced his war helmet and dragged off his coat of mail. The Conqueror was placed in a litter and carried slowly back to Rouen. The Norman peasants at work in the fields, as they saw the sad return of their Duke, are said to have burst into loud lamentations. The war against King Philip, which if successful might have changed Anglo-French history, had ended disastrously.

William was first taken to his palace, and there his physicians, among them the learned Gilbert Maminot, Bishop of Lisieux, and Gontard, Abbot of Jumièges, both men skilled in medicine, examined his condition. But it was clear to them, and probably to the Conqueror himself, that his internal wound was fatal. He lingered six weeks in great pain. From the first day to the last, in spite of his sufferings, which he bore stoically, he never lost his mental powers nor his faculty of speech. When the noise and tumult of Rouen, the grinding of cart wheels, the clangor of the craftsmen hammering on iron and copper, and the cries of the market-vendors, disturbed his peace, he caused himself to be carried outside the walls of the city to the little priory of St. Gervais on the hill overlooking Rouen from the west. There, in the ancient crypt of the church, lay the remains of a British bishop named Mellon, the first bishop appointed to the metropolitan see of Normandy. And there in a small cell in the priory William lay on his deathbed.

The greatest men of Normandy surrounded him. Among the bishops and abbots only the faces of Lanfranc and Anselm were missing. The former was fully occupied with the cares of Church and state in England. The saintly Anselm, for whom William had sent when he knew that his last hour was near, had set out on the road to Rouen, but was himself overtaken by illness, and he never again saw William alive. Two of the sons of the dying Conqueror were at his side, William Rufus, his second son, and Henry, his youngest. Robert Curthose, the eldest, was living in banishment, either at the court of William's adversary Philip or in Flanders with his other enemy Robert the Frisian. William then sent for his notaries and prepared to dictate his last wishes. He ordered that the greater part of his treasure should be distributed among the churches and abbeys and the poor in his dominions, and the amounts he allocated for this purpose were duly written down. The churches of England received sums ranging from sixty pence to ten marks of gold, besides gold and silver vessels and ornaments. The clergy of Mantes, whose churches had been burned down by William's order, were allotted a special gift of money for the rebuilding of them.

The Conqueror is said to have made public profession of repentance of his misdeeds. The remarkable speech attributed to him by Orderic Vital is doubtless not literally exact, but it may be accepted as based on a series of confessions made by the dying man during his long agony. Orderic Vital was received into holy orders at Lisieux, whose bishop Gilbert Maminot ministered to the Conqueror to the last. He probably had access to the texts as well as to the verbal evocations in which his superiors preserved the memorable scene for posterity.

The spectators heard the dying King in a silence broken only by the scratching of the goose-quill of the monk who recorded the words. During the sixty years of his life, said the Conqueror, he had been the cause of much wrong-doing, and was now obliged to make account of it. He had been brought up from infancy to the profession of arms, and since then had been responsible for a great deal of bloodshed. When his father, the Duke Robert, had gone on his pilgrimage and left the duchy of Normandy in his hands, he was a boy not yet eight years old. For fifty-two years he had governed the duchy in the midst of wars. His own subjects had often caused him grave prejudice. They had conspired to the death of his tutor Turquetil, of Osbern Fitz-Herfast, Seneschal of Normandy, of the venerable Count Gilbert of Brionne, father of his country, and of many others of his supporters. Yet in the most perilous situations he had experienced the devotion of the humblest of his people. Often during the night he had been removed from his bed by his uncle Walter and concealed in the cottage of a peasant from the treacherous designs of his enemies. The Normans were a generous race if they were firmly governed, invincible in adversity and capable of vanquishing their enemies. But in the lack of just and firm government they fell into rebellion and sedition, as he knew to his cost. His own kinsmen had frequently made war against him, instead of rallying to his support.

William then reviewed in memory the conspiracies of his adolescence. His cousin Guy of Burgundy, whom he had treated as a brother, and to whom he had given the castles of Vernon and Brionne, with many lands in Normandy, had denounced him as a bastard and had rebelled against him, seducing from their allegiance Ralph of Bayeux, Hamon-le-Dentu, Nigel of Coutances and other barons. While still a beardless boy he had been forced to take arms against Guy. Then, with God's aid, he had vanquished his enemies at Val-ès-Dunes and had possessed his inheritance in freedom. Guy had fled the battlefield, and William had besieged him in the castle of Brionne until he surrendered.

Then came the revolts of William of Arques and his brother Malger, Archbishop of Rouen, both men his paternal uncles, and William's siege of Arques. The dying man fought his other battles over again: the defeat of Henry of France at Mortemer and Varaville, the wars with Geoffrey of Anjou and a more recent adversary, Robert the Frisian, Count of Flanders. In England, which he confessed had come to him by Divine grace, and not by hereditary right, he had had to overcome the resistance of the inhabitants of Exeter, of Chester and of the land north of the Humber, and had to fight the Scots, the Welsh, the Norwegians and the Danes. In all these situations his good fortune had given him the victory. But now he was stricken by mortal fear when he thought of how in all his actions cruelty had accompanied courage and bravery.

Yet he could claim that he had ever loved piety and defended the Church and her ministers. He had never violated the laws of the Church, which he revered as his mother. He had never sold ecclesiastical dignities for gold, and had always detested and opposed simony. He had confided the government of the Church to the most meritorious, notably to Lanfranc and to Anselm. He had always chosen the wisest men for his Council. He had sought truth and wisdom in their company. Since he governed the duchy seventeen houses of monks and six of nuns had been built, and Normandy had been covered with spiritual fortresses.

William now came to the last and the most embarrassing of his earthly problems: the heritage of his sons. He said that before he met Harold in battle at Hastings, he had accorded to Robert, the eldest, the duchy of Normandy. The barons had already done homage to him, and it was too late to deprive him of his inheritance. But he foresaw trouble ahead for the country subjected to Robert's power. He was proud, senseless and disorderly, and long would he suffer the cruelest misfortunes.

As to the throne of England, he would leave it to Divine Providence. He had not acquired it by hereditary right. He had taken it from the perjured Harold, after a hard battle and much shedding of blood, and he had subdued the land only with great difficulty. He had cruelly oppressed both the nobles and the people of England. He had dispossessed some unjustly, and had caused to perish by the sword and by famine a great multitude of people, especially in Yorkshire. After the people of Durham had killed Robert of Comines and a thousand Norman soldiers he had been overcome by a terrible rage. He had punished the people of northern England by burning their houses and their crops and by destroying their flocks and their herds, and had condemned many thousands of both sexes to die of starvation.

Having obtained possession of this land after so much shedding of blood, the Conqueror dared not bequeath the English throne lest a worse calamity befall after his death. Nevertheless he hoped that his son William Rufus, who had always been attached to him since his childhood, should, if it were the will of God, reign over England. For all his filial affection, the young man whom the English were to call the Red King did not hesitate. He had reached Wissant, the port at which Julius Caesar is believed by some writers to have embarked from Gaul for England, when a messenger sent after him in all haste informed him of his father's death. He continued his journey, and was crowned by Lanfranc. He reigned for nearly thirteen years, surviving rebellions, wars and scandal, and finally met with his mysterious end in the New Forest.

William's long monologue and the manner of his disposal of the thrones of Normandy and England had plunged his hearers into awe and stupefaction. For the first time they realized the changes that would come at the great King's death. England and Normandy, which had been united under William, would again be divided and the Norman barons who had lands in both countries would be faced with the choice of following either Robert or William Rufus. The Conqueror's youngest son Henry, called Beauclerc, seeing his two brothers each provided with a goodly inheritance, is said to have wept and to have protested to his father: "And what do you give me?" William replied: "I give you five thousand pounds in silver from my treasury." Whereupon the youth again complained: "But what shall I do with this money if I have no land of my own?"

William then ended this Old Testament dialogue between father and son with an amazingly clear glance into the future. "My son, be content with your lot and trust in the Lord. Wait patiently while your brothers precede you. Robert will have Normandy and William will have England. As for you, when the time comes you will have all the possessions that I have acquired, and you will surpass your brothers in wealth and power."

Reassured by this prophetic vision of the dying King, the future Henry I also received his father's blessing, and hastened to cross the sea in his turn. He rode to the royal treasury at Winchester, and doubtless displaying a letter sealed with William's seal, had his five thousand pounds of silver weighed out to him, and saw that the money was placed in security. Then he sought the company of friends in whom he could trust, and awaited the fulfilment of his father's prophecy.

Meanwhile the dying man had given orders for the release from their bonds of his prisoners, English and Norman. Wulfnoth, the youngest brother of King Harold, had been a captive in the tower of Rouen since William set out to conquer England twenty-one years earlier. The English Earl Morcar had been in William's power since the revolt of Ely. The Norman Earl Roger of Hereford was also held at Rouen and would die there. And last, but far from least, there was William's half-brother, the Earl-Bishop Odo, who had secretly aspired after William's throne, and failing that, had set his designs on the Papacy.

The Conqueror consented to the release of all but one, on condition that they swore to his ministers not to trouble the peace of England or Normandy. But Odo he would not set free. He told the great men around him, and especially his other half-brother Robert, Count of Mortain, who had pleaded for Odo's liberty, that they were ill-counselled to ask for the Bishop's release. Odo was frivolous, cruel and ambitious, attached to the lusts of the flesh, and he would never change. It was not the bishop whom he had cast into prison, but the tyrant and oppressor. If he recovered his liberty Odo would again trouble the peace and cause the deaths of many thousands. William spoke not with hatred, but as the father of his country, concerned with the welfare of his people.

In the end, wearied by their importunities, William consented against his better judgment to set Odo free, predicting nevertheless, and accurately, that death and disaster would follow. At the same moment that Odo was released and restored to his honors and dignities, one of William's more obscure kinsmen, Gilbert of Heugleville, who had fought with him at Hastings, died at Anfoi on 14 August. It was Gilbert's distinction to have been one of the rare companions of the Conqueror to refuse all reward or honor for his part in the battle of Hastings. He returned to Normandy to live and die a simple and honest knight.

William did not long survive this modest Bayard of the Conquest. He had lain in the priory of St. Gervais for six weeks, subject to intense pain which he bore patiently and with fortitude to the last. His hour was now come. On the morning of Thursday, 9 September 1087, the bell of the great minister of Rouen tolled. He awoke from a quiet sleep and asked why the bell rang. One who had watched during the night replied, "Lord, it rings for the hour of Prime in the church of Our Lady." The dying King then raised his eyes and lifted up his hands. "I commend myself to the Holy Mary, Mother of God, that by her prayers she may reconcile me with her Son, Our Lord Jesus Christ."

Having said this, he died. He was about sixty years old. He died in the twenty-first year of his reign over England, and the fifty-second year since Robert the Magnificent had left him the duchy of Normandy.

An extraordinary scene followed. The death of the great King created a mental and spiritual as well as a physical void. The prelates and the barons around the deathbed were dazed and even demented. His death, as William had sagely predicted during his weeks of tranquil reflection, would cause a great revolution in the world about him. The barons, and even the priests, fearing for their lives and possessions in the anarchy which would descend upon Normandy, fled from the death-chamber. Led by William's own brother Robert of Mortain, and his more distant kinsmen, every man hastened to his own house, to guard his treasure, and to defend his lands. The servants, seeing that their masters had gone, seized the opportunity to plunder the possessions of the dead King. They took the weapons, the gold and silver vessels, the linen and clothing, all the King's furniture, and even his bed. Abandoning the Conqueror of England alone and almost naked on the floor, they also took flight.

When the news was spread in the town of Rouen the citizens, it is said, were also seized with fear, as if a multitude of enemies threatened them. Each man left his occupation and sought counsel of his friends, his wife, and even of strangers in the street. Each man hastened to place his goods in security. At last the Archbishop and abbots of Rouen, regaining their senses, went in procession to the little church of St. Gervais and prayed for the soul of the King. The Archbishop then ordered the transport of the royal corpse to the abbey of St. Stephen in Caen, where William had long since announced his desire to be buried. But there was neither kinsman nor servant of the King left in Rouen to perform the last rites and prepare his body for interment.

Finally an obscure knight of the region named Herluin, "for the love of God and the honor of his people," offered to take charge of the last rites. At his own expense he engaged embalmers and professional mourners, and found a cart to carry the King to the banks of the Seine. There the body was embarked, sewn up in an ox-hide, according to tradition, like the corpse of a pagan warrior, and the faithful Herluin conveyed his lord on his last journey. As was historically fitting, the funeral ship of the greatest descendant of the Vikings sailed down the broad river which had been to his ancestors the highway of conquest.

The last stage of the journey to Caen was made by land. When Herluin and his illustrious charge reached the place in which William and Matilda had built their abbeys of penitence, a great crowd of priests and nobles waited. Bishop Odo had been released from his prison. William's youngest son had left his treasure in safe hands and had returned to Normandy. His brother Rufus was being crowned King of England. The pious Anselm had recovered from his illness. Only Robert of Mortain is not mentioned among the mourners. Archbishop William of Rouen, followed by the bishops and abbots of Normandy, and Abbot Gilbert of St. Stephen's and his monks, led the funeral procession through the city to the abbey outside the walls.

And then a curious and ominous incident occurred. Fire broke out in one of the half-timbered houses on the funeral route, and in an instant the flames had spread to a large part of the town. The citizens rushed to place their possessions in safety, and the clergy hurried to protect their churches. The monks of St. Stephen's, chanting the office for the dead, were left to pursue their course alone to the abbey William had built for them. Thus, amid the flames and the smoke which had accompanied his sieges, his Coronation in Westminster, and his last fatal orgy of destruction in Mantes, the Conqueror came to his eternal resting-place.

In the church a tomb had been made ready between the high altar and the choir. A stone sarcophagus or coffin had been placed in the tomb, but the corpse of William still lay on its bier before the high altar. The danger of fire having abated, the great concourse of priests and citizens entered the abbey church, and Gilbert, Bishop of Évreux, renowned for his eloquence and nicknamed "the Crane" for his height and his long thin legs, preached the funeral sermon. The good Norman in him praised William for having extended the power of Normandy. The dead man had raised his people higher than any of his predecessors had done. He had maintained justice and peace in all the states under his dominion. He had punished thieves and brigands and protected the defenceless. When the Bishop had finished his eulogy he invited the assembly to pray for the soul of the King and to forgive him freely if he had offended any one of them.

To the general astonishment, an angry protest was heard from a man in the crowd. Saying that he was called Ascelin, the son of Arthur, he spoke in a loud voice which penetrated to the very depths of the church. "This ground on which you stand," he shouted, "was the site of my father's house. This man for whom you pray, while still only Duke of Normandy, took it away from my father by violence, and having refused all compensation, he built this church on it in an abuse of his power. That is why I demand this ground and claim it publicly. In God's name, I forbid that the body of the robber should be covered with my earth and buried within my heritage."

On this violent incident the ceremony came to a abrupt halt. The Abbot Gilbert and the bishops interrogated the men who stood near Ascelin. When they confirmed the truth of his statement, the prelates took Ascelin aside and promised to recompense him for his loss. He was given on the spot a sum of sixty shillings for the site of the tomb, and he was promised, with the consent of the King's son, Henry, a hundred pounds, the value of the rest of the land which had been confiscated by William. Not long afterwards the money was paid.

One final mishap remained to complete the strangeness of this ceremony. When the royal corpse was lifted down from its bier to be placed in the stone sarcophagus, this was found to be too small for the vast bulk of the King. The grave-diggers attempted to force the body into the coffin, and the stomach burst. The honest Herluin's embalmers had not completed their task. The monks hurriedly heaped more incense on the smoking censers, but the stench was overpowering. Bishops and abbots, embarrassed and full of fear, hastened to terminate the rites, and to leave the church to the intimidating presence of its Founder.

Afterwards a monument emblazoned with gold and silver and precious stones, the work of the Englishman Otto the Goldsmith, was erected over the Conqueror's tomb through the affection, if not the piety, of his godless son William Rufus. It bore an inscription in ornate Latin composed by Thomas, Archbishop of York. The tomb was profaned in the course of the centuries, and the original monument and its gems have disappeared. As was said earlier in this work, the sarcophagus was opened in 1552 to satisfy the curiosity of an Italian cardinal and two bishops. The remains of William are said to have been found wonderfully preserved, and the features were still distinct enough to permit of a portrait being painted. Ten years later, during the religious wars in France, the tomb was broken into, the corpse demolished and dispersed. A monk of the abbey succeeded in concealing a thigh-bone, one-third longer, it is related, than that of an ordinary man. The bone was reinterred eighty years later, in another sarcophagus, but neither this nor its contents survived the fury of the French Revolution.

Today an empty tomb and an inscription in the church of St. Stephen, whose twin towers, gaunt and stark, an abiding illustration of his character, rise over the modern town of Caen, and a gigantic statue in his native Falaise, alone honor the memory of William the Conqueror.

Jerusalem Delivered

ZOÉ OLDENBOURG

1099. The First Crusade, the only crusade to achieve its purpose by force of arms, liberated Jerusalem from Moslem rule and established several Christian states in the land beyond the sea—outre-mer. Inspired by the preaching of Pope Urban II and of Peter the Hermit, led by powerful barons but by no kings, the crusaders assembled at Byzantium, fought their way across Turkey, captured the city of Antioch, and arrived before the walls of Jerusalem on June 7, 1099. In addition to her contributions to medieval history, Zoé Oldenbourg has written outstanding historical novels about medieval France, the two finest being The World Is Not Enough *and* The Cornerstone.

When at last the army came in sight of the towers and domes of Jerusalem, there was a veritable explosion of delirious excitement. Knights and soldiers fell on their knees, uttering cries of joy, and burst into floods of tears.

Chroniclers who witnessed this first encounter, the joy of at last beholding Jerusalem which was the culmination of so many hopes and prayers and dreams, give us some idea what it was like, though even this must still be a long way from the reality. The city, set among olive- and cypress-covered hills, was surrounded by a twisting belt of ramparts flanked by towers. With its great gardens, white-painted houses, domes, and minarets it was a beautiful place, but infinitely more modest than Constantinople or

Antioch. The pilgrims in their imagination may have confused it with the heavenly Jerusalem, but even so, they knew that the splendor of this Jerusalem was entirely spiritual, and in the words of William of Tyre, there was not a man among them so hardhearted that he could hold back his tears.

This wave of passion and mystical enthusiasm which swept with such sudden violence over a whole army was a unique phenomenon. Only the name of Jerusalem can explain it, and it was something which never occurred again. It was the first time such a vast crowd of pilgrims from the West had come to the Holy City, and they had endured years of suffering by the hope of reaching Jerusalem.

We have already seen that among the poor and the common people drawn by the preachers were plenty of fanatics who believed that they had only to enter a Jerusalem liberated from the pagan to see a new heaven and a new earth. They believed that the angels were fighting on the side of the Christians, and that the poor and just would reign peacefully in Jerusalem which had been purified forever and flowed with riches of all kinds. It is not easy to assess the exact nature of these dreams or to what extent the will to conquer was consciously mingled with the desire for martyrdom, but it is certain that the pilgrims and the bulk of the army envisaged something very different from the simple capture of a particularly venerable city. The whole adventure had a mystical rather than a warlike quality about it, and it was infinitely more important to them to touch the ground trodden by the Savior's feet than to cover themselves with glory. Certainly a greater degree of disinterested selflessness was to be found in that war at that particular moment than in any other war before or since. Now more than ever the army believed it was fighting for Christ. Its object was to defend Christ, to avenge Christ, and to win Christ, and Christ seemed to them as much present as if he had been reincarnated in fact. Simply to be in the very country, in the very place, where the Passion of Jesus Christ had taken place was, to some extent, to relive the mystery of the Incarnation. Whatever may be said of the future conduct of this army of God, it would be unjust to underestimate the grandeur of this experience and the sincerity of those who lived through it.

The Crusaders had not come to Jerusalem merely to pray and to worship. They were there to fight and to snatch the city from the infidel. Whatever their relations with these infidels, Turks or Arabs, had been over the previous two years (and as we have seen, they had not always been bad), once outside Jerusalem the entire nature of the war suddenly changed. The Moslem became, or became once more, the diabolical enemy of God in the full meaning of the word, because by his presence he was profaning and polluting the place which, to the Christians, was the Holy of Holies.

They had known the truth for a long time but now it suddenly dawned on God's soldiers in all its force. They could see it before their eyes in the churches which had been turned into Mosques and the Egyptian banners floating from the towers. The Moslems, who could never have borne even the idea of infidels inside Mecca, were making a mistake when they let the fanaticism of the Christians surprise them.

To keep up the morale of the army the priests were continually preaching sermons to remind the soldiers of the insults which the Moslems were inflicting not only on the local Christians—a minor detail—but on the person of Christ himself and on the most sacred shrines, crosses, and relics. The Moslems were in fact guilty of many fewer and less serious acts of sacrilege than the Christians imagined, but the mere fact of such a holy place being in the hands of a "pagan" faith was an intolerable scandal in itself (although Christianity had managed to tolerate it perfectly well for over four centuries), and it was particularly so to this horde of pilgrims who for years had been obsessed by the idea of Jerusalem.

The siege continued for one month and ten days. The torrid June heat in those parts, and the shortage of water due to the fact that the wells had all been poisoned or filled in by the enemy and nothing remained but the pool of Siloam, which could not supply enough water for a whole army, all helped to make it an extremely painful one. The city was fairly well defended. The Egyptian governor, Iftikhar ad-Daula, had had plenty of time to take steps to ensure that the besiegers had no means of obtaining supplies on the spot: the walls of Jerusalem were stout and the garrison composed of picked Arab and Sudanese troops. For fear of treachery, the majority of Christians in Jerusalem had been driven out of the city, making so many fewer useless mouths.

The assault launched on June 13 was unsuccessful: the Crusading army was ill-equipped and weak from thirst. For all their holy zeal and longing for martyrdom, the men were powerless against well-defended walls. Fulcher of Chartres asserts that the attack failed simply for lack of ladders. The assailants were forced to withdraw, leaving numerous dead on the field, and prepare for a siege which their lack of engines promised to make a difficult one. To find wood to build machines they had to comb the countryside for miles. With the help of a Genoese squadron which had successfully captured the port of Jaffa, the Crusaders did manage to build some mangonels and movable towers. Two big wooden "castles" were equipped, one by Godfrey of Bouillon, the other by Raymond of Saint-Gilles, and Tancred's Normans later constructed a third.

While the barons, with the help of the Genoese engineers and carpenters and their own teams of technicians, were building the battle engines and completing the encirclement of the city, the army waited for the final assault in a state of exaltation rendered still more intense by heat and thirst. Just as at Antioch, their suffering and physical exhaustion became a source of strength in themselves, giving rise to visions, outbreaks of mass hysteria, a longing for purification, and a belief in miracles. In spite of the bloody failure of his own crusade, Peter the Hermit still retained a certain ascendancy over the crowd, and led countless disciples down to the river Jordan where, carrying palms in their hands and singing hymns, the pilgrims washed away their sins in the waters of the river in which Jesus had been baptized. A clerk named Peter Desiderius saw an apparition of the defunct Bishop of Le Puy, the legate Adhemar, below the walls of Jerusalem. The Bishop had been admitted to the number of the Blessed, but he had returned to direct his army and on his instructions, interpreted by Peter Desiderius, a solemn procession was organized. This was on July 8, a month after the beginning of the siege. Everyone, clergy, barons, knights, archers, foot soldiers, and civilians, marched around the walls of the Holy City singing psalms, and although the walls of Jerusalem did not tumble down like those of Jericho, in the minds of the people, at least, this solemn investment of the beleaguered city was certainly a decisive step toward victory. This was how the Christians saw it as they walked barefoot, singing and praying, to the Mount of Olives, with memories of the Passion, love for the Holy City, and hatred of the pagans fused into a single fervent outburst of emotion.

From the summit of the walls, Iftikhar ad-Daula's garrison contemplated this demonstration of piety with misplaced cynicism. They were rough soldiers, recruited among the nomads of the Arabian desert and the warrior tribes of the Sudan, and they did not understand that in these religious songs, these tears, and these prayers chanted aloud lay the real strength of their adversaries, nor that the crosses held high in the air could well prove more dangerous than swords. Iftikhar's soldiers, simple, ignorant Moslems, raised answering crosses on the walls, pillaged from the churches of Jerusalem. To annoy the enemy they abused them, spat on them, and subjected them, in the words of William of Tyre, "to still greater shames, and outrages of which it is not decent to speak." Soldiers of every age and nation have always been given to such crude and stupid behavior, but to the devout pilgrims who were at that moment climbing the Mount of Olives, it must have seemed a living proof of the perversity of Satan, and the men who insulted Jesus Christ in this way in his own city, devils incarnate. In the words of William of Tyre: "their hearts swelled with desire *to avenge this shame done to Jesus Christ.*"

Five days later the general assault was launched. This was a full-scale attack including a massive bombardment of the walls and gates. After two days' fierce fighting in which the defenders hurled down fire to repel the attackers, Godfrey of Bouillon's men succeeded in making their way into the city by means of a footbridge slung from the movable tower to the outer wall at Bab al-Sahira, close to Herod's Gate. Godfrey and his elder brother, Count Eustace, were among the first Crusaders to set foot on the walls of Jerusalem.

This happened at about midday on July 15 and from that moment on the capture of the city was no more than a matter of hours. The Walloon and Brabançon troops commanded by the two brothers of Boulogne occupied the whole of the northern wall and penetrated into the interior of the city, driving the defenders before them through the town to fall back on the mosque of al-Aqsa (Solomon's Temple). Taking refuge in the great mosque, the soldiers of the garrison held out there all day long, and when the Flemings finally broke into the temple there was such slaughter there that (according to the *Anonymi*) "our men were wading in blood up to their ankles." Very soon the bulk of the Crusading army was inside the walls, including the Count of Flanders and the Duke of Normandy, Tancred, Godfrey's cousin Baldwin of Le Bourg, Gaston of Béarn, and Gerard of Roussillon. At this point a terrible battle broke out inside the city. The Egyptian garrison was large, and faced with adversaries whose numbers were ten times greater, was determined to make them pay dearly for their victory, while the victors themselves were determined to give no quarter.

To the south of the city, in the direction of the citadel, the resistance was more long drawn out. This was where Raymond of Saint-Gilles was attacking with his tower and his Provençal troops. There was still bitter fighting on the ramparts when the groups of terrified men fleeing through the city toward the citadel spread panic among the defenders of the Sion Gate. Now it was the turn of the Provençaux to gain a foothold in the city. The resistance was at an end and Jerusalem was in the hands of the Crusaders. The governor, Iftikhar ad-Daula, with a small party of the garrison, had managed to barricade himself inside the citadel and from there, surrounded by the men of Provence, he surrendered to the Count of Toulouse in return for a promise that his own and his men's lives should be spared. This promise was kept. It was the only one. If other similar promises had been given that day the commanders had no means of enforcing them, and there is no doubt that Iftikhar ad-Daula owed his life to the thickness of the walls of his citadel quite as much as to the honor of Raymond of Saint-Gilles.

The massacre perpetrated by the Crusaders in Jerusalem has been reckoned among the greatest crimes of history. There is no lack of psychological explanations for it, and all historians, those who favor the Crusade and those who do not, rightly blame the state of almost morbid excitement which gripped a rabble made fanatical by the preaching of the holy war. It does not seem as though blame can be attached to the leaders on this score. They had nothing to gain from a massacre, and would no doubt have preferred good ransoms to such a drastic revenge for the shame put upon Jesus Christ. Tancred is known to have promised their lives to several hundred Arab soldiers who had taken refuge on the roof of the al-Aqsa mosque, and he did not conceal his fury when he learned that the prisoners protected by his banner had been slaughtered. He had in fact been powerless to ensure their protection.

During the days of July 15 and 16 the "soldiers of Christ" were masters of the Holy City. They scoured streets and alleys, gardens and courtyards, breaking down doors of houses and mosques and killing, killing all who fell in their path, no longer the soldiers, who had been killed first, but civilians, men, women, children, and old people.

The Jews, or as many of them as the building would hold, were shut up in the synagogue, which was then set on fire. The entire Jewish community of Jerusalem perished in the flames. Ibn al-Athir also records that the Crusaders' rage was particularly directed against imams and ulemas, that they profaned mosques and destroyed Moslem holy books. What is certain is that these manifestations of fanaticism were only one aspect of the murderous rage which took hold of the army on that day, because it is a fact that women and children were massacred without mercy.

Some eminent historians have attempted to "excuse" this monstrous act by recalling that, a century earlier, Moslems and Jews in the same city had turned against the Christians and put to death the Patriarch of Jerusalem. The pilgrims and the soldiers were probably not unaware of this, but it would be assuming a great deal to credit them with a desire to avenge local Christians who had been dead for over a hundred years, especially since they were largely unconcerned about the fate of contemporary Syrians, Armenians, and Greeks. If there was any avenging to be done—and the desire was certainly very strong—the person to be avenged was Jesus Christ.

Possibly responsibility for the disaster—for disaster it was—rests with the ecclesiastical and lay preachers for arousing in the men not only a laudable zeal for their faith but also hatred for the enemies of that faith. The preaching of the clergy (beginning with Urban II's celebrated sermon) had certainly excited the indignation of those who volunteered for the Crusade by descriptions of the sufferings of the Holy Land, but it is questionable whether this indignation, consciously inflamed by the priests, could still be so strong after two years of war.

*   *   *

It is clear, however, from both Latin and Moslem historians that the population was more or less completely exterminated. This means that between July 15 and 16, 1099, the Crusaders who, according to the estimates of modern historians, numbered at most ten thousand, killed nearly forty thousand people, the great majority of whom were unarmed civilians. To achieve this the regular army must have gone to work with as much ardor as the "pilgrims." The knights must, at best, have looked on without interfering; the leaders must have allowed the troops to have their way without protest and even the priests evinced no indignation. At all events, eyewitnesses mention no appeals to clemency or reason on the part of the authorities, either ecclesiastical or secular, probably because any such appeals would have made no impression on the maddened horde which poured through every sector of the Holy City like a pack of ferocious hounds with the lust for blood upon them.

William of Tyre, writing ninety years afterward, describes the scene: "The city offered a spectacle of such slaughter of enemies, such a profusion of bloodshed, that the victors themselves could not help but be struck with horror and disgust." But that was afterward, when there was no longer anyone left to kill. In this reference to horror and disgust, the Archbishop of Tyre is almost certainly basing his conjecture on written evidence or on memories handed down by word of mouth. It is unlikely that he is merely crediting the heroes of the Crusade with his own feelings. But contemporary historians of the event make no mention of any feelings of remorse on the part of the Crusaders when they saw the monstrous deeds they had committed. On the contrary, Albert of Aix (himself a churchman) stresses the joy of the victors at the magnitude of their victory and makes no attempt to condemn or even to exonerate the authors of the massacre. God had triumphed. The streets of the Holy City were literally running with blood, and neither the *Anonymi* nor Raymond of Aguilers appears to have paused to reflect that this was the blood of innocent people. Yet they must have seen with their own eyes the piled-up corpses of women and children, not to mention the men, who by an age-old law were regarded as guilty a priori because able to defend themselves even if they were only peaceful citizens or artisans.

In fact, the only word of regret or blame connected with the whole affair is the anger of Tancred, and this is simply the anger of a soldier who, having promised other soldiers their lives, has to suffer the indignity of having his word broken for him, and also the anger of a man who finds himself deprived of the opportunity of collecting a considerable ransom. Raymond of Saint-Gilles did succeed in protecting his captives—the governor of the city with a number of his officers and a contingent of Mamelukes and Arabs—and in escorting them safe and sound as far as

97

Ascalon. Evidently Iftikhar was not ungrateful, and if Raymond accepted a ransom there was nothing in this contrary to the rules of war. But because he had been the only one who took prisoners, he was immediately accused of treachery by the Crusaders from the North. Albert of Aix voiced their opinion that the Count of Toulouse must have been bought off by the Moslems. How else were they to explain his clemency toward Christ's enemies? In actual fact Raymond had saved only a handful of soldiers from the massacre, but in the eyes of an army that was already drunk with blood and a religious frenzy amounting to madness, even this was unforgivable.

On the evening of that terrible July 15, while the massacre was still raging in the city, the barons went altogether to the Church of the Holy Sepulcher. Once the city had been taken they considered their job was done and had stopped thinking of killing anyone. Robert of Flanders, Robert of Normandy, Tancred, Godfrey of Bouillon, and Raymond of Saint-Gilles, accompanied by their knights, chaplains, and servants, were already moving into the conquered city with the calm adaptability which makes a soldier feel at home anywhere. Wounded, bleeding, drenched with sweat and broken with fatigue after a battle of unprecedented ferocity, they swiftly installed themselves in the fine city houses, deserted now for a very good reason, then hastily washed and changed their clothes, not of course to rest, but to go to the Holy Sepulcher and give thanks to God and to Jesus Christ.

They went, says William of Tyre, "barefoot, with sighs and tears, through the holy places of the city where Jesus Christ Our Savior lived in the flesh. Devoutly they kissed the places where his feet had trod." They were welcomed by the Christian clergy, who had remained in the city sheltering in churches and monasteries, and were led in procession to the Church of the Holy Sepulcher. William of Tyre again, on the basis of earlier witnesses, gives a deeply moving description of the religious fervor of these barons on reaching the end of their pilgrimage. They shed tears "of joy and pity" as they prostrated themselves before the Holy Sepulcher. "To each one it seemed as though he saw the body of Jesus Christ still lying there, all dead. . . . They felt as if they had entered into Paradise." Can we doubt the sincerity (one might almost say the purity) of the deep surge of love which suddenly took hold of these very mediocre Christians? Perhaps the Holy Sepulcher, the Holiest of Holies, could accomplish even that miracle.

Two hundred yards outside the Holy Sepulcher, men were still murdering others blindly and savagely, wading in blood and trampling on corpses belonging to people whose skins, it was true, were somewhat darker than their own and who did not dress like Christians. Drawing inspiration from the words of the Psalmist, soldiers may have been taking little children by the feet and dashing their heads against the stones because they were the "little children of Babylon." But the knights and barons were praying and weeping for joy as they received the blessings of Greek and Syriac priests, among the candles and the smell of incense. At the gates of Paradise.

Jerusalem was delivered. More accurately, it had simply changed masters once again. The massacre of the population of Jerusalem filled the entire Moslem world with horror. As soon as the news of the Crusaders' victory spread throughout Christendom, the hearts of the faithful everywhere in the West overflowed with joy. Urban II, the man who had promoted and been largely responsible for the Crusade, did not live to hear the great news. He died on July 29, before the letter announcing the capture of Jerusalem could reach him.

The Burghers of Calais

JEAN FROISSART

1346–1347. After his great victory over the French in the battle of Crécy, King Edward III of England attacked the city of Calais. He needed Calais as an entry port and base for further campaigns in France. Surrounded by a double wall and a double moat, Calais resisted stoutly. The siege and blockade lasted for ten months before starvation forced the heroic defenders to surrender. This story of one of the most famous incidents in medieval warfare is taken from Froissart's Chronicles, *a nearly contemporary work which ranks as one of the greatest histories ever written in French.*

After the departure of King Philip and his army, the people of Calais realized that the support on which they had been counting had failed them, and at the same time they were so weakened by hunger that the biggest and strongest among them could hardly stand. So they took counsel together and decided it would be better to throw themselves on the mercy of the King of England, if they could not obtain better terms, than to die one by one of starvation; for hunger might drive many of them frantic and cost them their souls with their bodies. They so entreated the Governor, Sir Jean de Vienne, to negotiate that at last he consented. He went on to the battlements and signalled to those outside that he wished to talk to them. When King Edward heard of this, he immediately sent out Sir Walter Manny and Lord Basset. They came to Sir Jean de Vienne and heard him say:

"My dear lords, you are very gallant knights with much experience of war, and you know that the King of France whom we serve sent us to this place to hold the town and castle for as long as our honor and his interests might require it. We have done everything in our power, but now our help has failed us and you are pressing us so hard that we have nothing left to eat. We must all die or go mad with hunger if the noble King whom you serve does not take pity on us. So I ask you, dear lords, to beg him humbly to have mercy on us and allow us to go away just as we are, taking for himself the town and citadel and all the things in them. He will find enough to satisfy him."

To this Sir Walter Manny replied: "Sir John, Sir John, we know something of the intentions of our lord the King, for he has told us of them. We must warn you that it is not his purpose to let you go free as you suggest. His intention rather is that you should put yourselves entirely in his hands, to be ransomed or put to death as he chooses. The people of Calais have caused him so much trouble and vexation, have cost him so much money and so many lives, that you cannot wonder that he should be enraged against them."

Sir Jean de Vienne replied: "It would be too hard for us to agree to such conditions. Inside here we are a little band of knights and squires who have served our master loyally to the best of our ability, as you would serve yours in the same case, and we have undergone many hardships and sufferings in so doing. But we would rather suffer more than any man has yet endured than consent that the humblest groom or servant in the town should be worse treated than the greatest among us. We beg you, in the kindness of your heart, to go back to the King of England and entreat him to spare us. That would be a chivalrous act on your part. And we hope that his noble heart will move him to have pity on us."

"Indeed, yes," said Sir Walter Manny, "I will do that willingly, Sir John. And I sincerely hope he will listen to me, for it will go better with all of you if he does."

The two English knights went off, leaving Sir Jean de Vienne standing on the battlements, for they were soon to return. King Edward was waiting for them at the entrance to his quarters, eager to have news of the state of Calais. With him were the Earl of Derby, the Earl of Northampton, the Earl of Arundel and several other English lords. His envoys bowed and went up to him and Sir Walter Manny began:

"Sire, we have seen the captain of Calais and have had a long conversation with him. It appears that he and his companions in arms as well as the citizens would be quite ready to surrender the town and castle and every-thing in them to you, on the sole condition that they be allowed to leave unharmed."

"Sir Walter," the King answered, "you know something of our intentions concerning Calais. What was your reply?"

"Before God, Sir," said Sir Walter, "I told them that you would agree to nothing, except that they should put themselves entirely in your hands, to live or die as you chose. When he heard this, Sir Jean de Vienne admitted that they were on the point of starvation but said that rather than sur-render on those terms they would sell their lives as dearly as men ever did."

"Sir Walter," replied the King, "there is not the slightest hope or prospect of my changing my mind."

Sir Walter Manny went closer to the King and reasoned with him, saying, to help the defenders of Calais: "My lord, you may well be mistaken, and you are setting a bad example for us. Suppose one day you send us to de-fend one of your fortresses, we should go less cheerfully if you have those people put to death, for then they would do the same to us if they had the chance." This argument did much to soften the King's heart, especially when most of his barons supported it. So he said: "My lords, I do not want to be alone against you all. Walter, go back to Calais and tell its commander that this is the limit of our clemency: six of the principal citizens are to come out, with their heads and their feet bare, halters around their necks and the keys of the town and castle in their hands. With these six I shall do as I please, and the rest I will spare."

"My lord," said Sir Walter, "I will do as you say."

He went back to Calais to where Sir Jean de Vienne was waiting and told him what the King had said, adding that that was the most he could obtain. "I am sure that is true," said Sir Jean. "Now I must ask you to be so good as to wait here while I report all this to the townspeople. It was they who sent me here to talk with you and they, I think, who must give you the answer."

Sir Jean left the battlements and went to the market-place, where he had the bells rung to summon the people together. They all came, men and women, eager to hear the news, though they were so weak with hunger that they could scarcely stand. When they were assembled, Jean de Vienne quietly repeated all that had been said, telling them that nothing more could be hoped for and asking them to consult together and give their answer quickly. When he had finished speaking they began to cry out and weep so bitterly that their lamentations would have moved the stoniest heart. For a time they were unable to say anything in reply and Sir Jean himself was so moved that he also was weeping.

At last the richest citizen of the town, by name Master Eustache de Saint-Pierre, stood up and said:

"Sirs, it would be a cruel and miserable thing to allow such a population as this to die, so long as some remedy can be found. To prevent such a misfortune would surely be an act of great merit in Our Savior's eyes and, for my part, I should have such strong hopes of receiving pardon for my sins if I died to save this people that I wish to be the first to come forward. I am willing to strip to my shirt, bare my head, put the rope around my neck, and deliver myself into the King of England's hands."

When Master Eustache de Saint-Pierre had said this, his hearers were ready to worship him. Men and women flung themselves at his feet weeping bitterly. It was indeed a pitiful scene.

Then another greatly respected and wealthy citizen, who had two beautiful daughters, stood up and said that he would go with his friend Master Eustache de Saint-Pierre. His name was Master Jean d'Aire. A third, called Master Jacques de Wissant, who owned a rich family estate, offered to accompany them. Then his brother, Master Pierre de Wissant, and a fifth and a sixth said that they would go, too.

These six burghers stripped to their shirts and breeches there and then in the market-place, placed halters round their necks as had been stipulated and took the keys in their hands, each holding a bunch of them. Sir Jean de Vienne mounted a pony—for he could only walk with great difficulty—and led them to the gates. Then men, women and children of Calais followed them weeping and wringing their hands. Sir Jean de Vienne had the gate opened and closed behind him, so that he stood with the six burghers between it and the outer barriers. He went to where Sir Walter Manny was waiting and said to him:

"Sir Walter, as the military commander of Calais and with the consent of the poor people of this town, I deliver up to you these six burghers. I swear to you that they have been and are to this day the most honorable and prominent citizens of Calais, by reason of their personal characters, their wealth and their ancestry, and that they carry with them all the keys of the town and citadel. And I beg you, noble sir, to intercede with the King of England not to have these good men put to death."

"I do not know," said Sir Walter, "what the King will decide to do with them, but I promise you that I will do all I can."

The barriers were then opened and Sir Walter Manny led off the six burghers, in the state I have described, straight to the King's quarters, while Sir Jean de Vienne went back into the town.

At that time the King was in his chamber with a large company of earls, barons and knights. Hearing that the men of Calais were coming as he had ordered, he went out to the open space before his quarters, followed by his nobles and by great numbers of others who were curious to see them and learn what would happen to them. Even the Queen of England, who was far advanced in pregnancy, went out with her lord the King. When

103

Sir Walter Manny arrived with the six burghers, he went up to the King and said: "Sire, here is the deputation from Calais at your orders."

The King kept quite silent and looked at them very fiercely, for he hated the people of Calais because of the losses they had inflicted on him at sea in the past. The six burghers knelt down before him and, clasping their hands in supplication, said: "Most noble lord and King, here before you are we six citizens of Calais, long established and wealthy merchants of the town. We surrender to you the keys of the town and the castle, to do with them as you will. We put ourselves as you see us entirely in your hands, in order to save the remaining inhabitants of Calais, who have already undergone great privations. We pray you by your generous heart to have mercy on us also."

None of the brave men present, lords, knights or men-at-arms, could refrain from shedding tears of pity when they heard this. It was indeed a moving sight to see men so humiliated and in such mortal danger.

But the King continued to glare at them savagely, his heart so bursting with anger that he could not speak. When at last he did, it was to order their heads to be struck off immediately.

All the nobles and knights who were there begged the King to have mercy, but he would not listen. Sir Walter Manny spoke up for them: "Noble Sire, curb your anger. You have a reputation for royal clemency. Do not perform an act which might tarnish it and allow you to be spoken of dishonorably. If you do not spare these men, the world will say that it was a cruel deed and that it was too harsh of you to put to death these honorable citizens who have voluntarily thrown themselves on your mercy to save others."

At this the King ground his teeth and said: "That is enough, Sir Walter, my mind is made up. Let the executioner be sent for. The people of Calais have killed so many of my men that it is right that these should die in their turn."

Then the noble Queen of England, pregnant as she was, humbly threw herself on her knees before the King and said, weeping: "Ah, my dear lord, since I crossed the sea at great danger to myself, you know that I have never asked a single favor from you. But now I ask you in all humility, in the name of the Son of the Blessed Mary and by the love you bear me, to have mercy on these six men."

The King remained silent for a time, looking at his gentle wife as she knelt in tears before him. His heart was softened, for he would not willingly have distressed her in the state she was in, and at last he said: "My lady, I could wish you were anywhere else but here. Your appeal has so touched me that I cannot refuse it. So, although I do this against my will, here, take them. They are yours to do what you like with."

The Queen thanked him from the bottom of her heart, then rose to her feet and told the six burghers to rise also. She had the halters taken from their necks and led them into her apartment. They were given new clothes and an ample dinner. Then each was presented with six nobles and they were escorted safely through the English army and went to live in various towns in Picardy.

After King Edward had handed over the six burghers to the Queen, he called Sir Walter Manny and his two Marshals and said to them: "Sirs, take these keys of the town and castle of Calais and go and assume possession of them. Take the knights who are there and make them prisoners or else put them on parole; they are gentlemen and I will trust them on their word. All other soldiers, who have been serving there for pay, are to leave the place just as they are, and so is everyone else in the town, men, women and children, for I wish to repopulate Calais with pure-blooded English." . . .

Now in my opinion it is very sad to reflect on the fate of those great burghers and their noble wives and their handsome children, who with their forefathers had been living for generations in Calais. There were many such on the day when it fell. It was harrowing for them to have to abandon their fine houses, their estates, their furniture and possessions; for they could take nothing away and they received no restitution or compensation from the King of France, for whose sake they had lost everything. I will say no more about them. They managed as well as they could, and the majority went to the town of Saint-Omer.* . . .

When King Edward returned to London, he gave serious thought to the repopulation of Calais, sending there thirty-six wealthy and responsible citizens with their families, and more than three hundred other men of lesser standing. Their numbers grew continually because the King granted them such great liberties and privileges that many became eager to settle there.

* It appears that many of the French inhabitants were either not dispossessed, or were re-admitted after a few weeks. One who was confirmed in his possessions and given a post of special responsibility was the heroic Eustache de Saint-Pierre. It is also established that Philip IV made efforts to compensate those who were expelled, by conferring various offices and rights upon them.

The Black Death

SIR ARTHUR BRYANT

1348–1349. Much history is a record of the disasters men bring upon themselves. But some of the worst misfortunes of mankind—floods, earthquakes, famines, and plagues—seem to be inherent in the natural scheme of things or acts of God. The most terrible of these of which we have knowledge was the Black Plague which ravaged Europe in the fourteenth century. This account of the plague in England was written by one of the fine contemporary English historians, a sound scholar with a rare feeling for the resources of the English language.

The summer of 1348 was exceptionally wet. The Leicester chronicler, Henry Knighton, attributed the incessant downpour to the wanton behavior of ladies at tournaments. Dressed in men's attire "in party-colored tunics, one color or pattern on the right side and another on the left, with short hoods that had pendants like ropes wound round their necks, and belts thickly studded with gold or silver," he complained, "a band of women would come to share the sport, sometimes to the number of forty or fifty ladies, of the fairest and comeliest (though I say not of the best) among the whole kingdom. There they spent and lavished their possessions and wearied their bodies with fooleries and wanton buffoonery . . . But

God in this matter, as in all others, brought marvellous remedy, for He harassed the places and times appointed for such vanities by opening the floodgates of heaven with rain and thunder and lurid lightning and by unwonted blasts of tempestuous winds."

Yet, as the monastic historian was quick to point out, the rain that wrecked the tournaments in honor of the Order of the Garter was the least of the evils awaiting England that summer. God had prepared a far more awful punishment for her. Eighteen months earlier, while the English were besieging Calais, another army two thousand miles away had been blockading a small Genoese grain port in the Crimea where a band of silk-traders, operating at the end of the seven-thousand-mile route to China, had taken refuge from the Tartar horsemen of the steppes. Suddenly the besiegers had been struck down by a pestilence which, spreading everywhere throughout Tartary and known as "the death," had begun, it was believed, in the putrefaction of unburied multitudes in earthquakes in China. Before they raised the siege the Tartars are said to have catapulted some infected corpses into the town.

What is certain is that the disease was carried into Europe at the end of 1347 or beginning of 1348 by Genoese ships trading with the Black Sea. No-one knew its cause or even its nature, but it is now believed to have been the bubonic plague—a flea-borne epidemic of the black rat which had invaded Europe from Asia at the time of the Crusades and with which the wooden trading ships of the day were heavily infested. By the time vessels that had called in the Crimea reached the Bosphorus and Mediterranean the plague was raging among their crews, and every port at which they touched became infected. It struck so suddenly that at first no-one had time to escape; at Constantinople the Byzantine emperor's heir was among its victims. The symptoms were a gangrenous inflammation of the lungs, vomiting and spitting blood, vilely infected breath and the appearance, on the second day, of hard black buboes in the arm-pits and groin which were almost always the heralds of death. Few who caught the disease in its first onslaught outlived the third day.

By the end of January 1348 the plague was raging in all the great ports of southern Europe, including Venice, Genoa, Marseilles and Barcelona. In the Mediterranean ships were found drifting with every member of the crew dead. One after another, despite frantic efforts to isolate themselves, the Italian cities went down before the pestilence. Terrifying stories circulated of its supernatural origin; of how "in the east, hard by Greater India, fire and stinking smoke had burned up all the cities" and how "between Cathay and Persia there had rained a vast rain of fire, falling in flakes like snow and burning up mountains and plains with men and women," and accompanied by a sinister black cloud that "whosoever beheld died within the space of half a day." Thence, borne by "a foul blast of wind from the south," the infection had invaded Europe.

In the spring, having made Venice and Genoa cities of the dead, the plague reached Florence. In the introduction to his *Decameron* Boccaccio left a first-hand picture of its horrors: the helplessness of the doctors, the stench of the sick, the cautious shutting themselves up in their houses until the infection crept in and the reckless drinking in taverns day and night, the multitude of corpses lying uncovered before every church and the pits into which the dead were packed in layers. The poor perished in the streets or among the crops, the swine that rooted in the deserted streets dropped dead as they nosed the bundles of rags stripped from the plague-stricken, and swarms of oxen, sheep and goats—"and even dogs, those most faithful friends to men"—wandered untended through the fields. The dying were abandoned, the dead were dragged out of the houses and stacked by the road-side, the houses of those who had fled were left open to all, "the reverend authority of the laws, divine and human, being almost wholly ruined and dissolved." It was the same everywhere: in Siena, in Piacenza, in Parma, in Rimini, where the chronicler, Agniolo di Tura, carried with his own hand his five little sons to the grave.

While the plague was devastating Italy, it spread in widening circles from the Mediterranean eastwards into Istria and Hungary and over the Alps into Bavaria, westwards across Spain where it struck down the Queen of Aragon and, later, the King of Castile, and northwards from Marseilles up the Rhone. It broke out in the convent of the Carmelite friars at Avignon before anyone ever realized what it was, slaying Laura, the adored of the poet Petrarch, and the abbot of the great Canterbury monastery of St. Augustine's who was visiting the *curia* at the time. "When anyone who is infected by it dies," wrote a Flemish canon from the city, "all who see him in his sickness or visit him or even carry him to the grave, quickly follow him there. The sick are served by their kinsfolk as dogs would be; food is put near the bed for them to eat and drink after which all fly. . . . Nor do priests hear confessions or give the sacraments." "Charity was dead," reported the pope's physician, who himself caught the disease and was one of the few to recover. "Even the doctors did not dare to visit the sick. As for me, to avoid infamy, I did not dare to absent myself but still I was in continual fear." The pope himself, ordering corpses to be dissected to find the cause of the disease, fled to his country seat near Valence, where he shut himself up in a single room, keeping fires constantly burning to stifle the infection and giving access to no one.

All that summer of 1348 the Black Death was drawing nearer to England. In the spring it reached Gascony where it struck down King Edward's youngest daughter, the Princess Jean, who was on her way to Spain to marry the heir of Castile. Soon afterwards it broke out in Paris where vast multitudes died, including the queens of France and Navarre. By July, creeping north through Poitou and Brittany and round the coasts, it was in Normandy, where "it came to such a pass that no-one could be found to carry the corpses to the tomb. People said that the end of the world had come." All the while clouds and continuous rain poured down on England and, towards the end of the month as men watched the ports, Archbishop Zouche of York wrote to his deputy ordering processions and litanies to be held in all parish churches twice a week "for the stay of pestilence and infection." Only by prayers, he declared, could the scourge be turned away.

The archbishop—the victor of Neville's Cross—spoke of man's life being a warfare, where "those fighting amidst the miseries of this world are troubled by the uncertainty of a future now propitious, now averse, the Lord Almighty permitting those whom he loves to be chastised so that strength by the infusion of spiritual grace may be made perfect in infirmity." But though the Bishop of Bath and Wells, equally apprehensive, ordered processions and stations in all his churches to "protect the people from the pestilence which had come from the East into the neighboring kingdom," life in England that summer seems to have gone on very much as usual. In days when news travelled only by word of mouth and was carried from village to village along the grass roadways by friars and pedlars, the people of an isolated northern island can have heard little of the fate that had befallen their fellow Christians beyond the Channel. Absorbed in their local affairs, they were more concerned about the weather, the ruin of their crops and the murrain that had broken out among their sheep and cattle. Even the king, who must have been fully aware of the danger, seemed obsessed with his magnificent building projects for housing the college of his new Order of the Garter. On August 6th, he issued orders for the conversion of St. Edward the Confessor's chapel, Windsor, into one "of befitting splendor" and for the provision of accommodation for the additional canons and twenty-four "helpless and indigent knights" whom he and his companions were to present on the next St. George's day "in honor of Almighty God and of His mother Mary the glorious Virgin and of St. George the Martyr."

It may have been on that very day that, despite every precaution by the port authorities, the plague crossed the Channel. Some time that August it broke out in the little Dorset coast town of Melcombe Regis, now Weymouth, "depriving it almost of inhabitants." Within a few weeks it reached Bristol, probably by sea, turning it into a cemetery. It treated England as it had treated western Europe, and the English reacted in the same way. At Bristol "the living were scarce able to bury the dead," and "the men of Gloucester would not suffer the Bristol men to have access to them."

But no constable's guard could stop the swift-running rats from infecting one another, or their parasites from deserting their putrescent bodies for living men and women. Nor had anyone any idea what caused the mortality: the pallor, the sudden shivering and retching, the dreadful scarlet blotches and black boils—"God's tokens"—the delirium and unbearable agony that came without warning and carried off its victims in a few hours.

During that autumn the plague struck down southern shire after shire. Dorset and its adjoining counties suffered terribly; Poole was so depopulated that it did not recover for more than a century—a hundred years ago a projecting strip of land known as the Baiter was still pointed out as the burial-place of its victims. In some villages, like Bishopstone in Wiltshire, scarcely a soul survived, and when life was renewed after the plague the site was left deserted. The crops rotted in the fields, the church bells were silent, and everywhere corpses were flung, blackened and stinking, into hastily dug pits. At his lonely episcopal manor of Wiveliscombe, where he and his *familia* remained during the visitation, the Bishop of Bath and Wells instituted an endless succession of incumbents to vacant benefices—some, like St. Laurence's Shaftesbury, denuded of its parson more than once, and one, Winterbourne St. Nicholas, no less than three times. In a pastoral letter to his flock, he enjoined the sick to make confession to a layman if no priest was available and, if need be, to a woman. When the sacrament of Extreme Unction could not be administered, he concluded, "faith must, as in other matters, suffice."

In the adjoining diocese of Winchester, comprising the counties of Hampshire and Surrey which, by some miracle, escaped the infection almost till Christmas, Bishop Edington, the treasurer, ordered the cathedral chapter to say the seven penitential and fifteen gradual psalms twice weekly and on Fridays to lead a procession of the clergy and people through the streets and market place, bare-footed and with bowed head, "whilst with pious hearts they repeat their prayers and, putting away vain conversation, say as often as possible the Lord's Prayer and Hail Mary." News most grave, he declared, had reached him; the cruel plague which had turned the cities of Europe into "dens of wild beasts" had "begun to afflict the coasts of the realm of England." Towns, castles and villages had been "stripped of their population by the pestilence, more cruel than any two-edged sword and become abodes of horror. . . . We are struck with the gravest fear lest, which God forbid, the fell disease ravage any part of our diocese." Already it was spreading through that of Exeter, falling first, as everywhere, on the seaports and estuaries and then following the course of the rivers inland. The clergy and laity of Devon and Cornwall went down like corn before the reaper; at the Cistercian abbey of Newenham twenty monks and three lay brothers died and only the abbot and two others survived. At the Augustinian priory of Bodmin two canons alone lived to tell the tale; the abbots of Hartland, Tavistock and St. Nicholas Exeter, all perished, the last house losing two heads in succession.

The plague reached London at the beginning of November—"about the feast of All Hallows." It took the great financier Sir Thomas Pulteney— four times mayor and builder of the parish church of Little All Hallows, Thames Street—the Princess Joan of Kent's uncle, Lord Wake of Liddel, four wardens of the Goldsmiths' Company, and the abbot and twenty-six monks of Westminster. The adjoining hospital of St. James's was left without inmates, all the brethren and sisters perishing; perhaps, like the brave nuns of the Hôtel Dieu at Paris, "tending the sick with all sweetness and humility, putting all fear behind their backs." Of the Bishop of Rochester's household, four priests, five esquires, seven acolytes, six pages and ten servingmen died. The courts of Kings Bench and Common Pleas came to a standstill; a parliament, summoned for January, was prorogued indefinitely. All through the winter the pestilence raged in the rat-haunted streets and alleys until, having carried off nearly half the population, "by the intervention of the grace of the Holy Spirit on Whit-Sunday it ceased." "The Cemeteries," a chronicler wrote, "were not big enough and fields had to be set aside for the burying of the dead. . . . Men and women bore their own offspring on their shoulders to the church and cast them into the common pit, from which there proceeded so great a stench that hardly any-one dared to cross." A croft near Smithfield given by the Bishop of London for the burial of the dead became known as Pardon churchyard; another just outside the north wall of the city bought by the defender of Aiguillon, Sir Walter Manny, was endowed with a Carthusian cell which was to become the site of the Charterhouse and the great London school which still bears its name.

* * *

Of the general public it is impossible to estimate with any certainty the proportion who died; the verdict of modern scholarship is that the first outbreak probably carried off about one in three of the population. Con-temporary chroniclers and eye-witnesses believed the casualty-rate to be much higher: Thomas Walsingham of St. Albans reckoned "well-nigh half of all mankind," and others as much as two-thirds or even three-quarters. As the authors of such first-hand accounts were mostly writing of places where the plague was fiercest and from which many of the inhabitants had already fled, the fatality rate of those who remained may have been almost as high as they supposed. What is certain is that, once established in the soil, the plague remained endemic. Dormant for perhaps a dozen years it would suddenly flare up, first in one city, then in another, at least once in a generation. For three hundred years—a period of time as great as that which divides us from the last outbreak in Charles II's reign—the red cross on the stricken door, the cart piled with corpses on its way to the plague-pit, the cry of "Bring out your dead!" formed a recurrent part of the background of English life. During the three centuries since the Norman conquest the population of England had probably doubled. The generation born in the middle of Edward III's reign saw it halved.

The Violent Tenor of Life

J. HUIZINGA

1350–1475. During the fourteenth and fifteenth centuries, the medieval addiction to violence continued unabated. In his distinguished work The Waning of the Middle Ages, *the Dutch historian Huizinga wrote primarily about France and the Netherlands, but the conditions he described prevailed everywhere in Europe. In his fascinating opening chapter, Huizinga showed how the violence of bloody deeds was the natural result of a universal violence of emotion, of thought, and even of ideals.*

To the world when it was half a thousand years younger, the outlines of all things seemed more clearly marked than to us. The contrast between suffering and joy, between adversity and happiness, appeared more striking. All experience had yet to the minds of men the directness and absoluteness of the pleasure and pain of child-life. Every event, every action, was still embodied in impressive and solemn forms, which raised them to the dignity of a ritual. For it was not merely the great facts of birth, marriage and death which, by the sacredness of the sacrament, were raised to the rank of mysteries; incidents of less importance, like a journey, a task, a visit, were equally attended by a thousand formalities: benedictions, ceremonies, formulae.

113

Calamities and indigence were more afflicting than at present; it was more difficult to guard against them, and to find solace. Illness and health presented a more striking contrast; the cold and darkness of winter were more real evils. Honors and riches were relished with greater avidity and contrasted more vividly with surrounding misery. We, at the present day, can hardly understand the keenness with which a fur coat, a good fire on the hearth, a soft bed, a glass of wine, were formerly enjoyed.

Then, again, all things in life were of a proud or cruel publicity. Lepers sounded their rattles and went about in processions, beggars exhibited their deformity and their misery in churches. Every order and estate, every rank and profession, was disinguished by its costume. The great lords never moved about without a glorious display of arms and liveries, exciting fear and envy. Executions and other public acts of justice, hawkings, marriages and funerals, were all announced by cries and processions, songs and music. The lover wore the colors of his lady; companions the emblem of their confraternity; parties and servants the badges and blazon of their lord. Between town and country, too, the contrast was very marked. A medieval town did not lose itself in extensive suburbs of factories and villas; girded by its walls, it stood forth as a compact whole, bristling with innumerable turrets. However tall and threatening the houses of noblemen or merchants might be, in the aspect of the town the lofty mass of the churches always remained dominant.

The contrast between silence and sound, darkness and light, like that between summer and winter, was more strongly marked than it is in our lives. The modern town hardly knows silence or darkness in their purity, nor the effect of a solitary light or a single distant cry.

All things presenting themselves to the mind in violent contrasts and impressive forms, lent a tone of excitement and of passion to everyday life and tended to produce that perpetual oscillation between despair and distracted joy, between cruelty and pious tenderness which characterize life in the Middle Ages.

One sound rose ceaselessly above the noises of busy life and lifted all things into a sphere of order and serenity: the sound of bells. The bells were in daily life like good spirits, which by their familiar voices, now called upon the citizens to mourn and now to rejoice, now warned them of danger, now exhorted them to piety. They were known by their names: big Jacqueline, or the the bell Roland. Every one knew the difference in meaning of the various ways of ringing. However continuous the ringing of the bells, people would seem not to have become blunted to the effect of their sound.

Throughout the famous judicial duel between two citizens of Valenciennes, in 1455, the big bell, "which is hideous to hear," says Chastellain, never stopped ringing. What intoxication the pealing of the bells of all the churches, and of all the monasteries of Paris, must have produced, sounding from morning till evening, and even during the night, when a peace was concluded or a pope elected.

The frequent processions, too, were a continual source of pious agitation. When the times were evil, as they often were, processions were seen winding along, day after day, for weeks on end. In 1412 daily processions were ordered in Paris to implore victory for the king, who had taken up the oriflamme against the Armagnacs. They lasted from May to July, and were formed by ever-varying orders and corporations, going always by new roads, and always carrying different relics. The Burgher of Paris calls them "the most touching processions in the memory of men." People looked on or followed, "weeping piteously, with many tears, in great devotion." All went barefooted and fasting, councillors of the Parlement as well as the poorer citizens. Those who could afford it, carried a torch or taper. A great many small children were always among them. Poor country-people of the environs of Paris came barefooted from afar to join the procession. And nearly every day the rain came down in torrents.

Then there were the entries of princes, arranged with all the resources of art and luxury belonging to the age. And, lastly, most frequent of all, one might almost say, uninterrupted, the executions. The cruel excitement and coarse compassion raised by an execution formed an important item in the spiritual food of the common people. They were spectacular plays with a moral. For horrible crimes the law invented atrocious punishments. At Brussels a young incendiary and murderer is placed in the center of a circle of burning fagots and straw, and made fast to a stake by means of a chain running round an iron ring. He addresses touching words to the spectators, "and he so softened their hearts that every one burst into tears and his death was commended as the finest that was ever seen." During the Burgundian terror in Paris in 1411, one of the victims, Messire Mansart du Bois, being requested by the hangman, according to custom, to forgive him, is not only ready to do so with all his heart, but begs the executioner to embrace him. "There was a great multitude of people who nearly all wept hot tears."

When the criminals were great lords, the common people had the satisfaction of seeing rigid justice done, and at the same time finding the inconstancy of fortune exemplified more strikingly than in any sermon or picture. The magistrate took care that nothing should be wanting to the effect of the spectacle: the condemned were conducted to the scaffold, dressed in the garb of their high estate. Jean de Montaigu, grand maître d'hôtel to the king, the victim of Jean sans Peur, is placed high on a cart, preceded by two trumpeters. He wears his robe of state, hood, cloak, and hose half red and half white, and his gold spurs, which are left on the feet of the beheaded and suspended corpse. By special order of Louis XI, the head of maître Oudart de Bussy, who had refused a seat in the Parlement, was dug up and exhibited in the market-place of Hesdin, covered with a scarlet hood lined with fur *"selon la mode des conseillers de Parlement,"* with explanatory verses.

* * *

Public mourning still presented the outward appearance of a general calamity. At the funeral of Charles VII, the people are quite appalled on seeing the cortège of all the court dignitaries, "dressed in the deepest mourning, which was most pitiful to see; and because of the great sorrow and grief they exhibited for the death of their master, many tears were shed and lamentations uttered throughout the town." People were especially touched at the sight of six pages of the king mounted on horses quite covered with black velvet. One of the pages, according to a rumor, had neither eaten nor drunk for four days. "And God knows what doleful and piteous plaints they made, mourning for their master."

Solemnities of a political character also led to abundant weeping. An ambassador of the king of France repeatedly bursts into tears while addressing a courteous harangue to Philip the Good. At the meeting of the kings of France and of England at Ardres, at the reception of the dauphin at Brussels, at the departure of John of Coimbre from the court of Burgundy, all the spectators weep hot tears. Chastellain describes the dauphin, the future Louis XI, during his voluntary exile in Brabant, as subject to frequent fits of weeping.

Unquestionably there is some exaggeration in these descriptions of the chroniclers. In describing the emotion caused by the addresses of the ambassadors at the peace congress at Arras, in 1435, Jean Germain, bishop of Châlons, makes the auditors throw themselves on the ground, sobbing and groaning. Things, of course, did not happen thus, but thus the bishop thought fit to represent them, and the palapable exaggeration reveals a foundation of truth. As with the sentimentalists of the eighteenth century, tears were considered fine and honorable. Even nowadays an indifferent spectator of a public procession sometimes feels himself suddenly moved to inexplicable tears. In an age filled with religious reverence for all pomp and grandeur, this propensity will appear altogether natural.

A simple instance will suffice to show the high degree of irritability which distinguishes the Middle Ages from our own time. One can hardly imagine a more peaceful game than that of chess. Still like the *chansons de gestes* of some centuries back, Oliver de la Marche mentions frequent quarrels arising over it: *"le plus sage y pert patience."*

A scientific historian of the Middle Ages, relying first and foremost on official documents, which rarely refer to the passions, except violence and cupidity, occasionally runs the risk of neglecting the difference of tone between the life of the expiring Middle Ages and that of our own days. Such documents would sometimes make us forget the vehement pathos of medieval life, of which the chroniclers, however defective as to the material facts, always keep us in mind.

In more than one respect life had still the colors of a fairy-story; that is to say, it assumed those colors in the eyes of contemporaries. The court chroniclers were men of culture, and they observed the princes, whose deeds they recorded, at close quarters, yet even they give these records a somewhat archaic, hieratic air. The following story, told by Chastellain, serves to prove this. The young count of Charolais, the later Charles the Bold, on arriving at Gorcum, in Holland, on his way from Sluys, learns that his father, the duke, has taken all his pensions and benefices from him. Thereupon he calls the whole court into his presence, down to the scullions, and in a touching speech imparts his misfortune to them, dwelling on his respect for his ill-informed father, and on his anxiety about the welfare of all his retinue. Let those who have the means to live remain with him awaiting the return of good fortune; let the poor go away freely, and let them come back when they hear that the count's fortune had been re-established: they will all return to their old places, and the count will reward them for their patience. "Then were heard cries and sobs, and with one accord they shouted: 'We all, we all, my lord, will live and die with thee.'" Profoundly touched, Charles accepts their devotion: "Well, then, stay and suffer, and I will suffer for you, rather than that you should be in want." The nobles then come and offer him what they possess, "one saying, I have a thousand, another, ten thousand; I have this, I have that to place at thy service, and I am ready to share all that may befall thee." And in this way everything went on as usual, and there was never a hen the less in the kitchen.

Clearly this story has been more or less touched up. What interests us is that Chastellain sees the prince and his court in the epic guise of a popular ballad. If this is a literary man's conception, how brilliant must royal life have appeared, when displayed in almost magic splendor, to the naïve imagination of the uneducated!

Although in reality the mechanism of government had already assumed rather complicated forms, the popular mind pictures it in simple and fixed figures. The current political ideas are those of the Old Testament, of the romaunt and the ballad. The kings of the time are reduced to a certain number of types, every one of which corresponds, more or less, to a literary motif. There is the wise and just prince, the prince deceived by evil counsellors, the prince who avenges the honor of his family, the unfortunate prince to whom his servants remain faithful. In the mind of the people political questions are reduced to stories of adventure. Philip the Good knew the political language which the people understands. To convince the Hollanders and Frisians that he was perfectly able to conquer the bishopric of Utrecht, he exhibits, during the festivities of the Hague, in 1456, precious plate to the value of thirty thousand silver marks. Everybody may come and look at it. Amongst other things, two hundred thousand gold lions have been brought from Lille contained in two chests which every one may try to lift up. The demonstration of the solvency of the state took the form of an entertainment at a fair.

Often we find a fantastic element in the life of princes which reminds us of the caliph of the *Arabian Nights*. Charles VI, disguised and mounted with a friend on a single horse, witnesses the entrance of his betrothed and is knocked about in the crowd by petty constables. Philip the Good, whom the physicians ordered to have his head shaved, issues a command to all the nobles to do likewise, and charges Pierre de Hagenbach with the cropping of any whom he finds recalcitrant. In the midst of coolly calculated enterprises princes sometimes act with an impetuous temerity, which endangers their lives and their policy. Edward III does not hesitate to expose his life and that of the prince of Wales in order to capture some Spanish merchantmen, in revenge for deeds of piracy. Philip the Good interrupts the most serious political business to make the dangerous crossing from Rotterdam to Sluys for the sake of a mere whim. On another occasion, mad with rage in consequence of a quarrel with his son, he leaves Brussels in the night alone, and loses his way in the woods. The knight Philippe Pot, to whom fell the delicate task of pacifying him on his return, lights upon the happy phrase: "Good day, my liege, good day, what is this? Art thou playing King Arthur, now, or Sir Lancelot?"

The custom of princes, in the fifteenth century, frequently to seek counsel in political matters from ecstatic preachers and great visionaries, maintained a kind of religious tension in state affairs which at any moment might manifest itself in decisions of a totally unexpected character.

At the end of the fourteenth century and at the beginning of the fifteenth, the political stage of the kingdoms of Europe was so crowded with fierce and tragic conflicts that the peoples could not help seeing all that regards royalty as a succession of sanguinary and romantic events: in England, King Richard II dethroned and next secretly murdered, while nearly at the same time the highest monarch in Christendom, his brother-in-law Wenzel, king of the Romans, is deposed by the electors; in France, a mad king and soon afterwards fierce party strife, openly breaking out with the appalling murder of Louis of Orléans in 1407, and indefinitely prolonged by the retaliation of 1419 when Jean sans Peur is murdered at Montereau. With their endless train of hostility and vengeance, these two murders have given to the history of France, during a whole century, a sombre tone of hatred. For the contemporary mind cannot help seeing all the national misfortunes which the struggle of the houses of Orléans and Burgundy was to unchain, in the light of that sole dramatic motive of princely vengeance. It finds no explanation for historic events save in personal quarrels and motives of passion.

In addition to all these evils came the increasing obsession of the Turkish peril, and the still vivid recollection of the catastrophe of Nicopolis in 1396, where a reckless attempt to save Christendom had ended in the wholesale slaughter of French chivalry. Lastly, the great schism of the West had lasted already for a quarter of a century, unsettling all notions about the stability of the Church, dividing every land and community. Two, soon three, claimants contending for the papacy! One of them, the obstinate Aragonese Peter of Luna, or Benedict XIII, was commonly called in France "le Pappe de la Lune." What can an ignorant populace have imagined when hearing such a name?

The familiar image of Fortune's wheel from which kings are falling with their crowns and their sceptres took a living shape in the person of many an expelled prince, roaming from court to court, without means, but full of projects and still decked with the splendor of the marvellous East whence he had fled—the king of Armenia, the king of Cyprus, before long the emperor of Constantinople. It is not surprising that the people of Paris should have believed in the tale of the Gipsies, who presented themselves in 1427, "a duke and a count and ten men, all on horseback," while others, to the number of 120, had to stay outside the town. They came from Egypt, they said; the pope had ordered them, by way of penance for their apostasy, to wander about for seven years, without sleeping in a bed; there had been 1,200 of them, but their king, their queen and all the others had died on the way; as a mitigation the pope had ordered that every bishop and abbot was to give them ten pounds *tournois*. The people of Paris came in great numbers to see them, and have their fortunes told by women who eased them of their money "by magic art or in other ways."

The inconstancy of the fortune of princes was strikingly embodied in the person of King René. Having aspired to the crowns of Hungary, of Sicily, and of Jerusalem, he had lost all his opportunities, and reaped nothing but a series of defeats, and imprisonments, chequered by perilous escapes. The royal poet, a lover of the arts, consoled himself for all his disappointments on his estates in Anjou and in Provence; his cruel fate had not cured him of his predilection for pastoral enjoyment. He had seen all his children die but one, a daughter for whom was reserved a fate even harder than his own. Married at sixteen to an imbecile bigot, Henry VI of England, Margaret of Anjou, full of wit, ambition and passion, after living for many years in that hell of hatred and of persecution, the English court, lost her crown when the quarrel between York and Lancaster at last broke out into civil war. Having found refuge, after many dangers and suffering, at the court of Burgundy, she told Chastellain the story of her adventures: how she had been forced to commit herself and her young son to the mercy of a robber, how at mass she had had to ask a Scotch archer a penny for her offering, "who reluctantly and with regret took a groat Scots for her out of his purse and lent it to her." The good historiographer, moved by so much misfortune, dedicated to her "a certain little treatise on fortune, based on its inconstancy and deceptive nature," which he entitled *Le Temple de Bocace.* He could not guess that still graver calamities were in store for the unfortunate queen. At the battle of Tewkesbury, in 1471, the fortunes of Lancaster went down for ever. Her only son perished there, probably slaughtered after the battle. Her husband was secretly murdered; she herself was imprisoned in the Tower of London, where she remained for five years, to be at last given up by Edward IV to Louis XI, who made her renounce her father's inheritance as the price of her liberty.

An atmosphere of passion and adventure enveloped the lives of princes. It was not popular fancy alone which lent it that color.

A present-day reader, studying the history of the Middle Ages based on official documents, will never sufficiently realize the extreme excitability of the medieval soul. The picture drawn mainly from official records, though they may be the most reliable sources, will lack one element: that of the vehement passion possessing princes and peoples alike. To be sure, the passionate element is not absent from modern politics, but it is now restrained and diverted for the most part by the complicated mechanism of social life. Five centuries ago it still made frequent and violent interruptions into practical politics, upsetting rational schemes. In princes this violence of sentiment is doubled by pride and the consciousness of power, and therefore operates with a twofold impetus. It is not surprising, says Chastellain, that princes often live in hostility, "for princes are men, and their affairs are high and perilous, and their natures are subject to many passions, such as hatred and envy; their hearts are veritable dwelling-places of these, because of their pride in reigning."

In writing the history of the house of Burgundy, the *leitmotiv* should constantly keep before our minds the spirit of revenge. Nobody, of course, will now seek the explanation of the whole conflict of power and interests, whence proceeded the secular struggle between France and the house of Austria, in the family feud between Orléans and Burgundy. All sorts of causes of a general nature—political, economic, ethnographic—have contributed to the genesis of that great conflict. But we should never forget that the apparent origin of it, and the central motive dominating it, was, to the men of the fifteenth century and even later, the thirst for revenge. To them Philip the Good is always, in the first place, the avenger, "he who, to avenge the outrage done to the person of Duke John, sustained the war for sixteen years." He had undertaken it as a sacred duty: "With the most violent and deadly hatred he would give himself up to revenge the dead, as far as ever God would permit him, submitting everything to Fortune, considering it more a salutary task and agreeable to God to undertake it, than to leave it."

Read the long list of expiatory deeds which the treaty of Arras demanded in 1435—chapels, monasteries, churches, chapters to be founded, crosses to be erected, masses to be chanted—then one realizes the immensely high rate at which men valued the need of vengeance and of reparations to outraged honor. The Burgundians were not alone in thinking after this fashion; the most enlightened man of his century, Aeneas Sylvius, in one of his letters praises Philip above all other princes of his time for his anxiety to avenge his father.

According to la Marche, this duty of honor and revenge was to the duke's subjects also the cardinal point of policy. All the dominions of the duke, he says, were clamoring for vengeance along with him. We shall find it difficult to believe this, when we remember, for instance, the commercial relations between Flanders and England, a more important political factor, it would seem, than the honor of the ducal family. But to understand the sentiment of the age itself, one should look for the avowed and conscious political ideas. There can be no doubt that no other political motive could be better understood by the people than the primitive motives of hatred and vengeance. Attachment to the princes had still an emotional character; it was based on the innate and immediate sentiments of fidelity and fellowship; it was still feudal sentiment at bottom. It was rather party feeling than political. The last three centuries of the Middle Ages are the time of the great party struggles. From the thirteenth century onward inveterate party quarrels arise in nearly all countries: first in Italy, then in France, the Netherlands, Germany and England. Though economic interests may sometimes have been at the bottom of these quarrels, the attempts which have been made to disengage them often smack of somewhat arbitrary construction. The desire to discover economic causes is to some degree a craze with us, and sometimes leads us to forget a much simpler psychological explanation of the facts.

In the feudal age the private wars between two families have no other discernible reason than rivalry of rank and covetousness of possessions. Racial pride, thirst of vengeance, fidelity, are their primary and direct motives. There are no grounds to ascribe another economic basis to them than mere greed of one's neighbor's riches. Accordingly as the central power consolidates and extends, these isolated quarrels unite, agglomerate to groups; large parties are formed, are polarized, so to say; while their members know of no other grounds for their concord or enmity than those of honor, tradition and fidelity. Their economic differences are often only a consequence of their relation toward their rulers.

Every page of medieval history proves the spontaneous and passionate character of the sentiments of loyalty and devotion to the princes. At Abbeville, in 1462, a messenger comes at night, bringing the news of a dangerous illness of the duke of Burgundy. His son requests the good towns to pray for him. At once the aldermen order the bells of the church of Saint Vulfran to be rung; the whole population wakes up and goes to church, where it remains all night in prayer, kneeling or prostrate on the ground, with *"grandes allumeries merveilleuses,"* while the bells keep tolling.

It might be thought that the schism, which had no dogmatic cause, could hardly awaken religious passions in countries distant from Avignon and Rome, in which the two popes were only known by name. Yet in fact it immediately engendered a fanatical hatred, such as exists between the faithful and infidels. When the town of Bruges went over to the "obedience" of Avignon, a great number of people left their house, trade or prebend, to go and live according to their party views in some diocese of the Urbanist obedience: Liége, Utrecht, or elsewhere. In 1382 the oriflamme, which might only be unfurled in a holy cause, was taken up against the Flemings, because they were Urbanists, that is, infidels. Pierre Salmon, a French political agent, arriving at Utrecht about Easter, could not find a priest there willing to admit him to the communion service, "because they said I was a schismatic and believed in Benedict the anti-pope."

The emotional character of party sentiments and of fidelity was further heightened by the powerfully suggestive effect of all the outward signs of these divergences: liveries, colors, badges, party cries. During the first years of the war between the Armagnacs and the Burgundians, these signs succeeded each other in Paris with a dangerous alternation: a purple hood with a cross of St. Andrew, white hoods, then violet ones. Even priests, women and children wore distinctive signs. The images of saints were decorated with them; it was asserted that certain priests, during mass and in baptizing, refused to make the sign of the cross in the orthodox way, but made it in the form of a Saint Andrew cross.

In the blind passion with which people followed their lord or their party, the unshakable sentiment of right, characteristic of the Middle Ages, is trying to find expression. Man at that time is convinced that right is absolutely fixed and certain. Justice should prosecute the unjust everywhere and to the end. Reparation and retribution have to be extreme, and assume the character of revenge. In this exaggerated need of justice, primitive barbarism, pagan at bottom, blends with the Christian conception of society. The Church, on the one hand, had inculcated gentleness and clemency, and tried, in that way, to soften judicial morals. On the other hand, in adding to the primitive need of retribution the horror of sin, it had, to a certain extent, stimulated the sentiment of justice. And sin, to violent and impulsive spirits, was only too frequently another name for what their enemies did. The barbarous idea of retaliation was reinforced by fanaticism. The chronic insecurity made the greatest possible severity on the part of the public authorities desirable; crime came to be regarded as a menace to order and society, as well as an insult to divine majesty. Thus it was natural that the late Middle Ages should become the special period of judicial cruelty. That the criminal deserved his punishment was not doubted for a moment. The popular sense of justice always sanctioned the most rigorous penalties. At intervals the magistrate undertook regular campaigns of severe justice, now against brigandage, now against sorcery or sodomy.

What strikes us in this judicial cruelty and in the joy the people felt at it, is rather brutality than perversity. Torture and executions are enjoyed by the spectators like an entertainment at a fair. The citizens of Mons bought a brigand, at far too high a price, for the pleasure of seeing him quartered, "at which the people rejoiced more than if a new holy body had risen from the dead." The people of Bruges, in 1488, during the captivity of Maximilian, king of the Romans, cannot get their fill of seeing the tortures inflicted, on a high platform in the market-place, on the magistrates suspected of treason. The unfortunates are refused the deathblow which they implore, that the people may feast again upon their torments.

Both in France and in England, the custom existed of refusing confession and the extreme unction to a criminal condemned to death. Sufferings and fear of death were to be aggravated by the certainty of eternal damnation. In vain had the council of Vienna in 1311 ordered to grant them at least the sacrament of penitence. Towards the end of the fourteenth century the same custom still existed. Charles V himself, moderate though he was, had declared that no change would be made in his lifetime. The chancellor Pierre d'Orgemont, whose "forte cervelle," says Philippe de Mézières, was more difficult to turn than a mill-stone, remained deaf to the remonstrances of the latter. It was only after Gerson had joined his voice to that of Mézières that a royal decree of the 12th of February, 1397, ordered that confession should be accorded to the condemned. A stone cross erected by the care of Pierre de Craon, who had interested himself in the decree, marked the place where the Minorite friars might assist penitents going to execution. And even then the barbarous custom did not disappear. Etienne Ponchier, bishop of Paris, had to renew the decree of 1311 in 1500.

The Last Days of Louis XI

PHILIPPE DE COMMINES

1483. When Louis XI, the crafty, cruel, and able monarch who did so much to unify the the Kingdom of France, died in his castle of Plessis-les-Tours, he was sixty—a sick old man frightened of his subjects and terrified by the prospect of death. His confidential aid Philippe de Commines was painfully aware of Louis's faults and weaknesses, but nevertheless admired his royal master and felt something like affection for him. Commines's Memoirs is a historical document of enduring interest. Medieval in its religious faith, it seems modern in its disillusioned view of politics and its objective analyses of character.

His last illness continued from Monday to Saturday night. Upon which account I will now make comparison between the evils and sorrows which he brought upon others, and those which he suffered in his own person: for I hope his torments here on earth have translated him into Paradise, and will be a great part of his purgatory: and if, in respect of their greatness and duration, his sufferings were inferior to those he had brought upon other people, yet, if you consider the grandeur and dignity of his office, and that he had never before suffered anything in his own person, but had been obeyed by all people, as if all Europe had been created for no other end, but to serve and be commanded by him; you will find that little which he endured was so contrary to his nature and custom that it was more grievous for him to bear.

His chief hope and confidence was placed in the good hermit I spoke of (who was at Plessis, and had come thither from Calabria); he sent continually to him, believing it was in his power to prolong his life if he pleased; for, notwithstanding all his precepts, he had great hopes of recovering; and if it had so happened, he would quickly have dispersed the throng he had sent to Amboise, to wait upon the new king. Finding his hopes rested so strongly upon this hermit, it was the advice of a certain grave divine, and others who were about him, that it should be declared to him that there was no hope left for him but in the mercy of God; and it was also agreed among them, that his physician, Master James Coctier (in whom he had great confidence), should be present when this declaration was made him. This Coctier received of him every month ten thousand crowns, in the hope that he would lengthen his life. This resolution was taken to the end that he should lay aside all other thoughts, and apply himself wholly to the settlement of his conscience. And as he had advanced them, as it were, in an instant, and against all reason, to employments beyond their capacities, so they took upon them fearlessly to tell him a thing that had been more proper for other people to communicate; nor did they observe that reverence and respect towards him, which was proper in such a case, and would have been used by those persons who had been brought up with him, or by those whom, in a mere whim, he had removed from court but a little before. But, as he had sent a sharp message of death to two great persons whom he had formerly beheaded (the Duke of Nemours, and the Count of St. Paul), by commissioners deputed on purpose, who in plain terms told them their sentence, appointed them confessors to arrange their consciences, and acquainted them that in a few hours they must resolve to die; so with the same bluntness, and without the least circumstance of introduction, these imprudent persons told our King: "Sire, we must do our duty; do not place your hopes any longer in this holy hermit, or anything else, for you are a dead man. Think therefore upon your conscience, for there is no remedy left." Every one added some short saying to the same purpose; to which he answered, "I hope God will assist me, for perhaps I am not so ill as you imagine."

What sorrow was this to him to hear this news! Never man was more fearful of death, nor used more means to prevent it. He had, all his life long, commanded and requested his servants, and me among the rest, that whenever we saw him in any danger of death, we should not tell him of it, but merely admonish him to confess himself, without ever mentioning that cruel and shocking word Death, for he did not believe he could ever endure to hear so cruel a sentence. However, he endured that virtuously, and several more things equally terrible, when he was ill; and indeed he bore them better than any man I ever saw die. He spoke several things, which were to be delivered to his son, whom he called king; and he confessed himself very devoutly, said several prayers suitable to the sacraments he received, and called for the sacraments himself. He spoke as judiciously as if he had never been ill, discoursed of all things which might be necessary for his son's instruction, and among the rest gave orders that the Lord des Cordes should not stir from his son for six months; and that he should be desired to attempt nothing against Calais, or elsewhere, declaring, that though he had designed himself to undertake such enterprises for the benefit of both the king and the kingdom, yet they were very dangerous, especially that against Calais, because the English might resent it; and he left it in especial charge that for five or six years after his death, they should, above all things, preserve the kingdom in peace, which during his life he had never suffered. And indeed it was no more than was necessary; for though the kingdom was large and fertile, yet it was grown very poor, upon account of the marching and counter-marching of the soldiers up and down, in their passage from one country to another, as they have done since, to an even worse extent. He also ordered that nothing should be attempted against Brittany, but that Duke Francis should be suffered to live in peace; that both he and his neighbors might be without fear, and the king and kingdom remain free from wars, till the king should be of age, to take upon himself the administration of affairs.

You have already heard with what indiscretion and bluntness they acquainted the King with his approaching death; which I have mentioned in a more particular manner, because in a preceding paragraph I began to compare the evils, which he had made others suffer, who lived under his dominion, with those he endured himself before his death; that it might appear that, though they were not perhaps of so long a duration, yet they were fully as great and terrible, considering his station and dignity, which required more obedience than any private person, and had found more; so that the least opposition was a great torment to him. Some five or six months before his death he began to suspect everybody, especially those who were most capable and deserving of the administration of affairs. He was afraid of his son, and caused him to be kept close, so that no man saw or discoursed with him, but by his special command. At last he grew suspicious of his daughter, and of his son-in-law the Duke of Bourbon, and required an account of what persons came to speak with them at Plessis, and broke up a council which the Duke of Bourbon was holding there, by his order.

At the time that the Count of Dunois and the said Duke of Bourbon returned from conducting the ambassadors, who had been at Amboise to attend the marriage of the Dauphin and the young queen, the King being in the gallery at Plessis, and seeing them enter with a great train into the castle, called for a captain of the guards, and commanded him to go and search the servants of those lords, to see whether they had any arms under their robes; and ordered him to do it in discourse, so as no notice might be taken. Behold, then, if he had caused many to live under him in continual fear and apprehension, whether it was not returned to him again; for of whom could he be secure when he was afraid of his son-in-law, his daughter, and his own son? I speak this not only of him, but of all other princes who desire to be feared, that vengeance never falls on them till they grow old, and then, as a just penance, they are afraid of everybody themselves; and what grief must it have been to the poor King to be tormented with such terrors and passions?

He was still attended by his physician, Master James Coctier, to whom in five months' time he had already given fifty-four thousand crowns in ready money, besides the bishopric of Amiens for his nephew, and other great offices and estates for himself and his friends; yet this doctor used him very roughly indeed; one would not have given such outrageous language to one's servants, as he gave the King, who stood in such awe of him, that he durst not forbid him his presence. It is true he complained of his impudence afterwards, but he durst not change him as he had done all the rest of his servants; because he had told him after a most audacious manner one day, "I know well that some time or other you will dismiss me from court, as you have done the rest; but be sure (and he confirmed it with a great oath) you shall not live eight days after it"; with which expression the King was so terrified that ever after he did nothing but flatter and bribe him, which must needs have been a great mortification to a prince who had been humbly obeyed all his life by so many good and brave men.

The King had ordered several cruel prisons to be made; some were cages of iron, and some of wood, but all were covered with iron plates both within and without, with terrible locks, about eight feet wide and seven high; the first contriver of them was the Bishop of Verdun, who was immediately put in the first that was made, where he continued fourteen years. Many bitter curses he has had since for his invention, and some from me as I lay in one of them eight months together in the minority of our present King. He also ordered heavy and terrible fetters to be made in Germany, and particularly a certain ring for the feet, which was extremely hard to be opened, and fitted like an iron collar, with a thick weighty chain, and a great globe of iron at the end of it, most unreasonably heavy, which engines were called the King's Nets. However, I have seen many eminent and deserving persons in these prisons, with these nets about their legs, who afterwards came forth with great joy and honor, and received great rewards from the King. Among the rest, a son of the Lord de la Grutuse, in Flanders (who was taken in battle), whom the King married very honorably afterwards, made him his chamberlain, and seneschal of Anjou, and gave him the command of a hundred lances. The Lord de Piennes, and the Lord de Vergy, both prisoners of war, also had commands given them in his army, were made his or his son's chamberlains, and had great estates bestowed on them. Monsieur de Richebourg, the constable's brother, had the same good fortune, as did also one Roquebertin, a Catalonian, likewise prisoner of war; besides others of various countries, too numerous to be mentioned in this place.

This by way of digression. But to return to my principal design. As in his time this barbarous variety of prisons was invented, so before he died he himself was in greater torment, and more terrible apprehension than those whom he had imprisoned; which I look upon as a great mercy towards him, and as part of his purgatory; and I have mentioned it here to show that there is no person, of what station or dignity soever, but suffers some time or other, either publicly or privately, especially if he has caused other people to suffer. The King, towards the latter end of his days, caused his castle of Plessis-les-Tours to be encompassed with great bars of iron in the form of thick grating, and at the four corners of the house four sparrow-nests of iron, strong, massy, and thick, were built. The grates were without the wall on the other side of the ditch, and sank to the bottom. Several spikes of iron were fastened into the wall, set as thick by one another as was possible, and each furnished with three or four points. He likewise placed ten bowmen in the ditches, to shoot at any man that durst approach the castle before the opening of the gates; and he ordered that they should lie in the ditches, but retire to the sparrow-nests upon occasion. He was sensible enough that this fortification was too weak to keep out an army, or any great body of men, but he had no fear of such an attack; his great apprehension was, that some of the nobility of his kingdom, having intelligence within, might attempt to make themselves masters of the castle by night, and having possessed themselves partly of it by favor and partly by force, might deprive him of the regal authority, and take upon themselves the administration of public affairs; upon pretense he was incapable of business, and no longer fit to govern.

The gate of the Plessis was never opened, nor the drawbridge let down, before eight o'clock in the morning, at which time the officers were let in; and the captains ordered their guards to their several posts, with pickets of archers in the middle of the court, as in a town upon the frontiers that is closely guarded: nor was any person admitted to enter except by the wicket and with the King's knowledge, unless it were the steward of his household, and such persons as were not admitted into the royal presence.

Is it possible then to keep a prince (with any regard to his quality) in a closer prison than he kept himself? The cages which were made for other people were about eight feet square; and he (though so great a monarch) had but a small court of the castle to walk in, and seldom made use of that, but generally kept himself in the gallery, out of which he went into the chambers on his way to mass, but never passed through the court. Who can deny that he was a sufferer as well as his neighbors, considering how he was locked up and guarded, afraid of his own children and relations, and changing every day those very servants whom he had brought up and advanced; and though they owed all their preferment to him, yet he durst not trust any of them, but shut himself up in those strange chains and enclosures. If the place where he confined himself was larger than a common prison, he also was much greater than common prisoners.

It may be urged that other princes have been more given to suspicion than he, but it was not in our time; and, perhaps, their wisdom was not so eminent, nor were their subjects so good. They might too, probably, have been tyrants, and bloody-minded; but our King never did any person a mischief who had not offended him first, though I do not say all who offended him deserved death. I have not recorded these things merely to represent our master as a suspicious and mistrustful prince; but to show, by the patience which he expressed in his sufferings (like those which he inflicted on other people), they may be looked upon, in my judgment, as a punishment which Our Lord inflicted upon him in this world, in order to deal with him more mercifully in the next, as well as in regard to those things before-mentioned, as to the distempers of his body, which were great and painful, and much dreaded by him before they came upon him; and, likewise, that those princes who may be his successors, may learn by his example to be more tender and indulgent to their subjects, and less severe in their punishments than our master had been: although I will not censure him, or say I ever saw a better prince; for though he oppressed his subjects himself, he would never see them injured by anybody else.

After so many fears, sorrows, and suspicions, God, by a kind of miracle, restored him both in body and mind, as is His divine method in such kind of wonders; for He took him out of this miserable world in perfect health of mind, and understanding, and memory; after having received the sacraments himself, discoursing without the least twinge or expression of pain, and repeating his paternosters to the very last moment of his life. He gave directions for his own burial, appointed who should attend his corpse to the grave, and declared that he desired to die on a Saturday of all days of the week; and that he hoped Our Lady would procure him that favor, for in her he had always placed great trust, and served her very devoutly. And so it happened; for he died on Saturday, the 30th of August, 1483, at about eight in the evening, in the Castle of Plessis, where his illness seized him on the Monday before. May Our Lord receive his soul, and admit it unto His kingdom of Paradise!

The Princes in the Tower

SIR THOMAS MORE

1483. Although numerous romanticists have tried to whitewash the evil reputation of King Richard III and even to deny his guilt in the murder of his nephews Edward V and Richard, Duke of York, in the Tower of London, most historians agree that Richard either connived in the murders or directly ordered them. Sir Thomas More, an honorable man who would not knowingly write falsehoods, was personally acquainted with a number of men who had held public office during Richard's reign. His History of King Richard III *was written only thirty-one years after the murders of the princes. Edward was only twelve, Richard about ten.*

King Richard after his coronation taking his way to Gloucester, to visit in his new honour the town of which he bare the name of his old, devised as he rode to fulfil the thing which he before had intended. And forasmuch as his mind gave him, that his nephews living, men would not reckon that he could have right to the realm, he thought therefore without delay to rid them, as though the killing of his kinsmen could amend his cause, and make him a kindly king. Whereupon he sent one John Green, whom he specially trusted, unto Sir Robert Brackenbury, constable of the Tower, with a letter and credence also, that the same Sir Robert should in any wise put the two children to death. This John Green did his errand to Brackenbury kneeling before our Lady in the Tower; who plainly answered that he would never put them to death to die therefore, with which answer John Green returning recounted the same to King Richard at Warwick yet in his way.

Wherewith he took such displeasure and thought, that the same night he said unto a secret page of his: Ah, whom shall a man trust? those that I have brought up myself, those that I had weaned would most truly serve me, even those fail me, and at my commandment will do nothing for me. Sir, quoth the page, there lieth one on your pallet without, that I dare well say, to do your Grace's pleasure, the thing were right hard that he would refuse; meaning by this Sir James Tyrell, which was a man of right goodly personage, and for nature's gifts, worthy to have served a much better prince, if he had well served God, and by grace obtained as much truth and good will as he had strength and wit. The man had an high heart, and sore longed upward, not rising yet so fast as he had hoped, being hindered and kept under by the means of Sir Richard Ratcliffe, and Sir William Catesby; which longed for no more partners of the prince's favor, and namely not for him, whose pride they wist would bear no peer, kept him by secret drifts out of all secret trust. Which thing this page well had marked and known.

Wherefore this occasion offered of very special friendship, he took his time to put him forward, and by such wise do him good, that all the enemies he had except the devil, could never have done him so much hurt. For upon this page's words King Richard arose (for this communication had he sitting at the draught, a convenient carpet for such a counsel), and came out into the pallet chamber, on which he found in bed Sir James and Sir Thomas Tyrell, of person like and brethren of blood, but nothing of kin in conditions.

Then said the King merrily to them: What, sirs, be ye in bed so soon? And calling up Sir James, brake to him secretly his mind in this mischievous matter. In which he found him nothing strange. Wherefore on the morrow he sent him to Brackenbury with a letter, by which he was commanded to deliver Sir James all the keys of the Tower for one night, to the end that he might there accomplish the King's pleasure, in such thing as he had given him commandment. After which letter delivered and the keys received, Sir James appointed the night next ensuing to destroy them, devising before and preparing the means.

The prince, as soon as the protector left that name and took himself as king, had it showed unto him, that he should not reign, but his uncle should have the crown. At which words the prince, sore abashed, began to sigh and said: Alas, I would my uncle would let me have my life yet, though I lose my kingdom. Then he that told him the tale, used him with good words, and put him in the best comfort he could. But forthwith was the prince and his brother both shut up, and all other removed from them, only one called Black Will or William Slaughter except, set to serve them and see them sure. After which time the prince never tied his own points, or ought wrought of himself, but with that young babe his brother, lingered in thought and heaviness till this traitorous death delivered them of that wretchedness.

For Sir James Tyrell devised that they should be murdered in their beds. To the execution thereof, he appointed Miles Forest, one of the four that kept them, a fellow fleshed in murder before time. To him he joined one John Dighton, his own horse-keeper, a big broad square strong knave. Then all the other being removed from them, this Miles Forest and John Dighton, about midnight (the silly children lying in their beds) came into the chamber, and suddenly lapped them up among the clothes, so bewrapped them and entangled them, keeping down by force the feather bed and pillows hard unto their mouths, that within a while smoored and stifled, their breath failing, they gave up to God their innocent souls into the joys of heaven, leaving to the tormentors their bodies dead in the bed. Which after that the wretches perceived, first by the struggling with the pains of death, and after long lying still, to be thoroughly dead; they laid their bodies naked out upon the bed and fetched Sir James to see them. Which, upon the sight of them, caused those murderers to bury them at the stair foot, meetly deep in the ground under a great heap of stones.

Then rode Sir James in great haste to King Richard, and showed him all the manner of the murder; who gave him great thanks and, as some say, there made him knight. But he allowed not, as I have heard, the burying in so vile a corner, saying that he would have them buried in a better place, because they were a king's sons. Lo, the honourable courage of a king!

Whereupon they say that a priest of Sir Robert Brackenbury took up the bodies again, and secretly interred them in such a place, as by the occasion of his death, which only knew it, could never since come to light. Very truth it is and well known, that at such time as Sir James Tyrell was in the Tower for treason committed against the most famous prince King Henry the Seventh, both Dighton and he were examined, and confessed the murder in manner above written, but whither the bodies were removed they could nothing tell.

And thus as I have learned of them that much knew and little cause had to lie, were these two noble princes, these innocent tender children, born of most royal blood, brought up in great wealth, likely long to live and reign and rule in the realm, by traitorous tyranny taken, deprived of their estate, shortly shut up in prison, and privily slain and murdered, their bodies cast God wot where by the cruel ambition of their unnatural uncle and his despiteous tormentors. Which things on every part pondered, God never gave this world a more notable example, neither in what unsurety standeth this worldly weal, or what mischief worketh the proud enterprise of an high heart, and finally what wretched end ensueth such despiteous cruelty.

For first, to begin with the ministers, Miles Forest at Saint Martin's piece-meal rotted away. Dighton indeed yet walketh on alive in good possibility to be hanged ere he dies. But Sir James Tyrell died at Tower Hill, beheaded for treason. King Richard himself, as ye shall hereafter hear, slain in the field, hacked and hewed of his enemies' hands, harried on horseback dead, his hair in despite torn and tugged like a cur dog: and the mischief that he took within less than three years of the mischief that he did. And yet all the meantime spent in much pain and trouble outward, much fear, anguish and sorrow within. For I have heard by credible report of such as were secret with his chambers, that after this abominable deed done, he never had quiet in his mind, he never thought himself sure. Where he went abroad, his eyes whirled about, his body privily fenced, his hand ever on his dagger, his countenance and manner like one always ready to strike again; he took ill rest a-nights, lay long waking and musing, sore wearied with care and watch, rather slumbered than slept, troubled with fearful dreams, suddenly sometimes start up, leap out of bed and run about the chamber, so was his restless heart continually tossed and tumbled with the tedious impression and stormy remembrance of his abominable deed.

The Character of Henry VII

FRANCIS BACON

1457–1509. Although Francis Bacon's History of the Reign of Henry VII *is not written with the stately eloquence of some of his essays, it is nevertheless a landmark in the writing of English history, notable for its astute and objective appraisal of the crafty monarch who defeated Richard III at Bosworth Field; who married Elizabeth of York, daughter of Edward IV, and so united the Houses of Lancaster and York; and who easily suppressed several revolts, including two by impostors (Lambert Simnel and Perkin Warbeck) who claimed to be Richard, Duke of York, the younger of the two little princes murdered in the Tower of London.*

The King (to speak of him in terms equal to his deserving) was one of the best sort of wonders; a wonder for wise men. He had parts (both in his virtues and his fortunes) not so fit for a common-place as for observation. Certainly he was religious, both in his affection and observance. But as he could see clear (for those times) through superstition; so he would be blinded now and then by human policy. He advanced churchmen. He was tender in the privilege of sanctuaries, though they wrought him much mischief. He built and endowed many religious foundations, besides his memorable hospital of the Savoy: and yet was he a great alms-giver in secret; which shewed that his works in public were dedicated rather to

God's glory than his own. He professed always to love and seek peace; and it was his usual preface in his treaties that when Christ came into the world peace was sung, and when he went out of the world peace was bequeathed. And this virtue could not proceed out of fear or softness, for he was valiant and active; and therefore no doubt it was truly Christian and moral. Yet he knew the way to peace was not to seem to be desirous to avoid wars. Therefore would he make offers and fames of wars, till he had mended the conditions of peace. It was also much, that one that was so great a lover of peace should be so happy in war. For his arms, either in foreign or civil wars, were never infortunate; neither did he know what a disaster meant. The war of his coming in, and the rebellions of the Earl of Lincoln and the Lord Audley, were ended by victory. The wars of France and Scotland by peace sought at his hands. That of Brittany by accident of the Duke's death. The insurrection of the Lord Lovell, and that of Perkin at Exeter and in Kent, by flight of the rebels before they came to blows. So that his fortune in arms was still inviolate. The rather sure, for that in the quenching of the commotions of his subjects he ever went in person: sometimes reserving himself to back and second his lieutenants, but ever in action. And yet that was not merely forwardness, but partly distrust of others.

He did much maintain and countenance his laws; which (nevertheless) was no impediment to him to work his will. For it was so handled that neither prerogative nor profit went to diminution. And yet as he would sometimes strain up his laws to his prerogative, so would he also let down his prerogative to his Parliament. For mint and wars and martial discipline (things of absolute power) he would nevertheless bring to Parliament. Justice was well administered in his time, save where the King was party; save also that the counsel-table intermeddled too much with *meum* and *tuum*. For it was a very court of justice during his time; especially in the beginning. But in that part both of justice and policy which is the durable part, and cut as it were in brass or marble, which is the making of good laws, he did excel. And with his justice he was also a merciful prince: as in whose time there were but three of the nobility that suffered; the Earl of Warwick; the Lord Chamberlain; and the Lord Audley: though the first two were instead of numbers in the dislike and obloquy of the people. But there were never so great rebellions expiated with so little blood drawn by the hand of justice, as the two rebellions of Blackheath and Exeter. As for the severity used upon those which were taken in Kent, it was but upon a scum of people. His pardons went ever both before and after his sword. But then he had withal a strange kind of interchanging of large and inexpected pardons with severe executions: which (his wisdom considered) could not be imputed to any inconstancy or inequality; but either to some reason which we do not know, or to a principle he had set unto himself, that he would vary, and try both ways in turn. But the less blood he drew the more he took in treasure: and as some construed it, he was the more sparing in the one that he might be the more pressing in the other; for both would have been intolerable. Of nature assuredly he coveted to accumulate treasure; and was a little poor in admiring riches. The people (into whom there is infused for the preservation of monarchies a natural desire to discharge their Princes, though it be with the unjust charge of their counsellors and ministers) did impute this unto Cardinal Morton and Sir Reginald Bray; who, as it after appeared (as counsellors of ancient authority with him) did so second his humours, as nevertheless they did temper them. Whereas Empson and Dudley that followed, being persons that had no reputation with him otherwise than by servile following of his bent, did not give way only (as the first did) but shape his way to those extrimeties, for which himself was touched with remorse at his death; and which his successor renounced, and sought to purge. This excess of his had at that time many glosses and interpretations. Some thought the continual rebellions wherewith he had been vexed had made him grow to hate his people: Some thought it was done to pull down their stomachs and to keep them low: Some, for that he would leave his son a golden fleece: Some suspected he had some high design upon foreign parts. But those perhaps shall come nearest the truth that fetch not their reasons so far off; but rather impute it to nature, age, peace, and a mind fixed upon no other ambition or pursuit: whereunto I should add, that having every day occasion to take notice of the necessities and shifts for money of other great Princes abroad, it did the better by comparison set off to him the felicity of full coffers. As to his expending of treasure, he never spared charge which his affairs required: and in his buildings was magnificent; but his rewards were very limited. So that his liberality was rather upon his own state and memory than upon the deserts of others. He was of an high mind, and loved his own will and his own way; as one that revered himself, and would reign indeed. Had he been a private man he would have been termed proud: but in a wise Prince it was but keeping of distance; which indeed he did towards all; not admitting any near or full approach either to his power or to his secrets. For he was governed by none. His Queen (notwithstanding she had presented him with divers children; and with a crown also, though he would not acknowledge it) could do nothing with him. His mother he reverenced much, heard little. For any person agreeable to him for society (such as was Hastings to King Edward the Fourth, or Charles Brandon after to King Henry the Eighth), he had none; except we should account for such persons Foxe and Bray and Empson, because they were so much with him. But it was but as the instrument is much with the workman. He had nothing in him of vain-glory, but yet kept state and majesty to the height; being sensible that majesty maketh the people bow, but vain-glory boweth to them.

To his confederates abroad he was constant and just; but not open. But rather such was his inquiry and such his closeness, as they stood in the light towards him, and he stood in the dark to them; yet without strangeness, but with a semblance of mutual communication of affairs. As for little envies or emulations upon foreign Princes (which are frequent with many Kings), he had never any; but went substantially to his own business. Certain it is, that though his reputation was great at home, yet it was greater abroad. For foreigners that could not see the passages of affairs, but made their judgments upon the issues of them, noted that he was ever in strife and ever aloft. It grew also from the airs which the Princes and states abroad received from their ambassadors and agents here; which were attending the court in great numbers; whom he did not only content with courtesy, reward, and privateness; but (upon such conferences as passed with them) put them in admiration to find his universal insight into the affairs of the world: which though he did such chiefly from themselves, yet that which he had gathered from them all seemed admirable to every one. So that they did write ever to their superiors in high terms concerning his wisdom and art of rule. Nay when they were returned, they did commonly maintain intelligence with him; such a dexterity he had to impropriate himself all foreign instruments.

He was careful and liberal to obtain good intelligence from all parts abroad; wherein he did not only use his interest in the liegers here, and his pensioners which he had both in the court of Rome and other the courts of Christendom, but the industry and vigilancy of his own ambassadors in foreign parts. For which purpose his instructions were ever extreme curious and articulate; and in them more articles touching inquisition than touching negotiation: requiring likewise from his ambassadors an answer, in particular distinct articles, respectively to his questions.

As for his secret spials which he did employ both at home and abroad, by them to discover what practices and conspiracies were against him; surely his case required it; he had such moles perpetually working and casting to undermine him. Neither can it be reprehended; for if spials be lawful against lawful enemies, much more against conspirators and traitors. But indeed to give them credence by oaths or curses, they cannot be well maintained; for these are too holy vestments for a disguise. Yet surely there was this further good in his employing of those spies and familiars; that as the use of them was cause that many conspiracies were revealed, so the fame and suspicion of them kept (no doubt) many conspiracies from being attempted.

Towards his Queen he was nothing uxorious; nor scarce indulgent; but companionable and respective, and without jealousy. Towards his children he was full of paternal affection, careful of their education, aspiring to their high advancement, regular to see that they should not want of any due honour and respect; but not greatly willing to cast any popular lustre upon them.

To his counsel he did refer much, and sat oft in person; knowing it to be the way to assist his power and inform his judgment: in which respect also he was fairly patient of liberty both of advice and of vote, till himself were declared.

He kept a strait hand on his nobility, and chose rather to advance clergy-men and lawyers, which were more obsequious to him, but had less interest in the people; which made for his absoluteness, but not for his safety. Inso-much as I am persuaded it was one of the causes of his troublesome reign. For that his nobles, though they were loyal and obedient, yet did not co-operate with him, but let every man go his own way. He was not afraid of an able man, as Lewis the Eleventh was. But contrarywise he was served by the ablest men that then were to be found; without which his affairs could not have prospered as they did. For war, Bedford, Oxford, Surrey, Dawbeney, Brook, Poynings. For other affairs, Morton, Foxe, Bray, the Prior of Lanthony, Warham, Urswick, Hussey, Frowick, and others. Neither did he care how cunning they were that he did employ: for he thought himself to have the master-reach. And as he chose well, so he held them up well. For it is a strange thing, that though he were a dark Prince, and infinitely suspicious, and his times full of secret conspiracies and troubles; yet in twenty-four years of reign he never put down or discomposed coun-sellor or near servant, save only Stanley the Lord Chamberlain. As for the disposition of his subjects in general towards him, it stood thus with him; that of the three affections which naturally tie the hearts of the subjects to their sovereign—love, fear, and reverence—he had the last in height; the second in good measure; and so little of the first, as he was beholding to the other two.

He was a Prince, sad, serious and full of thoughts and secret observations; and full of notes and memorials of his own hand, especially touching per-sons; as whom to employ, whom to reward, whom to inquire of, whom to beware of, what were the dependencies, what were the factions, and the like; keeping (as it were) a journal of his thoughts. There is to this day a merry tale; that his monkey (set on as it was thought by one of his chamber) tore his principal note-book all to pieces, when by chance it lay forth: whereat the court which liked not those pensive accounts was almost tickled with sport.

He was indeed full of apprehensions and suspicions. But as he did easily take them, so he did easily check them and master them; whereby they were not dangerous, but troubled himself more than others. It is true, his thoughts were so many, as they could not well always stand together; but that which did good one way, did hurt another. Neither did he at some times weigh them aright in their proportions. Certainly that rumour which did him so much mischief (that the Duke of York should be saved and alive) was (at the first) of his own nourishing, because he would have more reason not to reign in the right of his wife. He was affable, and both well and fair spoken; and would use strange sweetness and blandishments of words, where he desired to effect or persuade any things that he took to heart. He was rather studious than learned; reading most books that were any of worth, in the French tongue. Yet he understood the Latin, as appeareth in that Cardinal Hadrian and others, who could very well have written French, did use to write to him in Latin.

For his pleasures, there is no news of them. And yet by his instructions to Marsin and Stile touching the Queen of Naples, it seemeth he could interrogate well touching beauty. He did by pleasures as great Princes do by banquets, come and look a little upon them, and turn away. For ne'r Prince was more wholly given to his affairs, nor in them more of himself: insomuch as in triumphs of justs and tourneys and balls and masks (which they then called disguises) he was rather a princely and gentle spectator than seemed much to be delighted.

No doubt, in him as in all men (and most of all in Kings) his fortune wrought upon his nature, and his nature upon his fortune. He attained to the crown, not only from a private fortune, which might endow him with moderation; but also from the fortune of an exiled man, which had quickened in him all seeds of observation and industry. And his times, being rather prosperous than calm, had raised his confidence by success, but almost marred his nature by troubles. His wisdom, by often evading from perils, was turned rather into a dexterity to deliver himself from dangers when they pressed him, than into a providence to prevent and remove them afar off. And even in nature, the sight of his mind was like some sights of eyes; rather strong at hand than to carry afar off. For his wit increased upon the occasion; and so much the more if the occasion were sharpened by danger. Again, whether it were the shortness of his foresight, or the strength of his will, or the dazzling of his suspicions, or what it was; certain it is that the perpetual troubles of his fortunes (there being no more matter out of which they grew) could not have been without some great defects and main errors in his nature, customs, and proceedings, which he had enough to do to save and help with a thousand little industries and watches. But those do best appear in the story itself. Yet take him with all his defects, if a man should compare him with the Kings his concurrents in France and Spain, he shall find him more politic than Lewis the Twelfth of France, and more entire and sincere than Ferdinando of Spain. But if you shall change Lewis the Twelfth for Lewis the Eleventh, who lived a little before, then the consort is more perfect. For that Lewis the Eleventh, Ferdinando, and Henry, may be esteemed for the *tres magi* of Kings of those ages. To conclude, if this King did no greater matters, it was long of himself; for what he minded he compassed.

He was a comely personage, a little above just stature, well and straight limbed, but slender. His countenance was reverend, and a little like a churchman: and as it was not strange or dark, so neither was it winning or pleasing, but as the face of one well disposed. But it was to the disadvantage of the painter, for it was best when he spake.

His worth may bear a tale or two, that may put upon him somewhat that may seem divine. When the Lady Margaret his mother had divers great suitors for marriage, she dreamed one night that one in the likeness of a bishop in pontifical habit did tender her Edmund Earl of Richmond (the King's father) for her husband. Neither had she ever any child but the King, though she had three husbands. One day when King Henry the Sixth (whose innocency gave him holiness) was washing his hands at a great feast, and cast his eye upon King Henry, then a young youth, he said; "This is the lad that shall possess quietly that that we now strive for." But that that was truly divine in him, was that he had the fortune of a true Christian as well as of a great King, in living exercised and dying repentant. So as he had an happy warfare in both conflicts, both of sin and the cross.

He was born at Pembroke Castle, and lieth buried at Westminster, in one of the stateliest and daintiest monuments of Europe, both for the chapel and for the sepulchre. So that he dwelleth more richly dead, in the monument of his tomb, than he did alive in Richmond or any of his palaces. I could wish he did the like in this monument of his fame.

The Personality of Erasmus

A. L. ROWSE

1466–1536. No contemporary historian writes a livelier, more blithely personal, and yet more finely polished prose than A. L. Rowse. His chief eminence rests upon a series of notable contributions to Elizabethan history. But these works are richly detailed and full of references which would be confusing in a short excerpt. So I have chosen from Mr. Rowse's writings this charming and characteristic tribute to a great and admirable man, whose once-enormous fame has so shrunk that many modern readers do not even nod politely when they meet his name.

Erasmus is one of the great names of Europe; but it is doubtful whether he is much more than a name to us today. There upon the library shelves stand the dozen or more tall folios of the Louvain edition of his works; there are the ten volumes of his *Letters*; in addition, his texts of the Fathers, Chrysostom, Cyprian, Jerome, Ambrose, Augustine, together with his life's crowning glory, the edition of the New Testament. Is it any wonder that the man should be buried under such a mountain of Latin and Greek?

In spite of all this, he comes through to us as a singularly modern personality: a sensitive, queasy, thin-skinned, human being, self-conscious and self-aware like a modern man, no medieval. His problems were very much ours; he was agonized by similar issues, extraordinarily contemporary in character; living as he did in that sickening period when the Renaissance passed over into the Reformation and the Wars of Religion, he was caught at a dangerous turning of the ways in Europe. It is fitting that we call him to mind: he was the first of modern writers, and his life holds a special significance for our age.

Let us begin by calling up his appearance. He was so famous in his life-time and so much painted, that his features at least are familiar to us. We see him as so often depicted, seated at a desk, for ever writing, writing, writing. There are usually books in the background, an open book before him. The face is deeply expressive: sensibility, refinement, self-awareness in every line of it. It is the face of a very clever man, who is also a valetudinarian; something of an invalid, perpetually over-working, nervous, alert; querulousness in the brow, no satisfaction in the tight repressed lips. It all bespeaks the life of incessant worrying labor this man lived; beneath the surface appearances, the sparse greying hair, the thin worn cheeks, the mobile hands heavy with rings, there is yet unmistakable determination, tenacity of purpose, the eager, anxious spirit. The expression of the face has something ambivalent about it: at once grave, yet on the verge of a smile; half tender, half querulous: evidently a personality with a sharp edge to it, the more fascinating to study because of the touchiness, the one skin too few, the combination of extreme sensibility with nervous tenacity.

All this mirrors the man we know him to have been. He was first and foremost the scholar, prince among the scholars of the Renaissance. He won this position after an apprenticeship over years, at school at Gouda and Deventer, at the Augustinian monastery of Steyn of which he was a canon, in Paris teaching himself Greek, at Oxford where Colet inspired him with a sense of his vocation, at Cambridge where he lectured and taught and studied. It was not until he was a man of thirty that he began to reap the rewards of his industry in a growing fame. In addition to his scholarship he was a brilliant original writer. Few had handled the Latin language as he since the Dark Ages closed down upon Europe, a resuscitation of the classical Latin of Cicero. If less of a living language than medieval Latin, at least it was living to Erasmus, who took pains not to speak his native Dutch and as far as possible to converse in Latin only, so as not to spoil his natural style.

No-one had more arresting things to say: he was a preternaturally sharp observer of events and persons, an acute commentator upon opinions, essentially moralist and critic, with a biting wit. He belongs to the small, well-defined class of writers to which Voltaire and Swift belong. But not even Voltaire's European reputation equalled Erasmus' recognized position in his lifetime. He was the admired of scholars, churchmen and princes, sought after by Charles V, Francis I, Henry VIII and successive Popes, the friend of Sir Thomas More and Fisher, since promoted saints; different countries competed for the honor of his presence, their leading men loaded him with presents and kindnesses.

Of the works that went to justify this immense reputation, we cannot here deal with those of pure scholarship; let us take his own original writings. I suppose the *Moriae Encomium (The Praise of Folly)* to be his most characteristic work, that one which best speaks for the man. The idea of the book occurred to him while journeying over the mountains from Italy to Northern Europe, on his way to England in 1509; arrived in London, he wrote it in the space of a few days in More's house in Bucklersbury—a characteristic play upon More's name gives it its title. The subject of the book is the foolery of mankind, the tragic condition that lies at the root of human nature. Why is it that man, the one animal gifted with reason, should choose the irrational, the foolish, the obviously absurd course? One sees that the book belongs to the same class as *Gulliver's Travels*, Voltaire's *Candide*, and Grimmelshausen's *Simplicissimus*. Why the Renaissance should have been so much concerned with the subject of human folly is an interesting, and perhaps profitable, speculation; there is a large Fool-literature of the time, of which the *Ship of Fools* and Rabelais's works are examples. The perfect expression of all that literature is, however, Erasmus' *Praise of Folly*.

The treatment of the subject is appropriately ironical, and indeed at times one can hardly distinguish between what is seriously and what is frivolously intended. There is scarcely any form of human folly that is not touched upon, sometimes with a mock serious approval, sometimes with open castigation. The latter is employed for the abuses of the Church, the attention to forms instead of to things of the spirit, the concern with property and pomp instead of preaching the gospel, the character of secular priests who justify their name by being so much better acquainted with the affairs of this world than of the next. Let us take an example from the book:

To work miracles is old and antiquated, and not in fashion now; to instruct the people, troublesome; to interpret the Scripture, pedantic; to pray, a sign one has little else to do; to shed tears, silly and womanish; to be poor, base; to be defeated, dishonorable and little becoming him that scarce admits even kings to kiss his slipper [i.e., the Pope]; and lastly, to die, uncouth; and to be stretched on a Cross, infamous.

The desire for practical reform is constantly in evidence, but more philosophical, or even anthropological, is such a thought as this:

In a word, this Folly is that that laid the foundation of Cities; and by it, Empire, Authority, Religion, Policy and Public Actions are preserved: neither is there any thing in Human Life that is not a kind of pastime of Folly.

Nothing could be more far-reaching than the scepticism implied by that: human folly is the foundation of all politics, and provides the necessity for authority, religion, the state: if only men were reasonable there would be no need for empires, states, authority. These two tendencies in Erasmus, the reforming and evangelistic ardor, and a profound scepticism regarding life and men, were held together in a delicate equipoise which gives the whole character to his mind. The equipoise was broken by the irruption of Luther into the European scene. The conflict between these two sides to Erasmus' nature was tragically revealed in the conflict with Luther over the Reformation.

Up to 1518-19 all had gone well with Erasmus: he stood at the apex of his European reputation. As both humanist and reformer, he appeared at the head of the movement for reform within the Church; all men looked to him as such, yet he retained the favor of kings, Emperor and Pope. The revolutionary upheaval which Luther set in train destroyed all this. The confident Victorian age considered that Luther showed up Erasmus' weakness as but a Laodicean, as certainly he confessed that he was not the stuff that martyrs are made of. But the tragedy went deeper: it was that the sensible, moderate course of reasonable reform, within the framework of the universal Church, became impossible in the mad onrush of events with men's passions unleashed, their hatred aroused.

The essential point of Erasmus' position was that he was a rationalist, he wanted men to be guided by reason. He had been not unsympathetic to Luther in the beginnings of his movement for reform; but he foresaw as Luther went farther and farther in his challenge to the Church, that new dogmas were being set up against the old and that this would lead to disastrous conflicts and wars, leaving the world in a worse state than before, Europe riven in two. Erasmus was right, but could do nothing; his own views about the folly of men were being only too precisely justified in the destruction they were bringing on themselves and in the ruin of all his hopes of agreed reform in a spirit of moderation and forbearance. Erasmus was caught by the whirlwind out of the interior depths of barbaric Germany, in much the same way as the Girodins were caught by the French Revolution, or the Mensheviks by the Russian. The contemporary parallel is obvious. It is regrettable that human beings are unable to bring about obvious and necessary reforms without pulling the house down about their ears. There is a discerning phrase of Froude's in his book on Erasmus, to the effect that two centuries of religious wars were to vindicate the rightness of his judgment.

Similarly with his views on internationalism and peace. He had a horror of war and killing which went with his shrinking, unmasculine temperament and civilized preferences. A modern German scholar has called him "the first of pacifists"; and some of his finest writings are denunciations of war and war-mongers. The fiercest exposure of all, the *Julius Exclusus*, is reserved for the most eminent offender, the war-like Pope Julius II, author of a general European war, whom Erasmus had seen entering Bologna in triumph and never forgot the spectacle. He is depicted clamoring for admission at the gate of Heaven: to be rejected.

Erasmus was a citizen of Europe, equally at home in the Netherlands, France, Italy, Germany or England, in Paris or London, Antwerp, Venice or Basel. Perhaps in the end equally homeless, for the city of the mind in which he dwelt was that Europe of which he was such a good citizen, but which has not even yet come to be.

The Golden Age of Spain

PAUL HORGAN

1500–1600. During the reign of Charles V and Philip II, Spain fought inter-minable wars in Europe and conquered a vast empire in the New World of the Americas. Then was Spain's Golden Age, the days of her power and glory, and also of her economic attrition. Several aspects of that Golden Age are described by Paul Horgan in these selections from his magnificent history Great River: The Rio Grande in North American History.

ARTS

A passion for study filled the century of the Golden Age. In Spain, thirty-four universities were at work, and others were founded in the New World within a few years of the conquest. The German Jacob Cromberger and his sons established their printing house at Seville in 1500, reading became an indispensable part of living, and all because a complicated machine held together many rows of reversed little metal letters and pressed them into damp paper, again and again, until many copies of the same words and ideas were at hand. Because her language went everywhere with Spain's power, printers in Italy, France, the Netherlands and the Indies printed books in Spanish.

Everything found its way into print, even the ballads that previously passed through generations by word of mouth. People made them up in inns and on travels and marching in wars, telling droll stories or love stories or wicked scandals, and the rude narratives were sung wherever somebody had an instrument to pluck. Seeing how such efforts looked in print, men of letters began to write ballads in the style of the old popular ones, that had gone on always changing as one man's memory revised the residue of another's. The new poetic ballads sang of the courts of chivalry; imaginary histories that revealed Spanish ideals of noble kingship, knightly valor, reverence for womanhood and death to monsters. True histories were also written in rhyme, long chronicles of heroes, as when Captain Pérez de Villagra, the alumnus of the University of Salamanca, sat down to write the history of Oñate's first year on the Río del Norte, he wrote it in heroic verse. The Spanish world grew not only in range but also in meaning as the people saw its likeness in all that was made by writers and artists.

As his father the Emperor admired Titian of Venice, so King Philip admired and employed Domenico Theotocópuli, known as the Greek, who came from Greece by way of long studies and labors in Venice and Rome. He was a learned man and a pious one, and for the Escorial and churches elsewhere he painted many pictures that swept the eye and mind of the beholder upward to heaven. Often even the very eyes of the kings and saints he painted were gazing heavenward and shining with great diamond tears of desire, and seeing them so, the beholder cast his desires upward also. The skies of his pictures of martyrdoms and sufferings and triumphs were like the skies of Good Friday afternoon, torn apart and blowing aloft in black and white clouds through which the Spanish temperament could see the immortal soul of Christ as it flew to His Father from the cross. The Greek painted many likenesses of people of circumstance, who without their starch and black velvet and swords, their armor and ribbons, or their violet mantelletas and trains, would have looked very much like everybody else in the Spanish populace, even those on the northern river of the latest and farthest Crown colony. All countenances which he limned were grave and melancholy, even that of the Madonna in the Nativity. The Spaniards were a people who did not often smile, but more often laughed outright or possessed their faces in calm, when most faces look sad. The Greek was much seen in Toledo, where he painted the town many times, making odd changes in exactly how it looked, yet by so doing, making the city's image combine with the beholder's feeling to produce a rise of the soul.

It was the same rise which Spaniards knew from music in the High Mass, when the dark high vaults of the church where candlelight never reached would be filled with the singing of choirs, plain, without instruments. They heard the masses composed by the great Tomas Luis de Victoria of Ávila, and Cristóbal of Morales, and Francesco Guerrero. The voices of boys came like shafts of heaven, and in the polyphonic style, the voices of men rose under them and turned with melody, and the two qualities met and divided, the one qualifying the other, now with one long note held against several notes in a figure, again with highs against lows, and again with syllables against whole words, and loud against soft, so that in heavenly laws known to music alone an experience of meaning and delivery struck all who truly listened, and the stone arches and the drift of incense and the possibility of divinity in mankind and the Mass at the altar all became intermingled with the soul that rose. How, lost in dark choir stalls under lofting stone, could boys, having yet so little of life, strike so purely to the darkest self with their shining voices that seemed to come from beyond all flesh?

And there was other music that used the very flesh itself, spoke to it, enlivened it, cozened it with coarse jokes, and pulled its nose and made the hearers laugh and clap and stamp their feet. It was heard at the inns, in public squares, and in the theatres, when ballads were sung or skits and plays given by actors and dancers. They came out on a stage bringing sackbuts, or dulcimers, harps, lutes or vihuelas, or combinations of all of these, and struck up a tune to which they sang a story with many verses. They plucked, beat, blew and nodded together, and often repeated with each verse a clever effect in which one musician gave a little variation at the same place each time, so that the audience listened for it in following verses. Such players entertained anyone who called for them and displayed a coin. They went from one tavern to another, ready to stand in a half-circle facing a table and play to a private party much to the advantage of any others in the place. Their music went with the Spaniards wherever in the world they might go.

If popular balladry was the poor man's comfort, there was much to sing about as the world moved and poor times befell Spain in her might. Great fortunes shrank, and the high state of many nobles lost its quality because it could not be paid for, and wage earners found their coins worth very little, and poor people lived always hungry. It was the very outpouring of wealth from the New World which caused such trouble. When so much more gold than usual came to be circulated, each little coin or bit of gold spent in trade was worth much less than usual, as gold itself became too common. In giving civilization to the New World, Spain seemed to give up its own strength as the new land found the lusty power to grow by itself. In the home kingdom, while all graces were maintained, the substance behind them shrank, and for great numbers of Spaniards the graces which they aired came to be pretentions and little else.

149

STYLE AND HUNGER

And yet there was that in the Spanish spirit which made of each Spaniard his own castle, and it was very like them all that as the wealth that sustained public nobility began to shrink, and as every hidalgo by birth disdained to reveal his poor estate, so many another man who had no title or claim to nobility adopted the airs and styles of the hidalgo, until the land became a parade of starving lords, real and false, who the lower they fell in worldly affairs, the more grandly they behaved. Going hungry, they would loll against a wall in public, picking their teeth to convince the passer-by that they had just dined on sweet carrots and turnips, sharp cheese, pungent bacon, fresh eggs, crusty roast kid, tart wine from Spanish grapes, and a covered dish of baked gazpacho, that was made out of wheat bread, olive oil, vinegar, onions, salt, and red peppers hot enough to make the eyes water.

There was little else for such a gentleman to do. If he had talents that could be employed, there was hardly anybody to pay him for them. He was a man of honor and to make a living could not stoop to improper ways, which no matter how hard the times seemed always to prosper. If his shanks were thin and bare, and his sitting bones almost showed in his threadbare britches, and his belly was puffy with windy hunger, then he still had his ragged cloak to throw about such betrayals. Within his cloak he could stand a noble stance, and at a little distance, who was the wiser? As the proverb said, "Under a bad cloak there may hide a good drinker," which gave comfort to fallen swagger; and to comfort the dream of impossible valor, there spoke another proverb, saying, "Under my cloak I kill the king."

But no patch ever failed to show, however lovingly stitched, even a patch on a man's pride. To cloak his spirit, the mangy gentleman had another sort of possession left to him from his better days. This was the high thought of chivalry, that gave to human life, all human life, so great a dignity and such an obligation of nobility on behalf of all other persons. There was a poor sweetness in this extravagant spending of spirit, that the more a man lacked simply to keep him alive, the more he disdained his own trouble and grandly swore to demolish the trouble of another. In his ironic self-knowledge the Spaniard knew such men, and smiled at the antic capers they cut in their hungry pretensions. And yet he bowed to their spirit that stated that, "he is only worth more than another who does more than another." It was no surprise to him that a champion should vow the rescue of anyone in distress, without reference to rank or station. If there were different levels of life, then one man in his own was worth as much as another in his, and was free to state as much, and act accordingly. And as every soul originated in God, and so was equal to every other in worth, so its offerings on earth deserved succor without discrimination. The Spaniard knew that the grandeur of God did not disdain the humblest surroundings, and could say with Saint Teresa of Avila, *"Entre los pucheros anda el Señor"*—God moves among the kitchen pots.

But all came back to hunger. Private soldiers who went to America were experienced in that condition. It was a marvel how far they could march, how hard they could fight, and how long they could cling to unknown country on empty stomachs. Núñez Cabeza de Vaca, Coronado's soldiers, Castaño de Sosa pillaging at Pecos, Zaldivar crawling over deserts toward the river, all gnawed on tradition when rations were low. Certainly the adventurers did not enlist for the pay, for the pay was meagre and always in arrears, even that owed to the commanders in silver-gilt armor. Nor did they venture forth for commerce as it could affect the ordinary individual, for the risks were too great for uncertain profits, and in any case the Spanish gift for business fulfilled itself not in the largest but in the smallest affairs, face to face with another man. For the pleasures of business were firstly social—little exchanges of desire and deceit, indifference and truth, the study of human nature, the flourish of bargaining, the satisfaction of the righteous swindle, in buyer and seller alike. Nor was it inordinate love of adventure that took Spaniards past oceans and shores, and up the river, for adventure could be had anywhere, even at home. Perhaps more than any one other motive it was a belief in their own inherent greatness that took the men of the Golden Age to their achievements in geography and colonization.

For to them it was finer to make greatness than to inherit it; and after they made it, they could in all justice cry with the True Chronicler of the conquest of Mexico, "I say again that I—I, myself—I am a true conqueror; and the most ancient of all . . . and I also say, and praise myself therein, that I have been in as many battles and engagements as, according to history, the Emperor Henry IV." In such spirit, what they did they did with style.

THE SWORDS

Even the swords that were extensions not only of their right arms but also of their personalities came out of humble means through fire and water to strength and beauty. Ovid sang the praises of Toledo blades, the best of which were made of old used metal, such as horseshoes. The Spaniard's sword was born at nighttime, through fire, of a river and the south wind.

In the city hall of Toledo the master steelworkers—Sahagún the Elder,

Julian del Rey, Menchaca, Hortuno de Aguirre, Juanes de la Horta—kept their metal punches when these were not in use to stamp the maker's name on a new blade. Every blade had its *alma*, and this soul was the core of old iron on whose cheeks were welded new plates of steel. Standing ready were the two gifts of the river Tagus that flowed below the high rocks of Toledo. These were its white sand and its clear water. The blades were born only in the darkest nights, the better to let the true or false temper of the steel show when red-hot; and of the darkest nights, only those when the south wind blew, so that in passing the blade from fire to water it might not cool too rapidly as a north wind would cool it. The clumsy weld was put into the coals where the bellows hooted. When it came red-hot the master took it from the fire. It threw sparks on meeting the air. Casting river sand on it which extinguished the sparks, the master moved to the anvil. There with taps of hammer and sweeps of the steel against the anvil he shaped the blade, creating a perfectly straight ridge down the center of each side, until squinted at edgewise the blade looked like a flattened lozenge. Now the blade was put again into the fire and kept there until it began to color again, when the master lifted it into the darkness to see if it showed precisely cherry-red. If so, it was ready for the river. There stood handy a tall wooden pail filled with water from the Tagus. Into this, point down, went the blade for its first immersion. To keep the exact right time for each immersion, and to bring blessings, the master or one of his boys sang during the first one, "Blessed be the hour in which Christ was born," and then the blade was lifted out. Heated again, it was returned to the water, and they sang, "The iron is hot!" and the next, "The water hisses!" and the next, "The tempering will be good," and the last, "If God wills." Then once more the blade went into the fire, but this time only until it became dull red, liver-colored. Then with pincers the master held it by the tang which would later fit into the hilt, and had the boy smear the blade with raw whole fat cut from the sac about the kidneys of a male goat or a sheep. The fat burst into flame. They took the blade to the rack and set it there against the wall point downward. The fat burned away, the blade darkened and cooled through several hours. In daytime they sharpened and polished it, and if it was to bear an inscription, it went to the bench of the engraver, who chiselled his letters on one of the flat faces, or perhaps both, spelling out a pious or patriotic motto, like one on a sword found in Texas not far from the Rio Grande, that read, on one side, "POR MY REY," and on the other, "POR MY LEY," thus swearing protection to king and law. The hilt, with guard and grip, then was joined to the tang, and those for plain soldiers were of well-turned iron, but without inlays of gold or silver, or studdings of smooth jewels, or wrappings with silver-gilt wire that variously went onto the swords of officers and nobles.

And at last the maker sent for his stamp from the city hall and let his device be punched into the blade at its thickest part near the guard, and the proud work was done, and the Spanish gesture could be sharpened and elongated across the world.

SOUL AND BODY

Both within the Spaniard and without him lay the country which Lope de Vega called "sad, spacious Spain." If Spaniards enacted their literature, it was because, like all people, they both created literature and were created by it. So it was with memories and visions in the colony of the river wilderness. Their hopes of what was to be were no less full of meanings than their certainties of what they had done, and both found their center of energy in a moral sense that gave a sort of secret poetry to the hard shape of life. The Spaniard was cruel but he loved life, and his melancholy brutality seemed to issue forth almost involuntarily through the humanitarian laws and codes with which he surrounded himself. If his nature was weak his conscience was strong, and if he sinned his first act of recovery was to recognize his guilt. When one of the most brutal of the conquerors of the New World was dying of wounds given to him by Indians he was asked where he ached, and he replied, "In my soul."

So the baggage of personality brought by the colonists told of their origin, their faith, the source of their power, the human types by which they perpetuated their tradition; and forecast much about how they would live along the river.

The Great Montezuma

BERNAL DÍAZ DEL CASTILLO

1519–1520. Some forty years after the conquest of Mexico, one of Cortés's veterans, Bernal Díaz del Castillo, occupied his old age by writing a personal narrative of that extraordinary adventure. He seems to have forgotten little. His artless prose has such evocative emotional power that his True History of the Conquest of Mexico *ranks with the great works of historical memoirs. This excerpt describes the Aztec emperor as he was in 1519 when the Spaniards were his guests in Mexico City. The concluding episode occurred in 1520 after Cortés had treacherously imprisoned Montezuma and the Mexicans had furiously attacked the Spaniards.*

The Great Montezuma was about forty years old, of good height and well proportioned, slender and spare of flesh, not very swarthy, but of the natural color and shade of an Indian. He did not wear his hair long, but so as just to cover his ears, his scanty black beard was well shaped and thin. His face was somewhat long, but cheerful, and he had good eyes and showed in his appearance and manner both tenderness and, when necessary, gravity. He was very neat and clean and bathed once every day in the afternoon. He had many women as mistresses, daughters of Chieftains, and he had two great Cacicas as his legitimate wives. He was free from unnatural offenses. The clothes that he wore one day, he did not put on again until four days later. He had over two hundred Chieftains in his guard, in other rooms close to his own, not that all were meant to converse with him, but only one or another, and when they went to speak to him they were obliged to take off their rich mantles and put on others of little worth, but they had to be clean, and they had to enter barefoot with their eyes lowered to the ground, and not to look up in his face. And they made him three obeisances, and said: "Lord, my Lord, my Great Lord," before they came up to him, and then they made their report and with a few words he dismissed them, and on taking leave they did not turn their backs, but kept their faces towards him with their eyes on the ground, and they did not turn their backs until they left the room. I noticed another thing, that when other great chiefs came from distant lands about disputes or business, when they reached the apartments of the Great Montezuma, they had to come barefoot and with poor mantles, and they might not enter directly into the Palace, but had to loiter about a little on one side of the Palace door, for to enter hurriedly was considered to be disrespectful.

For each meal, over thirty different dishes were prepared by his cooks according to their ways and usage, and they placed small pottery braziers beneath the dishes so that they should not get cold. They prepared more than three hundred plates of the food that Montezuma was going to eat, and more than a thousand for the guard. When he was going to eat, Montezuma would sometimes go out with his chiefs and stewards, and they would point out to him which dish was best, and of what birds and other things it was composed, and as they advised him, so he would eat, but it was not often that he would go out to see the food, and then merely as a pastime.

I have heard it said that they were wont to cook for him the flesh of young boys, but as he had such a variety of dishes, made of so many things, we could not succeed in seeing if they were of human flesh or of other things, for they daily cooked fowls, turkeys, pheasants, native partridges, quail, tame and wild ducks, venison, wild boar, reed birds, pigeons, hares and rabbits, and many sorts of birds and other things which are bred in this country, and they are so numerous that I cannot finish naming them in a hurry; so we had no insight into it, but I know for certain that after our Captain censured the sacrifice of human beings, and the eating of their flesh, he ordered that such food should not be prepared for him henceforth.

Let us cease speaking of this and return to the way things were served to him at meal-times. It was in this way: if it was cold they made up a large fire of live coals of a firewood made from the bark of trees which did not give off any smoke, and the scent of the bark from which the fire was made was very fragrant, and so that it should not give off more heat than he required, they placed in front of it a sort of screen adorned with figures of idols worked in gold. He was seated on a low stool, soft and richly worked, and the table, which was also low, was made in the same style as the seats, and on it they placed the table cloths of white cloth and some rather long napkins of the same material. Four very beautiful cleanly women brought water for his hands in a sort of deep basin which they call *xicales*, and they held others like plates to catch the water, and they brought him towels. And two other women brought him tortilla bread, and as soon as he began to eat they placed before him a sort of wooden screen painted over with gold, so that no one should watch him eating. Then the four women stood aside, and four great Chieftains who were old men came and stood beside them, and with those Montezuma now and then conversed, and asked them questions, and as a great favor he would give to each of these elders a dish of what to him tasted best. They say that these elders were his near relations, and were his counsellors and judges of law suits, and the dishes and food which Montezuma gave them they ate standing up with much reverence and without looking at his face. He was served on Cholula earthenware either red or black. While he was at his meal the men of his guard who were within the rooms near to that of Montezuma, never dreamed of making any noise or speaking aloud. They brought him fruit of all the different kinds that the land produced, but he ate very little of it. From time to time they brought him, in cup-shaped vessels of pure gold, a certain drink made from cacao, and the women served this drink to him with great reverence.

Sometimes at meal-times there were present some very ugly humpbacks, very small of stature and their bodies almost broken in half, who are their jesters, and other Indians, who must have been buffoons, who told him witty sayings, and others who sang and danced, for Montezuma was fond of pleasure and song, and to these he ordered to be given what was left of the food and the jugs of cacao. Then the same four women removed the table cloths, and with much ceremony they brought water for his hands. And Montezuma talked with those four old Chieftains about things that interested him, and they took leave of him with the great reverence in which they held him, and he remained to repose.

As soon as the Great Montezuma had dined, all the men of the guard had their meal and as many more of the other house servants, and it seems to me that they brought out over a thousand dishes of the food of which I have spoken, and then over two thousand jugs of cacao all frothed up, as they make it in Mexico, and a limitless quantity of fruit, so that with his women and female servants and bread makers and cacao makers his expenses must have been very great.

Let us cease speaking about the expenses and the food for his household and let us speak of the Stewards and the Treasures and the stores and pantries and of those who had charge of the houses where the maize was stored. I say that there would be so much to write about, each thing by itself, that I should not know where to begin, but we stood astonished at the excellent arrangements and the great abundance of provisions that he had in all, but I must add what I had forgotten, for it is as well to go back and relate it, and that is, that while Montezuma was at table eating, as I have described, there were waiting on him two other graceful women to bring him tortillas, kneaded with eggs and other sustaining ingredients, and these tortillas were very white, and they were brought on plates covered with clean napkins, and they also brought him another kind of bread, like long balls kneaded with other kinds of sustaining food, and *pan pachol*, for so they call it in this country, which is a sort of wafer. There were also placed on the table three tubes much painted and gilded, which held *liquidamber* mixed with certain herbs which they call tobacco, and when he had finished eating, after they had danced before him and sung and the table was removed, he inhaled the smoke from one of those tubes, but he took very little of it and with that he fell asleep.

I remember that at that time his steward was a great Cacique to whom we gave the name of Tapia, and he kept the accounts of all the revenue that was brought to Montezuma, in his books which were made of paper which they call *amal*, and he had a great house full of these books. Now we must leave the books and the accounts for it is outside our story, and say how Montezuma had two houses full of every sort of arms, many of them richly adorned with gold and precious stones. There were shields great and small, and a sort of broad-swords, and others like two-handed swords set with stone knives which cut much better than our swords, and lances longer than ours are, with a fathom of blade with many knives set in it, which even when they are driven into a buckler or shield do not come out, in fact they cut like razors so that they can shave their heads with them. There were very good bows and arrows and double-pointed lances and others with one point, as well as their throwing sticks, and many slings and round stones shaped by hand, and some sort of artful shields which are so made that they can be rolled up, so as not to be in the way when they are not fighting, and when they are needed for fighting they let them down, and they cover the body from top to toe. There was also much quilted cotton armor, richly ornamented on the outside with colored feathers, used as devices and distinguishing marks, and there were casques or helmets made of wood and bone, also highly decorated with feathers on the outside, and there were other arms of other makes which, so as to avoid prolixity, I will not describe, and there were artisans who were skilled in such things and worked at them, and stewards who had charge of the arms.

Let us leave this and proceed to the Aviary, and I am forced to abstain from enumerating every kind of bird that was there and its peculiarity, for there was everything from the Royal Eagle and other smaller eagles, and many other birds of great size, down to tiny birds of many-colored plumage, also the birds from which they take the rich plumage which they use in their green feather work. The birds which have these feathers are about the size of the magpies in Spain, they are called in this country *Quezales,* and there are other birds which have feathers of five colors— green, red, white, yellow and blue; I don't remember what they are called; then there were parrots of many different colors, and there are so many of them that I forgot their names, not to mention the beautifully marked ducks and other larger ones like them. From all these birds they plucked the feathers when the time was right to do so, and the feathers grew again. All the birds that I have spoken about breed in these houses, and in the setting season certain Indian men and women who look after the birds, place the eggs under them and clean the nests and feed them, so that each kind of bird has its proper food. In this house that I have spoken of there is a great tank of fresh water and in it there are other sorts of birds with long stilted legs, with body, wings and tail all red; I don't know their names, but in the island of Cuba they are called *Ypiris,* and there are others something like them, and there are also in that tank many other kinds of birds which always live in the water.

Let us leave this and go on to another great house, where they keep many Idols, and they say that they are their fierce gods, and with them many kinds of carnivorous beasts of prey, tigers and two kinds of lions, and animals something like wolves and foxes, and other smaller carnivorous animals, and all these carnivores they feed with flesh, and the greater number of them breed in the house. They give them as food deer and fowl, dogs and other things they are used to hunt, and I have heard it said that they feed them on the bodies of the Indians who have been sacrificed. It is in this way: you have already heard me say that when they sacrifice a wretched Indian they saw open the chest with stone knives and hasten to tear out the palpitating heart and blood, and offer it to their Idols, in whose name the sacrifice is made. Then they cut off the thighs, arms and head and eat the former at feasts and banquets, and the head they hang up on some beams, and the body of the man sacrificed is not eaten but given to these fierce animals. They also have in that cursed house many vipers and poisonous snakes which carry on their tails things which sound like bells. These are the worst vipers of all, and they keep them in jars and great pottery vessels with many feathers, and there they lay their eggs and rear their young, and they give them to eat the bodies of the Indians who have been sacrificed, and the flesh of dogs which they are in the habit of breeding.

Let me speak now of the infernal noise when the lions and tigers roared and the jackals and foxes howled and the serpents hissed, it was horrible to listen to and it seemed like hell. Let us go on and speak of the skilled workmen Montezuma employed in every craft that was practised among them. We will begin with lapidaries and workers in gold and silver and all the hollow work, which even the great goldsmiths in Spain were forced to admire, and of these there were a great number of the best in a town named Atzcapotzalco, a league from Mexico. Then for working precious stones and chalchihuites, which are like emeralds, there were other great artists. Let us go on to the great craftsmen in feather work, and painters and sculptors who were most refined; then to the Indian women who did the weaving and the washing, who made such an immense quantity of fine fabrics with wonderful feather work designs; the greater part of it was brought daily from some towns of the province on the north coast near Vera Cruz called Cotaxtla.

In the house of the Great Montezuma himself, all the daughters of Chieftains whom he had as mistresses always wore beautiful things, and there were many daughters of Mexican citizens who lived in retirement and wished to appear to be like nuns, who also did weaving but it was wholly of feather work. These nuns had their houses near the great Cue of Huichilobos and out of devotion to it, or to another Idol, that of a woman was said to be their mediatrix in the matter of marriage, their fathers placed them in that religious retirement until they married, and they were only taken out thence to be married.

Let us go on and tell about the great number of dancers kept by the Great Montezuma for his amusement, and others who used stilts on their feet, and others who flew when they danced up in the air, and others like Merry-Andrews, and I may say that there was a district full of these people who had no other occupation. Let us go on and speak of the workmen that he had as stone cutters, masons and carpenters, all of whom attended to the work of his houses, I say that he had as many as he wished for. We must not forget the gardens of flowers and sweet-scented trees, and the many kinds that there were of them, and the arrangements of them and the walks, and the ponds and the tanks of fresh water where the water entered at one end and flowed out of the other; and the baths which he had there, and the variety of small birds that nested in the branches, and the medicinal and useful herbs that were in the gardens. It was a wonder to see, and to take care of it there were many gardeners. Everything was made in masonry and well-cemented, baths and walks and closets, and apartments like summer houses where they danced and sang. There was as much to be seen in these gardens as there was everywhere else, and we could not tire of witnessing his great power. Thus as a consequence of so many crafts being practised among them, a large number of skilled Indians were employed.

* * *

It was decided to sue for peace so that we could leave Mexico, and as soon as it was dawn many more squadrons of Mexicans arrived and very effectually surrounded our quarters on all sides, and if they had discharged many stones and arrows before, they came much thicker and with louder howls and whistles on this day, and other squadrons endeavoured to force an entrance in other parts, and cannon and muskets availed nothing, although we did them damage enough.

When Cortés saw all this, he decided that the Great Montezuma should speak to them from the roof and tell them that the war must cease, and that we wished to leave his city. When they went to give this message from Cortés to the Great Montezuma, it is reported that he said with great grief: "What more does Malinche want with me? I neither wish to live nor listen to him, to such a pass has my fate brought me because of him."

And he did not wish to come, and it is even reported that he said he neither wished to see nor hear him, nor listen to his false words, promises or lies. Then the Padre de la Merced and Cristóbal de Olid went and spoke to him with much reverence and in very affectionate terms, and Montezuma said: "I believe that I shall not obtain any result towards ending this war, for they have already raised up another Lord and have made up their minds not to let you leave this place alive, therefore I believe that all of you will have to die."

Montezuma was placed by a battlement of the roof with many of us soldiers guarding him, and he began to speak to his people, with very affectionate expressions telling them to desist from the war, and that we would leave Mexico. Many of the Mexican Chieftains and Captains knew him well and at once ordered their people to be silent and not to discharge darts, stones or arrows, and four of them reached a spot where Montezuma could speak to them, and they to him, and with tears they said to him: "Oh! Señor, and our great Lord, how all your misfortunes and injury and that of your children and relations afflicts us, we make known to you that we have already raised one of your kinsmen to be our Lord," and there he stated his name, that he was called Cuitláhuac, the Lord of Ixtapalapa, and moreover they said that the war must be carried through, and that they had vowed to their Idols not to relax it until we were all dead, and that they prayed every day to their Huichilobos and Texcatepuca to guard him free and safe from our power, and that should it end as they desired, they would not fail to hold him in higher regard as their Lord than they did before, and they begged him to forgive them. They had hardly finished this speech when suddenly such a shower of stones and darts were discharged that (our men who were shielding him having neglected for a moment their duty, because they saw how the attack ceased while he spoke to them) he was hit by three stones, one on the head, another on the arm and another on the leg, and although they begged him to have the wounds dressed and to take food, and spoke kind words to him about it, he would not. Indeed, when we least expected it, they came to say that he was dead. Cortés wept for him, and all of us Captains and soldiers, and there was no man among us who knew him and was intimate with him, who did not bemoan him, as though he were our good father, and it is not to be wondered at, considering how good he was. It was stated that he had reigned for seventeen years and that he was the best king there had ever been in Mexico, and that he had conquered in person, in three wars which he had carried on in the countries he had subjugated.

The "Noche Triste"

WILLIAM H. PRESCOTT

1520. Whether Montezuma's death was intentional or accidental is unknown. The Mexicans attacked Cortés's approximately 1,250 Spaniards and perhaps 8,000 Tlascalan Indian allies not only because their emperor was treacherously imprisoned, but also because the Spaniards had desecrated their temples and had brutally massacred 600 of their nobles peacefully participating in a religious ceremony. The flight of Cortés and his little army from the island city of Mexico is one of the unforgettable episodes in one of the greatest and most popular histories ever written by an American, Prescott's History of the Conquest of Mexico, *first published in 1843. A New England aristocrat, Prescott became a distinguished historian in spite of being so nearly blind that he could not read for more than ten minutes at a time.*

There was no longer any question of the expediency of evacuating the capital. The only doubt was as to the time of doing so, and the route. The Spanish commander called a council of officers to deliberate on these matters. It was his purpose to retreat on Tlascala, and in that capital to decide, according to circumstances, on his future operations. After some discussion, they agreed on the causeway of Tlacopan as the avenue by which to leave the city. It would, indeed, take them back by a circuitous route, considerably longer than either of those by which they had approached the capital. But, for that reason, it would be less likely to be guarded, as least suspected; and the causeway itself, being shorter than either of the other entrances, would sooner place the army in comparative security on the main land.

There was some difference of opinion in respect to the hour of departure. The daytime, it was argued by some, would be preferable, since it would enable them to see the nature and extent of their danger and to provide against it. Darkness would be much more likely to embarrass their own movements than those of the enemy, who were familiar with the ground. A thousand impediments would occur in the night, which might prevent their acting in concert, or obeying, or even ascertaining, the orders of the commander. But, on the other hand, it was urged that the night presented many advantages in dealing with a foe who rarely carried his hostilities beyond the day. The late active operations of the Spaniards had thrown the Mexicans off their guard, and it was improbable they would anticipate so speedy a departure of their enemies. With celerity and caution they might succeed, therefore, in making their escape from the town, possibly over the causeway, before their retreat should be discovered; and, could they once get beyond that pass of peril, they felt little apprehension for the rest.

These views were fortified, it is said, by the counsels of a soldier named Botello, who professed the mysterious science of judicial astrology. He had gained credit with the army by some predictions which had been verified by the events; those lucky hits which make chance pass for calculation with the credulous multitude. This man recommended to his countrymen by all means to evacuate the place in the night, as the hour most propitious to them, although he should perish in it. The event proved the astrologer better acquainted with his own horoscope than with that of others.

It is possible Botello's predictions had some weight in determining the opinion of Cortés. Superstition was the feature of the age, and the Spanish general, as we have seen, had a full measure of its bigotry. Seasons of gloom, moreover, dispose the mind to a ready acquiescence in the marvellous. It is, however, quite as probable that he made use of the astrologer's opinion, finding it coincided with his own, to influence that of his men and inspire them with higher confidence. At all events, it was decided to abandon the city that very night.

The general's first care was to provide for the safe transportation of the treasure. Many of the common soldiers had converted their share of the prize, as we have seen, into gold chains, collars, or other ornaments, which they easily carried about their persons. But the royal fifth, together with that of Cortés himself, and much of the rich booty of the principal cavaliers, had been converted into bars and wedges of solid gold, and deposited in one of the strong apartments of the palace. Cortés delivered the share belonging to the crowd to the royal officers, assigned them one of the strongest horses, and a guard of Castilian soldiers to transport it. Still, much of the treasure, belonging both to the crown and to individuals, was necessarily abandoned, from the want of adequate means of conveyance. The metal lay scattered in shining heaps along the floor, exciting the cupidity of the soldiers. "Take what you will of it," said Cortés to his men. "Better you should have it, than these Mexican hounds. But be careful not to overload yourselves. He travels safest in the dark night who travels lightest." His own more wary followers took heed to his counsel, helping themselves to a few articles of least bulk, though, it might be, of greatest value. But the troops of Narváez, pining for riches of which they had heard so much and hitherto had seen so little, showed no such discretion. To them it seemed as if the very mines of Mexico were turned up before them, and, rushing on the treacherous spoil, they greedily loaded themselves with as much of it, not merely as they could accommodate about their persons, but as they could stow away in wallets, boxes, or any other means of conveyance at their disposal.

Cortés next arranged the order of march. The van, composed of two hundred Spanish foot, he placed under the command of the valiant Gonzalo de Sandoval, supported by Diego de Ordaz, Francisco de Lujo, and about twenty other cavaliers. The rear-guard, constituting the strength of the infantry, was intrusted to Pedro de Alvarado and Velásquez de León. The general himself took charge of the "battle," or center, in which went the baggage, some of the heavy guns, most of which, however, remained in the rear, the treasure, and the prisoners. These consisted of a son and two daughters of Montezuma, Cacama, the deposed lord of Tezcuco, and several other nobles, whom Cortés retained as important pledges in his future negotiations with the enemy. The Tlascalans were distributed pretty equally among the three divisions; and Cortés had under his immediate command a hundred picked soldiers, his own veterans most attached to his service, who, with Cristóbal de Olid, Francisco de Morla, Alonso de Ávila, and two or three other cavaliers, formed a select corps, to act wherever occasion might require.

The general had already superintended the construction of a portable bridge to be laid over the open canals in the causeway. This was given in charge to an officer named Magarino, with forty soldiers under his orders, all pledged to defend the passage to the last extremity. The bridge was to be taken up when the entire army had crossed one of the breaches, and transported to the next. There were three of these openings in the causeway, and most fortunate would it have been for the expedition if the foresight of the commander had provided the same number of bridges. But the labor would have been great, and time was short.

At midnight the troops were under arms, in readiness for the march. Mass was performed by Father Olmedo, who invoked the protection of the Almighty through the awful perils of the night. The gates were thrown open, and on the first of July, 1520, the Spaniards for the last time sallied forth from the walls of the ancient fortress, the scene of so much suffering and such indomitable courage.

The night was cloudy, and a drizzling rain, which fell without intermission, added to the obscurity. The great square before the palace was deserted, as indeed, it had been since the fall of Montezuma. Steadily, and as noiselessly as possible, the Spaniards held their way along the great street of Tlacopan, which so lately had resounded with the tumult of battle. All was now hushed in silence; and they were only reminded of the past by the occasional presence of some solitary corpse, or a dark heap of the slain, which too plainly told where the strife had been hottest. As they passed along the lanes and alleys which opened into the great street, or looked down the canals, whose polished surface gleamed with a sort of ebon lustre through the obscurity of night, they easily fancied that they discerned the shadowy forms of their foe lurking in ambush and ready to spring on them. But it was only fancy; and the city slept undisturbed even by the prolonged echoes of the tramp of the horses and the hoarse rumbling of the artillery and baggage-trains. At length, a lighter space beyond the dusty line of buildings showed the van of the army that it was emerging on the open causeway. They might well have congratulated themselves on having thus escaped the dangers of an assault in the city itself, and that a brief time would place them in comparative safety on the opposite shore. But the Mexicans were not all asleep.

As the Spaniards drew near the spot where the street opened on the causeway, and were preparing to lay the portable bridge across the uncovered breach, which now met their eyes, several Indian sentinels, who had been stationed at this, as at other approaches to the city, took the alarm, and fled, rousing their countrymen by their cries. The priests, keeping their night watch on the summit of the *teocallis*, instantly caught the tidings and sounded their shells, while the huge drum in the desolate temple of the war-god sent forth those solemn tones, which, heard only in seasons of calamity, vibrated through every corner of the capital. The Spaniards saw that no time was to be lost. The bridge was brought forward and fitted with all possible expedition. Sandoval was the first to try its strength, and, riding across, was followed by his little body of chivalry, his infantry, and Tlascalan allies, who formed the first division of the army. Then came Cortés and his squadrons, with the baggage, ammunition-wagons, and a part of the artillery. But before they had time to defile across the narrow passage, a gathering sound was heard, like that of a mighty forest agitated by the winds. It grew louder and louder, while on the dark waters of the lake was heard a splashing noise, as of many oars. Then came a few stones and arrows striking at random among the hurrying troops. They fell every moment faster and more furious, till they thickened into a terrible tempest, while the very heavens were rent with the yells and war-cries of myriads of combatants, who seemed all at once to be swarming over land and lake.

The Spaniards pushed steadily on through the arrowy sleet, though the barbarians, dashing their canoes against the sides of the causeway, clambered up and broke in upon their ranks. But the Christians, anxious only to make their escape, declined all combat except for self-preservation. The cavaliers, spurring forward their steeds, shook off their assailants and rode over their prostrate bodies, while the men on foot with their good swords or the butts of their pieces drove them headlong again down the sides of the dike.

But the advance of several thousand men, marching, probably, on a front of not more than fifteen or twenty abreast, necessarily required much time, and the leading files had already reached the second breach in the causeway before those in the rear had entirely traversed the first. Here they halted, as they had no means of effecting a passage, smart-ing all the while under unintermitting volleys from the enemy, who were clustered thick on the waters around this second opening. Sorely dis-tressed, the van-guard sent repeated messages to the rear to demand the portable bridge. At length the last of the army had crossed, and Magarino and his sturdy followers endeavored to raise the ponderous framework. But it stuck fast in the sides of the dike. In vain they strained every nerve. The weight of so many men and horses, and above all the heavy artillery, had wedged the timbers so firmly in the stones and earth that it was beyond their power to dislodge them. Still they labored amidst a torrent of missiles, until, many of them slain, and all wounded, they were obliged to abandon the attempt.

The tidings soon spread from man to man, and no sooner was their dreadful import comprehended than a cry of despair arose, which for a moment drowned all the noise of conflict. All means of retreat were cut off. Scarcely hope was left. The only hope was in such desperate exertions as each man could make for himself. Order and subordination were at an end. Intense danger produced intense selfishness. Each thought only of his own life. Pressing forward, he trampled down the weak and the wounded, heedless whether it were friend or foe. The leading files, urged on by the rear, were crowded on the brink of the gulf. Sandoval, Ordaz, and the other cavaliers dashed into the water. Some succeeded in swimming their horses across. Others failed, and some, who reached the opposite bank, rolled headlong with their steeds into the lake. The infantry followed pellmell, heaped promiscuously on one another, frequently pierced by the shafts or struck down by the war-clubs of the Aztecs; while many an unfortunate victim was dragged half stunned on board their canoes, to be reserved for a protracted but more dreadful death.

The carnage raged fearfully along the length of the causeway. Its shadowy bulk presented a mark of sufficient distinctness for the enemy's missiles, which often prostrated their own countrymen in the blind fury of the tempest. Those nearest the dike, running their canoes alongside, with a force that shattered them to pieces, leaped on the land, and grappled with the Christians, until both came rolling down the side of the causeway together. But the Aztec fell among his friends, while his antagonist was borne away in triumph to the sacrifice. The struggle was long and deadly. The Mexicans were recognized by their white cotton tunics, which showed faint through the darkness. Above the combatants rose a wild and discordant clamor, in which horrid shouts of vengeance were mingled with groans of agony, with invocations of the saints and the blessed Virgin, and with the screams of women; for their were several women, both natives and Spaniards, who had accompanied the Christian camp. Among those, one named Maria de Estrada is particularly noticed for the courage she displayed, battling with broadsword and target like the stanchest of the warriors.

The opening of the causeway, meanwhile, was filled up with the wreck of matter which had been forced into it, ammunition-wagons, heavy guns, bales of rich stuffs scattered over the waters, chests of solid ingots, and bodies of men and horses, till over this dismal ruin a passage was gradually formed, by which those in the rear were enabled to clamber to the other side. Cortés, it is said, found a place that was fordable, where, halting, with the water up to his saddle-girths, he endeavored to check the confusion, and lead his followers by a safer path to the opposite bank. But his voice was lost in the wild uproar, and finally, hurrying on with the tide, he pressed forwards with a few trusty cavaliers, who remained near his person, to the van; but not before he had seen his favorite page, Juan de Salazar, struck down, a corpse, by his side. Here he found Sandoval and his companions, halting before the third and last breach, endeavoring to cheer on their followers to surmount it. But their resolution faltered. It was wide and deep; though the passage was not so closely beset by the enemy as the preceding ones. The cavaliers again set the example by plunging into the water. Horse and foot followed as they could, some swimming, others with dying grasp clinging to the manes and tails of the struggling animals. Those fared best, as the general had predicted, who travelled lightest; and many were the unfortunate wretches who, weighed down by the fatal gold which they loved so well, were buried with it in the salt floods of the lake. Cortés, with his gallant comrades, Olid, Morla, Sandoval, and some few others, still kept in the advance, leading his broken remnant off the fatal causeway. The din of battle lessened in the distance; when the rumor reached them that the rear-guard would be wholly overwhelmed without speedy relief. It seemed almost an act of desperation; but the generous hearts of the Spanish cavaliers did not stop to calculate danger when the cry for succor reached them. Turning their horses' bridles, they galloped back to the theatre of action, worked their way through the press, swam the canal, and placed themselves in the thick of the *mêlée* on the opposite bank.

The first gray of the morning was now coming over the waters. It showed the hideous confusion of the scene which had been shrouded in the obscurity of night. The dark masses of combatants, stretching along the dike, were seen struggling for mastery, until the very causeway on which they stood appeared to tremble, and reel to and fro, as if shaken by an earthquake; while the bosom of the lake, as far as the eye could reach, was darkened by canoes crowded with warriors, whose spears and bludgeons, armed with blades of "volcanic glass," gleamed in the morning light.

The cavaliers found Alvarado unhorsed, and defending himself with a poor handful of followers against an overwhelming tide of the enemy. His good steed, which had borne him through many a hard fight, had fallen under him. He was himself wounded in several places, and was striving in vain to rally his scattered column, which was driven to the verge of the canal by the fury of the enemy, then in possession of the whole rear of the causeway, where they were reinforced every hour by fresh combatants from the city. The artillery in the earlier part of the engagement had not been idle, and its iron shower, sweeping along the dike, had mowed down the assailants by hundreds. But nothing could resist their impetuosity. The front ranks, pushed on by those behind, were at length forced up to the pieces, and, pouring over them like a torrent, overthrew men and guns in one general ruin. The resolute charge of the Spanish cavaliers, who had now arrived, created a temporary check, and gave time for their countrymen to make a feeble rally. But they were speedily borne down by the returning flood. Cortés and his companions were compelled to plunge again into the lake—though all did not escape. Alvarado stood on the brink for a moment, hesitating what to do. Unhorsed as he was, to throw himself into the water, in the face of the hostile canoes that now swarmed around the opening, afforded but a desperate chance of safety. He had but a second for thought. He was a man of powerful frame, and despair gave him unnatural energy. Setting his long lance firmly on the wreck which strewed the bottom of the lake, he sprung forward with all his might, and cleared the wide gap at a leap! Aztecs and Tlascalans gazed in stupid amazement, exclaiming as they beheld the incredible feat, "This is truly the *Tonatiuh*—the child of the sun!" The breadth of the opening is not given. But it was so great that the valorous captain Díaz, who well remembered the place, says the leap was impossible to any man. Other contemporaries, however, do not discredit the story. It was, beyond doubt, matter of popular belief at the time; it is to this day familiarly known to every inhabitant of the capital; and the name of the *Salto de Alvarado*, "Alvarado's Leap," given to the spot, still commemorates an exploit which rivalled those of the demi-gods of Grecian fable.

Cortés and his companions now rode forward to the front, where the troops, in a loose, disorderly manner, were marching off the fatal causeway. A few only of the enemy hung on their rear, or annoyed them by occasional flights of arrows from the lake. The attention of the Aztecs was diverted by the rich spoil that strewed the battle-ground; fortunately for the Spaniards, who, had the enemy pursued with the same ferocity with which he had fought, would, in their crippled condition, have been cut off, probably, to a man. But little molested, therefore, they were allowed to defile through the adjacent village, or suburbs, it might be called, of Popotla.

The Spanish commander there dismounted from his jaded steed, and, sitting down on the steps of an Indian temple, gazed mournfully on the broken files as they passed before him. What a spectacle did they present! The cavalry, most of them dismounted, were mingled with the infantry, who dragged their feeble limbs along with difficulty; their shattered mail and tattered garments dripping with the salt ooze, showing through their rents many a bruise and ghastly wound; their bright arms soiled, their proud crests and banners gone, the baggage, artillery, all, in short, that constitutes the pride and panoply of glorious war, forever lost. Cortés, as he looked wistfully on their disordered ranks, sought in vain for many a familiar face, and missed more than one dear companion who had stood side by side with him through all the perils of the Conquest. Though accustomed to control his emotions, or, at least, to conceal them, the sight was too much for him. He covered his face with his hands, and the tears, which trickled down, revealed too plainly, the anguish of his soul.

He found some consolation, however, in the sight of several of the cavaliers on whom he most relied. Alvarado, Sandoval, Olid, Ávila were yet safe. He had the inexpressible satisfaction, also, of learning the safety of the Indian interpreter, Marina, so dear to him, and so important to the army. She had been committed, with a daughter of a Tlascalan chief, to several of that nation. She was fortunately placed in the van, and her faithful escort had carried her securely through all the dangers of the night. Aguilar, the other interpreter, had also escaped. And it was with no less satisfaction that Cortés learned the safety of the ship-builder, Martín López. The general's solicitude for the fate of this man, so indispensable, as he proved, to the success of his subsequent operations, showed that, amidst all his affliction, his indomitable spirit was looking forward to the hour of vengeance.

* * *

What agitating thoughts must have crowded on the mind of their commander as he beheld his poor remnant of followers thus huddled together in this miserable bivouac! And this was all that survived of the brilliant array with which but a few weeks since he had entered the capital of Mexico! Where now were his dreams of conquest and empire? And what was he but a luckless adventurer, at whom the finger of scorn would be uplifted as a madman? Whichever way he turned, the horizon was almost equally gloomy, with scarcely one light spot to cheer him. He had still a weary journey before him, through perilous and unknown paths, with guides of whose fidelity he could not be assured. And how could he rely on his reception at Tlascala, the place of his destination—the land of his ancient enemies, where, formerly as a foe, and now as a friend, he had brought desolation to every family within its borders?

Yet these agitating and gloomy reflections, which might have crushed a common mind, had no power over that of Cortés; or, rather, they only served to renew his energies and quicken his perceptions, as the war of the elements purifies and gives elasticity to the atmosphere. He looked with an unblenching eye on his past reverses; but, confident in his own resources, he saw a light through the gloom which others could not. Even in the shattered relics which lay around him, resembling in their haggard aspect and wild attire a horde of famished outlaws, he discerned the materials out of which to reconstruct his ruined fortunes. In the very hour of discomfiture and general despondency, there is no doubt that his heroic spirit was meditating the plan of operations which he afterwards pursued with such dauntless constancy.

The loss sustained by the Spaniards on this fatal night, like every other event in the history of the Conquest, is reported with the greatest discrepancy. If we believe Cortés' own letter, it did not exceed one hundred and fifty Spaniards and two thousand Indians. But the general's bulletins, while they do full justice to the difficulties to be overcome and the importance of the results, are less scrupulous in stating the extent either of his means or of his losses. Thoan Cano, one of the cavaliers present, estimates the slain at eleven hundred and seventy Spaniards and eight thousand allies. But this is a greater number than we have allowed for the whole army. Perhaps we come nearer the truth by taking the computation of Gómara, who was the chaplain of Cortés, and who had free access, doubtless, not only to the general's papers, but to other authentic sources of information. According to him the number of Christians killed and missing was four hundred and fifty, and that of natives four thousand. This, with the loss sustained in the conflicts of the previous week, may have reduced the former to something more than a third, and the latter to a fourth, or perhaps fifth, of the original force with which they entered the capital. The brunt of the action fell on the rear-guard, few of whom escaped. It was formed chiefly of the soldiers of Narváez, who fell the victims, in some measure, of their cupidity. Forty-six of the cavalry were cut off, which with previous losses reduced the number in this branch of the service to twenty-three, and some of these in very poor condition. The greater part of the treasure, the baggage, the general's papers, including his accounts, and a minute diary of transactions since leaving Cuba—which, to posterity at least, would have been of more worth than the gold—had been swallowed up by the waters. The ammunition, the beautiful little train of artillery with which Cortés had entered the city, were all gone. Not a musket even remained, the men having thrown them away, eager to disencumber themselves of all that might retard their escape on that disastrous night. Nothing, in short, of their military apparatus was left, but their swords, their crippled cavalry, and a few damaged cross-bows, to assert the superiority of the European over the barbarian.

The prisoners, including, as already noticed, the children of Montezuma and the cacique of Tezcuco, all perished by the hands of their ignorant countrymen, it is said, in the indiscriminate fury of the assault. They were, also, some persons of consideration among the Spaniards whose names were inscribed on that same bloody roll of slaughter. Such was Francisco de Morla, who fell by the side of Cortés on returning with him to the rescue. But the greatest loss was that of Juan Velásquez de León, who, with Alvarado, had command of the rear. It was the post of danger on that night, and he fell, bravely defending it, at an early part of the retreat. He was an excellent officer, possessed of many knightly qualities, though somewhat haughty in his bearing, being one of the best-connected cavaliers in the army. The near relation of the governor of Cuba, he looked coldly, at first, on the pretensions of Cortés; but, whether from a conviction that the latter had been wronged, or from personal preference, he afterwards attached himself zealously to his leader's interests. The general requited this with a generous confidence, assigning him, as we have seen, a separate and independent command, where misconduct, or even a mistake, would have been fatal to the expedition. Velásquez proved himself worthy of the trust;

and there was no cavalier in the army, with the exception, perhaps, of Sandoval and Alvarado, whose loss would have been so deeply deplored by the commander. Such were the disastrous results of this terrible passage of the causeway; more disastrous than those occasioned by any other reverse which has stained the Spanish arms in the New World; and which have branded the night on which it happened, in the national annals, with the name of the *noche triste,* "the sad or melancholy night."

The Terrible Duke of Alva

JOHN LOTHROP MOTLEY

1508–1582. When Philip II, King of Spain and of the Netherlands, realized that his Dutch subjects were in full revolt against his tyrannical government and particularly against the horrors of the Inquisition, he sent the Duke of Alva to suppress rebellion and to destroy Protestant heresies. This portrait and assessment of the great soldier and religious fanatic reflects the Protestant and democratic convictions of a distinguished nineteenth-century American historian.

It was determined at last that the Netherland heresy should be conquered by force of arms. The invasion resembled both a crusade against the infidel and a treasure-hunting foray into the auriferous Indies, achievements by which Spanish chivalry had so often illustrated itself. The banner of the cross was to be replanted upon the conquered battlements of 300 infidel cities, and a torrent of wealth, richer than ever flowed from Mexican or Peruvian mines, was to flow into the royal treasury from the perennial fountains of confiscation. Who so fit to be the Tancred and the Pizarro of this bicolored expedition as the Duke of Alva, the man who had been devoted from his earliest childhood, and from his father's grave, to hostility against unbelievers and who had prophesied that treasure would flow in a stream a yard deep from the Netherlands as soon as the heretics began to meet with their deserts? An army of chosen troops was forthwith collected, by taking the four legions, or terzios, of Naples, Sicily, Sardinia and Lombardy, and filling their places by fresh levies. About ten thousand picked and veteran soldiers were thus obtained, of which the Duke of Alva was appointed general-in-chief.

Fernando Álvarez de Toledo, Duke of Alva, was now in his sixtieth year. He was the most successful and experienced general of Spain or of Europe. No man had studied more deeply or practised more constantly the military science. In the most important of all arts at that epoch he was the most consummate artist. In the only honorable profession of the age he was the most thorough and the most pedantic professor. Since the days of Demetrius Poliorcetes no man had besieged so many cities. Since the days of Fabius Cunctator no general had avoided so many battles, and no soldier, courageous as he was, ever attained to a more sublime indifference to calumny or depreciation. Having proved in his boyhood at Fontarabia, and in his maturity at Mühlberg, that he could exhibit heroism and headlong courage when necessary, he could afford to look with contempt upon the witless gibes which his enemies had occasionally perpetrated at his expense. Conscious of holding his armies in his hand by the power of an unrivaled discipline and the magic of a name illustrated by a hundred triumphs, he could bear with patience and benevolence the murmurs of his soldiers when their battles were denied them.

He was born in 1508, of a family which boasted imperial descent. A Palaeologus, brother of a Byzantine emperor, had conquered the city of Toledo and transmitted its appellation as a family name. The father of Fernando, Don García, had been slain on the isle of Gerbes, in battle with the Moors, when his son was but four years of age. The child was brought up by his grandfather, Don Frederick, and trained from his tenderest infancy to arms. Hatred to the infidel, and a determination to avenge his father's blood, crying to him from a foreign grave, were the earliest of his instincts. As a youth he was distinguished for his prowess. His maiden sword was fleshed at Fontarabia, where, although but sixteen years of age, he was considered, by his constancy in hardship, by his brilliant and desperate courage, and by the example of military discipline which he afforded to the troops, to have contributed in no small degree to the success of the Spanish arms.

In 1530 he accompanied the emperor in his campaign against the Turks. Charles, instinctively recognizing the merit of the youth who was destined to be the lifelong companion of his toils and glories, distinguished him with his favor at the opening of his career. Young, brave, and enthusiastic,

Fernando de Toledo at this period was as interesting a hero as ever illustrated the pages of a Castilian romance. His mad ride from Hungary to Spain and back again, accomplished in seventeen days, for the sake of a brief visit to his newly married wife, is not the least attractive episode in the history of an existence which was destined to be so dark and sanguinary. In 1535 he accompanied the emperor on his memorable expedition to Tunis. In 1546 and 1547 he was generalissimo in the war against the Smalkaldic League. His most brilliant feat of arms—perhaps the most brilliant exploit of the emperor's reign—was the passage of the Elbe and the battle of Mühlberg, accomplished in spite of Maximilian's bitter and violent reproaches and the tremendous possibilities of a defeat. That battle had finished the war. The gigantic and magnanimous John Frederick, surprised at his devotions in the church, fled in dismay, leaving his boots behind him, which for their superhuman size were ridiculously said afterward to be treasured among the trophies of the Toledo house. The rout was total. "I came, I saw, and God conquered," said the emperor, in pious parody of his immortal predecessor's epigram. Maximilian, with a thousand apologies for his previous insults, embraced the heroic Don Fernando over and over again, as, arrayed in a plain suit of blue armor, unadorned save with streaks of his enemies' blood, he returned from pursuit of the fugitives. So complete and so sudden was the victory that it was found impossible to account for it, save on the ground of miraculous interposition. Like Joshua in the vale of Ajalon, Don Fernando was supposed to have commanded the sun to stand still for a season, and to have been obeyed. Otherwise, how could the passage of the river, which was only concluded at six in the evening, and the complete overthrow of the Protestant forces, have all been accomplished within the narrow space of an April twilight? The reply of the duke to Henry II of France, who questioned him subsequently upon the subject, is well known: "Your Majesty, I was too much occupied that evening with what was taking place on the earth beneath to pay much heed to the evolutions of the heavenly bodies." Spared as he had been by his good fortune from taking any part in the Algerine expedition, or in witnessing the ignominious retreat from Innsbruck, he was obliged to submit to the intercalation of the disastrous siege of Metz in the long history of his successes. Doing the duty of a field-marshal and a sentinel, supporting his army by his firmness and his discipline when nothing else could have supported them, he was at last enabled, after half the hundred thousand men with whom Charles had begun the siege had been sacrificed, to induce his imperial master to raise the siege before the remaining fifty thousand had been frozen or starved to death.

The culminating career of Alva seemed to have closed in the mist which gathered around the setting star of empire. Having accompanied Philip to England in 1554 on his matrimonial expedition, he was destined in the following years, as viceroy and generalissimo of Italy, to be placed in a series of false positions. A great captain engaged in a little war, the champion of the cross in arms against the successor of St. Peter, he had extricated himself at last with his usual adroitness, but with very little glory. To him had been allotted the mortification, to another the triumph. The luster of his own name seemed to sink in the ocean, while that of a hated rival, with new-spangled ore, suddenly "flamed in the forehead of the morning sky." While he had been paltering with a dotard, whom he was forbidden to crush, Egmont had struck down the chosen troops of France and conquered her most illustrious commanders. Here was the unpardonable crime which could only be expiated by the blood of the victor. Unfortunately for his rival, the time was now approaching when the long-deferred revenge was to be satisfied.

On the whole, the Duke of Alva was inferior to no general of his age. As a disciplinarian he was foremost in Spain, perhaps in Europe. A spendthrift of time, he was an economist of blood, and this was, perhaps, in the eye of humanity, his principal virtue. "Time and myself are two," was a frequent observation of Philip, and his favorite general considered the maxim as applicable to war as to politics. Such were his qualities as a military commander. As a statesman he had neither experience nor talent. As a man his character was simple. He did not combine a great variety of vices, but those which he had were colossal, and he possessed no virtues. He was neither lustful nor intemperate, but his professed eulogists admitted his enormous avarice, while the world has agreed that such an amount of stealth and ferocity, of patient vindictiveness and universal bloodthirstiness, was never found in a savage beast of the forest, and but rarely in a human bosom. His history was now to show that his previous thrift of human life was not derived from any love of his kind. Personally he was stern and overbearing. As difficult of access as Philip himself, he was even more haughty to those who were admitted to his presence. He addressed everyone with the deprecating second person plural. Possessing the right of being covered in the presence of the Spanish monarch, he had been with difficulty brought to renounce it before the German emperor. He was of an illustrious family, but his territorial possessions were not extensive. His duchy was a small one, furnishing him with not more than fourteen thousand crowns of annual income, and with four hundred soldiers. He had, however, been a thrifty financier all his life, never having been without a handsome sum of ready money at interest. Ten years before his arrival in the Netherlands he was supposed to have already increased his income to forty thousand a year by the proceeds of his investments at Antwerp. As already intimated, his military character was sometimes profoundly misunderstood. He was often considered rather a pedantic than a practical commander, more capable to discourse of battles than to gain them. Notwithstanding that his long life had been an almost unbroken campaign, the ridiculous accusation of timidity was frequently made against him. A gentleman of the court of the Emperor Charles once addressed a letter to the duke with the title of "General of His Majesty's armies in the duchy of Milan in time of peace, and majordomo of the household in time of war." It was said that the lesson did the duke good, but that he rewarded very badly the nobleman who gave it, having subsequently caused his head to be taken off. In general, however, Alva manifested a philosphical contempt for the opinions expressed concerning his military fame, and was especially disdainful of criticism expressed by his own soldiers. "Recollect," said he, at a little later period, to Don John of Austria, "that the first foes with whom one has to contend are one's own troops, with their clamors for an engagement at this moment, and their murmurs about results at another; with their 'I thought that the battle should be fought,' or, 'It was my opinion that the occasion ought not to be lost. Your Highness will have opportunity enough to display valor, and will never be weak enough to be conquered by the babble of soldiers."

In person he was tall, thin, erect, with a small head, a long visage, lean yellow cheeks, dark twinkling eyes, a dust complexion, black bristling hair, and a long sable-silvered beard, descending in two waving streams upon his breast.

* * *

As his administration drew to a close, it was marked by disaster and disgrace on land and sea. The brilliant exploits by which he had struck terror into the heart of the Netherlanders, at Jemmingen and in Brabant, had been effaced by a handful of Hollanders, without discipline or experience. To the patriots the opportune capture of so considerable a personage as the admiral and governor of the northern province was of great advantage. Such of the hostages from Haarlem as had not yet been executed now escaped with their lives. Moreover, Sainte-Aldegonde, the eloquent patriot and confidential friend of Orange, who was taken prisoner, a few weeks later, in an action at Maaslandsluis, was preserved from inevitable destruction by the same cause. The prince hastened to assure the Duke of Alva that the same measure would be dealt to Bossu as should be meted to Sainte-Aldegonde. It was therefore impossible for the governor-general to execute his prisoner, and he was obliged to submit to the vexation of seeing a leading rebel and heretic in his power whom he dared not strike. Both the distinguished prisoners eventually regained their liberty.

The duke was doubtless lower sunk in the estimation of all classes than he had ever been before, during his long and generally successful life. The reverses sustained by his army, the belief that his master had grown cold toward him, the certainty that his career in the Netherlands was closing without a satisfactory result, the natural weariness produced upon men's minds by the contemplation of so monotonous and unmitigated a tyranny during so many years, all contributed to diminish his reputation. He felt himself odious alike to princes and to plebeians. With his cabinet councilors he had long been on unsatisfactory terms. President Tisnacq had died early in the summer, and Viglius, much against his will, had been induced, provisionally, to supply his place. But there was now hardly a pretense of friendship between the learned Frisian and the governor. Each cordially detested the other. Alva was weary of Flemish and Frisian advisers, however subservient, and was anxious to fill the whole council with Spaniards of the Vargas stamp. He had forced Viglius once more into office, only that, by a little delay, he might expel him and every Netherlander at the same moment. "Till this ancient set of dogmatizers be removed," he wrote Philip, "with Viglius, their chief, who teaches them all their lessons, nothing will go right. 'Tis of no use adding one or two Spaniards to fill vacancies; that is only pouring a flask of good wine into a hogshead of vinegar; it changes to vinegar likewise. Your Majesty will soon be able to reorganize the council at a blow, so that Italians or Spaniards, as you choose, may entirely govern the country."

Such being his private sentiments with regard to his confidential advisers, it may be supposed that his intercourse with his council during the year [1573] was not like to be amicable. Moreover, he had kept himself, for the most part, at a distance from the seat of government. During the military operations in Holland his headquarters had been at Amsterdam. Here, as the year drew to its close, he had become as unpopular as at Brussels. The time-serving and unpatriotic burghers, who, at the beginning of the spring, set up his bust in their houses and would give large sums for his picture in little, now broke his images and tore his portraits from their walls, for it was evident that the power of his name was gone, both with prince and people. Yet, certainly, those fierce demonstrations which had formerly surrounded his person with such an atmosphere of terror had not slackened or become less frequent than heretofore. He continued to prove that he could be barbarous, both on a grand and a minute scale, even as in preceding years he could ordain wholesale massacres with a breath and superintend in person the executions of individuals. This was illustrated, among other instances, by the cruel fate of Uitenhoove. That unfortunate nobleman, who had been taken prisoner in the course of the summer, was accused of having been engaged in the capture of Brill, and was therefore condemned by the duke to be roasted to death before a slow fire. He was accordingly fastened by a chain, a few feet in length, to a stake, around which the fagots were lighted. Here he was kept in slow torture for a long time, insulted by the gibes of the laughing Spaniards who surrounded him, until the executioner and his assistants, more humane than their superior, despatched the victim with their spears—a mitigation of punishment which was ill received by Alva. The governor had, however, no reason to remain in Amsterdam. Haarlem had fallen; Alkmaar was relieved; and Leyden—destined in its second seige to furnish so signal a chapter to the history of the war—was beleaguered, it was true, but, because known to be imperfectly supplied, was to be reduced by a blockade rather than by active operations. Don Francis Valdéz was accordingly left in command of the siege, which, however, after no memorable occurrences, was raised, as will soon be related.

The duke had contracted in Amsterdam an enormous amount of debt, both public and private. He accordingly, early in November, caused a proclamation to be made throughout the city, by sound of trumpet, that all persons having demands upon him were to present their claims in person, upon a specified day. During the night preceding the day so appointed, the duke and his train very noiselessly took their departure, without notice or beat of drum. By this masterly generalship his unhappy creditors were foiled upon the very eve of their anticipated triumph; the heavy accounts which had been contracted upon the faith of the king and the governor remained for the most part unpaid, and many opulent and respectable families were reduced to beggary. Such was the consequence of the unlimited confidence which they had reposed in the honor of their tyrant.

* * *

On the 18th of December the Duke of Alva departed from the provinces forever. With his further career this history has no concern, and it is not desirable to enlarge upon the biography of one whose name certainly never excites pleasing emotions. He had kept his bed for the greater part of the time during the last few weeks of his government—partly on account of his gout, partly to avoid being seen in his humiliation, but mainly, it was said, to escape the pressing demands of his creditors. He expressed a fear of traveling homeward through France, on the ground that he might very probably receive a shot out of a window as he went by. He complained pathetically that, after all his labors, he had not "gained the approbation of the king," while he had incurred "the malevolence and universal hatred of every individual in the country." Mondoucet, to whom he made the observation, was of the same opinion, and informed his master that the duke "had engendered such an extraordinary hatred in the hearts of all persons in the land that they would have fireworks in honor of his departure if they dared."

On his journey from the Netherlands he is said to have boasted that he had caused eighteen thousand six hundred inhabitants of the provinces to be executed during the period of his government. The number of those who had perished by battle, siege, starvation, and massacre defied computation. The duke was well received by his royal master, and remained in favor until a new adventure of Don Frederick brought father and son into disgrace. Having deceived and abandoned a maid of honor, he suddenly espoused his cousin, in order to avoid that reparation by marriage which was demanded for his offense. In consequence, both the duke and Don Frederick were imprisoned and banished, nor was Alva released till a general of experience was required for the conquest of Portugal. Thither, as it were with fetters on his legs, he went. After having accomplished the military enterprise intrusted to him, he fell into a lingering fever, at the termination of which he was so much reduced that he was only kept alive by milk, which he drank from a woman's breast. Such was the gentle second childhood of the man who had almost literally been drinking blood for seventy years. He died on the 12th of December, 1582.

The preceding pages have been written in vain if an elaborate estimate be now required of his character. His picture has been painted, as far as possible, by his own hand. His deeds, which are not disputed, and his written words, illustrate his nature more fully than could be done by the most eloquent pen. No attempt has been made to exaggerate his crimes or to extenuate his superior qualities. Virtues he had none, unless military excellence be deemed, as by the Romans, a virtue. In war, both as a science and a practical art, he excelled all the generals who were opposed to him in the Netherlands, and he was inferior to no commander in the world during the long and belligerent period to which his life belonged. Louis of Nassau possessed high reputation throughout Europe as a skilful and daring general. With raw volunteers he had overthrown an army of Spanish regulars, led by a Netherland chieftain of fame and experience; but when Alva took the field the scene was totally changed. The duke dealt him such a blow at Jemmingen as would have disheartened forever a less indomitable champion. Never had a defeat been more absolute. The patriot army was dashed out of existence, almost to a man, and its leader, naked and beggared, though not disheartened, sent back into Germany to construct his force and his schemes anew.

Having thus flashed before the eyes of the country the full terrors of his name and vindicated the ancient military renown of his nation, the duke was at liberty to employ the consummate tactics in which he could have given instruction to all the world against his most formidable antagonist. The country, paralyzed with fear, looked anxiously but supinely upon the scientific combat between the two great champions of Despotism and Protestantism which succeeded. It was soon evident that the conflict could terminate in but one way. The prince had considerable military abilities and enthusiastic courage; he lost none of his well-deserved reputation by the unfortunate issue of the campaign; he measured himself in arms with the great commander of the age, and defied him, day after day, in vain, to mortal combat. But it was equally certain that the duke's quiet game was played in the most masterly manner. His positions and his encampments were taken with faultless judgment, he skirmished wisely and coldly kept within the prescribed control, while the inevitable dissolution of the opposing force took place exactly as he had foreseen, and within the limits which he had predicted. Nor in the disastrous commencement of the year 1572 did the duke less signally manifest his military genius. Assailed as he was at every point, with the soil suddenly upheaving all around him, as by an earthquake, he did not lose his firmness nor his perspicacity. Certainly, if he had not been so soon assisted by that other earthquake which on St. Bartholomew's day caused all Christendom to tremble, and shattered the recent structure of Protestant freedom in the Netherlands, it might have been worse for his reputation. With Mons safe, the Flemish frontier guarded, France faithful, and thirty thousand men under the Prince of Orange in Brabant, the heroic brothers might well believe that the duke was "at their mercy." The treason of Charles IX "smote them as with a club," as the prince exclaimed in the bitterness of his spirit. Under the circumstances, his second campaign was a predestined failure, and Alva easily vanquished him by a renewed application of those dilatory arts which he so well understood.

The duke's military fame was unquestionable when he came to the provinces, and both in stricken fields and in long campaigns he showed how thoroughly it had been deserved; yet he left the Netherlands a baffled man. The prince might be many times defeated, but he was not to be conquered. As Alva penetrated into the heart of the ancient Batavian land he found himself overmatched as he had never been before, even by the most potent generals of his day. More audacious, more inventive, more desperate than all the commanders of that or any other age, the spirit of national freedom now taught the oppressor that it was invincible, except by annihilation. The same lesson had been read in the same thickets by the Nervii to Julius Caesar, by the Batavians to the legions of Vespasian; and now a loftier and a purer flame than that which inspired the national struggles against Rome glowed within the breasts of the descendants of the same people, and inspired them with the strength which comes from religious enthusiasm. More experienced, more subtle, more politic than Hermann; more devoted, more patient, more magnanimous than Civilis, and equal to either in valor and determination, William of Orange was a worthy embodiment of the Christian national resistance of the German race to a foreign tyranny. Alva had entered the Netherlands to deal with them as with conquered provinces. He found that the conquest was still to be made, and he left the land without having accomplished it. Through the sea of blood the Hollanders felt that they were marching to the promised land. More royal soldiers fell during the seven months' siege of Haarlem than the rebels had lost in the defeat of Jemmingen and in the famous campaign of Brabant. At Alkmaar the rolling waves of insolent conquest were stayed, and the tide then ebbed forever.

The accomplished soldier struggled hopelessly with the wild and passionate hatred which his tyranny had provoked. Neither his legions nor his consummate strategy availed him against an entirely desperate people. As a military commander, therefore, he gained, upon the whole, no additional laurels during his long administration of the Netherlands. Of all the other attributes to be expected of a man appointed to deal with a free country in a state of incipient rebellion, he manifested a signal deficiency. As a financier he exhibited a wonderful ignorance of the first principles of political economy. No man before ever gravely proposed to establish confiscation as a permanent source of revenue to the state; yet the annual product from the escheated property of the slaughtered heretics was regularly relied upon, during his administration, to replenish the king's treasury and to support the war of extermination against the king's subjects. Nor did statesman ever before expect a vast income from the commerce of a nation devoted to almost universal massacre. During the daily decimation of the people's lives he thought a daily decimation of their industry possible. His persecutions swept the land of those industrious classes which had made it the rich and prosperous commonwealth it had been so lately, while, at the same time, he found a "Peruvian mine," as he pretended, in the imposition of a tenth penny upon every one of its commercial transactions. He thought that a people crippled as this had been by the operations of the Blood-Council could pay ten per cent, not annually, but daily; not upon its income, but upon its capital; not once only, but every time the value constituting the capital changed hands. He had boasted that he should require no funds from Spain, but that, on the contrary, he should make annual remittances to the royal treasury at home from the proceeds of his imposts and confiscations; yet, notwithstanding these resources, and notwithstanding twenty-five millions of gold in five years sent by Philip from Madrid, the exchequer of the provinces was barren and bankrupt when his successor arrived. Requeséns found neither a penny in the public treasury nor the means of raising one.

As an administrator of the civil and judicial affairs of the country, Alva at once reduced its institutions to a frightful simplicity. In the place of the ancient laws of which the Netherlanders were so proud he substituted the Blood-Council. This tribunal was even more arbitrary than the Inquisition. Never was a simpler apparatus for tyranny devised than this great labor-saving machine. Never was so great a quantity of murder and robbery achieved with such despatch and regularity. Sentences, executions, and confiscations, to an incredible extent, were turned out daily with appalling precision. For this invention Alva is alone responsible. The tribunal and its councilors were the work and the creatures of his hand, and faithfully did they accomplish the dark purpose of their existence. Nor can it be urged, in extenuation of the governor's crimes, that he was but the blind and fanatically loyal slave of his sovereign. A noble nature could not have contaminated itself with such slaughter-house work, but might have sought to mitigate the royal policy without forswearing allegiance. A nature less rigid than iron would have at least manifested compunction as it found itself converted into a fleshless instrument of massacre. More decided than his master, however, he seemed by his promptness to rebuke the dilatory genius of Philip. The king seemed at times to loiter over his work, teasing and tantalizing his appetite for vengeance before it should be gratified. Alva, rapid and brutal, scorned such epicureanism. He strode with gigantic steps over haughty statutes and popular constitutions, crushing alike the magnates who claimed a bench of monarchs for their jury, and the ignoble artisans who could appeal only to the laws of their land. From the pompous and theatrical scaffolds of Egmont and Horn, to the nineteen halters prepared by Master Karl to hang up the chief bakers and brewers of Brussels on their own thresholds; from the beheading of the twenty nobles on the Horse Market, in the opening of the governor's career, to the roasting alive of Uitenhoove at its close; from the block on which fell the honored head of Antony Straalen, to the obscure chair in which the ancient gentlewoman of Amsterdam suffered death for an act of vicarious mercy; from one year's end to another's; from the most signal to the most squalid scenes of sacrifice, the eye and hand of the great master directed, without weariness, the task imposed by the sovereign.

No doubt the work of almost indiscriminate massacre had been duly mapped out. Not often in history has a governor arrived to administer the affairs of a province where the whole population, three millions strong, had been formally sentenced to death. As time wore on, however, he even surpassed the bloody instructions which he had received. He waved aside the recommendations of the Blood-Council to mercy; he dissuaded the monarch from attempting the path of clemency, which, for secret reasons, Philip was inclined at one period to attempt. The governor had, as he assured the king, been using gentleness in vain, and he was now determined to try what a little wholesome severity could effect. These words were written immediately after the massacre at Haarlem.

With all the bloodshed at Mons and Naarden and Mechlin, and by the Council of Tumults, daily for six years long, still crying from the ground, he taxed himself with a misplaced and foolish tenderness to the people. He assured the king that when Alkmaar should be taken he would not spare a "living soul among its whole population"; and, as his parting advice, he recommended that *every city in the Netherlands should be burned to the ground*, except a few which could be occupied permanently by royal troops. On the whole, so finished a picture of a perfect and absolute tyranny has rarely been presented to mankind by history as in Alva's administration of the Netherlands.

The tens of thousands in those miserable provinces who fell victim to the gallows, the sword, the stake, the living grave, or to living banishment, have never been counted, for those statistics of barbarity are often effaced from human record. Enough, however, is known, and enough has been recited in the preceding pages. No mode in which human beings have ever caused their fellow creatures to suffer was omitted from daily practice. Men, women, and children, old and young, nobles and paupers, opulent burghers, hospital patients, lunatics, dead bodies, all were indiscriminately made to furnish food for the scaffold and the stake. Men were tortured, beheaded, hanged by the neck and by the legs, burned before slow fires, pinched to death with red-hot tongs, broken upon the wheel, starved, and flayed alive. Their skins, stripped from the living body, were stretched upon drums, to be beaten in the march of their brethren to the gallows. The bodies of many who had died a natural death were exhumed, and their festering remains hanged upon the gibbet, on pretext that they had died without receiving the sacrament, but in reality that their property might become the legitimate prey of the treasury. Marriages of long standing were dissolved by order of government, that rich heiresses might be married against their will to foreigners whom they abhorred. Women and children were executed for the crime of assisting their fugitive husbands and parents with a penny in their utmost need, and even for consoling them with a letter in their exile. Such was the regular course of affairs as administered by the Blood-Council. The additional barbarities committed amid the sack and ruin of those blazing and starving cities are almost beyond belief: unborn infants were torn from the living bodies of their mothers; women and children were violated by the thousands, and whole populations burned and hacked to pieces by soldiers in every mode which cruelty, in its wanton ingenuity, could devise. Such was the administration of which Vargas affirmed, at its close, that too much mercy—*"nimia misericordia"*—had been its ruin.

Even Philip, inspired by secret views, became wearied of the governor, who, at an early period, had already given offense by his arrogance. To commemorate his victories, the viceroy had erected a colossal statue, not to his monarch, but to himself. To proclaim the royal pardon, he had seated himself upon a golden throne. Such insolent airs could be ill forgiven by the absolute king. Too cautious to provoke an open rupture, he allowed the governor, after he had done all his work, and more than all his work, to retire without disgrace, but without a triumph. For the sins of that administration, master and servant are in equal measure responsible.

The character of the Duke of Alva, so far as the Netherlands are concerned, seems almost like a caricature. As a creation of fiction, it would seem grotesque; yet even that hardy historical skepticism, which delights in reversing the judgment of centuries and in re-establishing reputations long since degraded to the dust, must find it difficult to alter this man's position. No historical decision is final; an appeal to a more remote posterity, founded upon more accurate evidence, is always valid; but when the verdict has been pronounced upon facts which are undisputed, and upon testimony from the criminal's lips, there is little chance of a reversal of the sentence. It is an affectation of philosophical candor to extenuate vices which are not only avowed, but claimed as virtues.

A Queen Possessed by a Hundred Thousand Devils

JOHN RICHARD GREEN

1533–1603. Green's A Short History of the English People *published in 1874, was one of the most popular histories ever written. It is still one of the best. A writer of great skill, Green was interested in cultural, economic, and social matters as well as in politics and war. This excerpt from his* A History of the English People, *an expanded version of his* Short History, *is a provocative appraisal of a great and complex character, Elizabeth I. It is strongly colored by the romanticism and righteous moral judgments of the Victorians.*

There was little indeed in her outward demeanor to give any indication of her greatness. To the world about her the temper of Elizabeth recalled in its strange contrasts the mixed blood within her veins. She was at once the daughter of Henry and of Anne Boleyn. From her father she inherited her frank and hearty address, her love of popularity and of free intercourse with the people, her dauntless courage and her amazing self-confidence. Her harsh, manlike voice, her impetuous will, her pride, her furious outbursts of anger came to her with her Tudor blood. She rated great nobles as if they were schoolboys; she met the insolence of Lord Essex with a box on the ear; she broke now and then into the gravest deliberations to swear

186

at her ministers like a fishwife. Strangely in contrast with these violent outlines of her father's temper stood the sensuous, self-indulgent nature she drew from Anne Boleyn. Splendor and pleasure were with Elizabeth the very air she breathed. Her delight was to move in perpetual progresses from castle to castle through a series of gorgeous pageants, fanciful and extravagant as a caliph's dream. She loved gaiety and laughter and wit. A happy retort or a finished compliment never failed to win her favor. She hoarded jewels. Her dresses were innumerable. Her vanity remained, even to old age, the vanity of a coquette in her teens. No adulation was too fulsome for her, no flattery of her beauty too gross. She would play with her rings that her courtiers might note the delicacy of her hands; or dance a coranto that an ambassador, hidden dexterously behind a curtain, might report her sprightliness to his master. Her levity, her frivolous laughter, her unwomanly jests gave color to a thousand scandals. Her character in fact, like her portraits, was utterly without shade. Of womanly reserve or self-restraint she knew nothing. No instinct of delicacy veiled the voluptuous temper which broke out in the romps of her girlhood and showed itself almost ostentatiously through her later life. Personal beauty in a man was a sure passport to her liking. She patted handsome young squires on the neck when they knelt to kiss her hand, and fondled her "sweet Robin," Lord Leicester, in the face of the Court.

It was no wonder that the statesmen whom she outwitted held Elizabeth to be little more than a frivolous woman, or that Philip of Spain wondered how "a wanton" could hold in check the policy of the Escurial. But the Elizabeth whom they saw was far from being all of Elizabeth. Wilfulness and triviality played over the surface of a nature hard as steel, a temper purely intellectual, the very type of reason untouched by imagination or passion. Luxurious and pleasure-loving as she seemed, the young Queen lived simply and frugally, and she worked hard. Her vanity and caprice had no weight whatever with her in state affairs. The coquette of the presence-chamber became the coolest and hardest of politicians at the council-board. Fresh from the flattery of her courtiers, she would tolerate no flattery in the closet; she was herself plain and downright of speech with her counsellors, and she looked for a corresponding plainness of speech in return. The very choice of her advisers indeed showed Elizabeth's ability. She had a quick eye for merit of any sort, and a wonderful power of enlisting its whole energy in her service. The sagacity which chose Cecil and Walsingham was just as unerring in its choice of the meanest of her agents. Her success indeed in securing from the beginning of her reign to its end, with the single exception of Leicester, precisely the right men for the work she set them to do sprang in great measure from the noblest characteristic of her intellect. If in loftiness of aim the Queen's temper fell below many of the tempers of her time, in the breadth of its range, in the universality of its sympathy it stood far above them all. Elizabeth could talk poetry with Spenser and philosophy with Bruno; she could discus Euphuism with Lyly, and enjoy the chivalry of Essex; she could turn from talk of the last fashions to pore with Cecil over despatches and treasury books; she could pass from tracking traitors with Walsingham to settle points of doctrine with Parker, or to calculate with Frobisher the chances of a north-west passage to the Indies. The versatility and many-sidedness of her mind enabled her to understand every phase of the intellectual movement about her, and to fix by a sort of instinct on its higher representatives.

It was only on its intellectual side indeed that Elizabeth touched the England of her day. All its moral aspects were simply dead to her. It was a time when men were being lifted into nobleness by the new moral energy which seemed suddenly to pulse through the whole people, when honor and enthusiasm took colors of poetic beauty, and religion became a chivalry. But the finer sentiments of the men about her touched Elizabeth simply as the fair tints of a picture would have touched her. She made her market with equal indifference out of the heroism of William of Orange or the bigotry of Philip. The noblest aims and lives were only counters on her board. She was the one soul in her realm whom the news of St. Bartholomew stirred to no thirst for vengeance; and while England was thrilling with the triumph over the Armada, its Queen was coolly grumbling over the cost, and making her profit out of the spoiled provisions she had ordered for the fleet that saved her. No womanly sympathy bound her even to those who stood closest to her life. She loved Leicester indeed; she was grateful to Cecil. But for the most part she was deaf to the voices either of love or gratitude. She accepted such services as were never rendered to any other English sovereign without a thought of return. Walsingham spent his fortune in saving her life and her throne, and she left him to die a beggar. But, as if by a strange irony, it was to this very lack of womanly sympathy that she owed some of the grandest features of her character. If she was without love she was without hate. She cherished no petty resentments; she never stooped to envy or suspicion of the men who served her. She was indifferent to abuse. Her good humor was never ruffled by the charges of wantonness and cruelty with which the Jesuits filled every Court in Europe. She was insensible to fear. Her life became at last a mark for assassin after assassin, but the thought of peril was the thought hardest to bring home to her. Even when Catholic plots broke out in her very household she would listen to no proposals for the removal of Catholics from her Court.

If any trace of her sex lingered in the Queen's actual statesmanship, it was seen in the simplicity and tenacity of purpose that often underlies a woman's fluctuations of feeling. It was the directness and steadiness of her aims which gave her her marked superiority over the statesmen of her time. No nobler group of ministers ever gathered round a council-board than those who gathered round the council-board of Elizabeth. But she was the instrument of none. She listened, she weighed, she used or put by the counsels of each in turn, but her policy as a whole was her own. It was a policy, not of genius, but of good sense. Her aims were simple and obvious: to preserve her throne, to keep England out of war, to restore civil and religious order. Something of womanly caution and timidity perhaps backed the passionless indifference with which she set aside the larger schemes of ambition which were ever opening before her eyes. In later days she was resolute in her refusal of the Low Countries. She rejected with a laugh the offers of the Protestants to make her "head of the religion" and "mistress of the seas." But her amazing success in the end sprang mainly from this wise limitation of her aims. She had a finer sense than any of her counsellors of her real resources; she knew instinctively how far she could go and what she could do. Her cold, critical intellect was never swayed by enthusiasm or by panic either to exaggerate or to under-estimate her risks or her power. Of political wisdom indeed in its larger and more generous sense Elizabeth had little or none; but her political tact was unerring. She seldom saw her course at a glance, but she played with a hundred courses, fitfully and discursively, as a musician runs his fingers over the key-board, till she hit suddenly upon the right one. Her nature was essentially practical and of the present. She distrusted a plan in fact just in proportion to its speculative range or its outlook into the future. Her notion of statesmanship lay in watching how things turned out around her, and in seizing the moment for making the best of them.

Such a policy as this, limited, practical, tentative as it always was, had little of grandeur and originality about it; it was apt indeed to degenerate into mere trickery and finesse. But it was a policy suited to the England of her day, to its small resources and the transitional character of its religious and political belief, and it was eminently suited to Elizabeth's peculiar powers. It was a policy of detail, and in details her wonderful readiness and ingenuity found scope for their exercise. "No War, my Lords," the Queen used to cry imperiously at the council-board, "No War!" but her hatred of war sprang not so much from aversion to blood or to expense, real as was her aversion to both, as from the fact that peace left the field open to the diplomatic manoeuvres and intrigues in which she excelled. Her delight in the consciousness of her ingenuity broke out in a thousand puckish freaks, freaks in which one can hardly see any purpose beyond the purpose of sheer mystification. She revelled in "bye-ways" and "crooked ways." She played with grave cabinets as a cat plays with a mouse, and with much of the same feline delight in the mere embarrassment of her victims. When she was weary of mystifying foreign statesmen she turned to find fresh sport in mystifying her own ministers. Had Elizabeth written the story of her reign she would have prided herself, not on the triumph of England or the ruin of Spain, but on the skill with which she had hoodwinked and outwitted every statesman in Europe during fifty years. Nothing is more revolting, but nothing is more characteristic of the Queen than her shameless mendacity. It was an age of political lying, but in the profusion and recklessness of her lies Elizabeth stood without a peer in Christendom. A falsehood was to her simply an intellectual means of meeting a difficulty; and the ease with which she asserted or denied whatever suited her purpose was only equalled by the cynical indifference with which she met the exposure of her lies as soon as their purpose was answered. Her trickery in fact had its political value. Ignoble and wearisome as the Queen's diplomacy seems to us now, tracking it as we do through a thousand despatches, it succeeded in its main end, for it gained time, and every year that was gained doubled Elizabeth's strength. She made as dexterous use of the foibles of her temper. Her levity carried her gaily over moments of detection and embarrassment where better women would have died of shame. She screened her tentative and hesitating statesmanship under the natural timidity and vacillation of her sex. She turned her very luxury sports to good account. There were moments of grave danger in her reign when the country remained indifferent to its peril, as it saw the Queen give her days to hawking and hunting, and her nights to dancing and plays. Her vanity and affectation, her womanly fickleness and caprice, all had their part in the diplomatic comedies she played with the successive candidates for her hand. If political necessities made her life a lonely one, she had at any rate the satisfaction of averting war and conspiracies by love sonnets and romantic interviews, or of gaining a year of tranquillity by the dexterous spinning out of a flirtation.

As we track Elizabeth through her tortuous mazes of lying and intrigue, the sense of her greatness is almost lost in a sense of contempt. But wrapped as they were in a cloud of mystery, the aims of her policy were throughout temperate and simple, and they were pursued with a rare tenacity. The sudden acts of energy which from time to time broke her habitual hesitation proved that it was no hesitation of weakness. Elizabeth could wait and finesse; but when the hour was come she could strike, and strike hard. Her natural temper indeed tended to a rash self-confidence rather than to self-distrust. "I have the heart of a King," she cried at a moment of utter peril, and it was with a kingly unconsciousness of the dangers about her that she fronted them for fifty years. She had, as strong natures always have, an unbounded confidence in her luck. "Her Majesty counts much on Fortune," Walsingham wrote bitterly; "I wish she would trust more in Almighty God."

The diplomatists who censured at one moment her irresolution, her delay, her changes of front, censured at the next her "obstinacy," her iron will, her defiance of what seemed to them inevitable ruin. "This woman," Philip's envoy wrote after a wasted remonstrance, "this woman is possessed by a hundred thousand devils." To her own subjects, who knew nothing of her manoeuvres and flirtations, of her "bye-ways" and "crooked ways," she seemed the embodiment of dauntless resolution. Brave as they were, the men who swept the Spanish Main or glided between the icebergs of Baffin's Bay never doubted that the palm of bravery lay with their Queen.

The Execution at Fotheringhay Castle

JAMES ANTHONY FROUDE

1587. The beautiful and reckless Mary Queen of Scots was a prisoner in various English castles for nineteen years, ever since she fled across the border from her rebellious nobles. As the rightful heir to the English throne when Elizabeth should die and as an ardent Catholic in a Protestant country with a large Catholic minority, Mary was inevitably involved in the schemes of Philip II of Spain. She herself expressly approved the murder of Elizabeth in the Babington conspiracy. Today no historian questions Mary's devotion to the Catholic faith. Yet the distinguished Victorian historian James Anthony Froude was so fierce in his Protestant bias that he did question Mary's sincerity and damaged only a little the quality of his famous and brilliant account of Mary's execution.

The end had come. She had long professed to expect it, but the clearest expectation is not certainty. The scene for which she had affected to prepare she was to encounter in its dread reality, and all her busy schemes, her dreams of vengeance, her visions of a revolution, with herself ascending out of the convulsion and seating herself on her rival's throne—all were gone. She had played deep, and the dice had gone against her.

Yet in death, if she encountered it bravely, victory was still possible. Could she but sustain to the last the character of a calumniated suppliant accepting heroically for God's sake and her creed's the concluding stroke of a long series of wrongs, she might stir a tempest of indignation which, if it could not save herself, might at least overwhelm her enemy. Persisting, as she persisted to the last, in denying all knowledge of Babington, it would be affectation to credit her with a genuine feeling of religion; but the imperfection of her motive exalts the greatness of her fortitude. To an impassioned believer death is comparatively easy.

Her chaplain was lodged in a separate part of the castle. The Commissioners, who were as anxious that her execution should wear its real character as she was herself determined to convert it into a martyrdom, refused, perhaps unwisely, to allow him access to her, and offered her again the assistance of an Anglican Dean. They gave her an advantage over them which she did not fail to use. She would not let the Dean come near her. She sent a note to the chaplain telling him that she had meant to receive the sacrament, but as it might not be she must content herself with a general confession. She bade him watch through the night and pray for her. In the morning when she was brought out she might perhaps see him, and receive his blessing on her knees. She supped cheerfully, giving her last meal with her attendants a character of sacred parting; afterwards she drew aside her apothecary M. Gorion, and asked him if she might depend upon his fidelity; when he satisfied her that she might trust him, she said she had a letter and two diamonds which she wished to send to Mendoza. He undertook to melt some drug and conceal them in it where they would never be looked for, and promised to deliver them faithfully. One of the jewels was for Mendoza himself; the other and the largest was for Philip. It was to be a sign that she was dying for the truth, and was meant also to bespeak his care for her friends and servants. Every one of them so far as she was able, without forgetting a name, she commended to his liberality. Arundel, Paget, Morgan, the Archbishop of Glasgow, Westmorland, Throgmorton, the Bishop of Ross, her two secretaries, the ladies who had shared the trials of her imprisonment, she remembered them all, and specified the sums which she desired Philip to bestow upon them. And as Mary Stuart then and throughout her life never lacked gratitude to those who had been true to her, so then as always she remembered her enemies. There was no cant about her, no unreal talk of forgiveness of injuries. She bade Gorion tell Philip it was her last prayer that he should persevere, notwithstanding her death, in the invasion of England. It was God's quarrel, she said, and worthy of his greatness; and as soon as he had conquered it, she desired him not to forget how she had been treated by Cecil, and Leicester, and Walsingham; by Lord Huntingdon, who had ill-used her fifteen years before at Tutbury; by Sir Amyas Paulet, and Secretary Wade.

Her last night was a busy one. As she said herself there was much to be done and the time was short. A few lines to the King of France were dated two hours after midnight. They were to insist for the last time that she was innocent of the conspiracy, that she was dying for religion, and for having asserted her right to the Crown; and to beg that out of the sum

which he owed her, her servants' wages might be paid, and masses provided
for her soul. After this she slept for three or four hours, and then rose and
with the most elaborate care prepared to encounter the end.

At eight in the morning the Provost-Marshal knocked at the outside
door which communicated with her suite of apartments. It was locked
and no one answered, and he went back in some trepidation lest the fears
might prove true which had been entertained the preceding evening. On
his returning with the Sheriff, however, a few minutes later, the door was
open, and they were confronted with the tall majestic figure of Mary Stuart
standing before them in splendor. The plain grey dress had been exchanged
for a robe of black satin; her jacket was of black satin also, looped and
slashed and trimmed with velvet. Her false hair was arranged studiously
with a coif, and over her head and falling down over her back was a white
veil of delicate lawn. A crucifix of gold hung from her neck. In her hand
she held a crucifix of ivory, and a number of jewelled paternosters were
attached to her girdle. Led by two of Paulet's gentlemen, the Sheriff walking before her, she passed to the chamber of presence in which she had
been tried, where Shrewsbury, Kent, Paulet, Drury and others were waiting
to receive her. Andrew Melville, Sir Robert's brother, who had been master
of her household, was kneeling in tears. "Melville," she said, "you should
rather rejoice than weep that the end of my troubles is come. Tell my
friends I die a true Catholic. Commend me to my son. Tell him I have
done nothing to prejudice his kingdom of Scotland, and so good Melville,
farewell." She kissed him, and turning asked for her chaplain du Preau. He
was not present. There had been a fear of some religious melodrama which
it was thought well to avoid. Her ladies, who had attempted to follow her,
had been kept back also. She could not afford to leave the account of her
death to be reported by enemies and Puritans, and she required assistance
for the scene which she meditated. Missing them she asked the reason for
their absence, and said she wished them to see her die. Kent said he feared
they might scream or faint, or attempt perhaps to dip their handkerchiefs
in her blood. She undertook that they should be quiet and obedient. "The
Queen," she said, "would never deny her so slight a respect"; and when
Kent still hesitated, she added with tears, "You know I am cousin to your
Queen, of the blood of Henry the Seventh, a married Queen of France, and
anointed Queen of Scotland."

It was impossible to refuse. She was allowed to take six of her own people
with her, and selected them herself. She chose her physician Burgoyne,
Andrew Melville, the apothecary Gorion, and her surgeon, with two ladies,
Elizabeth Kennedy and Curle's young wife Barbara Mowbray, whose child
she had baptized.

"*Allons donc,*" she then said—"Let us go," and passing out attended by the Earls, and leaning on the arm of an officer of the guard, she descended the great staircase to the hall. Thousands of people were collected outside the walls. About three hundred knights and gentlemen of the county had been admitted to witness the execution. The tables and forms had been removed, and a great wood fire was blazing in the chimney. At the upper end of the hall, above the fire-place, but near it, stood the scaffold, twelve feet square and two feet and a half high. It was covered with black cloth; a low rail ran round it covered with black cloth also, and the Sheriff's guard of halberdiers were ranged on the floor below on the four sides to keep off the crowd. On the scaffold was the block, black like the rest; a square black cushion was placed behind it, and behind the cushion a black chair; on the right were two other chairs for the Earls. The axe leant against the rail, and two masked figures stood like mutes on either side at the back. The Queen of Scots as she swept in seemed as if coming to take a part in some solemn pageant. Not a muscle of her face could be seen to quiver; she ascended the scaffold with absolute composure, looked round her smiling, and sat down. Shrewsbury and Kent followed and took their places, the Sheriff stood at her left hand, and Beale then mounted a platform and read the warrant aloud.

In all the assembly Mary Stuart seemed the person least interested in the words which were assigning her to death.

"Madam," said Lord Shrewsbury to her, when the reading was ended, "you hear what we are commanded to do."

"You will do your duty," she answered, and rose as if to kneel and pray.

The Dean of Peterborough, Dr. Fletcher, approached the rail. "Madam," he began with a low obeisance, "the Queen's most excellent Majesty"; "Madam, the Queen's most excellent Majesty"—thrice he commenced his sentence, wanting words to pursue it. When he repeated the words a fourth time, she cut him short.

"Mr. Dean," she said, "I am a Catholic, and must die a Catholic. It is useless to attempt to move me, and your prayers will avail me but little."

"Change your opinion, Madam," he cried, his tongue being loosed at last; "repent of your sins, settle your faith in Christ, by him to be saved."

"Trouble not yourself further, Mr. Dean," she answered; "I am settled in my own faith, for which I mean to shed my blood."

"I am sorry, Madam," said Shrewsbury, "to see you so addicted to Popery."

"That image of Christ you hold there," said Kent, "will not profit you if he be not engraved in your heart."

She did not reply, and turning her back on Fletcher knelt for her own devotions.

He had been evidently instructed to impair the Catholic complexion of the scene, and the Queen of Scots was determined that he should not succeed. When she knelt he commenced an extempore prayer in which the assembly joined. As his voice sounded out in the hall she raised her own, reciting with powerful deep-chested tones the penitential psalms in Latin, introducing English sentences at intervals, that the audience might know what she was saying, and praying with especial distinctness for her holy father the Pope.

From time to time, with conspicuous vehemence, she struck the crucifix against her bosom, and then, as the Dean gave up the struggle, leaving her Latin, she prayed in English wholly, still clear and loud. She prayed for the Church which she had been ready to betray, for her son, whom she had disinherited, for the Queen whom she had endeavored to murder. She prayed God to avert his wrath from England, that England which she had sent a last message to Philip to beseech him to invade. She forgave her enemies, whom she had invited Philip not to forget, and then, praying to the saints to intercede for her with Christ, and kissing the crucifix and crossing her own breast, "Even as thy arms, oh Jesus," she cried, "were spread upon the cross, so receive me into thy mercy and forgive my sins."

With these words she rose; the black mutes stepped forward, and in the usual form begged her forgiveness.

"I forgive you," she said, "for now I hope you shall end all my troubles." They offered their help in arranging her dress. "Truly, my lords," she said with a smile to the Earls, "I never had such grooms waiting on me before." Her ladies were allowed to come up upon the scaffold to assist her; for the work to be done was considerable, and had been prepared with no common thought.

She laid her crucifix on her chair. The chief executioner took it as a perquisite, but was ordered instantly to lay it down. The lawn veil was lifted carefully off, not to disturb the hair, and was hung upon the rail. The black robe was next removed. Below it was a petticoat of crimson velvet. The black jacket followed, and under the jacket was a body of crimson satin. One of her ladies handed her a pair of crimson sleeves, with which she hastily covered her arms; and thus she stood on the black scaffold with the black figures all around her, blood-red from head to foot.

Her reasons for adopting so extraordinary a costume must be left to conjecture. It is only certain that it must have been carefully studied, and that the pictorial effect must have been appalling.

The women, whose firmness had hitherto born the trial, began now to give way, spasmodic sobs bursting from them which they could not check. "*Ne criez vous*," she said, "*j'ay promis pour vous*." Struggling bravely, they crossed their breasts again and again, she crossing them in turn and bidding them pray for her. Then she knelt on the cushion. Barbara Mowbray bound her eyes with a handkerchief. "*Adieu*," she said, smiling for the last time and waving her hand to them, *"Adieu, au revoir."* They stepped back from off the scaffold and left her alone. On her knees she repeated the Psalm, *In te, Domine, confido,* "In thee, oh Lord, have I put my trust." Her shoulders being exposed, two scars became visible, one on either side, and the Earls being now a little behind her, Kent pointed to them with his white wand and looked enquiringly at his companion. Shrewsbury whispered that they were the remains of two abscesses from which she had suffered while living with him at Sheffield.

When the psalm was finished she felt for the block, and laying down her head muttered: *"In manus, Domine, tuas, commendo animam meam."* The hard wood seemed to hurt her, for she placed her hands under her neck. The executioners gently removed them, lest they should deaden the blow, and then one of them holding her slightly, the other raised the axe and struck. The scene had been too trying even for the practised headsman of the Tower. His arm wandered. The blow fell on the knot of the handkerchief, and scarcely broke the skin. She neither spoke nor moved. He struck again, this time more effectively. The head hung by a shred of skin, which he divided without withdrawing the axe; and at once a metamorphosis was witnessed, strange as was ever wrought by wand of fabled enchanter. The coif fell off and the false plaits. The labored illusion vanished. The lady who had knelt before the block was in the maturity of grace and loveliness. The executioner, when he raised the head, as usual, to shew it to the crowd, exposed the withered features of a grizzled, wrinkled old woman.

"So perish all enemies of the Queen," said the Dean of Peterborough. A loud Amen rose over the hall. "Such end," said the Earl of Kent, rising and standing over the body, "to the Queen's and the Gospel's enemies."

Orders had been given that everything which she had worn should be immediately destroyed, that no relics should be carried off to work imaginary miracles. Sentinels stood at the doors, who allowed no one to pass out without permission; and after the first pause, the Earls still keeping their places, the body was stripped. It then appeared that a favorite lapdog had followed its mistress unperceived, and was concealed under her clothes; when discovered it gave a short cry, and seated itself between the head and the neck, from which the blood was still flowing. It was carried away and carefully washed, and then beads, paternosters, handkerchief—each particle of dress which the blood had touched, with the cloth on the block and on the scaffold, was burnt in the hall fire in the presence of the crowd. The scaffold was next removed: a brief account of the execution was drawn up, with which Henry Talbot, Lord Shrewsbury's son, was sent to London, and then every one was dismissed. Silence settled down on Fotheringhay, and the last scene of the life of Mary Stuart, in which tragedy and melodrama were so strangely intermingled, was over.

A spectator, who was one of her warmest admirers, describes her bearing as infinitely transcending the power of the most accomplished actor to represent. The association of the stage was, perhaps, unconsciously suggested by what was in fact, notwithstanding the tremendous reality with which it closed, the most brilliant acting throughout. The plain grey dress would have sufficed, had she cared only to go through with simplicity the part which was assigned her. She intended to produce a dramatic sensation, and she succeeded. The self-possession was faultless, the courage splendid. Never did any human creature meet death more bravely; yet, in the midst of the admiration and pity which cannot be refused her, it is not to be forgotten that she was leaving the world with a lie upon her lips. She was a bad woman, disguised in the livery of a martyr, and, if in any sense at all she was suffering for her religion, it was because she had shewn herself capable of those detestable crimes which in the sixteenth century appeared to be the proper fruits of it.

To assume and carry through the character of a victim of religious intolerance, to exhibit herself as an example of saintliness, suffering for devotion to the truth, would be to win the victory over Elizabeth, even in defeat and death to fasten upon her the reputation of a persecutor which she had most endeavored to avoid, to stamp her name with infamy, and possibly to drag her down to destruction.

Nor can it be said that she failed. She could not, indeed, stay the progress of the Reformation, make England a province of Spain, or arrest the dissolution of an exploded creed; but she became a fitting tutelary saint for the sentimental Romanism of the modern world. She has had her revenge, if not on Elizabeth living, yet on her memory in the annals of her country, and English history will continue, probably to the end of time, to represent the treatment of Mary Stuart, which, if it erred at all, erred from the beginning on the side of leniency and weakness, as the one indelible stain on the reputation of the great Queen.

"Who now doubts," writes an eloquent modern writer, "that it would have been wiser in Elizabeth to spare her life?" Rather, the political wisdom of a critical and difficult act has never in the world's history been more signally justified. It cut away the only interest on which the Scotch and English Catholics could possibly have combined. It determined Philip upon the undisguised pursuit of the English throne, and it enlisted against him and his projects the passionate patriotism of the English nobility, who refused to be tempted, even by their creed, to betray the independence of their country. At once and forever it destroyed the hope that the Spanish Armada would find a party to welcome it. The entire Catholic organization, as directed against England, was smitten with paralysis; and the Queen found herself, when the invader arrived at last, supported by the loyal enthusiasm of an undivided nation.

San Lorenzo de Escorial

GARRETT MATTINGLY

1587. Philip II, who could authorize atrocities and assassinations in the sincere belief that they would be pleasing to God, was a conscientious, industrious, and pious monarch. This glimpse of him in his secluded retreat in the Escorial shortly after he received word of the execution of Mary Queen of Scots is taken from The Armada, *one of the finest histories of recent years, a notable combination of original scholarship and literary craftsmanship.*

Mendoza's dispatches for Spain may have arrived as soon as those for Rome. The Venetian ambassador finally heard that the news of Mary Stuart's death had reached the Escorial on the night of March 23rd. It should have. From Paris the route to Madrid was tougher than to Rome, more dangerous in Gascony, bleaker and steeper in Old Castile, but rather shorter. The courier for Spain had started first, he would have had the best mounts in the ambassador's stable, and as soon as he reached the border his pouch would have been sped southward by the royal post. But we cannot be sure. Although he tried, Philip II could not repair with his own pen every error and omission of his underlings. This dispatch lacks a date of receipt. The diplomatic corps knew nothing of Mary's death until March

31st, but they were shivering in Madrid, nearly thirty miles by road from the Escorial, and even when these miles were not foul and slippery with rain and snow, court gossip was often a week stale before the ambassador heard it. They could only wonder meanwhile what the king was doing up there on his mountain.

Whenever the news came, up to March 31st Philip was doing nothing. For that there could be more than one reason. When a diplomatic pouch reached the Escorial, its contents, however urgent, were receipted by the appropriate official, decyphered by the appropriate clerk and placed, along with the originals, on the appropriate corner of the long table in the cheerless little room in which the king now spent most of his waking hours. All sorts of official papers lay piled on that long table. It held the correspondence of ambassadors, the reports of viceroys and governors, of customs and treasury and municipal officials; it held petitions and memorials and the findings of judicial investigations, the accounts of dock-yards and mints and mines, and of the royal household. Every day the papers came in from all the kingdoms of Castile and of the crowns of Aragon, from Portugal now, too, and from Philip's other dominions, from Naples and Sicily and Milan, from Franche-Comté and the Belgian provinces, from Mexico and Peru and Brazil, from Golden Goa and African Sofala and the islands of the eastern and western seas. And nobody, surely, had ever had so many papers to read. Sooner or later Philip read, if not all, at least a very great many of them, leaving in his spidery scrawl in their margins shrewd statesmanlike comments and trivial corrections of spelling and grammar, each annotation a witness to posterity of his appalling, his stupefying industry. Naturally, he sometimes got a little behind. If the message that Mendoza sent off with such haste had remained unread for days and even weeks on the king's desk it would not have been the first dispatch, or the last, to be treated so.

Usually, however, the more important dispatches got fairly prompt attention. Usually, if Philip delayed action, it was because he made a habit of second thought. He liked to review methodically all the arguments for and against a given step, preferably outlined in writing and supported by relevant files. Among his councilors he listened, but rarely spoke. Afterwards, in silence, entrenched behind comforting stacks of papers, while candles flickered and an under-secretary yawned in a corner, slowly and stubbornly Philip made up his mind alone.

For this trait of the royal character, as for others, the monastery of San Lorenzo de Escorial provides a symbol and a revelation. Philip had dreamed of San Lorenzo while he was still fighting his father's wars in the Netherlands. Even in those first dreams the monastery-palace had always been in Spain. He had begun to search for its site almost as soon as he returned to his kingdom. He had paced the bare hillside above the wretched village of Escorial before a peg had been driven or a trench dug, had drunk from the mountain springs, sniffed the keen air, felt the wind and rain on his cheek. Once decided, he had hurried an army of workmen to his chosen spot, and a somewhat confused and irritated convent of Hieronymite monks along with them. Thereafter Philip could not keep himself away. He preferred this pastoral austerity to stately Toledo or soft, delicious Aranjuez, the parish priest's spare bedroom or an improvised cell in a makeshift wooden monastery to his pleasantest palaces. In the twenty years San Lorenzo was abuilding he constantly pored over the plans with the architect, scrambled about scaffolds with the master builder, and encouraged the workmen with more interest and affability than he ever showed to his grandees. The main outlines of the building and many of its details were intimately his.

Early he had planned for the center of the structure a noble church where his father's bones and his own might lie, and where masses could be said for their souls, many masses daily, until the end of time. From then on Philip seemed obsessed with the fear that he might not live to see his tomb. He pressed the work so urgently that his councilors grumbled about a king who spent as much time on one monastery as he did on all his kingdoms. Now, although the decoration of the interior would never be finished as long as the king's agents could find another painting in Venice, another tapestry in Flanders or another piece of classical sculpture in Naples or Rome, the last stone had been placed and the last tile laid for more than two years. Philip had begun to live inside his dream. The vast stone pile which he had drawn about him like a garment spoke of his peculiar self as no other building in Europe had ever echoed the spirit of a single man.

The building is seated on the knees of the mountains, the saw-toothed rock ridge of the Guadarramas rising steeply behind it and the rolling piedmont falling swiftly away before. It stands like a monument held out on a pedestal for the admiration of the Spanish plain. In its elevation, its distant prospects, its savage backdrop to the north, and the light and air and silence all around it, there is an overpowering sense of solitude, of isolation. The massive, unornamented walls, built of the local granite, might almost have grown up out of the mountain. Their meager, deeply recessed windows might be the mouths of caves or the embrasures of cannon.

At the center of the building rises the dome of the monastery church. Its shape suggests St. Peter's, a resemblance which did not escape contemporaries, which probably was meant not to escape them. Whoever might be emperor by the choice of the German electors, Philip felt that he was emperor by God's election and so a sacred personage, the equal of the pope. The church which says so is smaller than its Roman rival, but there was no stand of buildings in sixteenth century Europe which compared in size with the Escorial except the complex of St. Peter's and the Vatican. Both combined, conspicuously, a palace and a church. Both were, for Europe in the 1580's, modern buildings in the latest architectural fashion. Both breathed the spirit of the Counter Reformation. But here the resemblance ceased. The church of San Lorenzo in Philip's time had none of St. Peter's gaiety and lavish popular magnificence within. It has never had St. Peter's air of open, all-embracing welcome without. Philip's San Lorenzo is shut away at the center of the massive walled monastery like the innermost citadel of a fortress, like a sacred standard in the middle of a phalanx. St. Peter's stands for the spiritual counteroffensive of Rome, the confident, magniloquent advertisement of a Catholic faith. The church of San Lorenzo stands for the embattled defense of orthodoxy by the temporal sword.

That the great monastery actually seemed to Philip a defiance and a threat to the heretics of Europe which those wicked revolutionaries would risk anything to spoil is more than a fantasy. He often said so, attributing every accident or delay to the machinations of heretic spies, and a building thought of in those terms could hardly fail to resemble a fortress. That the church at the center should be at the same time a tomb where, according to plans which affected the whole complex structure, masses in overpowering numbers were to be said for the soul of Philip and his relatives tells us less of the king's spiritual views than it does of his sense of the unique position which he and his family occupied in Christendom—just as the site he selected is eloquent of his elevation above even the greatest of his subjects. But the Escorial reveals more than Philip's public image of his public self. At the sacred heart of the great building, right next to the monastery church, a meager suite of rooms is hidden. The most important pieces are a sort of study or workroom decently lighted but somehow meanly proportioned, and off it an alcove bedroom which has a shuttered little window opening into the church near the high altar. Monastery, palace and tomb prove only so many masks concealing a retreat, a refuge, almost a hiding place.

It was not enough that the site Philip had chosen for the Escorial insured isolation. On the bare, rocky slope where he had built it, there was no decent human habitation except San Lorenzo itself, and the use of the land around left no room for any. Moreover, vast as the building was, the king's plans had so filled it with activities, a school, a library, a workshop, a hospital, that it would barely hold the enlarged congregation of Hieronymite monks and a reduced royal household. There was no room for the swarms of courtiers, of suppliants and projectors who closed in on the king as soon as court moved to Madrid or Valladolid. His overpowering courtesy cousins, the grandees, and the watchful, importunate envoys of his clients and allies could neither impose on his hospitality here nor set up their households at his doorstep.

Yet inside the isolated pile Philip had managed a further isolation. The unkingly little huddle of rooms where Philip now spent a longer time each year had been designed to keep people out. The chambers were too small, the corridors too narrow for any crowd. The approaches were easily controlled; the eye could sweep each room at a glance; there was no chance of an unexpected encounter. Philip was an affectionate family man, but his family lodged elsewhere. Philip loved and trusted his monks, but his way into their choir was by a hidden door and a secret stairway. Even the public entrance to his apartments had something closed and secretive about it. Once inside it Philip could enjoy real privacy. In the sixteenth century, as throughout the middle ages, privacy had been the unenvied prerogative of hermits. The greater a man was the larger the crowd in the midst of which he was expected to pass most of his waking life. It was probably his increasing passion for privacy rather than his conventional piety which led people to feel, as he grew older, that there was something monkish about Philip.

In a sense there was. There was true asceticism in the way he toiled, eyes red-rimmed, bones aching, fingers stiff, at his self-imposed task of chief clerk of the Spanish empire. Increasingly, as he grew older, he gave up for it not only the hunting, dancing and feasting which were the conventional diversions of kings, but the things he really loved, flowers and pictures, country excursions and the company of his children. And there may have been true religious meditation in the agony of doubt with which he confronted every major decision of his reign. We know that he believed God expected more of kings than of other men, and far more of the king of Spain than of any other king. He was conscious of bearing a terrible, a unique burden. Perhaps the solitude of that cell-like cabinet, within sound of the chanting of the Hours, was as necessary to him as he wrestled with the problem of what God wanted him to do as it might have been to the lonely wrestling of any other monk.

There, in his cell-like cabinet, Philip sat for a week, as far as we know without writing a line touching England, or consulting anyone, except his confessor about a funeral service for the queen.

The Tragic Folly of the Earl of Essex

DAVID HUME

1599–1601. Robert Devereux, Earl of Essex, hero, courtier, and arrogant favorite of Queen Elizabeth, was the victim of his own presumption and folly. In 1598, in a quarrel with the Queen, he dared to turn his back on her. She boxed his ears. Thenceforward he marched to his doom. This account of his last days was written by the eighteenth-century Scots skeptic and philosopher who was also a distinguished historian. His History of England *was the first notably well-written, general history in English literature.*

Essex left London in the month of March, attended with the acclamations of the populace; and, what did him more honor, accompanied by a numerous train of nobility and gentry, who, from affection to his person, had attached themselves to his fortunes, and sought fame and military experience under so renowned a commander. The first act of authority which he exercised after his arrival in Ireland, was an indiscretion, but of the generous kind; and in both these respects suitable to his character. He appointed his intimate friend, the earl of Southampton, general of the horse; a nobleman who had incurred the queen's displeasure by secretly marrying without her consent, and whom she had therefore enjoined Essex not to employ in any command under him. She no sooner heard of this instance of disobedience, than she reprimanded him, and ordered him to recall his commission to Southampton. But Essex, who had imagined that some reasons which he opposed to her first injunctions had satisfied her, had the imprudence to remonstrate against these second orders; and it was not till she reiterated her commands that he could be prevailed upon to displace his friend.

Essex, on his landing at Dublin, deliberated with the Irish council concerning the proper methods of carrying on the war against the rebels; and here he was guilty of a capital error, which was the ruin of his enterprise. He had always, while in England, blamed the conduct of former commanders, who artfully protracted the war, who harassed their troops in small enterprises, and who, by agreeing to truces and temporary pacifications with the rebels, had given them leisure to recruit their broken forces. In conformity to these views, he had ever insisted on leading his forces immediately into Ulster against Tyrone, the chief enemy; and his instructions had been drawn agreeably to these his declared resolutions. But the Irish counselors persuaded him that the season was too early for the enterprise, and that as the morasses, in which the Northern Irish usually sheltered themselves, would not as yet be passable to the English forces, it would be better to employ the present time in an expedition into Munster. Their secret reason for this advice was, that many of them possessed estates in that province, and were desirous to have the enemy dislodged from their neighborhood; but the same selfish spirit which had induced them to give this counsel, made them soon after disown it, when they found the bad consequences with which it was attended.

Essex obliged all the rebels of Munster either to submit or to fly into the neighboring provinces: but the Irish, from the greatness of the queen's preparations, had concluded that she intended to reduce them to total subjection, or even utterly to exterminate them, they considered their defense as a common cause; and the English forces were no sooner withdrawn, than the inhabitants of Munster relapsed into rebellion, and renewed their confederacy with their other countrymen. The army, meanwhile, by the fatigue of long and tedious marches, and by the influence of the climate, was become sickly; and on its return to Dublin, about the middle of July, was surprisingly diminished in number. The courage of the soldiers was even much abated: for though they had prevailed in some lesser enterprises against Lord Cahir and others, yet had they sometimes met with more stout resistance than they expected from the Irish, whom they were wont to despise; and as they were raw troops and unexperienced, a considerable body of them had been put to flight at the Glins by an inferior number of the enemy. Essex was so enraged at this misbehavior, that he cashiered all the officers, and decimated the private men. But this act of severity, though necessary, had intimidated the soldiers, and increased their aversion to the service.

The queen was extremely disgusted, when she heard that so considerable a part of the season was consumed in these frivolous enterprises; and was still more surprised, that Essex persevered in the same practice which he had so much condemned in others, and which he knew to be so much contrary to her purpose and intention. That nobleman, in order to give his troops leisure to recruit from their sickness and fatigue, left the main army in quarters, and marched with a small body of fifteen hundred men into the country of the O'Connors and O'Mores, whom he forced to a submission: but, on his return to Dublin, he found the army so much diminished that he wrote to the English council an account of its condition, and informed them, that if he did not immediately receive a reinforcement of two thousand men, it would be impossible for him this season to attempt anything against Tyrone. That there might be no pretence for further inactivity, the queen immediately sent over the number demanded; and Essex began at last to assemble his forces for the expedition into Ulster. The army was so averse to the enterprise, and so terrified with the reputation of Tyrone, that many of them counterfeited sickness, many of them deserted; and Essex found, that after leaving the necessary garrisons, he could scarcely lead four thousand men against the rebels. He marched, however, with this small army; but was soon sensible, that in so advanced a season, it would be impossible for him to effect anything against an enemy who, although superior in number, was determined to avoid every decisive action. He hearkened, therefore, to a message sent him by Tyrone, who desired a conference; and a place near the two camps was appointed for that purpose. The generals met without any of their attendants; and a river ran between them, into which Tyrone entered to the depth of his saddle; but Essex stood on the opposite bank. After half an hour's conference, where Tyrone behaved with great submission to the lord lieutenant, a cessation of arms was concluded to the first of May, renewable from six weeks to six weeks; but which might be broken off by either party upon a fortnight's warning. Essex also received from Tyrone proposals for a peace, in which that rebel had inserted many unreasonable and exorbitant conditions: and there appeared afterwards some reason to suspect that he had here commenced a very unjustifiable correspondence with the enemy.

So unexpected an issue of an enterprise, the greatest and most expensive that Elizabeth had ever undertaken, provoked her extremely against Essex; and this disgust was much augmented by other circumstances of that nobleman's conduct. He wrote many letters to the queen and council, full of peevish and impatient expressions; complaining of his enemies, lamenting that their calumnies should be believed against him, and discovering symptoms of a mind equally haughty and discontented. She took care to inform him of her dissatisfaction; but commanded him to remain in Ireland till further orders.

Essex heard at once of Elizabeth's anger, and of the promotion of his enemy, Sir Robert Cecil, to the office of master of the wards, an office to which he himself aspired: and dreading that, if he remained any longer absent, the queen would be totally alienated from him, he hastily embraced a resolution which, he knew, had once succeeded with the earl of Leicester, the former favorite of Elizabeth. Leicester, being informed, while in the Low Countries, that his mistress was extremely displeased with his conduct, disobeyed her orders by coming over to England; and having pacified her by his presence, by his apologies, and by his flattery and insinuation, disappointed all the expectations of his enemies. Essex, therefore, weighing more the similarity of circumstances than the difference of character between himself and Leicester, immediately set out for England; and making speedy journeys, he arrived at court before any one was in the least appraised of his intentions. Though besmeared with dirt and sweat, he hastened up stairs to the presence chamber, thence to the privy chamber; nor stopped until he was in the queen's bed chamber, who was newly risen, and was sitting with her hair about her face. He threw himself on his knees, kissed her hand, and had some private conference with her; where he was so graciously received, that on his departure he was heard to express great satisfaction, and to thank God that, though he had suffered much trouble and many storms abroad, he found a sweet calm at home.

But this placability of Elizabeth was merely the result of her surprise, and of the momentary satisfaction which she felt on the sudden and unexpected appearance of her favorite: after she had leisure for recollection, all his faults recurred to her; and she thought it necessary, by some severe discipline, to subdue that haughty, imperious spirit, who, presuming on her partiality, had pretended to domineer in her councils, to engross all her favor, and to act, in the most important affairs, without regard to her orders and instructions. When Essex waited on her in the afternoon, he found her extremely altered in her carriage towards him: she ordered him to be confined to his chamber; to be twice examined by the council; and though his answers were calm and submissive, she committed him to the custody of Lord Keeper Egerton, and held him sequestered from all company, even from that of his countess, nor was so much as the intercourse of letters permitted between them. Essex dropped many expressionss of humiliation and sorrow, none of resentment: he professed an entire submission to the queen's will; declared his intention of retiring into the country, and of leading thenceforth a private life remote from courts and business: but though he affected to be so entirely cured of his aspiring ambition, the vexation of this disappointment, and of the triumph gained by his enemies, preyed upon his haughty spirit, and he fell into a distemper which seemed to put his life in danger.

The queen had always declared to all the world, and even to the earl himself, that the purpose of her severity was to correct, not to ruin him; and when she heard of his sickness, she was not a little alarmed with his situation. She ordered eight physicians of the best reputation and experience to consult of his case; and being informed that the issue was much to be apprehended, she sent Dr. James to him with some broth, and desired that physician to deliver him a message, which she probably deemed of still greater virtue, that if she thought such a step consistent with her honor, she would herself pay him a visit. The bystanders, who carefully observed her countenance, remarked, that in pronouncing these words her eyes were suffused with tears.

When these symptoms of the queen's returning affection towards Essex were known, they gave a sensible alarm to the faction which had declared their opposition to him. Sir Walter Raleigh in particular, the most violent as well as the most ambitious of his enemies, was so affected with the appearance of this sudden revolution, that he was seized with sickness in his turn; and the queen was obliged to apply the same salve to his wound, and to send him a favorable message, expressing her desire of his recovery.

The medicine which the queen administered to these aspiring rivals was successful with both; and Essex, being now allowed the company of his countess, and having entertained more promising hopes of his future fortunes, was so much restored in his health as to be thought past danger. A belief was instilled into Elizabeth, that his distemper had been entirely counterfeit, in order to move her compassion; and she relapsed into her former rigor against him. He wrote her a letter, and sent her a rich present on new-year's day, as was usual with the courtiers at that time: she read the letter but rejected the present. After some interval, however, of severity, she allowed him to retire to his own house; and though he remained still under custody, and was sequestered from all company, he was so grateful for this mark of lenity that he sent her a letter of thanks on the occasion. "This further degree of goodness," said he, "doth sound in my ears as if your majesty spake these words: 'Die not Essex; for yet will I one day be served again by thee.' My prostrate soul makes this answer: 'I hope for that blessed day.' And in expectation of it, all my afflictions of body and mind are humbly, patiently, and cheerfully borne by me." The countess of Essex, daughter of Sir Francis Walsingham, possessed, as well as her husband, a refined taste in literature; and the chief consolation which Essex enjoyed, during this period of anxiety and expectation, consisted in her company, and in reading with her those instructive and entertaining authors, which, even during the time of his greatest prosperity, he had never entirely neglected.

There were several incidents which kept alive the queen's anger against Essex. Every account which she received from Ireland, convinced her more and more of his misconduct in that government, and of the insignificant purposes to which he had employed so much force and treasure. Tyrone, so far from being quelled, had thought proper, in less than three months, to break the truce, and joining with O'Donnell and other rebels, had over-run almost the whole kingdom. He boasted that he was certain of receiving a supply of men, money, and arms from Spain: he pretended to be champion of the Catholic religion: and he openly exulted in the present of a phoenix plume, which the pope, Clement VIII, in order to encourage him in the prosecution of so good a cause, had consecrated, and had conferred upon him. The queen, that she might check his progress, returned to her former intention of appointing Mountjoy lord deputy; and though that nobleman, who was an intimate friend of Essex, and desired his return to the government of Ireland, did at first very earnestly excuse himself on account of his bad state of health, she obliged him to accept of the employment. Mountjoy found the island almost in a desperate condition; but being a man of capacity and vigor, he was so little discouraged, that he immediately advanced against Tyrone in Ulster. He penetrated into the heart of that country, the chief seat of the rebels; he fortified Derry and Mount-Norris, in order to bridle the Irish: he chased them from the field, and obliged them to take shelter in the woods and morasses: he employed, with equal success, Sir George Carew in Munster: and by these promising enterprises, he gave new life to the queen's authority in that island.

As the comparison of Mountjoy's administration with that of Essex contributed to alienate Elizabeth from her favorite, she received additional disgust from the partiality of the people, who, prepossessed with an extravagant idea of Essex's merit, complained of the injustice done him by his removal from the court, and by his confinement. Libels were secretly dispersed against Cecil and Raleigh and all his enemies: and his popularity, which was always great, seemed rather to be increased than diminished by his misfortunes. Elizabeth, in order to justify to the public her conduct with regard to him, had often expressed her intentions of having him tried in the star chamber for his offences: but her tenderness for him prevailed at last over her severity; and she was contented to have him only examined by the privy council. The attorney-general, Coke, opened the cause against him, and treated him with the cruelty and insolence which that great lawyer usually exercised against the unfortunate. He displayed in the strongest colors all the faults committed by Essex in his administration of

Ireland: his making Southampton general of the horse, contrary to the queen's injunctions; his deserting the enterprise against Tyrone, and marching to Leinster and Munster; his conferring knighthood on too many persons; his secret conference with Tyrone; and his sudden return from Ireland, in contempt of her majesty's commands. He also exaggerated the indignity of the conditions which Tyrone had been allowed to propose; odious and abominable conditions, said he; a public toleration of an idolatrous religion, pardon for himself and every traitor in Ireland, and full restitution of lands and possessions to all of them. The solicitor-general, Fleming, insisted upon the wretched situation in which the earl had left that kingdom; and Francis, son of Sir Nicholas Bacon, who had been lord keeper in the beginning of the present reign, closed the charge with displaying the undutiful expressions contained in some letters written by the earl.

Essex, when he came to plead in his own defense, renounced, with great submission and humility, all pretensions to an apology; and declared his resolution never, on this or any other occasion, to have any contest with his sovereign. He said, that having severed himself from the world, and abjured all sentiments of ambition, he had no scruple to confess every failing or error to which his youth, folly, or manifold infirmities might have betrayed him; that his inward sorrow for his offenses against her majesty was so profound, that it exceeded all his outward crosses and afflictions, nor had he any scruple of submitting to a public confession of whatever she had been pleased to impute to him; that in his acknowledgments he retained only one reserve, which he never would relinquish but with his life, the assertion of a loyal and unpolluted heart, of an unfeigned affection, of an earnest desire ever to perform to her majesty the best service which his poor abilities would permit; and that, if this sentiment were allowed by the council, he willingly acquiesced in any condemnation of sentence which they could pronounce against him. This submission was uttered with so much eloquence, and in so pathetic a manner, that it drew tears from many of the audience. All the privy counselors, in giving their judgment, made no scruple of doing the earl justice with regard to the loyalty of his intentions. Even Cecil, whom he believed his capital enemy, treated him with regard and humanity. And the sentence pronounced by the lord keeper (to which the council assented) was in these words: "If this cause," said he, "had been heard in the star chamber, my sentence must have been for as great a fine as ever was set upon any man's head in that court, together with perpetual confinement in that prison which belongeth to a man of his quality, the Tower. But since we are now in another place, and in a course of favor, my censure is, that the earl of Essex is not to execute the office of a counselor, nor that of an earl marshal of England, nor of master of the ordinance; and to return to his own house, there to continue a prisoner till it shall please her majesty to release this and all the rest of his sentence." The earl of Cumberland made a slight opposition to this sentence; and said, that if he thought it would stand, he would have required a little more time to deliberate; that he deemed it somewhat severe; and that any commander-in-chief might easily incur a like penalty. "But however," added he, "in confidence of her majesty's mercy, I agree with the rest." The earl of Worcester delivered his opinion in a couple of Latin verses; importing, that where the gods are offended, even misfortunes ought to be imputed as crimes, and that accident is no excuse for transgressions against the Divinity.

Bacon, so much distinguished afterwards for his high offices, and still more for his profound genius for the sciences, was nearly allied to the Cecil family, being nephew to Lord Burleigh, and cousin-german to the secretary: but not withstanding his extraordinary talents, he had met with so little protection from his powerful relations, that he had not yet obtained any preferment in the law, which was his profession. But Essex, who could distinguish merit, and who passionately loved it, had entered into an intimate friendship with Bacon; had zealously attempted, although without success, to procure him the office of solicitor-general; and in order to comfort his friend under the disappointment, had conferred on him a present of land to the value of eighteen hundred pounds. The public could ill excuse Bacon's appearance before the council against so munificent a benefactor, though he acted in obedience to the queen's commands: but she was so well pleased with his behavior, that she imposed on him a new task, of drawing a narrative of that day's proceedings, in order to satisfy the public of the justice and lenity of her conduct. Bacon, who wanted firmness of character more than humanity, gave to the whole transaction the most favorable turn for Essex; and, in particular, pointed out, in elaborate expression, the dutiful submission which that nobleman discovered in the defence that he made for his conduct. When he read the paper to her, she smiled at that passage, and observed to Bacon, that old love, she saw, could not easily be forgotten. He replied, that he hoped she meant that of herself.

All the world, indeed, expected that Essex would soon be reinstated in his former credit; perhaps, as is usual in reconcilements founded on inclination, would acquire an additional ascendant over the queen, and after all his disgraces would again appear more a favorite than ever. They were confirmed in this hope, when they saw that, although he was still prohibited from appearing at court, he was continued in his office of master of horse, and was restored to his liberty, and that all his friends had access to him. Essex himself seemed determined to persevere in that conduct which had hitherto been so successful, and which the queen, by all this discipline, had endeavored to render habitual to him: he wrote to her, that he kissed her majesty's hands, and the rod with which she had corrected him; but that he could never recover his wonted cheerfulness, till she deigned to admit him to that presence which had ever been the chief source of his happiness and enjoyment: and that he had now resolved to make amends for his past errors, to retire into a country solitude, and say with Nebuchadnezzar, "Let my dwelling be with the beasts of the field; let me eat grass as an ox, and be wet with the dew of heaven; till it shall please the queen to restore me to my understanding." The queen was much pleased with these sentiments; and replied, that she heartily wished his actions might correspond with his expressions; that he had tried her patience for a long time, and it was but fitting she should now make some experiment of his submission; that her father would never have pardoned so much obstinacy; but that, if the furnace of affliction produced such good effects, she should ever after have the better opinion of her chemistry.

The earl of Essex possessed a monopoly of sweet wines; and as his patent was near expiring, he patiently expected that the queen would renew it; and he considered this event as the critical circumstance of his life, which would determine whether he could ever hope to be reinstated in credit and authority. But Elizabeth, though gracious in her deportment, was of a temper somewhat haughty and severe; and being continually surrounded with Essex's enemies, means were found to persuade her, that his lofty spirit was not yet sufficiently subdued, and that he must undergo this further trial, before he could again be safely received into favor. She therefore denied his request; and even added, in a contemptuous style, that an ungovernable beast must be stinted in his provender.

This rigor, pushed one step too far, proved the final ruin of this young nobleman, and was the source of infinite sorrow and vexation to the queen herself. Essex, who had with great difficulty so long subdued his proud spirit, and whose patience was now exhausted, imagining that the queen was entirely inexorable, burst at once all restraints of submission and of prudence, and determined to seek relief by proceeding to the utmost extremities against his enemies. Even during his greatest favor, he had ever been accustomed to carry matters with a high hand towards his sovereign; and as this practise gratified his own temper, and was sometimes successful, he had imprudently imagined that it was the only proper method of managing her: but being now reduced to despair, he gave entire reins to his violent disposition, and threw off all appearance of duty and respect. Intoxicated with the public favor which he already possessed, he practised anew every art of popularity; and endeavored to increase the general good will by a hospitable manner of life, little suited to his situation and circumstances. His former employments had given him great connections with men of the military profession; and he now entertained, by additional caresses and civilities, a friendship with all desperate adventurers, whose attachment, he hoped, might, in his present views, prove serviceable to him. He secretly courted the confidence of the Catholics; but his chief trust lay in the Puritans, whom he openly caressed, and whose manners he seemed to have entirely adopted. He engaged the most celebrated preachers of that sect to resort to Essex House; he had daily prayers and sermons in his family; and he invited all the zealots in London to attend those pious exercises. Such was the disposition now beginning to prevail among the English, that, instead of feasting and public spectacles, the methods anciently practised to gain the populace, nothing so effectively ingratiated an ambitious leader with the public as these fanatical entertainments. And as the Puritanical preachers frequently inculcated in their sermons the doctrine of resistance to the civil magistrate, they prepared the minds of their hearers for those seditious projects which Essex was secretly meditating.

But the greatest imprudence of this nobleman proceeded from the openness of his temper, by which he was ill qualified to succeed in such difficult and dangerous enterprises. He indulged himself in great liberties of speech, and was even heard to say of the queen, that she was now grown an old woman, and was become as crooked in her mind as in her body. Some court ladies, whose favors Essex had formerly neglected, carried her these stories, and incensed her to a high degree against him. Elizabeth was ever remarkably jealous on this head; and though she was now approaching to her seventieth year, she allowed her courtiers, and even foreign ambassadors, to compliment her upon her beauty; nor had all her good sense been able to cure her of this preposterous vanity.

There was also an expedient employed by Essex, which, if possible, was more provoking to the queen than those sarcasms on her age and deformity; and that was, his secret applications to the king of Scots, her heir and successor. That prince had this year very narrowly escaped a dangerous though ill-formed conspiracy of the earl of Gowrie; and even his deliverance was attended with this disagreeable circumstance, that the obstinate ecclesiastics persisted, in spite of the most incontestable evidence, to maintain to his face, that there had been no such conspiracy. James, harassed with his turbulent and factious subjects, cast a wishful eye to the succession of England; and in proportion as the queen advanced in years, his desire increased of mounting that throne, on which, besides acquiring a great addition of power and splendor, he hoped to govern a people so much more tractable and submissive. He negotiated with all the courts of Europe, in order to insure himself friends and partisans: he even neglected not the court of Rome and that of Spain; and though he engaged himself in no positive promise, he flattered the Catholics with hopes that, in the event of his succession, they might expect some more liberty than was at present indulged them. Elizabeth was the only sovereign in Europe to whom he never dared to mention his right of succession: he knew that, though her advanced age might now invite her to think of fixing an heir to the crown, she never could bear the prospect of her own death without horror, and was determined still to retain him, and all other competitors, in an entire dependence upon her.

Essex was descended by females from the royal family; and some of his sanguine partisans had been so imprudent as to mention his name among those of other pretenders to the crown; but the earl took care, by means of Henry Lee, whom he secretly sent to Scotland, to assure James, that so far from entertaining such ambitious views, he was determined to use every expedient for extorting an immediate declaration in favor of that monarch's right of succession.

* * *

A select council of malcontents was formed, who commonly met at Drury House, and were composed of Sir Charles Davers, to whom the house belonged, the earl of Southampton, Sir Ferdinando Gorges, Sir Christopher Blount, Sir John Davies, and John Littleton; and Essex, who boasted that he had a hundred and twenty barons, knights, and gentlemen of note at his devotion, and who trusted still more to his authority with the populace, communicated to his associates those secret designs with which his confidence in so powerful a party had inspired him. Among other criminal projects, the result of blind rage and despair, he deliberated with them concerning the method of taking arms; and asked their opinion, whether he had best begin with seizing the palace or the Tower, or set out with making himself master of both places. The first enterprise being preferred, a method was concerted for executing it. It was agreed, that Sir Christopher Blount, with a choice detachment, should possess himself of the palace gates; that Davies should seize the hall, Davers the guard chamber and presence chamber; and that Essex should rush in from the Meuse, attended by a body of his partisans; should entreat the queen, with all demonstrations of humility, to remove his enemies; should oblige her to assemble a parliament; and should, with common consent, settle a new plan of government.

While these desperate projects were in agitation, many reasons of suspicion were carried to the queen; and she sent Robert Sackville, son of the treasurer, to Essex House, on pretence of a visit, but, in reality, with a view of discovering whether there were in that place any unusual concourse of people, or any extraordinary preparations which might threaten an insurrection. Soon after, Essex received a summons to attend the council, which met at the treasurer's house; and while he was musing on this circumstance, and comparing it with the late unexpected visit from Sackville, a private note was conveyed to him, by which he was warned to provide for his own safety. He concluded, that all his conspiracy was discovered, at least suspected; and that the easiest punishment which he had reason to apprehend, was a new and more severe confinement: he therefore excused himself to the council on pretence of an indisposition; and he immediately dispatched messages to his more intimate confederates, requesting their advice and assistance in the present critical situation of his affairs. They deliberated, whether they should abandon all their projects, and fly the kingdom; or instantly seize the palace with the force which they could assemble; or rely upon the affections of the citizens, who were generally known to have a great attachment to the earl. Essex declared against the first expedient, and professed himself determined to undergo any fate rather than to live the life of a fugitive. To seize the palace seemed impracticable without more preparations; especially as the queen seemed now aware of their projects, and, as they heard, had used the precaution of doubling her ordinary guards. There remained, therefore, no expedient but that of betaking themselves to the city; and while the prudence and feasibility of this resolution was under debate, a person arrived, who, as if he had received a commission for the purpose, gave them assurance of the affections of the Londoners, and affirmed, that they might securely rest any project on that foundation. The popularity of Essex had chiefly buoyed him up in all his vain undertakings; and he fondly imagined, that, with no other assistance than the good will of the multitude, he might overturn Elizabeth's government, confirmed by time, revered for wisdom, supported by vigor, and concurring with the general sentiments of the nation. The wild project of raising the city was immediately resolved on; the execution of it was delayed till next day; and emissaries were dispatched to all Essex's friends, informing them that Cobham and Raleigh had laid schemes against his life, and entreating their presence and assistance.

Next day, there appeared at Essex House the earls of Southampton and Rutland, the lords Sandys and Monteagle, with about three hundred gentlemen of good quality and fortune; and Essex informed them of the danger to which, he pretended, the machinations of his enemies exposed him. To some, he said that he would throw himself at the queen's feet, and crave her justice and protection; to others, he boasted of his interest in the city, and affirmed that, whatever might happen, this resource could never fail him. The queen was informed of these designs, by means of intelligence conveyed, as is supposed, to Raleigh by Sir Ferdinando Gorges;

and having ordered the magistrates of London to keep the citizens in readiness, she sent Egerton, lord keeper, to Essex House, with the earl of Worcester, Sir William Knollys, comptroller, and Popham, chief justice, in order to learn the cause of these unusual commotions. They were with difficulty admitted through a wicket; but all their servants were excluded, except the purse-bearer. After some altercation, in which they charged Essex's retainers, upon their allegiance, to lay down their arms, and were menaced in their turn by the angry multitude who surrounded them, the earl, who found that matters were past recall, resolved to leave them prisoners in his house, and to proceed to the execution of his former project. He sallied forth with about two hundred attendants, armed only with walking swords; and in his passage to the city was joined by the earl of Bedford and Lord Cromwell. He cried aloud, "For the queen! for the queen! a plot is laid for my life"; and then proceeded to the house of Smith the sheriff, on whose aid he had great reliance. The citizens flocked about him in amazement; but though he told them that England was sold to the infanta, and exhorted them to arm instantly, otherwise they could not do him any service, no one showed a disposition to join him. The sheriff, on the earl's approach to his house, stole out at the back door, and made the best of his way to the mayor. Essex, meanwhile, observing the coldness of the citizens, and hearing that he was proclaimed a traitor by the earl of Cumberland and Lord Burleigh, began to despair of success, and thought of retreating to his own house. He found the streets in his passage barricaded and guarded by the citizens under the command of Sir John Levison. In his attempt to force his way, Tracy, a young gentleman to whom he bore great friendship, was killed, with two or three of the Londoners; and the earl himself, attended by a few of his partisans (for the greater part began secretly to withdraw themselves) retired towards the river, and taking boat, arrived at Essex House. He there found that Gorges, whom he had sent before to capitulate with the lord keeper and the other counselors, had given all of them their liberty, and had gone to court with them. He was now reduced to despair; and appeared determined, in prosecution of Lord Sandys' advice, to defend himself to the last extremity, and rather to perish like a brave man, with his sword in his hand, than basely by the hands of the executioner: but after some parley, and after demanding in vain, first hostages, then conditions, from the besiegers, he surrendered at discretion; requesting only civil treatment, and a fair and impartial hearing.

The queen, who, during all this commotion, had behaved with as great tranquillity and security as if there had only passed a fray in the streets, in which she was in no wise concerned, soon gave orders for the trial of the most considerable of the criminals. The earls of Essex and Southampton were arraigned before a jury of twenty-five peers, where Buckhurst acted as lord steward. The guilt of the prisoners was too apparent to admit of any doubt; and, besides the insurrection known to every body, the treasonable conferences at Drury House were proved by undoubted evidence. Sir Ferdinando Gorges was produced in court: the confessions of the earl of Rutland, of the lords Cromwell, Sandys and Monteagle, of Davers, Blount, and Davies, were only read to the peers, according to the practice of that age. Essex's best friends were scandalized at his assurance in insisting so positively on his innocence, and the goodness of his intentions, and still more at his vindictive disposition, in accusing, without any appearance of reason, Secretary Cecil as a partisan of the infanta's title. The secretary, who had expected this charge, stepped into the court, and challenged Essex to produce his authority, which, on examination, was found extremely weak and frivolous. When sentence was pronounced, Essex spoke like a man who expected nothing but death; but he added, that he should be sorry if he were represented to the queen as a person who despised her clemency; though he should not, he believed, make any cringing submissions to obtain it. Southampton's behavior was more mild and submissive; he entreated the good offices of the peers in so modest and becoming a manner, as excited compassion in every one.

The most remarkable circumstance in Essex's trial was Bacon's appearance against him. He was none of the crown lawyers; so was not obliged by his office to assist at this trial: yet he did not scruple, in order to obtain the queen's favor, to be active in bereaving of life his friend and patron, whose generosity he had often experienced. He compared Essex's conduct, in pretending to fear the attempts of his adversaries, to that of Pisistratus the Athenian, who cut and wounded his own body, and, making the people believe that his enemies had committed the violence, obtained a guard for his person, by whose assistance he afterwards subdued the liberties of his country.

After Essex had spent some days in the solitude and reflections of a prison, his proud heart was at last subdued, not by the fear of death, but by the sentiments of religion; a principle which he had before attempted to make the instrument of his ambition, but which now took a more firm hold on his mind, and prevailed over every other motive and consideration. His spiritual directors persuaded him, that he could never obtain the pardon of Heaven, unless he made a full confession of his disloyalty; and he gave in to the council an account of all his criminal design, as well as of his correspondence with the king of Scots. He spared not even his most intimate friends, such as Lord Mountjoy, whom he had engaged in these conspiracies; and he sought to pacify his present remorse by making such atonements as, in any other period of his life, he would have deemed more blamable than those attempts themselves which were the objects of his penitence. Sir Henry Nevil, in particular, a man of merit, he accused of a correspondence with the conspirators; though it appears that this gentleman had never assented to the proposals made him, and was no further criminal than in not revealing the earl's treason; an office to which every man of honor naturally bears the strongest reluctance. Nevil was thrown into prison, and underwent a severe persecution: but as the queen found Mountjoy an able and successful commander, she continued him in his government, and sacrificed her resentment to the public service.

Elizabeth affected extremely the praise of clemency; and in every great example which she had made during her reign, she had always appeared full of reluctance and hesitation: but the present situation of Essex called forth all her tender affections, and kept her in the most real agitation and irresolution. She felt a perpetual combat between resentment and inclination, pride and compassion, the care of her own safety and concern for her favorite; and her situation, during this interval, was perhaps more an object of pity than that to which Essex himself was reduced. She signed the warrant for his execution; she countermanded it; she again resolved on his death; she felt a new return of tenderness. Essex's enemies told her, that he himself desired to die, and had assured her, that she could never be in safety while he lived: it is likely that this proof of penitence and concern for her would produce a contrary effect to what they intended, and would revive all the fond affection which she had so long indulged towards the unhappy prisoner. But what chiefly hardened her heart against him was his supposed obstinacy, in never making, as she hourly expected, any application to her for mercy; and she finally gave her consent to his execution. He discovered at his death symptoms rather of penitence and piety than fear; and willingly acknowledged the justice of the sentence by which he suffered. The execution was private in the Tower, agreeably to his own request. He was apprehensive, he said, lest the favor and compassion of the people would too much raise his heart in those moments, when humiliation under the afflicting hand of Heaven was the only proper sentiment which he could indulge. And the queen, no doubt, thought that prudence required the removing of so melancholy a spectacle from the public eye. Sir Walter Raleigh, who came to the Tower on purpose, and who beheld Essex's execution from a window, increased much by this action the general hatred under which he already labored: it was thought, that his sole intention was to feast his eyes with the death of an enemy; and no apology which he could make for so ungenerous a conduct could be accepted by the public. The cruelty and animosity with which he urged on Essex's fate, even when Cecil relented, were still regarded as the principles of this unmanly behavior.

The earl of Essex was but thirty-four years of age, when his rashness, imprudence, and violence brought him to this untimely end. We must here, as in many other instances, lament the inconstancy of human nature, that a person endowed with so many noble virtues—generosity, sincerity, friendship, valor, eloquence and industry—should, in the latter period of his life, have given reins to his ungovernable passions, and involved, not only himself, but many of his friends, in utter ruin. The queen's tenderness and passion for him, as it was the cause of those premature honors which he attained, seems, on the whole, the chief circumstance which brought on his unhappy fate. Confident of her partiality towards him, as well as of his own merit, he treated her with a haughtiness which neither her love nor her dignity could bear; and as her amorous inclinations, in so advanced an age, would naturally make her appear ridiculous, if not odious, in his eyes, he was engaged, by an imprudent openness, of which he made profession, to discover too easily those sentiments to her. The many reconciliations and returns of affection, of which he had still made advantage, induced him to venture on new provocations, till he pushed her beyond all bounds of patience; and he forgot, that though the sentiments of the woman were ever strong in her, those of the sovereign had still in the end appeared predominant.

Sir John Harington

LYTTON STRACHEY

1561–1612. Lytton Strachey once wrote that an essential part of the historian's equipment is a point of view. No writer of history ever had a more personal point of view than Strachey—an urbane, condescending, sophisticated detachment enlivened by a sort of sneering elegance. This combined with a style of captivating grace and charm made his historical biographies and essays superbly good reading, even though they were occasionally inaccurate and sometimes unfair. This essay appeared in Strachey's Portraits in Miniature, *which was published in 1931.*

An old miniature shows a young man's face, whimsically Elizabethan, with tossed-back curly hair, a tip-tilted nose, a tiny point of a beard, and a long single earring, falling in sparkling drops over a ruff of magnificent proportions. Such was John Harington, as he appeared in the happy fifteen-eighties, at Greenwich, or at Nonsuch—a courtier, a wit, a scholar, a poet, and a great favorite with the ladies. Even Gloriana herself usually unbent when he approached her. She liked the foolish fellow. She had known him since he was a child; he was her godson—almost, indeed, a family connection, for his father's first wife had been a natural daughter of her own indefatigable sire. Through this lady the young man had inherited his fine

Italian house at Kelston, in Somersetshire, where one day Elizabeth, on her way to Bath, paid him the honor of an extremely expensive visit. He had felt himself obliged to rebuild half the house to lodge his great guest fittingly; but he cared little for that—he wrote a rhyming epigram about it all, which amused the ladies of the bedchamber. He wrote, he found, with extraordinary ease and pleasure; the words came positively running off the end of his pen; and so—to amuse the ladies again, or to tease them —he translated the twenty-eighth book of Ariosto's *Orlando Furioso*, in which the far from decorous history of the fair Fiammetta is told. The Queen soon got wind of this. She read the manuscript and sent for the poet. She was shocked, she said, by this attempt to demoralize her household; and she banished the offender from Court until—could there be a more proper punishment—he should have completed the translation of the whole poem. Harington hurried off to Kelston, worked away for a month or two, and returned with a fine folio containing the entire *Orlando* in English, together with notes, a life of Ariosto, "a general allegory of the whole," and "apologie of Poetrie," and "epistle dedicatorie to the Queenes Majestie," and an engraved title-page with the portrait of himself and his dog Bungay. The book was printed in 1591. The exquisite elegance and mature serenity of the original are nowhere to be found in it; but Harington himself, bringing with him the natural abundance, the charming ingenuousness, the early morning freshness of his wonderful generation, comes to us delightfully on every page.

The translation was well received, and the gay young man looked about for new worlds to conquer. Not to be talked of was his only fear. A curious notion struck him. His nose was sensitive as well as impudent, and he had been made to suffer agonies by the sanitary arrangements in the houses of the great. Suddenly inspired, he invented the water-closet. Then, seizing his pen, he concocted a pamphlet after the manner of Rabelais—or, as he preferred to call him, "the reverent Rabbles"—in which extravagant spirits, intolerable puns, improper stories, and sly satirical digs at eminent personages were blended together into a preposterous rhapsody, followed by an appendix—written, of course, by his servant—could a gentleman be expected to discuss such details?—containing a minute account, with measurements, diagrams and prices, of the new invention. *The Metamorphosis of Ajax*—for so the book, with a crowningly deplorable pun, was entitled—created some sensation. Queen Elizabeth was amused. But then some malicious courtier told her that one of the satirical digs was aimed at the memory of Leicester, whereupon her smiles changed to frowns, the Star Chamber was talked of, and Harington made a strategic retreat to Somersetshire. "The merry poet, my godson," the Queen declared, "must not come to Greenwich, till he hath grown sober and leaveth the ladies' sports and frolics." But before very long she relented. With her supreme sense of the practical, she saw that, as she put it, "the marrow of the book" was not entirely ludicrous; she sent down word to the poet that she approved of his invention; and eventually she set the fashion for the new contrivances by installing one of them in Richmond Palace, with a copy of the *Ajax* hanging from the wall.

Harington's next adventure was more serious. He was summoned by Essex to join his ill-fated expedition to Ireland, in command of a troop of horse. In Ireland, with a stretch of authority which was bitterly resented by the Queen, Harington was knighted by the rash Lord Deputy, and afterwards, when disaster came thick upon disaster, he followed his patron back to London. In fear and trembling, he presented himself before the enraged Elizabeth. "What!" she cried, "did the fool bring you too?" The terrified poet fell upon his knees, while the Queen, as he afterwards described it, "chafed much, walked fastly to and fro, and looked with discomposure in her visage." Then, suddenly rushing towards him, she caught hold of his girdle. "By God's Son," she shouted, "I am no Queen, and that man is above me!" His stammering excuses were cut short with a "Go back to your business!" uttered in such a tone that Sir John, not staying to be bidden twice, fled out of the room, and fled down to Kelston, "as if all the Irish rebels had been at his heels."

It is clear that poor Harington never quite recovered from the shock of that terrific scene. The remainder of his life passed in ineffectiveness and disillusionment. In the bosom of his family he did his best to forget the storms and shipwrecks of "the Essex coast"; he wrote incessantly; he cracked scandalous jokes with his mother-in-law, old Lady Rogers; he busied himself over the construction of a curious lantern for King James of Scotland. But his happy vein had deserted him. His *Discourse shewing that Elyas must personally come before the Day of Judgment* could never get finished, and he threw aside his *Treatise on Playe* as a failure. His epigrams, no doubt, were more successful; he scribbled them down on every possible occasion, and the most scurrilous he invariably dispatched to old Lady Rogers. She roared with laughter, but omitted to leave him a legacy. He dashed into her house as she was dying, broke open the chests, tried to get possession of everything, and was at last ignominiously ejected by his brother-in-law. King James was equally disappointing. Even the curious lantern, even a learned, elaborate, and fantastic dissertation *On the Succession to the Crown*, failed to win him. After he had been a year in London, the new King granted Sir John an interview, but, though his Majesty was polite, he was not impressed. "Sir John," he said, with much gravity, "do you truly understand why the Devil works more with ancient women than others?" And, unluckily, on that, Sir John "could not refrain from a scurvy jest." Nevertheless, though he felt that he had made no headway, he would not despair; a little later the Lord Chancellorship of Ireland and the Archbishopric of Dublin fell vacant, and the author of *Ajax* bravely requested that he should be appointed to both offices. Oddly enough, his application received no answer. He solaced himself with an endeavor to win the good graces of the young Prince Henry, to whom he addressed a discourse, full of pleasant anecdotes, concerning all the bishops of his acquaintance, followed by a letter describing "the good deedes and straunge feats" of his "rare Dogge," Bungay—how he used to carry messages from London to Kelston, and how, on one occasion, he took a pheasant from a dish at the Spanish Ambassador's table, and then returned it to the very same dish, at a secret sign from his master.

But in truth the days of Bungay were over, and the new times were uncomfortable and strange. "I ne'er did see such lack of good order, discretion, and sobriety." There had been jollities and junketings, no doubt, in his youth, but surely, they were different. He remembered the "heroicall dames," the "stately heroyns" whom he had celebrated aforetime—

> These entertayn great Princes; these have learned
> The tongues, toys, tricks of Rome, of Spayn, of Fraunce;
> These can correntos and lavoltas daunce,
> And though they foote it false 'tis ne'er discerned.

More and more his thoughts reverted to his old mistress. "When she smiled, it was a pure sunshine, that every one did choose to bask in, if they could; but anon came a storm from a sudden gathering of clouds, and the thunder fell in wondrous manner on all alike." Yes! Those were great times indeed! And now . . . he was "olde and infirme"; he was forty-five; he must seek a quiet harbor and lay up his barque. He lingered at Kelston, impoverished, racked by various diseases; he vainly took the Bath waters; he became "stricken of a dead palsy"; until, in 1612, at the age of fifty-one, he passed into oblivion. And in oblivion he has remained. Nobody reads his *Orlando*; his letters are known to none but a few learned historians; his little books of epigrams lie concealed in the grim recesses of vast libraries; and Englishmen today, reflecting on many things, as they enjoy the benefits of a sanitary system unknown to the less fortunate inhabitants of other countries, give never a thought to Sir John Harington.

John Hampden

EDWARD HYDE, FIRST EARL OF CLARENDON

1594–1643. Patriot, statesman, and officer in the Parliamentary army, Hampden was fatally wounded at the battle of Chalgrove Field, June 18, 1643, and died six days later. This sketch of him was written by another patriot and statesman who was a loyal supporter of the Stuarts, a great historian and a fair-minded man who recognized the admirable qualities and abilities of one of his most formidable political foes.

Mr. Hampden was a man of much greater cunning, and it may be of the most discerning spirit, and of the greatest address and insinuation to bring anything to pass which he desired, of any man of that time, and who laid the design deepest. He was a gentleman of a good extraction, and a fair fortune, who, from a life of great pleasure and license, had on a sudden retired to extraordinary sobriety and strictness, and yet retained his usual cheerfulness and affability; which, together with the opinion of his wisdom and justice, and the courage he has shewed in opposing the ship-money, raised his reputation to a very great height, not only in Buckinghamshire, where he lived, but generally throughout the kingdom. He was not a man of many words, and rarely begun the discourse, or made the first entrance upon any business that was assumed; but a very weighty speaker, and after he had heard a full debate, and observed how the house was like to be inclined, took up the argument, and shortly, and clearly, and craftily, so stated it, that he commonly conducted it to the conclusion he desired; and if he found he could not do that, he was never without the dexterity to divert the debate to another time, and to prevent the determining any thing in the negative, which might prove inconvenient in the future. He made so great a show of civility, and modesty, and humility, and always of mistrusting his own judgment, and of esteeming his with whom he conferred for the present, that he seemed to have no opinions or resolutions, but such as he contracted from the information and instruction he received upon the discourses of others, whom he had a wonderful art of governing, and leading into his principles and inclinations, whilst they believed that he wholly depended upon their counsel and advice. No man had ever a greater power over himself, or was less the man that he seemed to be, which shortly after appeared to every body, when he cared less to keep on the mask.

The Battle of Chalgrove Field, in which Hampden received his mortal wound, was a Royalist victory.

But that which would have been looked upon as a considerable recompense for a defeat, could not but be thought a glorious crown of victory, which was the death of Mr. Hampden; who, being shot into the shoulder with a brace of bullets, which brake the bone, within three weeks after died with extraordinary pain; to as great a consternation of all that party, as if their whole army had been defeated, or cut off.

Many men observed (as upon signal turns of great affairs, as this was, such observations are frequently made) that the field in which the late skirmish was, and upon which Mr. Hampden received his death's wound, Chalgrove Field, was the same place in which he had first executed the ordinance of the militia, and engaged that county, in which his reputation was very great, in this rebellion: and it was confessed by the prisoners that were taken that day, and acknowledged by all, that upon the alarm that morning, after their quarters were beaten up, he was exceedingly solicitous to draw forces together to pursue the enemy; and, being himself a colonel of foot, put himself among those horse as a volunteer, who were first ready; and that when the prince made a stand, all the officers were of opinion to stay until their body came up, and he alone (being second to none but the general himself in the observance and application of all men) persuaded, and prevailed with them to advance, so violently did his fate carry him, to pay the mulct in the place where he had committed the transgression, about a year before.

He was a gentleman of good family in Buckinghamshire, and born to a fair fortune, and of a most civil and affable deportment. In his entrance into the world, he indulged to himself all the license in sports and exercises, and company, which was used by men of the most jolly conversation. Afterwards, he retired to a more reserved and melancholy society, yet preserving his own natural cheerfulness and vivacity, and above all, a flowing courtesy to all men; though they who conversed nearly with him, found him growing into a dislike of the ecclesiastical government of the church, yet most believed it rather a dislike of some churchmen, and of some introducements of theirs, which he apprehended might disquiet the public peace. He was rather of reputation in his own country, than of public discourse, or fame in the kingdom, before the business of ship-money; but then he grew the argument of all tongues, every man inquiring who and what he was, that durst, at his own charge, support the liberty and property of the kingdom, and rescue his country, as he thought, from being made a prey to the court. His carriage, throughout this agitation, was with that rare temper and modesty, that they who watched him narrowly to find some advantage against his person, to make him less resolute in his cause, were compelled to give him a just testimony. And the judgment that was given against him infinitely more advanced him, than the service for which it was given. When this parliament begun (being returned knight of the shire for the county, where he lived) the eyes of all men were fixed on him, as their *patriae pater*, and the pilot that must steer the vessel through the tempests and rocks which threatened it. And I am persuaded, his power and interest, at that time, was greater to do good or hurt, than any man's in the kingdom, or than any man of his rank hath had in any time: for his reputation of honesty was universal, and his affections seemed so publicly guided, that no corrupt or private ends could bias them.

He was of that rare affability and temper in debate, and of that seeming humility and submission of judgment, as if he brought no opinion with him, but a desire of information and instruction; yet he had so subtle a way of interrogating, and, under the notion of doubts, insinuating his objections, that he left his opinions with those from whom he pretended to learn and receive them. And even with them who were able to preserve themselves from his infusions, and discerned those opinions to be fixed in him, with which they could not comply, he always left the character of an ingenious and conscientious person. He was indeed a very wise man, and of great parts, and possessed with the most absolute spirit of popularity, that is, the most absolute faculties to govern the people, of any man I ever knew. For the first year of the parliament, he seemed rather to moderate and soften the violent and distempered humours, than to inflame them. But wise and dispassioned men plainly discerned, that that moderation proceeded from prudence, and observation that the season was not ripe, rather than that he approved of the moderation; and that he begat many opinions and motions, the education whereof he committed to other men; so far disguising his own designs, that he seemed seldom to wish more than was concluded: and in many gross conclusions, which would hereafter contribute to designs not yet set on foot, when he found them sufficiently backed by majority of voices, he would withdraw himself before the question, that he might seem not to consent to so much visible unreasonableness; which produced as great a doubt in some, as it did approbation in others, of his integrity. What combination soever had been originally with the Scots for the invasion of England, and what farther was entered into afterwards in favour of them, and to advance any alteration [of the government] in parliament, no man doubts was at least with the privity of this gentleman.

After he was among those members accused by the king of high treason, he was much altered; his nature and carriage seeming much fiercer than it did before. And without question, when he first drew the sword, he threw away the scabbard, for he passionately opposed the overture made by the king for a treaty from Nottingham, and as eminently, any expedients that might have produced accommodations in this that was at Oxford; and was principally relied on, to prevent any infusions which might be made into the earl of Essex towards peace, or to render them ineffectual, if they were made; and was indeed much more relied on by that party, than the general himself. In the first entrance into the troubles, he undertook the command of a regiment of foot, and performed the duty of a colonel, on all occasions most punctually. He was very temperate in diet, and a supreme governor over all his passions and affections, and had thereby a great power over other men's. He was of an industry and vigilance not to be tired out, or wearied by the most laborious; and of parts not to be imposed upon by the most subtle or sharp; and of a personal courage equal to his best parts; so that he was an enemy not to be wished wherever he might have been made a friend; and as much to be apprehended where he was so, as any man could be deserved to be. And therefore his death was no less congratulated on the one party, than it was condoled in the other. In a word, what was said of Cinna might well be applied to him; "he had a head to contrive, and a tongue to persuade, and a hand to execute, any mischief." His death therefore seemed to be a great deliverance to the nation.

The Thirtieth of January

JOHN BUCHAN

1649. Charles I—whose grandmother, Mary Queen of Scots, was beheaded; whose son James II was driven out of England by successful revolutionists— was a stupid politician, a bad soldier, and a man whose word could never be trusted. He was also kind, decent, devout, and brave. His composure and courage while being tried by an illegal court composed of his declared enemies and while upon the scaffold where he was executed won him admiration and sympathy in his own time, and continue to do so. John Buchan, Baron Tweedsmuir, from whose biography of Cromwell published in 1934 this selection is taken, was a Scots novelist, historian, and statesman.

On January 6 the Commons passed a new act by a majority of six, which arrogated to a single House the legislative power. The court established by it consisted of one hundred and thirty-five commissioners, with no judges among its members, and no peers. The act set forth that Charles Stuart had wickedly designed to subvert the ancient laws and liberties of the people, and had shown himself impenitent in these causes; wherefore he must stand his trial "for prevention of the like and greater inconveniences, and to the end no chief officer or magistrate whatever may hereafter presume traitorously and maliciously to imagine or contrive the enslaving and destroying of the English nation and to expect impunity for so doing."

228

These words in which we may detect the influence of Oliver, put the thing in its true light as a political act, to meet a present emergency and to provide for the future—a step founded not on legal or constitutional niceties but on a desperate need.

Under any possible definition of law there was no shadow of legality in the business. It was an act of state based upon that necessity which is assumed to be above the laws, an act of war like a drumhead court martial. The commissioners were army officers, members of parliament, and aldermen of London. Since there was no judge to preside, an obscure lawyer of Gray's Inn, one John Bradshaw, was chosen as president. There were independent colonels like Pride and Whalley and Harrison, and other parliamentary commanders like Ludlow and Hutchinson and Grey of Groby. Fairfax and Ireton and Oliver were members. But when the first meeting was held in the Painted Chamber on January 8 only fifty-two attended. Half of the nominees refused the task. Some were aghast at the constitutional absurdity of a tribunal founded upon a resolution of a disconsidered fragment of a single branch of parliament. Others felt the scandal of an action taken professedly in the name of the English people, when the people by a great majority were notoriously hostile to its originators. Others dreaded the tyranny of the army, remembering perhaps that clause in the Petition of Right which forbade martial law. Fairfax attended the first meeting, but no others, and some of his old officers, like Skippon, Lambert and Disbrowe, followed his example. The court, after several sparsely attended meetings, decided that the trial should begin on the 20th.

On the 19th Charles was brought from Windsor to the palace of St. James's, guarded by troops of horse, and with Hugh Peters prancing in mountebank triumph before his coach. London was in the grip of a black frost and its Christmas had been dismal. Troopers were everywhere, riding in grim posses, or off duty and sombrely puffing tobacco, vast silent men, lean from the wars. The citizens did not linger in the streets, for none knew his neighbor's mind. Whitehall was full of soldiers, and now and then there was an outbreak and broken heads. St. Paul's, if we are to believe the royalist journalists, was a curious spectacle; "they have turned it into an ale-house, a barber's-shop, a smith's forge, a scullery, and, I blush to think of it, into a bawdy house." Everywhere there was an epidemic of preaching, Hugh Peters and his friends in St. Margaret's and the Whitehall courtyard, while the London ministers, like Marshall and Calamy, from their own pulpits fulminated against the army.

Meanwhile the great hall of Westminster had been set in order for the trial. That hall remains today though all its environs have suffered change, and it is easy to reconstruct the scene. The booths of the tradespeople were cleared from the floor, and the south end, where the courts of Chancery and King's Bench usually sat, was filled with a wooden platform three feet high. Beneath it was a broad gangway, and another ran at right angles down to the main door, and both gangways were to be lined with pikemen and musketeers. The spectators were to be crowded in the space between the gangways and the walls, but there were also two little galleries above the dais itself. The judges were to sit on benches covered with scarlet cloth at the back of the dais under the great south window. In the middle of the front row was a raised desk for the president; the clerks sat at a table beneath him, where lay the mace and the sword of state; at the edge of the dais there were pews for the prosecuting counsel and a crimson-velvet armchair for the king, who would sit with his back to the body of spectators. On the left of the dais, looking toward the judges, a door led to St. Stephen's Chapel where the Commons met; at the back there was a way through by the Court of Requests to the Painted Chamber, splendid in gilding and frescoes and black-letter Scripture texts, where the court held its private sessions. The windows of the Painted Chamber looked out on the gardens of Sir Robert Cotton's house, where the king was to lodge.

About two o'clock on the 20th Charles was carried to Whitehall in a sedan-chair and thence by water to Cotton house. The commissioners in the Painted Chamber saw him arrive before they had decided upon the authority upon which they should found their case, for they were well aware of its legal flimsiness. A certain Sir Purbeck Temple, a royalist who was planning the king's escape, was hidden behind the arras, and at the trial of the regicides deposed as follows:

When their prayer was over there came news that the King was landing at Sir Robert Cotton's Stairs, at which Cromwell ran to a window, looking on the King as he came up the garden. He turned as white as the wall. Returning to the board . . . he said thus: "My masters, he is come, he is come and now we are doing that great work that the whole nation will be full of. Therefore I desire you to let us resolve here what answer we shall give the King when he comes before us, for the first question that he will ask will be by what authority as commissioners we do try him." To which none answered presently. Then after a little space Henry Marten rose up and said: "In the name of the Commons in parliament assembled, and all the good people of England."

We may discredit certain details, such as Oliver's white face, but there is no reason to disbelieve the substance of the tale. Headed by Bradshawe in his shot-proof hat, the court, having got its formula, marched with its men-at-arms and ushers into Westminster hall.

Charles, in a dark suit and wearing the insignia of the Garter, remained covered and paid no respect to the court. When the roll of judges was called sixty-eight responded; when Fairfax's name was spoken Lady Fairfax in one of the galleries called out that he had too much wit to be there.

While the charge was read the king's stern face relaxed, and he laughed when he heard himself proclaimed a traitor. He tried to interrupt the clerk by touching him with his cane; its silver head fell off and he had to pick it up himself. Bradshawe called on him to answer, using Henry Marten's new-made formula. Again there was an interruption, a woman's voice crying out, that it was a lie, that not half nor a quarter of the people of England was with them, and that the charge was made by rebels and traitors. There was a delay while the gallery was cleared, and then Charles asked the expected question—by what authority he was being tried. England, he said, had never been an elective kingdom; he was monarch not by election but by inheritance, and to acknowledge a usurped authority would be betrayal of his trust. As he was removed the soldiers by order shouted "Justice," but the mass of the spectators cried "God save the King."

He was next brought before the court on the 22nd, and again refused to plead. His objection was unanswerable by those who tried to give a color of legality to what was an act of revolutionary statecraft. "It is not my case alone, it is the freedom and liberty of the people of England, and, do you pretend what you will, I stand more for their liberties. For if power without law make law, may alter the fundamental laws of the kingdom, I do not know what subject he is in England can be assured of his life or anything he can call his own." So completely did the court fail to overawe the prisoner that Hewson, one of the commanders of the guards, is said to have lost his temper and spat in Charles's face. "God hath justice in store," said the king gently, "both for you and me." Again on the 23rd he was before the court with the same result. The commissioners accordingly sat in private in the Painted Chamber, and heard condemnatory evidence in the absence of the prisoner—how he had been seen in arms against the parliament and had invited foreign armies to enter England. All this was farcical, but time was needed to convince doubting members of the court. On the 25th it was resolved in a small house that they should proceed to sentence against the king as tyrant, traitor, murderer and public enemy to the commonwealth of England, and that the sentence should be death; and a fuller court next day confirmed the decision. The king was to be brought into Westminster hall on the morrow to hear his doom.

That day, Saturday the 27th, saw the end of the judicial travesty. That morning Bradshawe's wife implored her husband to spare the king, and was told that he would do him no harm save what the Lord commanded. Bradshawe believed sincerely that he had a good legal case, and, when four years later the rump of the Commons was turned out on the ground that it was no parliament but an oligarchy, he is said to have lamented, "If this be no parliament, then am I the king's murderer?" When he took his seat in a scarlet gown that afternoon in Westminster hall there was further interruption by women. Charles demanded that he should be heard in his defence by the Lords and Commons, since he had something to say "most material for the peace of the kingdom." What that something was we cannot tell, but it may be that he meant to offer to abdicate in favor of his son on certain terms. One of the commissioners, John Downes, was inclined to agree to the proposal, but the rest of the court refused. Bradshawe delivered a vast rambling speech, in which he quoted the Scriptures and the classics, medieval lawyers like Bracton, Mariana, Father Parsons and George Buchanan, and made but a poor job of it. Charles asked permission to answer him, but was told that it was too late. The clerk read the sentence, and the prisoner still struggling to speak, was removed by the guards. The soldiers in the hall and outside it, pursuant to orders, shouted "Justice" and "Execution" and blew tobacco-smoke in his face. "Poor souls," said the king, "for sixpence they would do the same for their commanders." But in the streets the common people were weeping.

As the news of the verdict flew abroad, and the first trestles were set up outside the Banqueting House in Whitehall, a silence of horror fell upon the city. The death-sentence was not the work of the people of England; it was carried through by a small, resolute and armed minority in the face of a stupefied nation. Visionaries besieged the council of officers with commands from Heaven for Charles's safety. All that was most stable in the land, all who were reverent of old sanctities and "fearful for the laws" were shocked to the core not only by the barbarity of the deed but by its futility. Many pointed out—not quite truly—that England's true grievance was not against the king's person but against "the power that is made up in the kingly office by the corrupt constitution"; the sword could end Charles's life, but not the monarchy. Staunch reformers and tried servants of parliament went into opposition. Fairfax was one; he did his best in his slow way to save the king's life, and, like Montrose, he wrote verses of passionate regret to his memory. Vane was another, and he had gone to extreme lengths in his anti-monarchist fervor. Lawyers like St. John and Pierrepoint were naturally hostile, and young Algernon Sidney put the thing squarely to the judges—"First, the king can be tried by no court; second, no man can be tried by this court." The presbyterians were scandalized and enraged; the Scottish commissioners in London made vigorous protests; the Assembly of Divines pled for a respite, as did the London clergy. The gentility, the reason, the moderation, the wealth of England were flung into the scale.

Fruitlessly, for in the other was the sword. A knot of determined men, who see their course with the terrible simplicity of the fanatic, and have armed forces to do their bidding, are more than a match for a million puzzled civilians. They were so deeply in earnest that they made a sacrament out of their vengeance. "The gentlemen that were appointed his judges," Lucy Hutchinson wrote, and divers others, saw in the King a disposition so bent on the ruin of all that opposed him, and of all the righteous and just things they had contended for, that it was upon the conscience of many of them that, if they did not execute justice upon him, God would require at their hands all the blood and desolation which should ensue by their suffering him to escape, when God had brought him into their hands." Against such assurance there could be no argument, for it had the compelling power of a mandate from Heaven. The logic of events had convinced Ireton and Oliver, but they saw it not as a conclusion of cold reason but as a flash of divine revelation.

But Oliver, unlike his colleagues, had the plain good sense of the countryman and a mind ruled more by instinct than by syllogisms. He had reached his decision by crushing down his practical wisdom and closing his eyes to ultimate consequences. He had no doubts, but the consciousness that his certainty had been won by doing violence to other sides of his nature left him in a strained, neurotic temper. He argued his case fiercely to Fairfax, to the Scots, to every doubter; his inflexible will coerced the waverers, and it is said that in the signing of the death-warrant he guided some of their pens. The strain of rustic buffoonery in him came out, for on that grim occasion he inked Henry Marten's face and got his own inked in return. It was the natural rebound from his long months of torturing indecision. The man, too, was physically and mentally over-strung; an indecent nervous hilarity was the proof of his new-won confidence, and he dismissed with horse-play or with a horse-laugh the scruples of the timid. "I tell you," he boasted to Algernon Sidney, "we will cut off his head with the crown on it."

On the evening of the 27th, after sentence, Charles was taken to Sir Robert Cotton's house, and thence to Whitehall, where he spent the night. His spirits were equable, almost gay. He gave orders that his dogs should be removed and sent to his wife, that nothing might distract his mind from grave contemplation. On Sunday Juxon, who had been bishop of London, was permitted to attend him, and the day was spent in prayer. Charles refused to see any of his friends on the ground that the time left to him on earth was short and precious. He sent for a little casket of jewels, which was in the care of his laundress, and which was all that he had to bequeath to his children. On the Sunday evening, through a sudden mercifulness in his gaolers, he was taken to St. James's palace that he might not hear the scaffold being hammered together in Whitehall. Colonel Hacker, who commanded his guards, was induced also to keep the soldiers out of his room, so that the last nights of his life were spent in peace. All that Sunday the London pulpits rang with presbyterian denunciations of his judges, while Hugh Peters of St. James's poured forth Hebraic frenzies in their honor. He found an apt text—"All the kings of the nations, even all of them, lie in glory, every one in his own house. But thou art cast out of thy grave like an abominable branch, and as the raiment of those that are slain, thrust through with a sword, that go down to the stones of the pit; as a carcass trodden under foot. Thou shalt not be joined with them in burial, because thou hast destroyed thy land, and slain thy people."

On the Monday the king set about disposing of his few belongings, while the scaffold was rising in Whitehall, and the commissioners were playing strange pranks to secure an adequately signed death-warrant. To his family and his friends he gave his books and jewels. His two younger children were admitted to see him, Princess Elizabeth and the Duke of Gloucester. He took them on his knees, dried their tears, and gravely comforted and counselled them. The delicate little girl of thirteen has left her own record of his words: "He wished me not to grieve or torment myself for him, for that would be a glorious death he should die, it being for the laws and liberties of this land, and for maintaining the true Protestant religion. He bid me read Bishop Andrewes's sermons, Hooker's *Ecclesiastical Polity*, and Bishop Laud's book against Fisher, which would ground me against Popery. He told me he had forgiven all his enemies, and hoped God would forgive them also, and commanded us and all the rest of my brothers and sisters to forgive them. He bid us tell my mother that his thoughts had never strayed from her, and that his love should be the same to the last." To the boy he spoke more simply, for he was only ten. "Sweetheart, now they will cut off thy father's head; mark, child, what I say: they will cut off my head and perhaps make thee a king. But mark what I say. You must not be a king so long as your brothers Charles and James do live; for they will cut off your brothers' heads when they can catch them, and cut off thy head too at the last, and therefore I charge you do not be made a king by them." "I will be torn to pieces first," was the child's answer. He shared among them his trinkets, which were mainly broken Georges and Garter stars.

Tuesday the 30th dawned grey and very cold; so keen was the frost that ice-floes jostled in the Thames. Charles rose shortly after five. He bade Herbert dress him carefully, giving him an extra shirt; "by reason the season is so sharp as probably may make me shake, which some will imagine proceeds from fear. I would have no such imputation. I fear not death, death is not terrible to me. I bless my God I am prepared." Herbert told of a dream he had had in the night of Laud entering the room, but Charles only said that it was remarkable; he was more concerned about his clothes, which were black (but not mourning), and he put on the George and the Garter riband. "This is my second marriage day," he said. "I would be as trim today as may be, for before night I hope to be espoused to my blessed Jesus." Presently Juxon arrived to pray with him and read the lesson of the day, and a little later Hacker knocked at the door and bade him get ready to go to Whitehall.

In the bitter morning, attended by Juxon and Herbert and a guard of halberdiers, the king walked across the park, briskly, as was his custom. He arrived at Whitehall about ten o'clock. There was no chance of talk on the way, for drums beat continually. At Whitehall he received the sacrament from Juxon and was allowed to rest in a bedchamber for some hours, while parliament was passing an act to forbid the proclamation of any successor. He was offered a meal but refused; the bishop, however, warned him that he might faint in the cold, so he ate a crust of bread and drank a glass of claret.

About half-past one Hacker summoned him to die. He walked to the Banqueting House through the Whitehall galleries which were lined with spectators; most of them were praying, and the guards did not forbid them, "seeming by their silence and dejected faces afflicted rather than insulting." From one of the windows he stepped out onto the scaffold. This was railed in, and it and the railings were covered with black cloth. In the centre was the low block. Charles's refusal to plead had led to the fear that he might resist at the last moment, so staples had been fixed in the floor so that if necessary he might be held down by ropes. By the block lay the axe, brought from the Tower, perhaps the very one which had been used at Stafford's death, and beside it stood two masked men, dressed in close-fitting tunics, rough-looking fellows like sailors or butchers, one of them short, and one of them tall with a grey wig. Around the scaffold were lines of horse and foot, and beyond them a packed multitude, while every window and housetop were crowded.

On the scaffold were six figures, the king and Juxon and the two heads-men, Colonel Hacker and Colonel Tomlinson. Since Charles could not speak to the people, he addressed himself to Tomlinson and Juxon. Re-membering Stafford, he said that an unjust sentence to which he had been a party was now punished by an unjust sentence upon himself. He sub-mitted himself humbly to God's judgement. He prayed that his enemies might be pardoned, and that the land should be freed from the tyranny of the sword. There could be no peace till men paid their duties to God, people and king. And then in a few sentences he expounded his political philosophy, sentences which afterwards must have come ominously to Oliver's mind.

For the people I desire their liberty and freedom as much as anybody whom-soever; but I must tell you that this liberty and freedom consists in having government, those laws by which their lives and goods may be most their own. It is not their having a share in the government, that is nothing pertaining to them. A subject and a sovereign are clean different things; and, therefore, until you do this—I mean that you put the people in that liberty—they will never enjoy themselves. . . . If I would have given way to have all changed according to the power of the sword, I needed not to have come here; and therefore I tell you (and I pray God that it be not laid to your charge) that I am the martyr of the people.

With the assistance of the executioners he put his long hair under a white satin nightcap. For a little he spoke aside with Juxon, handing him the George which he took from his neck, with instructions for its disposal. He removed his cloak and doublet and laid himself down on the scaffold with his head on the block. For a few minutes he lay there praying, his eye, said a watcher, "as brisk and lively as ever he had seen it." Then he stretched out his hands, and the grizzled executioner brought down the axe and severed his head. The other held it up in silence to the people. A groan of horror rent the stillness, and the next minute troops of horse were on the move, splitting up the crowd and driving it towards Charing Cross and Westminster.

Then followed a hideous scene. Men and women were permitted—on payment—to dip their handkerchiefs in the king's blood, and his long locks were shorn and sold as keepsakes. The body was put in a plain deal coffin costing six pounds, covered with a black velvet pall, and remained for some days in a Whitehall bedroom. Then it was embalmed, the head being sewn on, and afterwards removed to St. James's palace. An application to bury it in Henry VII's chapel was refused, but permission was given to lay it in St. George's chapel at Windsor. Thither, on Friday, February 9th, it was taken by Herbert and Juxon, Richmond and a few other nobles attending, and placed in the vault which held the remains of Jane Seymour and Henry VIII. No service was read, for the governor of Windsor would not permit the use of the prayerbook. The prophecy of Merlin was fulfilled, and Charles, who had chosen to be crowned in white, went in white to his tomb. "This is memorable," Herbert wrote, "that at such time as the King's body was brought out of St. George's hall the sky was serene and clear; but presently it began to snow, and so fast as, by the time they came to the west end of the royal chapel, the black velvet pall was all white (the color of innocency) being thick covered with snow. So went the white King to his grave, in the forty-eighth year of his age and the twenty-second year and tenth month of his reign."

In Bossuet's great sermon at the funeral of Henrietta Maria he spoke some words of her husband. "I am scarce able to contemplate the greatness of his courage in those last trials; but assuredly he plainly evidenced that it is not in the power of rebels to make a king who knows himself to lose his majesty." The tribute was just. None of the shortcomings of Charles's life can detract from the splendor of his death. He had the gift of his strange race of leaving the world with a noble gesture, with no act or word to mar the final tragic perfection. On the paradoxes of his character men will argue till the end of time. Of his personal charm there is no doubt; on that Clarendon and Philip Warwick have written with a lover's passion. Nor are his virtues and vices in dispute—his piety and fortitude; his inability to read a plain lesson, his lack of candor, his craze for blundering intrigues, his gentle but unshakable obstinacy. He was a tragic figure, because he was born into times which he could not understand and to a task which was too hard for him. The tragedy is there rather than in his death, for his execution was largely his own blame. It was beyond his power, beyond the power of anyone, to revive the Tudor monarchy, and Charles realized this; he was willing to make concessions, and it is certain that during the first nine months of 1747 he could have got from Oliver and Ireton and the army terms which would have safeguarded the things for which he ultimately died, episcopal government and a reasonable degree of royal authority. But in his folly he tried to bluff those with whom he dealt, the game went against him, and after the second Civil War men's tempers were soured and all hope of accommodation departed. As a legal act his death was a travesty of justice; as an incident in a revolutionary war it was as just or as unjust as the other details of that war. Charles lost and had to pay the penalty; if he had won, Oliver, Ireton and many others would have been shorter by their heads.

The Persecution of the Protestants by Louis XIV

VOLTAIRE

1681–1685. The French Protestants, variously called Huguenots, Calvinists, and members of the Reformed Religion, enjoyed a limited freedom from the passage of the Edict of Nantes by Henry IV in 1598 until its revocation in 1685. Voltaire in his celebrated Age of Louis XIV, *published in 1751, devoted most of his attention to praising economic progress, political and legal reforms, and cultural achievements. But the great skeptic, much as he admired Louis, was shocked by his religious fanaticism. As a hater of cruelty, he sympathized with the victims of Louis's persecution, but he deplored their fanaticism also.*

Louis XIV was roused to anger against the reformers by the continual remonstrances of his clergy, by the insinuations of the Jesuits, by the court of Rome and lastly by the chancellor Le Tellier and his son Louvois, who were both enemies of Colbert and who wanted to root out the Calvinists as rebels because Colbert was protecting them as useful subjects. Louis XIV, who knew nothing of the fundamentals of their doctrine, looked on them, not without some reason, as former rebels who had been subdued with difficulty. He began by applying himself to the task of undermining from every side the edifice of their religion. Their churches were closed on the slightest pretext; they were forbidden to marry Catholic girls, a

238

prohibition which perhaps showed a lack of shrewdness in that it failed to take advantage of the power of a sex with which the court, nevertheless, was well acquainted. The intendants and bishops tried, on the most plausible grounds, to take Huguenot children away from their parents. In 1681 Colbert was ordered not to employ any man of this religion in the administration of taxation. They were excluded, as far as possible, from the guilds of arts and crafts. The King, however, while keeping them under the yoke, did not always make them feel the full weight of it. Decrees prohibited all acts of violence against them. Persuasion was mixed with severity, and it was not only in the formalities of justice that full rigor was employed.

One method of conversion which often proved effective was used more than all others: this was money; yet even this was not used enough. Pellisson was charged with this secret undertaking—the same Pellisson who had long been a Calvinist, and who was so well known for his writings, for his abundant eloquence and for his attachment to the superintendent Fouquet, of whom he had been both the secretary and favorite, and the victim. He had the good fortune to be enlightened and to change his religion at a time when this change could lead him to dignities and fortune. He entered orders and obtained benefices and a post of master of requests. About 1677 the King gave him the revenues of the abbeys of Saint-Germain-les-Prés and Cluny, together with the revenues of a third of the vacant benefices, so that he might distribute them to those who were willing to be converted. Cardinal Lecamus, Bishop of Grenoble, had already used this method. Pellisson, when he was put in charge of this department, sent money to the provinces, trying to secure a large number of conversions for very little money. Small sums distributed to the poor swelled the list that Pellisson presented every three months to the King, making him believe that nothing could resist his power and his generosity.

The Council, encouraged by these small successes, which time would have rendered more considerable, took a bold step in 1681 by issuing a declaration which required all children to renounce the Protestant religion at the age of seven; under the sanction of this declaration, large numbers of children were seized in the provinces in order to force them to abjure, and troops were billeted on their parents.

In 1681 this precipitate step, taken by the chancellor Le Tellier and his son Louvois, resulted in the desertion of many families from Poitou, Saintonge and the neighboring provinces. Foreign countries hastened to take advantage of these.

The Kings of England and Denmark, and above all the city of Amsterdam, invited the French Calvinists to take refuge in their states and assured them of a livelihood. Amsterdam even promised to build a thousand houses for the refugees.

The Council, seeing the dangerous consequences of this hasty assertion of their authority, thought it could remedy them by other measures equally authoritarian. They realized the importance of artisans in a commercially prosperous country, and of sailors at a time when a powerful navy was being built up. They therefore ordered that any members of these professions who tried to escape should be condemned to the galleys.

A number of Calvinist families were found to be selling their landed property. Immediately a declaration was issued confiscating all this property in the event the seller left the country within a year. There followed an intensification of the stern measures against the Protestant ministers. At the slightest infringement of the law, their churches were closed. All the income bequested to their consistories was used instead for the upkeep of hospitals throughout the kingdom.

Calvinist schoolmasters were forbidden to receive pensioners. Ministers were made subject to the taille [a tax on land or income not paid by nobles]; Protestant mayors were deprived of their nobility. Those officers of the royal household and King's secretaries who were Protestants were ordered to resign their offices. Adherents of this religion were no longer allowed to become notaries, advocates or even attorneys.

The clergy were enjoined to make converts, and the reformed pastors were forbidden to do so on pain of banishment for life. All these decrees had been pressed for openly by the French clergy. They were, after all, the children of the family, and they did not want to have to share with strangers introduced by force.

Pellisson continued to buy converts; but Mme. Hervart, widow of the controller general of the finances, animated by the sort of religious zeal to which women throughout the ages have always been prone, offered as much money to prevent conversions as Pellisson did to achieve them.

Finally, in 1682 the Huguenots in a number of places dared to disobey. They assembled together in Vivarais and in Dauphiné near the places where their churches had been demolished. They were attacked, and they defended themselves. This was but a dying spark of the old fire of civil war. Two or three hundred wretches, without leaders, without strongholds and even without plans, were dispersed in a quarter of an hour. Their defeat was followed by their torture and execution. The intendant of Dauphiné had the grandson of Pastor Chamier, who had drawn up the Edict of Nantes, broken on the wheel. He is among the most famous martyrs of the sect and his name has long been venerated by the Protestants.

In 1683 the intendant of Languedoc had the preacher Chomet broken on the wheel. Three others were condemned to the same torture, and ten more to hanging; they saved themselves by flight and were only executed in effigy.

All this inspired terror, but at the same time increased the stubbornness of resistance. It is well known that men become more attached to their religion the more they have to suffer for it.

It was then that the King was persuaded that after having sent missionaries into all the provinces, the next step was to send dragoons. These acts of violence seemed untimely; they resulted from the view, prevalent in the court at that time, that the very name of Louis XIV should suffice to silence all opposition. People did not reflect that the Huguenots were no longer what they had been at Jarnac, Moncontour and Coutras;* that the rage of civil war was spent; that this disease, which had lasted so long, was no longer virulent; that nothing human is unchanging and that if the fathers had been rebels under Louis XIII, the children were loyal subjects of Louis XIV. In England, Holland and Germany, one could witness the spectacle of several sects who had been busy cutting each other's throats in the previous century now living peacefully together in the same towns. Everything showed that an absolute monarch could be served equally well by Catholics and Protestants alike. The Lutherans of Alsace offered convincing proof of this. In short, it seems that Queen Christina was right when she wrote in one of her letters, referring to these acts of violence and to the emigrations: "I consider France to be like a sick man who is having his arms and legs cut off to cure a disease which could have been completely cured by kindness and patience."

Louis XIV, who protected Lutheranism when he occupied Strasbourg in 1681, could have tolerated Calvinism in the rest of the country, for time might well have abolished it just as it is gradually diminishing the number of Lutherans in Alsace. Did the government really never stop to think that by using force against a large number of the King's subjects, they might end by losing an even greater number, who, despite edicts and guards, would succeed in escaping from a violence which seemed to them horrible persecution? Finally, why should they have wished to make more than a million men hate a dear and precious name and one to which Protestants and Catholics, Frenchmen and foreigners alike had attached the epithet "great"? Even political considerations might have persuaded them to keep the Calvinists, for their presence would have helped them to resist the constant claims of the court of Rome. It was precisely at this time that the King was in open conflict with Innocent XI, the enemy of France. But Louis XIV, trying to conciliate the interests of his religion with those of his grandeur, wanted simultaneously to humiliate the Pope with one hand and crush Calvinism with the other.

In both these enterprises, he sought only the glory which he admired in all things. The bishops, several of the intendants and the whole Council

* These were famous battles of the civil wars of the sixteenth century.

persuaded him that his soldiers had only to show themselves in order to complete the work which his generosity and the missions had begun. He thought he was merely using his authority; but those to whom this authority was entrusted exercised it with extreme rigor.

Toward the end of 1684 and at the beginning of 1685, when Louis XIV still powerfully armed, had nothing to fear from his neighbors, troops were sent into all the towns and castles where the Protestants were strongest; and as the dragoons, who were rather badly disciplined in those days committed most excesses, this action was known as the *dragonnade.*

The frontiers were as carefully guarded as possible, to prevent the flight of those whom it was intended to convert. It was like a hunt carried out in a vast enclosure.

A bishop, an intendant, a subdelegate, a priest or some other authorized person marched at the head of the soldiers. The principal Calvinist families were gathered together, especially those who were thought most open to persuasion. They renounced their religion in the name of the others, and those who refused were handed over to the soldiers, who could do anything with them except kill them. A number of people, however, were so cruelly maltreated that they died. The children of the refugees in foreign countries still cry out in horror at the sufferings of their fathers, comparing them to the most violent persecutions of the early Church.

It was a strange contrast to see such harsh and pitiless orders emanating from a pleasure-loving court famous for its gentle manners, its graces and its social charm. Behind the actions taken, one could clearly detect the stern hand of the Marquis of Louvois, the man who had wanted to drown Holland beneath the sea and had reduced the Palatinate to ashes. There still exists a letter he wrote in this year 1685, which reads as follows: "His majesty wishes those who are unwilling to accept his religion to be treated with the utmost rigor; and those who are stupid enough to seek the glory of being the last should be reduced to the last extremity."

Paris was not exposed to these vexations; the sounds of distress would have been heard all too near the throne. It is all very well to make men suffer, but it is painful to have to listen to their cries.

While the Protestant churches were being destroyed everywhere, and armed force was being used in the provinces to make their adherents abjure, the Edict of Nantes itself was finally revoked in October, 1685, thereby completing the ruin of an edifice which was already undermined on every side.

The Chamber of the Edict had already been suppressed. The Calvinist councilors of the parliament were ordered to resign. In quick succession the King's Council issued a large number of decrees, all designed to stamp out the remains of the proscribed religion. The one which seemed cruelest was the order to seize the children of Protestants and hand them over to the nearest Catholic parents; this order was so blatantly unnatural that it was never executed.

However, this celebrated edict revoking that of Nantes in fact produced a result which was the complete opposite of the one aimed at. The intention was to reunite the Calvinists with the Church within the kingdom. We know that when Gourville, who was a most judicious man, was consulted by Louvois, he proposed that all the ministers should be locked up and that none should be released except those who, having been won over by secret bribes, would abjure their religion in public, thereby serving the cause of reunion much more effectively than the missionaries and the soldiers. Instead of following this shrewd advice, the government ordered that all ministers who refused to be converted should leave the country within a fortnight. It was blind folly to think that if they drove away the shepherds, a large portion of the flock would not follow. It showed a rash overestimation of their power and little understanding of human nature to think that all these wounded hearts and all these imaginations inflamed by the idea of martyrdom, especially in the south of France, would not take every risk to escape abroad, there to make known their constancy and the glory of their exile among the many nations who envied Louis XIV and were holding out their arms to these swarms of refugees.

When he signed the Edict, the old chancellor, Le Tellier, cried out in his joy: "*Nunc dimittis servum tuum, Domine . . . quia viderunt oculi salutare tuum.*"* He did not know that he was signing one of France's greatest misfortunes.

Louvois, his son, was equally deceived when he thought that an order signed by him would be sufficient to guard all the frontiers and all the coasts against those who decided it was their duty to escape. When people apply all their skill to breaking the law, they are always stronger than authority. It was enough to bribe a few guards to ensure the escape of a whole host of refugees. Nearly fifty thousand families left the country in three years, and they were later followed by others. They took with them, for the benefit of foreign countries, their skill, their industry and their wealth. Almost the whole of northern Germany, a land still rural and devoid of industries, was transformed by the arrival of these multitudes. They peopled whole towns. The cloths, the braids, the hats and the stockings which formerly had been bought from France were now made by them. A whole suburb of London was populated by French silk workers; others took there the art of making cut glass, which was then lost to

---

* "Now let thy servant depart, O Lord . . . for mine eyes have seen thy salvation." (Luke 2:25)

France. It is still common to find in Germany the gold circulated there by the refugees. And so France lost about five-hundred thousand inhabitants, a vast amount of money and above all the skills which went to enrich her enemies. Holland acquired some excellent officers and soldiers. The Prince of Orange and the Duke of Savoy and Piedmont who had treated their own reformers so cruelly took those of France into their pay; and it was certainly not because of religious zeal that the Prince of Orange enrolled them. Some of them even settled as far away as the Cape of Good Hope. The nephew of the famous Duquesne, lieutenant general of the navy, founded a little colony in this far-off land. It did not prosper, and the majority of those who set sail perished. Yet some remnants of this colony still remain as neighbors of the Hottentots. The French were dispersed even farther than the Jews had been.

The prisons and galleys were filled with those who were caught in flight; but in vain. What could be done with so many wretched people whose belief had been strengthened by their sufferings? How could one send lawyers and infirm old men to the galleys? Several hundred were shipped off to America. Finally the Council conceived the idea that once people were no longer forbidden to leave the country, and their minds were no longer influenced by the secret pleasure of disobedience, there would be fewer desertions. They were wrong again; and after having opened the frontiers, they closed them a second time, but to no avail.

In 1685 Calvinists were forbidden to have Catholic servants for fear that these might be converted by their masters; and in the following year another edict ordered them to get rid of Huguenot servants, who could then be arrested as vagabonds. There was no uniformity in the way they were persecuted, except in the general plan to use oppression as a means of conversion.

When all the Protestant churches were destroyed, and all their ministers banished, the question arose as to how those who had recanted, whether from persuasion or through fear, were to be kept within the Roman communion. Over four-hundred thousand of them remained in France. Some, who refused the sacrament after having first received it, were condemned to be burned alive. The bodies of those who refused the last rites were dragged on a hurdle through the streets and buried in the refuse dump.

When used against those filled with a burning enthusiasm, persecution often merely reinforces their convictions. Everywhere, the Calvinists gathered to sing their psalms despite the fact that such meetings were punishable by death. Death was also the punishment for any minister who returned to France and five thousand five-hundred francs reward was offered to anybody who denounced one of them. Several did return, and were either hanged or broken on the wheel.

Though it seemed crushed, the Calvinist sect lived on. In the war of 1689, it entertained the hope that King William, after he had dethroned his Catholic father-in-law, would come to the aid of the Protestants of France. The hope proved vain, but in the war of 1701 there was a real outbreak of rebellion and fanaticism in Languedoc and the neighboring areas.

This rebellion was stirred up by prophecies. Such predictions have always been used to delude the simple and inflame the fanatical. If a charlatan makes a hundred predictions and chance brings about the fulfillment of one of these, the others are forgotten and the one remains as a token of God's favor and as proof of a miracle. If none of them comes true, then explanations are offered, and a new interpretation put on the words; this is adopted by enthusiasts and believed by fools.

Justice Jeffreys and the Bloody Assizes

THOMAS BABINGTON MACAULAY

1685. After the failure of the rebellion against James II led by the Duke of Monmouth, an illegitimate son of Charles II, hundreds of the duke's followers were fined, whipped, hanged, and transported. Chief Justice of the King's Bench George Jeffreys presided over this infamous "justice." Macaulay's The History of England from the Accession of James II, *from which these selections are taken, is widely considered the second greatest history written in English, surpassed only by Gibbon's* The Decline and Fall of the Roman Empire—*and this in spite of Macaulay's notorious Whig bias.*

The depravity of this man has passed into a proverb. Both the great English parties have attacked his memory with emulous violence: for the Whigs considered him their most barbarous enemy; and the Tories found it convenient to throw on him the blame of all the crimes which had sullied their triumph. A diligent and candid inquiry will show that some frightful stories which have been told concerning him are false or exaggerated. Yet the disapassionate historian will be able to make very little deduction from the vast mass of infamy with which the memory of the wicked judge has been loaded.

He was a man of quick and vigorous parts, but constitutionally prone to insolence and to the angry passions. When just emerging from boyhood he had risen into practise at the Old Bailey bar, a bar where advocates have always used a license of tongue unknown in Westminster Hall. Here, during many years, his chief business was to examine and crossexamine the most hardened miscreants of a great capital. Daily conflicts with prostitutes and thieves called out and exercised his powers so effectually that he became the most consummate bully ever known in his profession. All tenderness for the feelings of others, all selfrespect, all sense of the becoming, were obliterated from his mind. He acquired a boundless command of the rhetoric in which the vulgar express hatred and contempt. The profusion of maledictions and vituperative epithets which composed his vocabulary could hardly have been rivalled in the fishmarket or the beargarden. His countenance and his voice must always have been unamiable. But these natural advantages—for such he seems to have thought them—he had improved to such a degree that there were few who, in his paroxysms of rage, could see or hear him without emotion. Impudence and ferocity sate upon his brow. The glare of his eyes had a fascination for the unhappy victim on whom they were fixed. Yet his brow and his eye were said to be less terrible than the savage lines of his mouth. His yell of fury, it was said by one who had often heard it, sounded like the thunder of judgment day. These qualifications he carried, while still a young man, from the bar to the bench. He early became Common Serjeant and then Recorder of London. As a judge at the City sessions he exhibited the same propensities which afterwards, in a higher post, gained for him an unenviable immortality. Already might be remarked in him the most odious vice which is incident to human nature, a delight in misery merely as misery. There was a fiendish exultation in the way in which he pronounced sentence on offenders. Their weeping and imploring seemed to titillate him voluptuously; and he loved to scare them into fits by dilating with luxuriant amplification on all the details of what they were to suffer. Thus, when he had an opportunity of ordering an unlucky adventuress to be whipped at the cart's tail, "Hangman," he would exclaim, "I charge you to pay particular attention to this lady! Scourge her soundly, man. Scourge her till the blood runs down! It is Christmas, a cold time for Madam to strip in! See that you warm her shoulders thoroughly!" He was hardly less facetious when he passed judgment on poor Lodowick Muggleton, the drunken tailor who fancied himself a prophet. "Impudent rogue!" roared Jeffreys, "thou shalt have an easy, easy, easy punishment!" One part of this easy punishment was the pillory, in which the wretched fanatic was almost killed with brickbats.

By this time the heart of Jeffreys had been hardened to that temper which tyrants require in their worst implements. He had hitherto looked for professional advancement to the corporation of London. He had therefore professed himself a Roundhead, and had always appeared to be in a higher state of exhilaration when he explained to Popish priests that they were to be cut down alive, and were to see their own bowels burned, than when he passed ordinary sentences of death. But, as soon as he had got all that the City could give, he made haste to sell his forehead of brass and his tongue of venom to the Court. Chiffinch, who was accustomed to act as broker in infamous contracts of more than one kind, lent his aid. He had conducted many amorous and many political intrigues; but he assuredly never rendered a more scandalous service to his masters than when he introduced Jeffreys to Whitehall. The renegade soon found a patron in the obdurate and revengeful James, but was always regarded with scorn and disgust by Charles, whose faults, great as they were, had no affinity with insolence and cruelty. "That man," said the King, "has no learning, no sense, no manners, and more impudence than ten carted streetwalkers." Work was to be done, however, which could be trusted to no man who reverenced law or was sensible of shame, and thus Jeffreys, at an age at which a barrister thinks himself fortunate if he is employed to conduct an important case, was made Chief Justice of the King's Bench.

His enemies could not deny that he possessed some of the qualities of a great judge. His legal knowledge, indeed, was merely such as he had picked up in practice of no very high kind. But he had one of those happily constituted intellects which, across labyrinths of sophistry, and through masses of immaterial facts, go straight to the true point. Of his intellect, however, he seldom had the full use. Even in civil causes his malevolent and despotic temper perpetually disordered his judgment. To enter his court was to enter the den of a wild beast, which none could tame, and which was as likely to be roused to rage by caresses as by attacks. He frequently poured forth on plaintiffs and defendants, barristers and attorneys, witnesses and jurymen, torrents of frantic abuse, intermixed with oaths and curses. His looks and tones had inspired terror when he was merely a young advocate struggling into practice. Now that he was at the head of the most formidable tribunal in the realm, there were few indeed who did not tremble before him. Even when he was sober, his violence was sufficiently frightful. But in general his reason was overclouded and his evil passions stimulated by the fumes of intoxication. His evenings were ordinarily given to revelry. People who saw him only over his bottle would have supposed him to be a man gross indeed, sottish, and addicted to low company and low merriment, but social and goodhumored. He was constantly surrounded on such occasions by buffoons selected, for the most part, from among the vilest pettifoggers who practised before him. These men bantered and abused each other for his entertainment. He joined in their ribald talk, sang catches with them, and, when his head grew hot, hugged and kissed them in an ecstasy of drunken fondness. But, though wine at first seemed to soften his heart, the effect a few hours later was very different. He often came to the judgment seat, having kept the court waiting long, and yet having but half slept off his debauch, his cheeks on fire, his eyes staring like those of a maniac. When he was in this state, his boon companions of the preceding night, if they were wise, kept out of his way: for the recollection of the familiarity to which he had admitted them inflamed his malignity; and he was sure to take every opportunity of overwhelming them with execration and invective. Not the least odious of his many odious peculiarities was the pleasure which he took in publicly browbeating and mortifying those whom, in his fits of maudlin tenderness, he had encouraged to presume on his favor.

The services which the government had expected from him were performed, not merely without flinching, but eagerly and triumphantly. His first exploit was the judicial murder of Algernon Sidney. What followed was in perfect harmony with this beginning. Respectable Tories lamented the disgrace which the barbarity and indecency of so great a functionary brought upon the administration of justice. But the excesses which filled such men with horror were titles to the esteem of James. Jeffreys, therefore, after the death of Charles, obtained a seat in the cabinet and a peerage. This last honor was a signal mark of royal approbation. For, since the judicial system of the realm had been remodelled in the thirteenth century, no Chief Justice had been a Lord of Parliament.

* * *

In Hampshire Alice Lisle was the only victim: but, on the day following her execution, Jeffreys reached Dorchester, the principal town of the country in which Monmouth had landed, and the judicial massacre began.

The court was hung, by order of the Chief Justice, with scarlet; and this innovation seemed to the multitude to indicate a bloody purpose. It was also rumored that, when the clergyman who preached the assize sermon inforced the duty of mercy, the ferocious mouth of the judge was distorted by an ominous grin. These things made men augur ill of what was to follow.

More than three hundred prisoners were to be tried. The work seemed heavy; but Jeffreys had a contrivance for making it light. He let it be understood that the only chance of obtaining pardon or respite was to plead guilty. Twenty-nine persons, who had put themselves on their country and were convicted, were ordered to be tied up without delay. The remaining prisoners pleaded guilty by scores. Two hundred and ninety-two received sentence of death. The whole number hanged in Dorchester amounted to seventy-four.

Justice Jeffreys and the Bloody Assizes

From Dorchester Jeffreys proceeded to Exeter. The civil war had barely grazed the frontier of Devonshire. Here, therefore, comparatively few persons were punished. Somersetshire, the chief seat of the rebellion, had been reserved for the last and most fearful vengeance. In this county two hundred and thirty-three prisoners were in a few days hanged, drawn and quartered. At every spot where two roads met, on every market place, on the green of every large village which had furnished Monmouth with soldiers, ironed corpses clattering in the wind, or heads and quarters stuck on poles, poisoned the air, and made the traveller sick with horror. In many parishes the peasantry could not assemble in the house of God without seeing the ghastly face of a neighbor grinning at them over the porch. The Chief Justice was all himself. His spirits rose higher and higher as the work went on. He laughed, shouted, joked, and swore in such a way that many thought him drunk from morning to night. But in him it was not easy to distinguish the madness produced by evil passions from the madness produced by brandy. A prisoner affirmed that the witnesses who appeared against him were not entitled to credit. One of them, he said, was a Papist, and another a prostitute. "Thou impudent rebel," exclaimed the judge, "to reflect on the King's evidence! I see thee, villain, I see thee already with the halter round thy neck." Another produced testimony that he was a good Protestant. "Protestant!" said Jeffreys; "you mean Presbyterian. I'll hold you a wager of it. I can smell a Presbyterian forty miles." One wretched man moved the pity even of bitter Tories. "My Lord," they said, "this poor creature is on the parish." "Do not trouble yourselves," said the judge, "I will ease the parish of the burden." It was not only on the prisoners that his fury broke forth. Gentlemen and noblemen of high consideration and stainless loyalty, who ventured to bring to his notice any extenuating circumstance, were almost sure to receive what he called, in the coarse dialect which he had learned in the pothouses of Whitechapel, a lick with the rough side of his tongue. Lord Stawell, a Tory peer, who could not conceal his horror at the remorseless manner in which his poor neighbors were butchered, was punished by having a corpse suspended in chains at his park gate. In such spectacles originated many tales of terror, which were long told over the cider by the Christmas fires of the farmers of Somersetshire. Within the last forty years peasants, in some districts, well knew the accursed spots, and passed them unwillingly after sunset.

Jeffreys boasted that he had hanged more traitors than all his predecessors together since the Conquest. It is certain that the number of persons whom he executed in one month, and in one shire, very much exceeded the number of all the political offenders who have been executed in our island since the Revolution. The rebellions of 1715 and 1745 were of longer duration, of wider extent, and of more formidable aspect than that which was put down at Sedgemoor. It has not been generally thought that, either after the rebellion of 1715, or after the rebellion of 1745, the House of Hanover erred on the side of clemency. Yet all the executions of 1715 and 1745 added together will appear to have been few indeed when compared with those which disgraced the Bloody Assizes. The number of the rebels whom Jeffreys hanged on this circuit was three hundred and twenty.

Such havoc must have excited disgust even if the sufferers had been generally odious. But they were, for the most part, men of blameless life, and of high religious profession. They were regarded by themselves, and by a large proportion of their neighbors, not as wrongdoers, but as martyrs who sealed with blood the truth of the Protestant religon. Very few of the convicts professed any repentance for what they had done. Many, animated by the old Puritan spirit, met death, not merely with fortitude, but with exultation. It was in vain that the ministers of the Established Church lectured them on the guilt of rebellion and on the importance of priestly absolution. The claim of the King to unbounded authority in things temporal, and the claim of the clergy to the spiritual power of binding and loosing, moved the bitter scorn of the intrepid sectaries. Some of them composed hymns in the dungeon, and chaunted them on the fatal sledge. Christ, they sang while they were undressing for the butchery, would soon come to rescue Zion and to make war on Babylon, would set up his standard, would blow his trumpet, and would requite his foes tenfold for all the evil which had been inflicted on his servants. The dying words of these men were noted down; their farewell letters were kept as treasures; and in this way, with the help of some invention and exaggeration, was formed a copious supplement to the Marian martyrology.

A few cases deserve special mention. Abraham Holmes, a retired officer of the parliamentary army, and one of those zealots who would own no King but King Jesus, had been taken at Sedgemoor. His arm had been frightfully mangled and shattered in the battle; and, as no surgeon was at hand, the stout old soldier amputated it himself. He was carried up to London, and examined by the King in Council, but would make no submission. "I am an aged man," he said; "and what remains to me of life is not worth a falsehood or a baseness. I have always been a republican; and I am so still." He was sent back to the West and hanged. The people remarked with awe and wonder that the beasts which were to drag him to the gallows became restive and went back. Holmes himself doubted not that the Angel of the Lord, as in the old time, stood in the way sword in hand, invisible to human eyes, but visible to the inferior animals. "Stop, gentlemen," he cried, "let me go on foot. There is more in this than you think. Remember how the ass saw him whom the prophet could not see." He walked manfully to the gallows, harangued the people with a smile, prayed fervently that God would hasten the downfall of Antichrist and the deliverance of England, and went up the ladder with an apology for mounting so awkwardly. "You see," he said, "I have but one arm."

Not less courageously died Christopher Battiscombe, a young Templar of good family and fortune who, at Dorchester, an agreeable provincial town proud of its taste and refinement, was regarded by all as the model of a fine gentleman. Great interest was made to save him. It was believed through the West of England that he was engaged to a young lady of gentle blood, the sister of the Sheriff, that she threw herself at the feet of Jeffreys to beg for mercy, and that Jeffreys drove her from him with a jest so hideous that to repeat it would be an offence against decency and humanity. Her lover suffered at Lyme piously and courageously.

A still deeper interest was excited by the fate of two gallant brothers, William and Benjamin Hewling. They were young, handsome, accomplished, and well connected. Their maternal grandfather was named Kiffin. He was one of the first merchants in London, and was generally considered as the head of the Baptists. The Chief Justice behaved to William Hewling on the trial with characteristic brutality. "You have a grandfather," he said, "who deserves to be hanged as richly as you." The poor lad, who was only nineteen, suffered death with so much meekness and fortitude, that an officer of the army who attended the execution, and who had made himself remarkable by rudeness and severity, was strangely melted and said, "I do not believe that my Lord Chief Justice himself could be proof against this." Hopes were entertained that Benjamin would be pardoned. One victim of tender years was surely enough for one house to furnish. Even Jeffreys was, or pretended to be, inclined to lenity. The truth was that one of his kinsmen, from whom he had large expectations, and whom, therefore, he could not treat as he generally treated intercessors, pleaded strongly for the afflicted family. Time was allowed for a reference to London. The sister of the prisoner went to Whitehall with a petition. Many courtiers wished her success; and Churchill, among whose numerous faults cruelty had no place, obtained admittance for her. "I wish well to your suit with all my heart," he said, as they stood together in the antechamber; "but do not flatter yourself with hopes. This marble," and he laid his hand on the chimney piece, "is not harder than the King." The prediction proved true. James was inexorable. Benjamin Hewling died with dauntless courage, amid lamentations in which the soldiers who kept guard around the gallows could not refrain from joining.

Yet those rebels who were doomed to death were less to be pitied than some of the survivors. Several prisoners to whom Jeffreys was unable to bring home the charge of high treason were convicted of misdemeanors, and were sentenced to scourging not less terrible than that which Oates had undergone. A woman for some idle words, such as had been uttered by half the women in the districts where the war had raged, was condemned to be whipped through all the market towns in the county of Dorset. She suffered part of her punishment before Jeffreys returned to London: but, when he was no longer in the West, the gaolers, with the humane connivance of the magistrates, took on themselves the responsibility of sparing her any further torture. A still more frightful sentence was passed on a lad named Tutchin, who was tried for seditious words. He was, as usual, interrupted in his defence by ribaldry and scurrility from the judgment seat. "You are a rebel; and all your family have been rebels since Adam. They tell me that you are a poet. I'll cap verses with you." The sentence was that the boy should be imprisoned for seven years, and should, during that period, be flogged through every market town in Dorsetshire every year. The women in the galleries burst into tears. The clerk of the arraigns stood up in great disorder. "My Lord," said he, "the prisoner is very young. There are many market towns in our country. The sentence amounts to whipping once a fortnight for seven years." "If he is a young man," said Jeffreys, "he is an old rogue. Ladies, you do not know the villain as well as I do. The punishment is not half bad enough for him. All the interest in England shall not alter it." Tutchin in his despair petitioned, and probably with sincerity, that he might be hanged. Fortunately for him he was, just at this conjuncture, taken ill of the small pox and given over. As it seemed highly improbable that the sentence would ever be executed, the Chief Justice consented to remit it, in return for a bribe which reduced the prisoner to poverty. The temper of Tutchin, not originally very mild, was exasperated to madness by what he had undergone. He lived to be known as one of the most acrimonius and pertinacious enemies of the House of Stuart and of the Tory party.

The number of prisoners whom Jeffreys transported was eight hundred and forty-one. These men, more wretched than their associates who suffered death, were distributed into gangs, and bestowed on persons who enjoyed favor at Court. The conditions of the gift were that the convicts should be carried beyond sea as slaves, that they should not be emancipated for ten years, and that the place of their banishment should be some West Indian island. This last article was studiously framed for the purpose of aggravating the misery of the exiles. In New England or New Jersey they would have found a population kindly disposed to them and a climate not unfavorable to their health and vigor. It was therefore determined that they should be sent to colonies where a laborer born in the temperate zone could hope to enjoy little health. Such was the state of the slave market that these bondmen, long as was the passage, and sickly as they were likely to prove, were still very valuable. It was estimated by Jeffreys that, on an average, each of them, after all charges were paid, would be worth from ten to fifteen pounds. There was therefore much angry competition for grants. Some Tories in the West conceived that they had, by their exertions and sufferings during the insurrection, earned a right to share in the profits which had been eagerly snatched up by the sycophants of Whitehall. The courtiers, however, were victorious.

The misery of the exiles equalled that of the negroes who are now carried from Congo to Brazil. It appears from the best information which is at present accessible that more than one fifth of those who were shipped were flung to the sharks before the end of the voyage. The human cargoes were stowed close in the holds of small vessels. So little space was allowed that the wretches, many of whom were still tormented by unhealed wounds, could not all lie down at once without lying on one another. They were never suffered to go on deck. The hatchway was constantly watched by sentinels armed with hangers and blunderbusses. In the dungeon below all was darkness, stench, lamentation, disease and death. Of ninety-nine convicts who were carried out in one vessel, twenty-two died before they reached Jamaica, although the voyage was performed with unusual speed. The survivors when they arrived at the house of bondage were mere skeletons. During some weeks coarse biscuit and fetid water had been doled out to them in such scanty measure that any one of them could easily have consumed the ration which was assigned to five. They were, therefore, in such a state that the merchant to whom they had been consigned found it expedient to fatten them before selling them.

Meanwhile the property both of the rebels who had suffered death, and of those more unfortunate men who were withering under the tropical sun, was fought for and torn to pieces by a crowd of greedy informers. By law a subject attainted of treason forfeits all his substance; and this law was enforced after the Bloody Assizes with a rigor at once cruel and ludicrous. The brokenhearted widows and destitute orphans of the laboring men whose corpses hung at the cross roads were called upon by the agents of the Treasury to explain what had become of a basket, of a goose, of a flitch of bacon, of a keg of cider, of a sack of beans, of a truss of hay. While the humble retainers of the government were pillaging the families of the slaughtered peasants, the Chief Justice was fast accumulating a fortune out of the plunder of a higher class of Whigs. He traded largely in pardons. His most lucrative transaction of this kind was with a gentleman named Edmund Prideaux. It is certain that Prideaux had not been in arms against the government; and it is probable that his only crime was the wealth which he had inherited from his father, an eminent lawyer who had been high in office under the Protector. No exertions were spared to make out a case for the crown. Mercy was offered to some prisoners on condition that they would bear evidence against Prideaux. The unfortunate man lay long in gaol, and at length, overcome by fear of the gallows, consented to pay fifteen thousand pounds for his liberation. This great sum was received by Jeffreys. He bought with it an estate, to which the people gave the name of Aceldama, from the accursed field which was purchased with the price of innocent blood.

He was ably assisted in the work of extortion by the crew of parasites who were in the habit of drinking and laughing with him. The office of these men was to drive hard bargains with convicts under the strong terror of death, and with parents trembling for the lives of their children. A portion of the spoil was abandoned by Jeffreys to his agents. To one of his boon companions, it is said, he tossed a pardon for a rich traitor across the table during a revel. It was not safe to have recourse to any intercession except that of his creatures; for he guarded his profitable monopoly of mercy with jealous care. It was even suspected that he sent some persons to the gibbet solely because they had applied for the royal clemency through channels independent of him.

The Duke of Marlborough

GEORGE M. TREVELYAN

1650–1722. In the opinion of many military historians, Marlborough was one of the great captains of history, the greatest of all English soldiers. But his cool and enigmatic personality deprived him of wide popularity in his own time and continues to deny him a hero's status to this day. Marlborough, the victor of Blenheim and Ramillies, who did more than any other man to prevent Louis XIV's domination of Europe, was immensely aided in his campaigns by the support of Queen Anne, the intimate friend of Marlborough's wife, Sarah. This appraisal of Marlborough's character is taken from the first volume of G. M. Trevelyan's thee-volume England Under Queen Anne. *The great-nephew of Macaulay and the son of the historian George Otto Trevelyan, G. M. Trevelyan was a historian by family tradition as well as by instinct and talent.*

Macaulay adopted his unfavorable reading of Marlborough's motives and character straight from Swift and the Tory pamphleteers of the latter part of Anne's reign. Macaulay, indeed, was less often misled by traditional Whig views than by his own over-confident, lucid mentality, which always saw things in black and white, but never in grey. The greatness of his history lies in his account of political situations and his narrative of the course of events; a public man himself, he understood these things better than most historians, and he could make them clear in his own unrivalled manner. But he was no psychologist, and the artist in him tended to delineate character by the unsafe method of dramatic antithesis. He in-

256

stinctively desired to make Marlborough's genius stand out bright against the background of his villainy. He had blacked in the background, but did not live to put in the full-length figure of the victor of Blenheim in all his magnificent panoply.

In place of Macaulay's villain of genius, what do we see in fact? Nothing quite so clear, except indeed the military genius, which shines the brighter the more clearly it is analysed. But Marlborough's motives often remain obscure and his character is not as sharply definable as that of Chatham, Nelson or Wellington. Unlike those occasionally talkative heroes, Marlborough kept a very strict guard on both his tongue and his pen. He liked to keep his own secret, and in keeping it from contemporaries he has kept it from posterity as well. He scorned or neglected to answer his libellers or to state his case in memoirs. His correspondence deals with the matter in hand and refrains from discursive remarks. The nearest approach to self-revelation and frank comment on events as he saw them, is to be found in the long sequence of love letters to his wife. Otherwise his actions alone speak for him. Sarah for her part told her story in the *Conduct of the Duchess*, with frankness worthy of Pepys and ability worthy of Defoe. She unpacked her heart in words; but her husband hid himself in the cloud of his mighty deeds.

It would be an error, in reaction against Swift and Macaulay, to picture Marlborough as a public servant of the same integrity and high-mindedness as Wellington. Born in 1650, John Churchill had been brought up in the very worst school of Restoration laxity. His father, Sir Winston Churchill, a West-county squire, had suffered heavily for the royalist cause, and John, when still of schoolboy age, was sent up to Whitehall to remake the family's fortunes there as best he might. His elder sister, Arabella, was mistress of James, Duke of York. If the brother had been a man of high principle, he would have felt his sister's shame and would not have attached himself to James's clientele. But Churchill had no higher standards than the world in which he found himself, and that world regarded a Prince's mistress as a grand lady. So, too, Whitehall thought that handsome Jack Churchill had done a fine thing when he cut out King Charles in the easy affections of Barbara, Duchess of Cleveland; nor would that Court have raised its eyebrows very high, if indeed the lady, as rumor afterwards averred, had rewarded her needy gallant with gold. But unlike the other harpies of Whitehall, Churchill was hardening his body and training his mind in the profession of arms, in the desert hills behind Tangier, and in Germany under Turenne himself.

A few years later, he married for love a Court lady of unspotted character, whose face and wit were her only fortune. This was not the act of a mercenary or coldly calculating man. And he loved Sarah Jennings, for all her disagreeable humors, every hour till he died. Between the ages of fifty and sixty he went through his great campaigns at the head of half the armies of Europe, with his thoughts as constantly turning home to Sarah as those of a young subaltern to his mistress. Of all the world's famous soldiers he seems to have had the warmest and most fixed domestic affections. In the campaign of 1702 he writes:

I do assure you that your letters are so welcome to me that if they should come in the time I was expecting the enemy to charge me, I could not forbear reading them.

And as he drew rein on the plateau of Blenheim, before the carnage of that great victory had ceased, he had two thoughts: one for his wife to whom he scribbled a pencil note from the saddle, the other for the wounded and prisoners who depended on his care. He was, like the Duke of Wellington, a humane man in war and in peace, and he was less stern than Wellington to his subordinates. Except the burning of Bavaria no act of cruelty stands against his name. He won Sedgemoor; others turned it into a butchery. He taught generals how their poor soldiers should be fed, clothed and cared for.

The successful military conspiracy which Marlborough organized against James II at the time of William's invasion saved England from the horrors of civil war. Macaulay, without denying the public usefulness of his action, regarded it as a piece of selfish treachery on Marlborough's part against his patron James II. But there is no reason to doubt that his devotion to the liberties of England and the Protestant religion was a motive with him at that crisis, as with the rest of his countrymen. And like them he thought that, in time of revolution, conspiracy is a legitimate weapon, and the method of conspiracy is deceit. Probably, indeed, his motives were to some extent personal in 1688 as at other times. He did not like the prospect of holding high command at the good-will of Jesuit fathers; and he had good private as well as public reasons to support a revolution which would secure the reversion of the crown to his wife's devoted friend, Princess Anne.

So, too, when she at length came to the throne, he took pleasure in his position as the greatest subject in England and in Europe. He enjoyed using in the largest field his unrivalled military talents, as everyone who is worth anything enjoys doing the thing he can do best. But it is clear from his letters to his wife that he cared deeply for the cause for which he fought—the cause of England, of Protestantism and of European liberty against the domination of France.

There are, indeed, bad incidents in his career, particularly in the troubled reign of William III. His deep intrigues with the Court of St. Germains*

* The court of King James II in exile in France.

are ugly reading. Whatever his precise motives in these mystifications, he was playing the knave—but so were many others, Whig and Tory, whom it is not the custom to set down simply as villains. Perhaps, like so many others, he was only insuring his head and his fortune against a Restoration which he did not desire but regarded as probable. In judging his actions we must consider the standards of a time when Russell, Shrewsbury and Somers thought fit to masquerade as Jacobite penitents. If indeed Marlborough sought to strengthen the impression of his loyalty to St. Germains by betraying to the national enemy the coming attack on Brest, he touched the lowest point of his career. But even if the story were true, the French had already had warning from others, and Marlborough knew it. Moreover Mr. Winston Churchill's recent researches and arguments have rendered it so doubtful whether Marlborough's alleged warning was not a Jacobite fabrication, that no case against him can be safely deduced from the still mysterious incident.

Apart from the charge of treachery, it is said that he was uxorious, ambitious and avaricious. He was uxorious in the sense that he lived long and happily with that woman whom no one else could charm or control. His ambition saved his country and Europe. And for every guinea that his avarice drew from England, he gave her back the value of a thousand. Nearly all the other statesmen of the day were engaged in founding families and amassing estates at the public expense. Marlborough only differed from Portland, Rochester, Danby and countless others, in that he gave the public very much fuller value for their money.

The talk about his avarice, grossly exaggerated for purposes of faction, arose in part from little, thrifty personal habits which never go down well in England. They would have passed unnoticed in Holland or France. But the English made it a crime in a man who had given them victory, that he blew out unnecessary candles, and walked home when other rich men would call a coach. These habits of life, innocent, if not actually laudable, he had acquired in his penurious youth, when he was living at Charles II's Court on his ensign's pay, and they clung to him when he grew rich.

Perhaps the secret of Marlborough's character is that there is no secret. Abnormal only in his genius, he may have been guided by motives very much like those that sway commoner folk. He loved his wife, with her witty talk and her masterful temper, which he was man enough to hold in check without quarrelling. He loved his country; he was attached to her religion and free institutions. He loved money, in which he was not singular. He loved, as every true man must, to use his peculiar talents to their full; and as in his case they required a vast field for their full exercise, he was therefor ambitious. Last, but not least, he loved his fellow men, if scrupulous humaneness and consideration for others are signs of loving one's fellows. He was the prince of courtesy. It is true that courtesy was one of his chief weapons in political and diplomatic negotiation; but it would not have been so effective if it had not been genuine, and based on kindly feelings. Old John Evelyn records on one of the last pages of his journal a scene in London society in the winter after Blenheim.

I went to wait on my Lord Treasurer, where was the victorious Duke of Marlborough, who came to me and took me by the hand, with extraordinary familiarity and civility, as formerly he was used to do, without any alteration of his good nature. He had a most rich George in sardonyx set in diamonds of real value: for the rest very plain. I had not seen him for some years, and believed he might have forgotten me.

Swift might suspect Marlborough of some deep-laid scheme of avarice or ambition, when he crossed the room to give pleasure to the old man by speaking to him. But what advancement could he hope from Evelyn? It is not so that the incident should be read.

The charm of Marlborough's manners was irresistible, and he used it to the full to hold together for ten years the Alliance of touchy Kings, Generals and Councillors. His patience was often tried by fools of importance—English, Dutch and German, in the cabinet and in the field. And his patience was as inexhaustible as his courage. Now patience is not only a weapon but a virtue.

Why, then, was he so hated by the Tories and so ill-defended by the Whigs? Chiefly for reasons of faction. Party spirit raged in the reign of Anne with a ferocity that devastated social life and human intercourse. Marlborough deserted the Tories, yet never fully became one of the Whigs. Yet in spite of his fall between the two stools of English public life, he would have found more friends and defenders if he had ever obtained a hold on the popular affection at all proportionate to his services. His soldiers loved him, because he cared for their wants, and led them to victory; they bitterly resented his treatment by the politicians at the end of the war. But, outside the army, the common people had so little feeling for him that they allowed the Tories to libel him and drive him from the country without protest. Patient, courageous, persuasive, humane, he lacked the spark that kindles devotion. His unbroken reserve, though we need not suspect it as a mask for designs invariably evil, acted as a screen between him and the multitude of his day, and still acts as a screen between him and historians seeking to know him. He never gave himself away, to friends in love or to foes in anger. Except by his achievements he has never fired the imagination, like Cromwell or Nelson. The flame of his spirit served for light, not heat. He stands on the threshold of the Eighteenth Century, one of the first-born of the Age of Reason, the armed champion of toleration and good sense.

The King's Selfishness

SAINT-SIMON

1708. Probably the most celebrated of all historical memoirs are those of the Duc de Saint-Simon, who lived at the Court of Versailles for many years. With untiring interest, considerable malice, and much skill, the snobbish courtier wrote about gossip, scandal, rank, personalities, etiquette, and daily doings; and left a first-hand record of immense importance. But Saint-Simon is often dull and often concerned with trivialities. So he is represented here by one short and chilling anecdote. Louis XIV was sixty-nine years old. The twenty-three-year-old Duchesse de Bourgogne was Marie-Adelaide of Savoy, wife of Louis's grandson. Usually Louis was very fond of her.

The Duchesse de Bourgogne was pregnant and far from well. The King had announced that, contrary to his usual custom, he intended to go to Fontainebleau as soon as the good weather came, and meantime he wanted to pay his customary visit to Marly. He could not do without the company of his granddaughter, who amused him, but in her condition so much travelling was not good for her. Mme. de Maintenon was worried about it and Fagon discreetly let it be known that he was against it. This annoyed the King, who was used to being indulged in every whim, and had been spoiled by his mistresses, who travelled anywhere when he wanted them to whether pregnant or only just arisen from childbed. The remarks about Marly rubbed him up the wrong way without shaking him in his resolution. The only concession he made was to put off his departure from Low Sunday to the middle of the following week, defying every effort, first to dissuade him, and then to get him to allow the Duchess to remain at Versailles.

The following Saturday the King was walking on the terrace after mass, amusing himself feeding the carp, when he saw the Duchesse de Lude coming toward him alone—without there being any ladies in attendance on her, which was unusual in the morning. The King realized that she had something urgent to tell him; he went to meet her, and everyone else fell back so that they could talk in private. Their conversation was not long. She left, and the King walked back toward us, beside the carp pool, without saying a word. Everyone realized what had happened, but no one wanted to say anything. Finally the King turned and looked at the senior individuals present, and, without addressing anyone in particular, said in an irritated tone, "The Duchesse de Bourgogne has had a miscarriage."

The Duc de la Rochefoucauld, M. de Bouillon, the Duc de Tresmes, and the Maréchal de Boufflers all expressed their deep regret. M. de la Rochefoucauld then added that it was such a pity as it had happened before, and everyone hoped it would not recur. "Well, what of it?" interrupted the King with a sudden burst of rage, "what do I care? Hasn't she got a son already? And if he dies, there's the Duc de Berry who is old enough to marry and have children. They're all my grandchildren, I don't care which of them succeeds me." Then he burst out: "Thank God, if she had to have a miscarriage, she's got it over with, and I shan't have my arrangements upset any more by nattering doctors and old women. I shall go and come as I please, and be left in peace."

Silence followed at these words, and you could have heard a pin drop. Everyone lowered his eyes and scarcely dared to breathe. Everyone was stupefied—even the builders and gardeners who were within earshot. Silence reigned for fully a quarter of an hour. The King broke it by leaning on the balustrade and remarking on the size of one of the carp; no one replied. Then he addressed some remark about the fish to the workmen, but they had nothing to say either. The silence hung heavy, and finally the King walked away.

Once he had gone, our eyes met and spoke volumes, and for a few minutes we all felt the same. Astonishment, distress, and shrugging of shoulders—as long as time lasts, I shall never forget that moment. M. de Rochefoucauld was seething with rage—for once, rightly. The First Equerry was faint with terror. I kept my eyes and ears open, watching them all, and I was not altogether displeased because I had long made up my mind that the King had no interest in anyone except himself, and had no regard for anyone else's feelings except his own.

The World

DAVID CECIL

Circa 1720–1820. The world described so brilliantly in this chapter from Lord David Cecil's biography of William Lamb, Viscount Melbourne, the Prime Minister who introduced the young Victoria to her queenly duties, was the world of the Whig aristocracy.

The great Whig country houses of the eighteenth and early nineteenth centuries are among the most conspicuous monuments of English history. Ornate and massive, with their pedimented porticoes, their spreading balustraded wings, they dominate the landscape round them with a magnificent self-assurance. Nor are their interiors less imposing. Their colonnaded entrance halls, whence the Adam staircase sweeps up beneath a fluted dome; their cream and gilt libraries piled with sumptuous editions of the classics; their orangeries peopled with casts from the antique; their saloons hung with yellow silk, and with ceiling and doorways painted in delicate arabesque by Angelica Kauffmann—all combine to produce an extraordinary impression of culture and elegance and established power.

Yet, they are not palaces. There is something easy-going and unofficial about them. Between library and saloon one comes on little rooms, full of sporting prints and comfortable untidiness; the bedrooms upstairs are friendly with chintz and flowered wallpaper. Even the great rooms themselves, with their roomy writing tables, their armchairs, their tables piled with albums and commonplace books, seemed designed less for state occasions than for private life—for leisure and lounging, for intimate talk and desultory reading. And the portraits that glow down from the walls exhibit a similar character. The gentlemen lean back in their hunting coats, the ladies stroll in their parks with spaniels snapping at the ribbons that dangle from the garden hats slung on their arms. In big and in detail these houses convey an effect of splendid naturalness. In this they are typical of the society which was their creator.

The Whig aristocracy was a unique product of English civilization. It was before all things a governing class. At a time when economic power was concentrated in the landed interest, the Whigs were among the biggest landowners: their party was in office for the greater part of the eighteenth century; during this period they possessed a large proportion of the seats in the House of Commons; they produced more ambassadors and officers of state than the rest of England put together. And they lived on a scale appropriate to their power. "A man," said one of their latest representatives, "can jog along on £40,000 a year." And jog very well they did. They possessed, most of them, a mansion in London and two or three in the country; they moved through the world attended by a vast retinue of servants, of secretaries and chaplains, of companions, librarians and general hangers-on; they never travelled but in their own carriages; they kept open house to a continuous stream of guests, whom they entertained in the baroque and lavish style approved by their contemporaries.

For the elaboration of their life was increased by the period they lived in. The eighteenth century, that accomplished age, did not believe in the artless and the austere. In its view the good man, or, as they would have phrased it, "the man of sense and taste," was he whose every activity was regulated in the light of a trained judgment and the experience of the wise in his own and former ages. From his earliest years the Whig nobleman was subjected to a careful education. He was grounded in the classics first by a tutor, then at Eton, then at the University. After this he went abroad for two years' grand tour to learn French and good manners in the best society of the Continent. His sisters learnt French and manners equally thoroughly at home; and their demeanor was further improved by a course of deportment. The Whigs' taste was in harmony with the ideal that guided their education. They learnt to admire the grand style in painting, the "correct" in letters, the Latin tradition in oratory. And in everything they paid strict attention to form. Since life to them was so secure and so pleasant, the Whig aristocrats tended to take its fundamental values very much for granted; they concentrated rather on how to live. And here again their ideal was not an artless one. Their customs, their mode of speech, their taste in decoration, their stylish stiff clothes, are alike marked by a character at once polished and precise, disciplined and florid. If one of them writes a note, it is rounded with a graceful phrase, their most extempore speeches are turned with a flourish of rotund rhetoric.

Yet—and here it is that it differs from those of similar societies on the Continent—theirs was not an unreal life, no Watteau-like paradise of exquisite trifling and fastidious idleness. For one thing it had its roots in the earth. Founded as their position was on landed property, the Whig aristocracy was never urban. They passed at least half the year in their country seats, and there they occupied themselves in the ordinary avocations of country life. The ladies interested themselves in their children and visited the poor; the gentlemen looked after their estates, rode to hounds and administered from the local bench justice to poachers and pilferers. Their days went by, active out-of-door, unceremonious; they wore riding boots as often as silk stockings. Moreover, they were always in touch with the central and serious current of contemporary life. The fact that they were a governing class meant that they had to govern. The Whig lord was often as not a minister, his eldest son an M.P., his second attached to a foreign embassy, so that their houses were alive with the effort and hurry of politics. Red Foreign Office boxes strewed the library tables; at any time of day or night a courier might come galloping up with critical news, and the minister must post off to London to attend a Cabinet meeting. He had his work in the country too. He was a landlord and magistrate, often a lord lieutenant, while every few years would come a general election when his sons, if not himself, might have to sally forth to stand on the hustings and be pelted with eggs and dead cats by the free and independent electors of the neighboring borough. Indeed his was not a protected existence. The eighteenth century was the age of clubs; and Whig society itself was a sort of club, exclusive, but in which those who managed to achieve membership lived on equal terms—a rowdy, rough-and-tumble club, full of conflict and plain speaking, where people were expected to stand up for themselves and take and give hard knocks. At Eton the little dukes and earls cuffed and bullied one another like street urchins. As mature persons in their country homes, or in the pillared rooms of Brooks's Club, their intercourse continued more politely, yet with equal familiarity, while their House of Commons life passed in a robust atmosphere of combat and crisis and defeat. The Whigs despised the royal family; and there was certainly none of the hush and punctilio of court existence about them. Within the narrow limits of their world they were equalitarians.

Their life, in fact, was essentially a normal life, compounded of the same elements as those of general humanity, astir with the same clamor and clash and aspiration and competition as filled the streets round their august dwellings. Only, it was normal life played out on a colossal stage and with magnificent scenery and costumes. Their houses were homes, but homes with sixty bedrooms, set in grounds five miles round; they fought to keep their jobs, but the jobs were embassies and prime ministerships; their sons went to the same universities as humbler students, but were distinguished from them there by a nobleman's gold-tasselled mortar-board. When the Duke of Devonshire took up botany, he sent out a special expedition to the East Indies to search for rare plants; Lord Egremont liked pictures, so he filled a gallery with Claudes and Correggios; young Lord Palmerston was offered the Chancellorship of the Exchequer a year or two after entering Parliament.

This curiously blended life produced a curiously blended type of character. With so many opportunities for action, its interests were predominantly active. Most of the men were engaged in politics. And the women—for they lived to please the men—were political too. They listened, they sympathized, they advised; through them two statesmen might make overtures to each other, or effect a reconciliation. But politics then were not the life sentence to hard labor that in our iron age they have become. Parliament sat for only a few months in the year; and even during the session, debates did not start till the late afternoon. The Whigs had the rest of their time to devote to other things. If they were sporting, they raced and hunted; if interested in agriculture, they farmed on an ambitious scale; if artistic, they collected marbles and medals; if intellectual, they read history and philosophy; if literary, they composed compliments in verse and sonorous, platitudinous orations. But the chief of their spare time was given up to social life. They gave balls, they founded clubs, they played cards, they got up private theatricals; they cultivated friendship and every variety, platonic and less platonic, of the art of love. Their ideal was the Renaissance ideal of the whole man, whose aspiration it is to make the most of every advantage, intellectual and sensual, that life has to offer.

In practice, of course, this ideal was not so broad as it sounds. The Whigs could not escape the limitations imposed by the splendor of their circumstances. Like all aristocrats they tended to be amateurs. When life is so free and so pleasant, a man is not likely to endure the drudgery necessary to make himself really expert in any one thing. Even in those affairs of state which took up most of the Whigs' time, they troubled little with the dry details of economic theory or administrative practice. Politics to them meant, first of all, personalities and, secondly, general principles. And general principles to them were an occasion for expression rather than thought. They did not dream of questioning the fundamental canons of Whig orthodoxy. Their only concern was to restate these indisputable truths in a fresh and effective fashion.

Again, their taste was a little philistine. Aristocratic taste nearly always is. Those whose ordinary course of life is splendid and satisfying find it hard to recognize the deeper value of the exercises of the solitary imagination; art to them is not the fulfilment of the soul, but an ornamental appendage to existence. Moreover, the English nobility were too much occupied with practical affairs to achieve the fullest intellectual life. They admired what was elegant, sumptuous and easy to understand: portraits that were good likenesses and pleasing decorations, architecture which appropriately housed a stately life. In books, they appreciated acute, wittily phrased observations of human nature, or noble sentiments expressed in flowing periods: Cicero, Pope, Horace, Burke. The strange and the harsh they dismissed immediately. Among contemporary authors they appreciated Jane Austen, condemned Crabbe, for the most part, as sordid and low, and neglected Blake almost entirely. If they had read him, they would not have liked him. For—it is another of their limitations—they were not spiritual. Their education did not encourage them to be; and, anyway, they found this world too absorbing to concern themselves much with the next. The bolder spirits among them were atheists. The average person accepted Christianity, but in a straightforward spirit, innocent alike of mysticism and theological exactitude.

Further, their circumstances did not encourage the virtues of self-control. Good living gave them zest; wealth gave them opportunity; and they threw themselves into their pleasures with an animal recklessness at once terrifying and exhilarating to a modern reader. The most respectable people often drank themselves under the table without shocking anyone. "Colonel Napier came in to-night as drunk as an owl," remarks Lady Sarah Napier of the staid middle-aged gentleman who was her husband. And their drinking was nothing to their gambling. Night after night they played loo and faro from early evening till the candles guttered pale in the light of the risen sun. Lord Stavordale lamented he had not been playing higher, on a night when he won £11,000 in a single hand at hazard. Georgiana, Duchess of Devonshire, cost her husband nearly £1,000,000 in card debts. Rich as they were, they often ruined themselves. The letters of the time are loud with lamentations about the duns coming in and the furniture going out. Nor was their sexual life of a kind to commend them to an austere morality. "I was afraid

I was going to have the gout the other day," writes Lord Carlisle to a friend. "I believe I live too chaste: it is not a common fault with me." It was not a common fault with any of them. In fact, an unmarried man was thought unpleasantly queer if he did not keep under his protection some sprightly full-bosomed Kitty Clive or Mrs. Bellamy, whose embraces he repaid with a house in Montpelier Square, a box at the opera and a smart cabriolet in which to drive her down to Brighthelmstone for a week's amorous relaxation. Nor did he confine himself to professional ladies of pleasure. Even unmarried girls like Lady Hester Stanhope were suspected of having lovers; among married women the practice was too common to stir comment. The historian grows quite giddy as he tries to disentangle the complications of heredity consequent on the free and easy habits of the English aristocracy. The Harley family, children of the Countess of Oxford, were known as the Harleian Miscellany on account of the variety of fathers alleged to be responsible for their existence. The Duke of Devonshire had three children by the Duchess and two by Lady Elizabeth Foster, the Duchess one by Lord Grey; and most of them were brought up together in Devonshire House, each set of children with a surname of its own. "Emily, does it never strike you," writes Miss Pamela Fitzgerald in 1816, "the vices are wonderfully prolific among the Whigs? There are such countless illegitimates, such a tribe of children of the mist." It is noteworthy that the author of this lively comment was a carefully brought-up young lady of the highest breeding. The free habits of these days encouraged free speech. "Comfortable girls," remarks a middle-aged lady of her growing nieces, "who like a dirty joke." And the men, as can be imagined, were a great deal freer than the women. For all their polish the Whigs were not refined people in the Victorian sense of the word.

It appears in other aspects of their lives. They could be extremely arrogant, treating their inferiors with a patrician insolence which seems to us the reverse of good breeding. Lady Catherine de Bourgh was not the caricature that an ignorant person might suppose. Fashionable young men of refined upbringing amused themselves by watching fights where the Game Chicken battered the Tutbury Pet into unconsciousness with bared and blood-stained fists. And the pamphlets, the squibs, the appalling political cartoons that lay open in the most elegant drawing-rooms show that the ladies of the day were not squeamish either.

Still, unseemly as some of its manifestations were, one must admit that there is something extremely attractive in this earthy exuberance. And, as a matter of fact, it was the inevitable corollary of their virtues. English society had the merits of its defects. Its wide scope, its strong root in the earth, gave it an astounding, an irresistible vitality. For all their dissipation there was nothing decadent about these eighteenth-century aristocrats.

Their excesses came from too much life, not too little. And it was the same vitality that gave them their predominance in public life. They took on the task of directing England's destinies with the same self-confident vigor that they drank and diced. It was this vigor that made Pitt Prime Minister at twenty-four years old,* that enabled the Foxites to keep the flag of liberty flying against the united public opinion of a panic-stricken nation. Nor did they let their pleasures interfere with these more serious activities. After eighteen hours of uninterrupted gambling, Charles Fox would arrive at the House of Commons to electrify his fellow members by a brilliant discourse on American taxation. Rakes and ladies of fashion intersperse their narratives of intrigue with discussions on politics, on literature, even on morals. For they were not unmoral. Their lapses came from passion, not from principle; and they are liable at times to break out in contrite acknowledgement of guilt and artless resolutions for future improvement. Indeed it was one of the paradoxes created by their mixed composition that, though they were worldly, they were not sophisticated. Their elaborate manners masked simple reactions. Like their mode of life, their characters were essentially natural: spontaneous, unintrospective, brimming over with normal feelings, love of home and family, loyalty, conviviality, desire for fame, hero-worship, patriotism. And they showed their feelings too. Happy creatures! They lived before the days of the stiff upper lip and the inhibited public-school Englishman. A manly tear stood in their eye at the story of a heroic deed; they declared their loves in a strain of flowery hyperbole. They were the more expressive from their very unself-consciousness. It never struck them that they needed to be inarticulate to appear sincere. They were equally frank about their less elevated sentiments. Eighteenth-century rationalism combined with rural common sense to make them robustly ready to face unedifying facts. And they declared their impressions with a brusque honesty, outstandingly characteristic of them. From Sir Robert Walpole, who encouraged coarse conversation on the ground that it was the only form of talk which everyone enjoyed, down to the Duke of Wellington, who described the army of his triumphs as composed of "the scum of the earth, enlisted for drink," the Augustan aristocracy, Whig and Tory alike, said what they thought with superb disregard for public opinion. For if they were not original they were independent-minded. The conventions which bounded their lives were conventions of form only. Since they had been kings of their world from birth, they were free from the tiresome inhibitions that are induced by a sense of inferiority. Within the locked garden of their society, individuality flowered riotous and rampant. Their typical figures show up beside the muted introverts of today as clear-

---

* Pitt diverged from the Whigs in later life, but he was brought up among them and is, so far, representative of the Whig tradition.

cut and idiosyncratic as characters in Dickens. They took for granted that you spoke your mind and followed your impulse. If these were odd, they were amused but not disapproving. They enjoyed eccentrics: George Selwyn, who never missed an execution, Beau Brummell, who took three hours to tie his cravat. The firm English soil in which they were rooted, the spacious freedom afforded by their place in the world, allowed personality to flourish in as many bold and fantastic shapes as it pleased.

But it was always a garden plant, a civilized growth. Whatever their eccentricities, the Whig nobles were never provincial and never uncouth. They had that effortless knowledge of the world that comes only to those who from childhood have been accustomed to move in a complex society, that delightful unassertive confidence possible only to people who have never had cause to doubt their social position. And they carried to the finest degree of cultivation those social arts which engaged so much of their time. Here we come to their outstanding distinction. They were the most agreeable society England has ever known. The character of their agreeability was of a piece with the rest of them; mundane, straightforward, a trifle philistine, largely concerned with gossip, not given to subtle analyses or flights of fancy. But it had all their vitality and all their sense of style. It was incomparably racy and spontaneous and accomplished, based solidly on a wide culture and experience, yet free to express itself in bursts of high spirits, in impulses of appreciation, in delicate movements of sentiment, in graceful compliments. For it had its grace—a virile classical grace like that of the Chippendale furniture which adorned its rooms, lending a glittering finish to its shrewd humor, its sharp-eyed observation, its vigorous disquisitions on men and things. Educated without pedantry, informal but not slipshod, polished but not precious, brilliant without fatigue, it combined in an easy perfection the charms of civilization and nature. Indeed the whole social life of the period shines down the perspective of history like some masterpiece of natural art—a prize bloom, nurtured in shelter and sunshine and the richest soil, the result of generations of breeding and blending, that spreads itself to the open sky in strength and beauty.

It was at its most characteristic in the middle of the century; it was at its most dazzling towards its close. By 1780 a new spirit was rising in the world. Ossian had taught people to admire ruins, Rousseau to examine the processes of the heart; with unpowdered heads and the ladies in simple muslin dresses, they paced the woods meditating, in Cowper-like mood, on the tender influences of nature. Though they kept the style and good sense of their fathers, their sympathies were wider. At the same time their feelings grew more refined. The hardness which had marred the previous age dwindled. Gainsborough, not Hogarth, mirrored the taste of the time; "sensibility" became a fashionable word. For a fleeting moment Whig society had a foot in two worlds and made the best of both of them. The lucid outline of eighteenth-century civilization was softened by the glow of the romantic dawn.

Dawn—but for them it was sunset. The same spirit which tinged them with their culminating glory was also an omen of their dissolution. For the days of aristocratic supremacy were numbered. By the iron laws which condition the social structure of man's existence, it could last as long as it maintained an economic predominance. With the coming of the Industrial Revolution this predominance began to pass from the landlords to other ranks of the community. Already by the close of the century go-ahead manufacturers in the north were talking of Parliamentary reform; already, in the upper rooms of obscure London alleys, working-men met together to clamor for liberty, equality and fraternity. Within forty years of its zenith the Whig world was completely swept away. Only a few survivors lingered on to illustrate to an uncomprehending generation the charm of the past. Of these the most distinguished was William Lamb, second Viscount Melbourne.

Major-General James Wolfe

FRANCIS PARKMAN

1727–1759. By general consent, Parkman is still considered the greatest **of** *American historians. His major work,* France and England in North America **,** *consists of seven volumes which were published from 1865 through 1892. Th**is** *and the following selection are both taken from his* Montcalm and Wolfe.

Never was the soul of a hero cased in a frame so incongruous. His face, when seen in profile, was singular as that of the Great Condé. The forehead and chin receded; the nose, slightly upturned, formed with the other features the point of an obtuse triangle; the mouth was by no means shaped to express resolution; and nothing but the clear, bright, and piercing eyes bespoke the spirit within. On his head he wore a black three-cornered hat; his red hair was tied in a queue behind; his narrow shoulders, slender body, and long, thin limbs were cased in a scarlet frock, with broad cuffs and ample skirts that reached the knee; while on his left arm he wore a band of crepe in mourning for his father, of whose death he had heard a few days before

James Wolfe was in his thirty-third year. His father was an officer of distinction, Major-General Edward Wolfe, and he himself, a delicate and sensitive child, but an impetuous and somewhat headstrong youth, had served the King since the age of fifteen. From childhood he had dreamed of the army and the wars. At sixteen he was in Flanders, adjutant of his regiment, discharging the duties of the post in a way that gained him early promotion and, along with a painstaking assiduity, showing a precocious faculty for commanding men. He passed with credit through several campaigns, took part in the victory of Dettingen, and then went to Scotland to fight at Culloden. Next we find him at Stirling, Perth and Glasgow, always ardent and always diligent, constant in military duty, and giving his spare hours to mathematics and Latin. He presently fell in love; and being disappointed, plunged into a variety of dissipations, contrary to his usual habits, which were far above the standard of that profligate time.

At twenty-three he was a lieutenant-colonel; commanding his regiment in the then dirty and barbarous town of Inverness, amid a disaffected and turbulent population whom it was his duty to keep in order: a difficult task, which he accomplished so well as to gain the special commendation of the King, and even the good-will of the Highlanders themselves. He was five years among these northern hills, battling with ill-health, and restless under the intellectual barrenness of his surroundings. He felt his position to be in no way salutary, and wrote to his mother: "The fear of becoming a mere ruffian and of imbibing the tyrannical principles of an absolute commander, or giving way insensibly to the temptations of power till I become proud, insolent, and intolerable,—these considerations will make me wish to leave the regiment before next winter; that by frequenting men above myself I may know my true condition, and by discoursing with the other sex may learn some civility and mildness of carriage." He got leave of absence, and spent six months in Paris, where he was presented at court and saw much of the best society. That did not prevent him from working hard to perfect himself in French, as well as in horsemanship, fencing, dancing, and other accomplishments, and from earnestly seeking an opportunity to study the various armies of Europe. In this he was thwarted by the stupidity and prejudice of the commander-in-chief; and he made what amends he could by extensive reading in all that bore on military matters.

His martial instincts were balanced by strong domestic inclinations. He was fond of children; and after his disappointment in love used to say that they were the only true inducement to marriage. He was a most dutiful son, and wrote continually to both his parents. Sometimes he would philosophize on the good and ill of life; sometimes he had questionings with his conscience; and once he wrote to his mother in a strain of self-accusation not to be expected from a bold and determined soldier. His nature was a compound of tenderness and fire, which last sometimes showed itself in sharp and unpleasant flashes. His excitable temper was capable almost of fierceness, and he could now and then be needlessly stern; but towards his father, mother, and friends he was a model of steady affection. He made friends readily, and kept them, and was usually a pleasant companion, though subject to sallies of imperious irritability which occasionally broke through his strong sense of good breeding. For this his susceptible constitution was largely answerable, for he was a living barometer, and his spirits rose and fell with every change of weather. In spite of his impatient outbursts, the officers whom he had commanded remained attached to him for life; and, in spite of his rigorous discipline, he was beloved by his soldiers, to whose comfort he was always attentive. Frankness, directness, essential good feeling, and a high integrity atoned for all his faults.

In his own view, as expressed to his mother, he was a person of very moderate abilities, aided by more than usual diligence; but this modest judgment of himself by no means deprived him of self-confidence, nor in time of need, of self-assertion. He delighted in every kind of hardihood and, in his contempt for effeminacy, once said to his mother: "Better be a savage of some use than a gentle, amorous puppy, obnoxious to all the world." He was far from despising fame; but the controlling principles of his life were duty to his country and his profession, loyalty to the King, and fidelity to his own ideal of the perfect soldier. To the parent who was the confidante of his most intimate thoughts he said: "All that I wish for myself is that I may at all times be ready and firm to meet that fate we cannot shun, and to die gracefully and properly when the hour comes." Never was wish more signally fulfilled. Again he tells her: "My utmost desire and ambition is to look steadily upon danger"; and his desire was accomplished. His intrepidity was complete. No form of death had power to daunt him. Once and again, when bound on some deadly enterprise of war, he calmly counts the chances whether or not he can compel his feeble body to bear him on insensible to danger; but forgetfulness of self, and the absorption of every faculty in the object before him, shut out the sense of fear. He seems always to have been at his best in the thick of battle; most complete in his mastery over himself and over others. . . .

His part in the taking of Louisbourg greatly increased his reputation. After his return he went to Bath to recruit his health; and it seems to have been here that he wooed and won Miss Katherine Lowther, daughter of an ex-governor of Barbados, and sister of the future Lord Lonsdale. A betrothal took place, and Wolfe wore her portrait till the night before his death. It was a little before this engagement that he wrote to his friend Lieutenant Colonel Rickson: "I have this day signified to Mr. Pitt that he may dispose of my slight carcass as he pleases, and that I am ready for any undertaking within the compass of my skill and cunning. I am in a very bad condition with the gravel and rheumatism; but I had much rather die than decline any kind of service that offers. If I followed my own taste it would lead me into Germany. However, it is not our part to choose, but to obey. My opinion is that I shall join the army in America."

Pitt chose him to command the expedition then fitting out against Quebec; made him a major-general, though, to avoid giving offense to older officers, he was to hold that rank in America alone; and permitted him to choose his own staff. Appointments made for merit, and not through routine and patronage, shocked the Duke of Newcastle, to whom a man like Wolfe was a hopeless enigma; and he told George II that Pitt's new general was mad. "Mad is he?" returned the old King; "then I hope he will bite some others of my generals."

At the end of January the fleet was almost ready, and Wolfe wrote to his uncle Walter: "I am to act a greater part in this business than I wished. The backwardness of some of the older officers has in some measure forced the Government to come down so low. I shall do my best, and leave the rest to fortune, as perforce we must when there are not the most commanding abilities. We expect to sail in about three weeks. A London life and little exercise disagrees entirely with me, but the sea still more. If I have health and constitution enough for the campaign, I shall think myself a lucky man; what happens afterwards is of no great consequence." He sent to his mother an affectionate letter of farewell, went to Spithead, embarked with Admiral Saunders in the ship *Neptune*, and set sail on the seventeenth of February. In a few hours the whole squadron was at sea, the transports, the frigates, and the great line-of-battle ships, with their ponderous armament and their freight of rude humanity armed and trained for destruction; while on the heaving deck of the *Neptune*, wretched with seasickness and racked with pain, stood the gallant invalid who was master of it all.

The Heights of Abraham

FRANCIS PARKMAN

1759. The English expeditionary force of 9,000 soldiers reached Quebec in late August and found the capital of French Canada defended by some 16,000 men —French regulars, indifferent Canadian militia, and some Indian allies. The Marquis de Vaudreuil, the governor, shared the command with the Marquis de Montcalm, the able military commander. The battle which decided the fate of Canada was fought on September 13th.

Meanwhile a deep cloud fell on the English. Since the siege began, Wolfe had passed with ceaseless energy from camp to camp, animating the troops, observing everything, and directing everything; but now the pale face and tall lean form were seen no more, and the rumor spread that the general was dangerously ill. He had in fact been seized by an access of the disease that had tortured him for some time past; and fever had followed. His quarters were at a French farmhouse in the camp at Montmorency; and here, as he lay in an upper chamber, helpless in bed, his singular and most unmilitary features haggard with disease and drawn with pain, no man could less have looked the hero. But as the needle, though quivering, points always to the pole, so, through torment and languor and the heats of fever, the mind of

Wolfe dwelt on the capture of Quebec. His illness, which began before the 20th of August, had so far subsided on the 25th that Knox wrote in his Diary of that day: "His Excellency General Wolfe is on the recovery, to the inconceivable joy of the whole army."

* * *

The brigadiers met in consultation, rejected the three plans proposed in the letter, and advised that an attempt should be made to gain a footing on the north shore above the town, place the army between Montcalm and his base of supply, and so force him to fight or surrender. The scheme was similar to that of the heights of St. Michel. It seemed desperate, but so did all the rest; and if by chance it should succeed, the gain was far greater than could follow any success below the town. Wolfe embraced it at once.

Not that he saw much hope in it. He knew that every chance was against him. Disappointment in the past and gloom in the future, the pain and exhaustion of disease, toils and anxieties "too great," in the words of Burke, "to be supported by a delicate constitution, and a body unequal to the vigorous and enterprising soul that it lodged," threw him at times into deep dejection. By those intimate with him he was heard to say that he would not go back defeated, "to be exposed to the censure and reproach of an ignorant populace." In other moods he felt that he ought not to sacrifice what was left of his diminished army in vain conflict with hopeless obstacles. But his final resolve once taken, he would not swerve from it. His fear was that he might not be able to lead his troops in person. "I know perfectly well you cannot cure me," he said to his physician; "but pray make me up so that I may be without pain for a few days, and able to do any duty: that is all I want."

* * *

On the next day, the last of August, he was able for the first time to leave the house. It was on this same day that he wrote his last letter to his mother: "My writing to you will convince you that no personal evils worse than defeats and disappointments have fallen upon me. The enemy puts nothing to risk, and I can't in conscience put the whole army to risk. My antagonist has wisely shut himself up in inaccessible intrenchments, so that I can't get at him without spilling a torrent of blood, and that perhaps to little purpose. The Marquis de Montcalm is at the head of a great number of bad soldiers, and I am at the head of a small number of good ones, that wish for nothing so much as to fight him; but the wary old fellow avoids an action, doubtful of the behavior of his army. People must be of the profession to understand the disadvantages and difficulties we labor under, arising from the uncommon natural strength of the country."

* * *

Some days later, he wrote to the Earl of Holderness: "The marquis of Montcalm has a numerous body of armed men (I cannot call it an army), and the strongest country perhaps in the world. Our fleet blocks up the river above and below the town, but can give no manner of aid in an attack upon the Canadian army. We are now here with about thirty-six hundred men, waiting to attack them when and wherever they can best be got at. I am so far recovered as to do business; but my constitution is entirely ruined, without the consolation of doing any considerable service to the state, and without any prospect of it." He had just learned through the letter brought from Amherst to Ensign Hutchins, that he could expect no help from that quarter.

Perhaps he was as near despair as his undaunted nature was capable of being. In his present state of body and mind he was a hero without the light and cheer of heroism. He flattered himself with no illusions, but saw the worst and faced it all. He seems to have been entirely without excitement. The languor of disease, the desperation of the chances, and the greatness of the stake may have wrought to tranquillize him. His energy was doubly tasked: to bear up his own sinking frame, and to achieve an almost hopeless feat of arms.

Audacious as it was, his plan cannot be called rash if we may accept the statement of two well-informed writers on the French side. They say that on the 10th of September the English naval commanders held a council on board the flagship, in which it was resolved that the lateness of the season required the fleet to leave Quebec without delay. They say further that Wolfe then went to the admiral, told him that he had found a place where the heights could be scaled, that he would send up 150 picked men to feel the way, and that if they gained a lodgement at the top, the other troop should follow; if, on the other hand, the French were there in force to oppose them, he would not sacrifice the army in a hopeless attempt, but embark them for home, consoled by the thought that all had been done that men could do. On this, concludes the story, the admiral and his officers consented to wait the result.

*   *   *

Wolfe had been very ill on the evening of the 4th of September. The troops knew it, and their spirits sank; but, after a night of torment, he grew better, and was soon among them again, rekindling their ardor, and imparting a cheer that he could not share. For himself he had no pity; but when he heard of the illness of two officers in one of the ships, he sent them a message of warm sympathy, advised them to return to Point Levi, and offered them his own barge and an escort. They thanked him, but replied that, come what might, they would see the enterprise to an end. Another

278

officer remarked in his hearing that one of the invalids had a very delicate constitution. "Don't tell me of constitution," said Wolfe, "he has good spirit, and good spirit will carry a man through everything." An immense moral force bore up his own frail body and forced it to his work.

Major Robert Stobo, who, five years before, had been given as a hostage to the French at the capture of Fort Necessity, arrived about this time in a vessel from Halifax. He had long been a prisoner at Quebec, not always in close custody, and had used his opportunities to acquaint himself with the neighborhood. In the spring of this year he and an officer of rangers named Stevens had made their escape with extraordinary skill and daring; and he now returned to give his countrymen the benefit of his local knowledge. His biographer says that it was he who directed Wolfe in the choice of a landing-place. Be this as it may, Wolfe in person examined the river and the shores as far as Pointe-aux-Trembles; till at length, landing on the south side a little above Quebec, and looking across the water with a telescope, he described a path that ran with a long slope up the face of the woody precipice, and saw at the top a cluster of tents. They were those of Vergor's guard at the Anse du Foulon, now called Wolfe's Cove. As he could see but ten or twelve of them, he thought that the guard could not be numerous, and might be overpowered. His hope would have been stronger if he had known that Vergor had once been tried for misconduct and cowardice in the surrender of Beauséjour, and saved from merited disgrace by the friendship of Bigot and the protection of Vaudreuil.

* * *

At last the time for action came. On Wednesday, 12 September, the troops of St. Nicolas were embarked again, and all were told to hold themselves in readiness. Wolfe, from the flagship *Sutherland*, issued his last general orders. "The enemy's force is now divided, great scarcity of provisions in their camp, and universal discontent among the Canadians. Our troops below are in readiness to join us; all the light artillery and tools are embarked at the Point of Levi; and the troops will land where the French seem least to expect it. The first body that gets on shore is to march directly to the enemy and drive them from any little post they may occupy; the officers must be careful that the succeeding do not by any mistake fire on those who go before them. The battalions must form on the upper ground with expedition, and be ready to charge whatever presents itself. When the artillery and troops are landed, a corps will be left to secure the landing-place, while the rest march on and endeavor to bring the Canadians and French to battle. The officers and men will remember what their country expects from them, and what a determined body of soldiers inured to war is capable of doing against five weak French battalions mingled with a disorderly peasantry."

The spirit of the army answered to that of its chief. The troops loved and admired their general, trusted their officers, and were ready for any attempt. "Nay, how could it be otherwise," quaintly asks honest Sergeant John Johnson, of the 58th regiment, "being at the heels of gentlemen whose whole thirst, equal with their general, was for glory? We had seen them tried, and always found them sterling. We knew that they would stand by us to the last extremity."

Wolfe had 3,600 men and officers with him on board the vessels of Holmes; and he now sent orders to Colonel Burton at Point Levi to bring to his aid all who could be spared from that place and the Point of Orleans. They were to march along the south bank, after nightfall, and wait further orders at a designated spot convenient for embarkation. Their number was about 1,200, so that the entire force destined for the enterprise was at the utmost 4,800. With these, Wolfe meant to climb the heights of Abraham in the teeth of an enemy who, though much reduced, were still twice as numerous as their assailants.

Admiral Saunders lay with the main fleet in the Basin of Quebec. This excellent officer, whatever may have been his views as to the necessity of a speedy departure, aided Wolfe to the last with unfailing energy and zeal. It was agreed between them that while the general made the real attack, the admiral should engage Montcalm's attention by a pretended one. As night approached, the fleet ranged itself along the Beauport shore; the boats were lowered and filled with sailors, marines, and the few troops that had been left behind; while ship signalled to ship, cannon flashed and thundered, and shot ploughed the beach, as if to clear a way for assailants to land. In the gloom of the evening the effect was imposing. Montcalm, who thought that the movements of the English above the town were only a feint, that their main force was still below it, and that their real attack would be made there, was completely deceived, and massed his troops in front of Beauport to repel the expected landing. But while in the fleet of Saunders all was uproar and ostentatious menace, the danger was ten miles away, where the squadron of Holmes lay tranquil and silent at its anchorage off Cap-Rouge.

It was less tranquil than it seemed. All on board knew that a blow would be struck that night, though only a few high officers knew where. Colonel Howe, of the light infantry, called for volunteers to lead the unknown and desperate venture, promising, in the words of one of them, "that if any of us survived we might depend on being recommended to the general." As many as were wanted—twenty-four in all—soon came forward. Thirty large bateaux and some boats belonging to the squadron lay moored alongside the vessels; and late in the evening the troops were ordered into them, the twenty-four volunteers taking their place in the foremost. They held in all about 1,700 men. The rest remained on board.

Bougainville could discern the movement, and misjudged it, thinking that he himself was to be attacked. The tide was still flowing; and, the better to deceive him, the vessels and boats were allowed to drift upward with it for a little distance, as if to land above Cap-Rouge.

The day had been fortunate for Wolfe. Two deserters came from the camp of Bougainville with intelligence that, at ebb tide on the next night, he was to send down a convoy of provisions to Montcalm. The necessities of the camp at Beauport, and the difficulties of transportation by land, had before compelled the French to resort to this perilous means of conveying supplies; and their boats, drifting in darkness under the shadows of the northern shore, had commonly passed in safety. Wolfe saw at once that, if his own boats went down in advance of the convoy, he could turn the intelligence of the deserters to good account.

He was still on board the *Sutherland*. Every preparation was made, and every order given; it only remained to wait the turning of the tide. Seated with him in the cabin was the commander of the sloop-of-war *Porcupine*, his former school-fellow, John Jervis, afterwards Earl St. Vincent. Wolfe told him that he expected to die in the battle of the next day; and taking from his bosom a miniature of Miss Lowther, his betrothed, he gave it to him with a request that he would return it to her if the presentiment should prove true.

Towards two o'clock the tide began to ebb, and a fresh wind blew down the river. Two lanterns were raised into the maintop shrouds of the *Sutherland*. It was the appointed signal: the boats cast off and fell down with the current, those of the light infantry leading the way. The vessels with the rest of the troops had orders to follow a little later.

To look for a moment at the chances on which this bold adventure hung. First, the deserters told Wolfe that provision-boats were ordered to go down to Quebec that night; secondly, Bougainville countermanded them; thirdly, the sentries posted along the heights were told of the order, but not of the countermand; fourthly, Vergor at the Anse du Foulon had permitted most of his men, chiefly Canadians from Lorette, to go home for a time and work at their harvesting, on condition, it is said, that they should afterwards work in a neighboring field of his own; fifthly, he kept careless watch, and went quietly to bed; sixthly, the battalion of Guienne, ordered to take post on the Plains of Abraham, had, for reasons unexplained, remained encamped by the St. Charles; and lastly, when Bougainville saw Holmes's vessels drift down the stream, he did not tax his weary troops to follow them, thinking that they would return as usual with the flood tide. But for these conspiring circumstances New France might have lived a little longer, and the fruitless heroism of Wolfe would have passed, with countless other heroisms, into oblivion.

For full two hours the procession of boats, borne on the current, steered silently down the St. Lawrence. The stars were visible, but the night was moonless and sufficiently dark. The general was in one of the foremost boats, and near him was a young midshipman, John Robison, afterwards professor of natural philosophy in the University of Edinburgh. He used to tell in his later life how Wolfe, with a low voice, repeated Gray's "Elegy in a Country Churchyard" to the officers about him. Among the rest was the verse which his own fate was soon to illustrate,

The paths of glory lead but to the grave.

"Gentlemen," he said, as his recital ended, "I would rather have written those lines than take Quebec." None were there to tell him that the hero is greater than the poet.

As they neared their destination, the tide bore them in towards the shore, and the mighty wall of rock and forest towered in darkness on their left. The dead stillness was suddenly broken by the sharp *"Qui vive!"* of a French sentry, invisible in the thick gloom. *France!* answered a Highland officer of Fraser's regiment from one of the boats of the light infantry. He had served in Holland, and spoke French fluently.

A quel regiment?

De la Reine, replied the Highlander. He knew that a part of that corps was with Bougainville. The sentry, expecting the convoy of provisions, was satisfied, and did not ask for the password.

Soon after, the foremost boats were passing the heights of Samos, when another sentry challenged them, and they could see him through the darkness running down to the edge of the water, within range of a pistol-shot. In answer to his questions, the same officer replied in French: "Provision boats. Don't make a noise; the English will hear us." In fact, the sloop-of-war *Hunter* was anchored in the stream not far off. This time, again, the sentry let them pass. In a few moments they rounded the headland above the Anse du Foulon. There was no sentry there. The strong current swept the boats of the light infantry a little below the intended landing-place. They disembarked on a narrow strand at the foot of heights as steep as a hill covered with trees can be. The twenty-four volunteers led the way, climbing with what silence they might, closely followed by a much larger body. When they reached the top they saw in the dim light a cluster of tents at a short distance, and immediately made a dash at them. Vergor leaped from his bed and tried to run off, but was shot in the heel and captured. His men, taken by surprise, made little resistance. One or two were caught, and the rest fled.

The main body of troops waited in their boats by the edge of the strand. The heights near by were cleft by a great ravine choked with forest trees; and in its depths ran a little brook called Ruisseau St. Denis, which, swollen by the late rains, fell splashing in the stillness over a rock. Other than this no sound could reach the strained ear of Wolfe but the gurgle of the tide and the cautious climbing of his advance-parties as they mounted the steeps at some distance from where he sat listening. At length from the top came the sound of musket shots, followed by loud huzzas, and he knew that his men were masters of the position. The word was given; the troops leaped from the boats and scaled the heights, some here, some there, clutching at trees and bushes, their muskets slung at their backs. Tradition still points out the place, near the mouth of the ravine, where the foremost reached the top. Wolfe said to an officer near him: "You can try it, but I don't think you'll get up." He himself, however, found strength to drag himself up with the rest. The narrow slanting path on the face of the heights had been made impassable by trenches and abattis; but all obstructions were soon cleared away, and then the ascent was easy. In the gray of the morning the long file of red-coated soldiers moved quickly upward, and formed in order on the plateau above.

Before many of them had reached the top, cannon were heard close on the left. It was the battery at Samos firing on the boats in the rear and the vessels descending from Cap-Rouge. A party was sent to silence it; this was soon effected, and the more distant battery at Sillery was next attacked and taken. As fast as the boats were emptied they returned for the troops left on board the vessels and for those waiting on the southern shore under Colonel Burton.

The 13th day of September broke in clouds and threatening rain. Wolfe's battalions were drawn up along the crest of the heights. No enemy was in sight, though a body of Canadians had sallied from the town and moved along the strand towards the landing-place, whence they were quickly driven back. He had achieved the most critical part of his enterprise; yet the success that he coveted placed him in imminent danger. On the one side was the garrison of Quebec and the army of Beauport, and Bougainville was on the other. Wolfe's alternative was victory or ruin; for if he should be overwhelmed by a combined attack, retreat would be hopeless. His feelings no man can know; but it would be safe to say that hesitation or doubt had no part in them.

He went to reconnoitre the ground, and soon came to the Plains of Abraham, so called from Abraham Martin, a pilot known as Maître Abraham, who had owned a piece of land here in the early times of the colony. The Plains were a tract of grass, tolerably level in most parts, patched here and there with cornfields, studded with clumps of bushes, and forming a part of the high plateau at the eastern end of which Quebec stood. On the south it was bounded by the declivities along the St. Lawrence; on the north by those along the St. Charles, or rather along the meadows through which that lazy stream crawled like a writhing snake. At the place that Wolfe chose for his battle-field the plateau was less than a mile wide.

Thither the troops advanced, marched by files till they reached the ground, and then wheeled to form their line of battle, which stretched across the plateau and faced the city. It consisted of six battalions and the detached grenadiers from Louisbourg, all drawn up in ranks three deep. Its right wing was near the brink of the heights along the St. Lawrence; but the left could not reach those along the St. Charles. On this side a wide space was perforce left open, and there was danger of being outflanked. To prevent this, Brigadier Townshend was stationed here with two battalions, drawn up at right angles with the rest, and fronting the St. Charles. The battalion of Webb's regiment, under Colonel Burton, formed the reserve; the 3rd battalion of Royal Americans was left to guard the landing; and Howe's light infantry occupied a wood far in the rear. Wolfe, with Monckton and Murray, commanded the front line, on which the heavy fighting was to fall, and which, when all the troops had arrived, numbered less than 3,500 men.

Quebec was not a mile distant, but they could not see it; for a ridge of broken ground intervened, called Buttes-à-Neveu, about 600 paces off. The first division of troops had scarcely come up when, about six o'clock, this ridge was suddenly thronged with white uniforms. It was the battalion of Guienne, arrived at the eleventh hour from its camp by the St. Charles. Some time after there was hot firing in the rear. It came from a detachment of Bougainville's command attacking a house where some of the light infantry were posted. The assailants were repulsed, and the firing ceased. Light showers fell at intervals, besprinkled the troops as they stood patiently waiting the event.

Montcalm had passed a troubled night. Through all the evening the cannon bellowed from the ships of Saunders, and the boats of the fleet hovered in the dusk off the Beauport shore, threatening every moment to land. Troops lined the intrenchments till day, while the general walked the field that adjoined his headquarters till one in the morning, accompanied by the Chevalier Johnstone and Colonel Poulariez. Johnstone says that he was in great agitation, and took no rest all night. At daybreak he heard the sound of cannon above the town. It was the battery at Samos firing on the English ships. He had sent an officer to the quarters of Vaudreuil, which were much nearer Quebec, with orders to bring him word at once should anything unusual happen. But no word came, and about six o'clock he mounted and rode thither with Johnstone. As they advanced, the country behind the town opened more and more upon their sight; till at length, when opposite Vaudreuil's house, they saw across the St. Charles, some two miles away, the red ranks of British soldiers on the heights beyond.

"This is a serious business," Montcalm said; and sent off Johnstone at full gallop to bring up the troops from the centre and left of the camp. Those of the right were in motion already, doubtless by the governor's order. Vaudreuil came out of the house. Montcalm stopped for a few words with him; then set spurs to his horse, and he rode over the bridge of the St. Charles to the scene of danger. He rode with a fixed look, uttering not a word.

The army followed in such order as it might, crossed the bridge in hot haste, passed under the northern rampart of Quebec, entered at the Palace Gate, and pressed on in headlong march along the quaint narrow streets of the warlike town: troops of Indians in scalp-locks and war-paint, a savage glitter in their deep-set eyes; bands of Canadians whose all was at stake—faith, country, and home; the colony regulars; the battalions of Old France, a torrent of white uniforms and gleaming bayonets, La Sarre, Languedoc, Roussillon, Béarn—victors of Oswego, William Henry, and Ticonderoga. So they swept on, poured out upon the plain, some by the gate of St. Louis, and some by that of St. John, and hurried, breathless, to where the banners of Guienne still fluttered on the ridge.

Montcalm was amazed at what he saw. He had expected a detachment, and he found an army. Full in sight before him stretched the lines of Wolfe: the close ranks of the English infantry, a silent wall of red, and the wild array of the Highlanders, with their waving tartans, and bagpipes screaming a defiance. Vaudreuil had not come; but not the less was felt the evil of a divided authority and the jealousy of the rival chiefs. Montcalm waited long for the forces he had ordered to join him from the left wing of the army. He waited in vain. It is said that the governor had detained them, lest the English should attack the Beauport shore. Even if they did so, and succeeded, the French might defy them, could they but put Wolfe to rout on the Plains of Abraham. Neither did the garrison of Quebec come to the aid of Montcalm. He sent to Ramesay, its commander, for twenty-five field-pieces which were on the Palace battery. Ramesay would give him only three, saying that he wanted them for his own defence. There were orders and counter-orders; misunderstanding, haste, delay, perplexity.

Montcalm and his chief officers held a council of war. It is said that he and they alike were for immediate attack. His enemies declare that he was afraid lest Vaudreuil should arrive and take command; but the governor was not a man to assume responsibility at such a crisis. Others say that his impetuosity overcame his better judgment; and of this charge it is hard to acquit him. Bougainville was but a few miles distant, and some of his troops were much nearer; a messenger sent by way of Old Lorette could have reached him in an hour and a half at most, and a combined attack in front and rear might have been concerted with him. If, moreover, Montcalm could have come to an understanding with Vaudreuil, his own force might have been strengthened by two or three thousand additional men from the town and the camp of Beauport; but he felt that there was no time to lose, for he imagined that Wolfe would soon be reinforced, which was impossible, and he believed that the English were fortifying themselves, which was no less an error. He has been blamed not only for fighting too soon, but for fighting at all. In this he could not choose. Fight he must, for Wolfe was now in a position to cut off all his supplies. His men were full of ardor, and he resolved to attack before their ardor cooled. He spoke a few words to them in his keen, vehement way. "I remember very well how he looked," one of the Canadians, then a boy of eighteen, used to say in his old age; "he rode a black or dark bay horse along the front of our line, brandishing his sword, as if to excite us to do our duty. He wore a coat with wide sleeves, which fell back as he raised his arms, and showed the white linen of the wristband."

The English waited the result with a composure which, if not quite real, was at least well feigned. The three field-pieces sent by Ramesay plied them with canister-shot, and 1,500 Canadians and Indians fusilladed them in front and flank. Over all the plain, from behind bushes and knolls and the edge of cornfields, puffs of smoke sprang incessantly from the guns of those hidden marksmen. Skirmishers were thrown out before the lines to hold them in check, and the soldiers were ordered to lie on the grass to avoid the shot. The firing was liveliest on the English left, where bands of sharp-shooters got under the edge of the declivity, among thickets, and behind scattered houses, whence they killed and wounded a considerable number of Townshend's men. The light infantry were called up from the rear. The houses were taken and retaken, and one or more of them was burned.

Wolfe was everywhere. How cool he was, and why his followers loved him, is shown by an incident that happened in the course of the morning. One of his captains was shot through the lungs; and on recovering consciousness he saw the general standing at his side. Wolfe pressed his hand, told him not to despair, praised his services, promised him early promotion, and sent an aide-de-camp to Monckton to beg that officer to keep the promise if he himself should fall.

It was towards ten o'clock when, from the high ground on the right of the line, Wolfe saw that the crisis was near. The French on the ridge had formed themselves into three bodies, regulars in the centre, regulars and Canadians on right and left. Two field-pieces, which had been dragged up the heights at Anse du Foulon, fired on them with grape-shot, and the troops, rising from the ground, prepared to receive them. In a few moments more they were in motion. They came on rapidly, uttering loud shouts, and firing as soon as they were within range. Their ranks, ill ordered at best, were further confused by a number of Canadians who had been mixed among the regulars, and who, after hastily firing, threw themselves on the ground to reload. The British advanced a few rods; then halted and stood still. When the French were within forty paces the word of command rang out, and a crash of musketry answered all along the line. The volley was delivered with remarkable precision. In the battalions of the centre, which had suffered least from the enemy's bullets, the simultaneous explosion was afterwards said by French officers to have sounded like a cannon-shot. Another volley followed, and then a furious clattering fire that lasted but a minute or two. When the smoke rose, a miserable sight was revealed: the ground cumbered with dead and wounded, the advancing masses stopped short and turned into a frantic mob, shouting, cursing, gesticulating. The order was given to charge. Then over the field rose the British cheer, mixed with the fierce yell of the Highland slogan. Some of the corps pushed forward with the bayonet; some advanced firing. The clansmen drew their broadswords and dashed on, keen and swift as bloodhounds. At the English right, though the attacking column was broken to pieces, a fire was still kept up, chiefly, it seems, by sharpshooters from the bushes and cornfields, where they had lain for an hour or more. Here Wolfe himself led the charge, at the head of the Louisbourg grenadiers. A shot shattered his wrist. He wrapped his handkerchief about it and kept on. Another shot struck him, and he still advanced, when a third lodged in his breast. He staggered, and sat on the ground. Lieutenant Brown, of the grenadiers, one Henderson, a volunteer in the same company, and a private soldier, aided by an officer of artillery who ran to join them, carried him in their arms to the rear. He begged them to lay him down. They did so, and asked if he would have a surgeon. "There's no need," he answered; "it's all over with me." A moment after, one of them cried out: "They run; see how they run!" "Who run?" Wolfe demanded, like a man roused from sleep. "The enemy, sir. Egad, they give way everywhere!" "Go, one of you, to Burton," returned the dying man; "tell him to march Webb's regiment down to Charles River, to cut off their retreat from the bridge." Then, turning on his side, he murmured, "Now, God be praised, I will die in peace!" and in a few moments his gallant soul had fled.

Montcalm, still on horseback, was borne with the tide of fugitives towards the town. As he approached the walls a shot passed through his body. He kept his seat; two soldiers supported him, one on each side, and led his horse through the St. Louis gate. On the open space within, among the excited crowd, were several women, drawn, no doubt, by eagerness to know the result of the fight. One of them recognized him, saw the streaming blood, and shrieked, "*O mon Dieu! mon Dieu! le Marquis est tué!*" "It's nothing, it's nothing," replied the death-stricken man; "don't be troubled for me, my good friends." ("*Ce n'est rien, ce n'est rien; ne vous affligez pas pour moi, mes bonnes amies.*")

Benjamin Franklin

GEORGE OTTO TREVELYAN

1706–1790. Sir George Otto Trevelyan, nephew and biographer of Macaulay, wrote history nearly as well as his famous uncle—with verve, grace, wit, many an outspoken moral judgment, and many a frank expression of his Liberal political opinions. He began his popular, six-volume work, The American Revolution, *when he was fifty-nine and finished it when he was seventy-six. Published between 1899 and 1914, it probably contains too much about English parliamentary politics for the tastes of most Americans; but it is rich with color and drama and brilliant portrait sketches. Trevelyan's affectionate profile of Franklin is one of his best. Though why he thought that one of the most extraordinary of all Americans was a typical American passes understanding.*

THE MOST TYPICAL AMERICAN WHO EVER LIVED

There was another celebrated colonist whose youth had been fostered at a greater distance still from the lap of luxury. The inventory of the effects owned by the great great grandfather of John Adams showed that there had been a silver spoon in the family four generations back. But Franklin ate his breakfast with pewter out of earthenware until, when he was already a mature householder, his wife bought him a China bowl and a silver spoon, on the grounds that her husband deserved to live as handsomely as any of his neighbors. If he inherited no plate, he derived a more valuable legacy from his ancestors, who in their history and their qualities were worthy forerunners of the most typical American who ever lived. England in the seventeenth century gave, or rather thrust upon, the New World much of what was staunch and true, and much also of what was quick-witted and enterprising, in her population. The Franklins, a Northamptonshire clan of very small freeholders, among whom the trade of blacksmith was as hereditary as in an Indian caste, were good Protestants in the worst of times. During the reign of Queen Mary the head of the household kept his English Bible fastened with tapes beneath the seat of a stool, and read it aloud with the stool reversed between his knees, while a child stood in the doorway to give the alarm in case an apparitor from the spiritual court was seen in the street. Benjamin Franklin's father was a stout and zealous nonconformist; and when conventicles were forbidden in England by laws cruelly conceived and rigorously enforced, he carried his wife and children to Massachusetts in order that they might enjoy the exercise of their religion in freedom. He set up at Boston first as a dyer, and then as a maker of soap and candles. The family character was marked by native ingenuity and homely public spirit. One of Franklin's uncles invented a shorthand of his own. Another, who remained at home in Northamptonshire, taught himself law; filled local offices of importance; was a prime mover in all useful undertakings in town and country; and was long remembered in his village as a benefactor, an advisor, and (by the more ignorant) as a reputed conjurer. He set on foot a subscription to provide a set of chimes, which his nephew heard with satisfaction three-quarters of a century afterwards; and he discovered a simple effective method of saving the common lands from being drowned by the river. "If Franklin says he knows how to do it, it will be done," was a phrase which had passed into a proverb for the neighborhood. He died four years to a day before his brother's famous child was born. "Had he died four years later," it was said, "one might have supposed a transmigration."

Benjamin Franklin had a right to be proud of the mental gifts which were born within him, when he looked back from the height of his fame to the material circumstances which surrounded him on his entrance into this world. Seldom did any man who started with as little accomplish so much, if we except certain august self-seekers in history whose career was carved out at great cost of human life and human freedom. He had a year at a grammar-school; and then he was taken into the family business, and set to serve at the counter and run errands. He disliked the life; and his father, who feared that he would break loose and go to sea, gravely took him a round of the shops in Boston, and showed him joiners, bricklayers, turners, braziers, and cutlers at their work, in order that, with knowledge of what he was about, he might choose his calling for himself. The boy, who was twelve years old, everywhere learned something which he never forgot, and which he turned to account in one or another of the seventy-two years that were before him. The combined good sense of parent and child led them to decide on the trade of a printer. He was bound apprentice, and from this time forward he read the books which passed under his hand. Others, which he loved better, he purchased to keep; dining, a joyful anchorite, on a biscuit or a handful of raisins, in order that he might spend his savings on his infant library. He gave himself a classical education out of an old volume of the "Spectator," re-writing the papers from memory, and correcting them by the original; or turning the tales into verse and back again into prose. He taught himself arithmetic thoroughly, and learned a little geometry and a little navigation; both of which in after days he made to go a long way, and put to great uses.

But, above all, he trained himself as a logician; making trial of many successive systems with amazing zest, until he founded an unpretentious school of his own in which his pre-eminence has never been questioned. He traversed with rapidity all the stages in the art of reasoning, from the earliest phase, when a man only succeeds in being disagreeable to his fellows, up to the period when he has become a proficient in the science of persuading them. He began by arguing to confute, "souring and spoiling the conversation," and making enemies, instead of disciples, at every turn. "I had caught this," he wrote, "by reading my father's books of dispute on religion. Persons of good sense, I have since observed, seldom fall into it, except lawyers, university men, and generally men of all sorts who have been bred at Edinburgh." He next lighted upon a copy of Xenophon's "Memorabilia," and, captivated by the charms of the Socratic dialogue, he dropped the weapons of abrupt contradiction and positive assertion, and put on the humble inquirer. He grew very expert into drawing people into concessions, the consequences of which they did not foresee—especially people who were not familiar with Shaftesbury's "Characteristics" and Collins's "Discourse on Free-Thinking." From his own study of those works he derived conclusions which made it safer for him to proselytise the Boston of that day by a process of suggestion and induction rather than by dogmatic exposition. At length he found that his friends grew wary, and would hardly reply to the most common question without asking first what he intended to infer from the answer. Then he once more changed his style of conversation, and this time for good. Keeping nothing of his former method except the habit of expressing himself "with modest diffidence," he refrained altogether from the words "certainly" and "undoubtedly," and from the air of aggressive superiority which generally accompanies them. The phrases with which he urged his point, and seldom failed to carry it, were "I conceive," or "I apprehend," or "It appears to me," or "It is so, if I am not mistaken." He made it a practice, likewise, to encourage his interlocutors to think that the opinion he aimed at instilling into them was theirs already. If, as he pleased himself with believing, he had learned these arts from Socrates, the teaching of the Academy had for once borne an abundant crop of Baconian fruit; for it would be hard to name a man who, over so long a space of time as Franklin, ever talked so many people into doing that which was for their own improvement and advantage.

The theatre of his beneficent operations was not his native city. Boston, in common with the world at large, gathered in due time some of the crumbs which fell from the table of his inventiveness; but she very soon lost the first claim upon one who was so clever a son as even she ever produced. At the age of seventeen Franklin walked into the capital of Pennsylvania, his pockets stuffed with shirts and stockings, but empty of money; carrying a roll under each arm, and eating as he went along. The expansive possibilities of an American's career may be traced in every page of his early story. The intimate companions of his poverty, young as he, made their way in the world soon and far. One, who went to England, got himself into a couplet of the "Dunciad"; wrote a history of William the Third which was praised by Charles Fox; and extracted from the Earl of Bute a pension twice as large as Dr. Johnson's. Another became an eminent lawyer, and died rich while he and Franklin were still below middle age. The two friends had agreed that the one who left the earth first should afterwards pay a visit to the other; but the ghost had yet to be found which had the courage to present itself to Franklin.

He worked hard, and lived very hardly indeed in Philadelphia, and in London for a while, and in Philadelphia again. At the end of ten years he was securely settled in business as a stationer and master-printer, and the owner of a newspaper which soon became an excellent property, which bore the trace of his hand in every corner of its columns. By a miracle of industry and thrift, he had paid out his first partners, and paid off his borrowed capital. It was no longer necessary for him to breakfast on gruel, and sup on half an anchovy and a slice of bread; to be at work when his neighbors returned at night from the club, and at work again before they rose in the morning; to wheel the paper for his Gazette home through the streets on a barrow, and to take neither rest nor recreation except when a book "debauched" him from his labors. From the moment that he had set his foot firmly on the path of fortune, he threw his vast energy, his audacious creativeness, his dexterity in the management of his fellow-creatures, and a good portion of his increased though still slender substance, into the service of his adopted city. One scheme followed hard upon another; each of them exactly suited to local wants which Franklin was quick to discern, and to a national taste with which he was entirely in sympathy. By the end of a quarter of a century Philadelphia lacked nothing that was possessed by any city in England, except a close corporation and bull-ring, and enjoyed in addition a complete outfit of institutions which were eagerly imitated throughout the Northern colonies.

Franklin's first project was a book-club; the mother, to use his own words, of those subscription libraries which perceptibly raised the standard of American conversation, "and made tradesmen and farmers as intelligent as the gentry of other countries." Then came, in rapid succession, a volunteer fire company; a paid police-force; a public hospital; a Philosophical Society; an Academy, which he lived to see develop itself into the University of Philadelphia; and a paper currency, which with his stern views on private and public credit, he fortunately for him did not live to see at the height of its notoriety in the shape of the memorable Pennsylvania Bonds. He turned his attention successfully to the paving and scavenging of the highways. When the city was first lighted, he designed the form of a street lamp which has long been in universal use wherever Anglo-Saxons now burn gas or once burned oil. He invented a hot-stove for sitting-rooms, and refused a patent for it, on the ground that he himself had profited so much by the discoveries of others that he was only too glad of an opportunity to repay his debt, and to repay it in a shape so peculiarly acceptable to his country-women. Whitefield, whom everybody except the clergy wished to hear, had been refused the use of the existing pulpits. Franklin, as his contribution to the cause of religion, promoted the building of a spacious meeting-house, vested in trustees, expressly for the use of any preacher of any denomination who might desire to say something to the people of Philadelphia.

In 1744, on the breaking out of war with France, Franklin excited the patriotism of Pennsylvania by voice and pen, and directed it into the practical channel of enrolling a State militia, and constructing a battery for the protection of the river. He raised the requisite funds by a lottery in which he was artful enough to induce the members of the Society of Friends to take tickets, knowing well that, without their support, no scheme appealing to the purse would be very productive in Philadelphia. In order to arm his embrasures, he applied to Governor Clinton of New York for cannon, who met him with a flat refusal. But Franklin sate with him over his Madeira until, as the bumpers went round, his Excellency consented to give six guns, then rose to ten, and ended by contributing to the defense of the Delaware no less than eighteen fine pieces, with carriages included. Eleven years afterwards, when Braddock marched to the attack of Fort Duquesne, Franklin, by the earnest request of the general, and at formidable risk to his own private fortune, organized the transport and commissariat with an ability and foresight in marked contrast to the military conduct of the ill-fated expedition. In the terrible panic which ensued when the news of the disaster reached Philadelphia, the authorities of the colony,—catching at the hope that, as he understood everything else, there was at least a chance of his understanding how to fight,—entrusted him with the defence of the North-West frontier against the imminent peril of an Indian invasion. He levied and commanded a respectable force, and threw up a line of forts, the planning and building of which gave him the most exquisite satisfaction; and, on his return home, he accepted the title of a true American by becoming a Colonel of Militia, and was greeted by his regiment with a salvo of artillery which broke several glasses of the electrical apparatus that had already made his name famous throughout the entire scientific world.

There were few military posts with regard to which Franklin, if he was not competent to fill them himself, could not give a useful hint to their holder. The chaplain of his troops complained that the men would not attend public worship. The commanding officer accordingly suggested that the chaplain should himself serve out the rum when prayers were over; "and never," said Franklin, "were prayers more generally and punctually attended. I think this method preferable to the punishment inflicted by some military laws for non-attendance on divine service." Wherever he went, and whatever he was engaged upon, he was always calculating, and never guessing. When he built his forts, he soon noticed that two men cut down a pine of fourteen inches in diameter in six minutes, and that each pine made three palisades eighteen feet in length. When he was collecting money for his battery, he satisfied himself, by means of an intricate computation, that out of every twenty-two Quakers only one sincerely disapproved of participation in a war of defence. And on an evening when Whitefield was delivering a sermon from the top of the Court-House steps, Franklin moved about in the crowd, and measured distances, until he had ascertained that the human voice, or at any rate Whitefield's voice, could be heard by more than thirty thousand people. "This," he said, "reconciled me to the newspaper accounts of his having preached to twenty-five thousand people in the fields, and to the history of generals haranguing whole armies, of which I had sometimes doubted."

His growing reputation brought him important public employment, though not any great amount of direct public remuneration. He was chosen Clerk of the Pennsylvania Assembly in 1736, and next year he was placed at the head of the Pennsylvania Post Office. As time went on, the British Government, finding that the postal revenue of the colonies had fallen to less than nothing, appointed Franklin Joint Postmaster-General of America, with a colleague to help him. The pair were to have six hundred pounds a year between them, if they could make that sum out of the profits of the office. For four years the balance was against them; but at the end of that time the department, managed according to the precepts of "The Way to Wealth" in *Poor Richard's Almanac*, began to pay, and paid ever better yearly, until it yielded the Crown a net receipt three times as large as that of the Post Office in Ireland. So much he did for himself, and so much more he enabled to do for others, by a strict obedience to the promptings of a mother-wit, which, in great things as in small, was all but infallible, and by a knowledge of human nature diplomatic even to the verge of wiliness. When he had a project on foot, he would put his vanity in the background, and would represent the matter as the plan of a number of friends, who had requested him to go about and recommend it to public favor and support. To conciliate an enemy, if all other means failed, he would beg of him a trifling service, which in decency could not be refused; relying on the maxim that "He who has once done you a kindness will be more ready to do you another than he whom you yourself have obliged." For the furtherance of all his undertakings, he had a powerful instrument in a newspaper as respectable as it was readable; which, with a fine prescience of the possible dangers of a free press to America, and not to America alone, he steadily refused to make the vehicle of scurrilous gossip and personal detraction. By such arts as these he fulfilled to the letter the augury of his good old father, who in past days loved to remind him that a man diligent in his calling should stand before Kings, and not before mean men. "I did not think," said Franklin, "that I should ever literally stand before Kings, which, however, has since happened; for I have stood before five, and even had the honor of sitting down with one, the King of Denmark, to dinner."

Franklin had the habit, which was the basis of his originality, of practising himself what he preached to others. He kept his accounts in morals as minutely as in business matters. He drew up a catalogue of twelve virtues which it was essential to cultivate, commencing with Temperance and ending with Chastity; to which at a subsequent period a Quaker friend, who knew him well, advised him to add Humility. "My intention," he wrote, "being to acquire the *habitude* of these virtues, I judged it would be well not to distract my attention by attempting the whole at once, but to fix it on one of them at a time; and, when I should be the master of that, then to proceed to another, till I should have gone through the thirteen. And, as the previous acquisition of some might facilitate the acquisition of certain others, I arranged them with that view." By the time he became Joint Postmaster-General of America, he had made his ground sure enough to justify him in relaxing his vigilance, though he carried his little book on all his voyages as a precaution and as a reminder. The

Joint Postmaster-General of England, who was no other than the Earl of Sandwich, would not have got very far along the list of virtues, at whichever end he began.

The early relations between the United States of America and the monarchies of Europe may be studied with advantage by those writers who attach little or no importance to the personal factor in history. The prospects of the young Republic were seriously, and to all appearance irretrievably, damnified by the mismanagement of Congress; but the position was saved by the ability, the discretion, and the force of character of one single man. Benjamin Franklin was now past seventy. He had begun to earn his bread as a child of ten; he commenced as an author at sixteen; and he had ever since been working with his hands, and taxing his brain, unintermittently, and at the top of his power. Such exertions were not maintained with impunity. He kept his strength of will unimpaired, his mind clear and lively, and his temper equable, by a life-long habit of rigid abstemiousness; but he already felt the approach of painful diseases that tormented him cruelly before the immense undertaking, which still lay before him, had been half accomplished. In September 1776 he was elected Commissioner to France, by a unanimous resolution of Congress. Franklin, in the highest sense of the term, was a professional diplomatist; for he had passed sixteen years in England as Agent for his colony; and his individual qualities had gained for him a political influence, and a social standing, out of all proportion to the comparatively humble interests which he represented at the British Court. The ambassadors of the Great Powers, who were resident in London, treated him as one of themselves. He was old enough to be the father of most among them, and wise enough to be the advisor of all; and, towards the end of his time, they united in regarding him as in some sort of the *doyen* of their body. Franklin's knowledge of European statesmen, and courtiers, taught him to anticipate nothing but failure and humiliation from the diplomatic methods which Congress favored; and he had no confidence whatever in the emissaries whom it thought fit to employ. The acceptance of the laborious and perilous mission, to which he was now invited, presented itself to his mind in the light of an absolute duty. His feelings remain on record in a letter which he subsequently addressed to a friend who urged him, in those "tempestuous times," to take some care of himself, and of his own safety. "I thank you," he wrote, "for your kind caution; but, having nearly finished a long life, I set but little value on what remains of it. Like a draper, when one chaffers with him for a remnant, I am ready to say: 'As it is only the fag end, I will not differ with you about it. Take it for what you please.' "

* * *

Franklin had come to Europe for the sole purpose of engaging in a stern and single-handed conflict with the difficulties and problems of a supreme crisis; and the old man's tale of work during the next eight years was a record which has seldom been beaten. Europe (it has been truely said) was henceforward the centre of action, where the funds for carrying on the Rebellion were raised, and the supplies required by the American armies were mainly purchased. In Europe, moreover, as a consequence of the impossibility of prompt and regular communication across the seas with Congress, the diplomacy of the Republic was necessarily moulded. American privateers were fitted out, their crews enlisted, and their prizes sold, in European ports; and all controverted questions about the legal validity of their captures were examined and decided in Europe, and not in America. "It was by Franklin alone that these various functions were exercised. It was on Franklin alone that fell the enormous labor of keeping the accounts connected with these various departments." He had no staff of clerks at his command, and no deft and devoted subordinates to collect information, to sift correspondence, to prepare despatches for signature, and to save their over-burdened chief from the infliction of a personal interview with all the idlers, the jobbers, and soldiers of fortune, and real or sham men of science, who daily thronged his door. His only assistant was his elder grandson,—a worthy youth who could write from dictation, and copy a letter in a good round hand; but who did not possess, and never acquired, the art of drafting an important paper.

* * *

Europe had welcomed and accepted him, not as a mere spokesman and agent of the government at Philadelphia, but as the living and breathing embodiment of the American Republic. No statesman would do business with anybody but Franklin. No financier would negotiate a loan except with him, pay over money into other hands than his. "It was to Franklin that both the French and English ministries turned, as if he were not only the sole representative of the United States in Europe, but as if he were endowed with plenipotentiary power." Nine-tenths of the public letters addressed to the American Commissioners were brought to his house; "and," (so his colleagues admitted,) "they would ever be carried wherever Dr. Franklin is." He transacted his affairs with Louis the Sixteenth's ministers on a footing of equality, and, (as time went on,) of unostentatious but unquestionable superiority. Thomas Jefferson, an impartial and most competent observer, had on one occasion been contending that American diplomatists were always spoiled for use after they had been kept seven years abroad. But this, (said Jefferson,) did not apply to Franklin, "who was America itself when in France, not subjecting himself to French influence," but imposing American influence upon France, and upon the whole course and conduct of her national policy.

The fact was that the French ministry, in its relations to Franklin, had to reckon with a political phenomenon of exceptional nature, and portentous significance. The royal authority in France was uncontrolled by any effective, and continuously operating, machinery of national self-government; but that very circumstance lent force and weight to public opinion, at those rare conjunctures when public opinion had been strongly moved. If ever the privileged, the moneyed, and the intellectual classes united in one way of thinking, their influence was all the more irresistible because it was not defined, and limited, by the provisions of a written constitution. The rest of the nation, below those classes, was a powerless and voiceless proletariat; while above them there was nothing except a handful of Viscounts and Marquises, the Royal ministers of the hour, who were drawn from their ranks, and lived in their society, and who were mortally afraid of their disapprobation, and still more of their ridicule. France, in the last resort, was ruled by fashion; and Franklin had become the idol of fashion like no foreigner, and perhaps no Frenchman, either before or since.

His immense and, (as he himself was the foremost to acknowledge,) his extravagant popularity was founded on a solid base of admiration and esteem. The origin of his fame dated from a time which seemed fabulously distant to the existing generation. His qualities and accomplishments were genuine and unpretentious; and his services to the world were appreciated by high and low, rich and poor, in every country where men learned from books, or profited by the discoveries of science. His *Poor Richard*,—which expounded and elucidated a code of rules for the everyday conduct of life with sagacity that never failed, and wit that very seldom missed the mark,—had been thrice translated into French, had gone through many editions, and had been recommended by priests and bishops for common use in their parishes and dioceses. As an investigator, and an experimentalist, he was more widely known even than as an author; for he had always aimed at making natural philosophy the handmaid of material progress. Those homely and practical inventions, by which he had done so much to promote the comfort and convenience of the average citizen, had caused him to be regarded as a public benefactor in every civilized community throughout the world. His reputation, (so

John Adams wrote,) was more universal than that of Leibnitz or Newton. "His name was familiar to government and people, to foreign countries,— to nobility, clergy, and philosophers, as well as to plebeians,—to such a degree that there was scarcely a peasant or a citizen, a valet, coachman, or footman, a day's chambermaid, or scullion in the kitchen, who did not consider him a friend to humankind." If Franklin, at seventy years of age, had visited France as a private tourist, his progress through her cities would have been one long ovation; and her enthusiasm transcended all bounds when, coming as an ambassador from a new world beyond the seas, he appealed to French chivalry on behalf of a young nation struggling for freedom. "His mission," (said a French writer who was no blind partisan of Franklin,) "flattered all the bright and generous ideas which animated France. He caressed our happiest hopes, our most gilded chimaeras. He came across the ocean to win liberty for his own country; and he brought liberty to us. He was the representative of a people still primitive and unsophisticated,—or who appeared so in our eyes. He professed no religious creed except tolerance, and kindliness of heart. France, moved by a thousand passions and a thousand caprices, prostrated herself at the feet of a man who had no caprices and no passions. She made him the symbol and object of her adoration; and Franklin took rank above Voltaire and Rousseau, by the side of Socrates."

One such account must serve for all. It would be tedious, and superfluous, to multiply quotations from contemporary authors who have recorded their passionate devotion, and, (what in parallel cases has been a rare feature,) the invincible constancy and fidelity with which French society abandoned itself to the worship of Franklin. The wise old American was keenly alive to the excess, and the occasional absurdity, of the adulation by which he was encompassed. He had measured, more accurately than any man then living, the true and exact worth of Benjamin Franklin; and he did nothing whatever to encourage the exaggerated estimate of that personage which most Frenchmen, and all French women, persisted in cherishing. He lived his own life, and talked his own talk, and allowed the imaginative and emotional Parisians to make what they chose both of the one and the other. The French government, anxious to keep their distinguished guest as far as possible removed from hostile supervision and impertinent curiosity, placed at his disposal a house and garden at Passy, which now is well within the circuit of the fortifications, but then was still "a neat village on high ground, half a mile from the city." Here Franklin dwelt, as pleasantly lodged as in an elm-shaded suburb of his own Philadelphia; superintending the education of his smaller grandson, who was a child of seven; entertaining Americans, young and old, at a quiet dinner on the Sunday afternoon; working, during odd hours, in the Royal Laboratory, which stood close at hand; and making a show of drinking the Passy waters. He was seldom seen on foot in the streets of the capital; and he took his exercise, with conscientious regularity, in his garden when the sun shone, and within doors during the months of winter. "I walk," (so he told John Adams in November 1782,) "every day in my chamber. I walk quick, and for an hour, so that I go a league. I make a point of religion of it." When he appeared in public he was dressed in good broadcloth of a sober tint; conspicuous with his long straight hair, whitened by age, and not by art; and wearing a pair of spectacles, to remedy an old man's dimness of vision, and a cap of fine marten's fur, because he had an old man's susceptibility to cold.

Franklin's costume had not been designed with any idea of pleasing the Parisians; but it obtained an extraordinary success, and has left a mark on history. Fine gentlemen, with their heads full of the new philosophy, regarded his unembroidered coat, and unpowdered locks, as a tacit, but visible, protest against those luxuries and artificialities which they all condemned, but had not the smallest intention of themselves renouncing. He reminded them of everything and everybody that Jean Jacques Rousseau had taught them to admire. The Comte de Ségur declared that "Franklin's antique and patriarchal aspect seemed to transport into the middle of an enervated, and servile, civilization a Republican of Rome of the time of Cato and Fabius, or a sage who had consorted with Plato." Some compared him to Diogenes, and some to Phocion,—about whom they can have known very little; for, if Phocion had been a Pennsylvanian of Anno Domini 1776, he would, beyond all question, have been a strenuous and uncompromising supporter of the British connection. Readers of *Emile*, who then comprised three-fourths of the fashionable world, delighted to recognize in the American stranger an express and living image of the Savoyard Vicar; and it was believed, with some reason, that his views on religion nearly corresponded to those of Rousseau's famous ecclesiastic, although Franklin would most certainly have compressed his Profession of Faith into much shorter compass. The great French ladies were attracted and fascinated by his quiet self-possession, his benign courtesy, and his playful, yet always rational, conversation. The ardor of Franklin's votaries sometimes manifested itself with an exuberance which made it difficult for him to keep his countenance. When he paid a visit to Madame d'Houdetot at her country residence in the Valley of Montmorency, his hostess,—attended by the solemn and imperturbable Marquis who then was her lover, as he was the lover in turn of the most celebrated blue-stockings of that generation,—came forth to meet him, as if he were a royal personage, before he entered the avenue. She greeted him with an address in verse; at dinner he was regaled by a rhymed compliment, from some Count or Viscount, between every course, and after the coffee; Monsieur d'Houdetot himself, "rising to the sublime of absurdity in his quality of husband," instituted an elaborate parallel between Franklin and William Tell, to the disadvantage of the Swiss patriot; and the departing guest was ultimately pursued to his coach door by a shower of laudatory couplets. To exhibit himself as the central figure in such scenes was not the least among the sacrifices which Franklin made upon the altar of his country.

Franklin dined abroad on every weekday; not because people thought it their duty to invite him, but because they could never have too much of his company. John Adams, before he himself spoke French at all, gave a disparaging account of Franklin's grammar and accent; but Frenchmen praised the ease and skill with which he employed their language; and that is the one point on which no true Parisian will ever condescend to flatter. The banquets which he attended did not afford him unmixed enjoyment; for he was almost sure of meeting some officer who wanted to become a Major General in the American army, or some chemist with an invention for blowing up the English fleet, and who only waited to begin their attack upon him until he had been "put in good humor by a glass or two of champagne." The world then dined at two in the afternoon; the party broke up as soon as the dinner had been eaten; and Franklin's evenings were very generally spent in the house of his neighbor, Madame Helvétius, who lived beyond him at Auteuil, in the direction of the Bois de Boulogne. In this lady's salon he consorted with the most prominent of his brother Academicians; for he had long ere this been elected a member of their august body. Diderot and Morellet, Lavoisier, d'Alembert, Condorcet, and Turgot were his habitual associates, and his attached friends. In Paris and at Auteuil alike, during the give and take of the best conversation which the continent of Europe then had to show, Franklin never missed an opportunity of interesting his companions in the cause of America, and re-assuring them about her future. An undaunted and persuasive optimist, speaking with the authority of one who was no mere amateur of war, he imparted to all around him his own loyal confidence in Washington's strategy; and, at the lowest moment of his country's fortunes, he boldly and cheerfully proclaimed his settled conviction that it was not the British who had taken Philadelphia, but Philadelphia which had taken the British. No less a writer than the Marquis de Condorcet has borne witness to the tact and ability, and the all but universal acceptance, with which Franklin handled the topic of America. "It was an honor," said Condorcet, "to have seen him. People repeated in all societies what they had heard him say. Every entertainment which he accepted, every house where he consented to go, gained him new admirers who became so many partisans of the American revolution."

He was a great ambassador, of a type which the world had never seen before, and will never see again until it contains another Benjamin Franklin. Tried by the searching test of practical performance, he takes high rank among the diplomatists of history. His claims to that position have been vindicated, in a manner worthy of the subject, by an eminent American publicist of our own generation. There were conspicuous statesmen, (writes Doctor Wharton,) at the Congress of Vienna; but the imposing fabric constructed by Metternich, and Nesselrode, and Talleyrand, with such lofty disregard for national liberties and popular rights, has long ago perished, while Franklin's work endures to this hour. It was Franklin who introduced America, on a footing of equality, into the councils of Europe, and who, in a truer sense than Canning, called the New World into existence to redress the balance of the Old. And the crown and coping-stone of his protracted labors was that final treaty of peace between Great Britain and the United States, which of all international settlements is "the one that has produced the greatest blessings to both the contracting parties, has been the greatest benefit to civilization as a whole, and has been least affected by the flow of time."

Thomas Jefferson: A Portrait

CLAUDE G. BOWERS

43–1826. Many books have been written about Jefferson, several of them
table works of scholarship. But none that I know of contains so fervently ad-
ring a portrait of the great man who became our third President as Bowers's
ferson and Hamilton. Published in 1925, it concentrates on the rivalry be-
een the two statesmen and stops short at Jefferson's first inauguration. Bowers
s an ardent Democrat, an ambassador, and the author of many volumes of
tory.

the personal appearance of Thomas Jefferson there was little to denote
: powerful, dominating leader and strict disciplinarian that he was.
like Hamilton, he did not look the commander so much as the rather
philosopher. The gruff Maclay, on seeing him for the first time, was
appointed with his slender frame, the looseness of his figure, and the
r of stiffness in his manner," while pleased with the sunniness of his
e. He was of imposing height, being more than six feet, and slender
hout being thin. All contemporaries who have left descriptions refer
the long, loosely jointed limbs, and none of them convey an impression
grace. His hair, much redder than that of Hamilton, was combed

loosely over the forehead and at the side, and tied behind. His complexic
was light, his eyes blue and usually mild in expression, his forehe:
broad and high. Beneath the eyes, his face was rather broad, the chee
bones high, the chin noticeably long, and the mouth of generous size. T
casual glance discovered more of benevolence than force, more of subtle
than of pugnacity. Nor, in that day of lace and frills, was there anythii
in his garb to proclaim him of the élite. His enemies then, and ev
since, have made too much of his loose carpet slippers and worn cloth
and the only thing they prove is that he may have had the Lincolni:
indifference to style. Long before he made his "pose" in the Presiden
house for the benefit of the groundlings, we find a critic who was to
numbered among his followers complaining because his clothes were t
small for his body. The truth, no doubt, is that he dressed conventiona}
because men must, and was careless of his attire.

Certain it is that when she first met him, Mrs. Bayard Smith, who h
been unduly impressed with the Federalist references to the "coarsenc
and vulgarity of his manners," was astonished at the contradiction of t
caricature by the man. "So meek and mild, yet dignified in his manne
while a voice so soft and low, with a countenance so benign and intelliger
she found him. In truth there was enough dignity in his manner to c
courage the stranger on a first approach, as Tom Moore found to his c
gust. Even Mrs. Smith thought his "dignified and reserved air" chill
first; and a French admirer who made a sentimental journey to Montice
thought him somewhat cold and reserved. "The cold first look he alw:
cast upon a stranger" appears too often in the observations of his cc
temporaries to have been imaginary.

As some have found fault with his dress, others have criticized a slover
way of sitting—"in a lounging manner, on one hip commonly, with c
of his shoulders elevated much above the other"; while another-
woman, too—was charmed at the "free and easy manner" in which
accepted a proffered chair. The natural deduction from the contradictic
is that he seated himself as comfortably as possible with little regard
the picture in the pose. There is a manifest absurdity in the idea t)
the man who moved familiarly in the most cultured circles of the m
polished capital in Europe could have been either impossible in dress
boorish in manner.

But there is one unpleasant criticism of his manner that cannot be
easily put aside—a shiftiness in his glance which bears out the charge
his enemies that he was lacking in frankness. The most democrs
member of the first Senate, meeting him for the first time, was e
appointed to find that "he had a rambling vacant look, and nothing
that firm collected deportment which I expected would dignify the prese

f a Secretary or Minister." Another found that "when speaking he did
ot look at his auditor, but cast his eyes toward the ceiling or anywhere
ut at the eye of his auditor." This weakness was possibly overemphasized,
ut he was notoriously shy.

Aside from this, there is abundant evidence that there was an in-
fable charm in his manner. One who objected to his "shifty glance"
as favorably impressed with "the simplicity and sobriety" of his de-
ortment, and found that while "he was quiet and unobtrusive . . . a
ranger would perceive that he was in the presence of one who was not a
mmon man." He was free of the affectations of pedantry, courteous and
ndly, modest and tolerant. Thus he appeared to excellent advantage in
nversation, and, with one exception, all who knew him and have left
eir impressions found him an entertaining and illuminating talker.
aclay, who was certainly not the most competent of judges, thought
s conversation "loose and rambling," and yet admitted that "he scattered
formation wherever he went, and some even brilliant sentiments sparkled
om him." It is probable that the gout-racked radical confused conversa-
on with set speeches, and quite as possible that on this particular oc-
sion, when Jefferson was meeting with a curious senatorial committee,
: was not inclined to tell all he knew.

Certainly the polished nobleman, familiar with the most intellectual
cles of Paris, who found his "conversation of the most agreeable kind,"
d that he possessed "a stock of information not inferior to that of any
her man," and "in Europe . . . would hold a distinguished rank among
en of letters," was quite as competent a judge as the Senator from the
lderness of Pennsylvania. Among men his manner of conversation was
lm and deliberate, without the Johnsonian *ex-cathedra* touch, and yet
"spoke like one who considered himself as entitled to deference."
nong friends, and particularly women, he appears to have been deferen-
l and captivating in his tactful kindness. Then when "with a manner
d voice almost femininely soft and gentle," he "entered into conversation
the commonplace topics of the day," at least one woman found that
ere was something in his manner, his countenance and voice that
once unlocked [her] heart."

Such was the Jefferson seen superficially by his contemporaries.

* * *

Such is the persistency of falsehood that Jefferson has come down to us
guely as an atheist and an enemy of the Christian religion. Since this
arge is to play a part in the political story we are about to tell, it calls
some attention. He was brought up in the Church of England, and
earliest recollection was of saying the Lord's Prayer when his dinner

was delayed. He planned at least one church and contributed to th
erection of others, gave freely to Bible Societies, and liberally to the suppo
of the clergy. He attended church with normal regularity, taking h
prayer book to the services and joining in the responses and prayers
the congregation. No human being ever heard him utter a word of pr
fanity. During the period of his social ostracism by the intolerant partisa
of Philadelphia, he passed many evenings with Dr. Rush in conversation o
religion. "I am a Christian," he once said, "in the only sense Jesus wishe
any one to be—sincerely attached to his doctrines in preference to a
others." On one occasion when a man of distinction expressed his di
belief in the truths of the Bible, he said, "Then, sir, you have studied
to little purpose." While the New England pulpits were ringing wit
denunciations of this "infidel," and old ladies, unable to detect the fal
witness of the partisan clergy, were solemnly hiding their Bibles to preve
their confiscation by the "atheist" in the President's house, he was spendir
his nights in the codification of the *Morals of Jesus,* and through th
remainder of his life he was to read from this every night before retirin
In his last days he spent much time reading the Greek dramatists and th
Bible, dwelling in conversation on the superiority of the moral system
Christ over all others. In his dying hour, after taking leave of his fami
he was heard to murmur, "Lord, now lettest Thy servant depart in peace."

The reason for the myth against him is not far to seek. Just as the land
aristocracy of Virginia pursued him with increasing venom because of h
land reforms, the clergy hated him for forcing the separation of Chur
and State. When he made the fight for this reform, it was a crime not
baptize a child into the Episcopal Church; a crime to bring a Quaker in
the colony; and, according to the law, a heretic could be burned. If t
latter law was not observed, that compelling all to pay tithes regardl
of their religious affiliations and opinions was rigidly enforced. This o
raged Jefferson's love of liberty. The Presbyterians, Baptists, and Meth
ists, who were making inroads on the membership of the Establish
Church, were prosecuted, and their ministers were declared disturbers
the peace and thrown into jail like common felons. Patrick Henry and h
followers fought Jefferson's plan for a disestablishment—but he won. T
"atheist" law, which was never forgiven by the ministers of Virginia a
Connecticut, was simple and brief:

No man shall be compelled to frequent or support any religious worship, pl
or ministry whatsoever, nor shall be enforced, restrained, molested or burde
in his mind or goods, nor shall otherwise suffer on account of his religi
opinions or belief; but all men shall be free to profess, and by argument to ma
tain, their opinions in matters of religion, and the same shall in no v
diminish, enlarge, or affect their civil capacities.

Here we have the secret of the animus of the clergy of the time—but 1ere were other reasons. In his *Notes on Virginia* he did not please the rthodox, and Dr. Mason, a fashionable political minister of New York City, exposed him in the pulpit, holding him up to scorn as a "profane hilosopher" and an "infidel." Discussing the theory that the marine 1ells found in the high mountains were proof of the universal deluge, fferson had rejected it. "Aha," cried Mason, "he derides the Mosaic count"; he "sneers at the Scriptures" and with "malignant sarcasm." Vhen Jefferson, referring to the tillers of the soil, wrote that they were the chosen people of God if ever He had a chosen people," and referred Christ as "good if ever a man was," the minister charged him with profane babbling."

His view of creation is set forth in a letter discussing a work by White-urst. He believed that a Supreme Being created the earth and its inhabit-1ts; that if He created both, He could have created both at once, or eated the earth and waited for ages for it to get form itself before He eated man; but he believed that it was created in a state of fluidity and ot in its present solid form. This was his infidelity. He probably did not elieve that Jonah was swallowed by the whale—and that was enough damn him. But if he was not a Christian, the pulpits are teeming with heists today.

* * *

This brings us to Jefferson the creator and leader of a party, and his ethods of management. Here he was without peer in the mastery of ,en. He intuitively knew men, and when bent upon it could easily bend em to his will. He was a psychologist and could easily probe the minds 1d hearts of those he met. In his understanding of mass psychology, he 1d no equal. When a measure was passed or a policy adopted in Phila-lphia, he knew the reactions in the woods of Georgia without waiting r letters and papers. This rare insight into the mass mind made him a illiantly successful propagandist. In every community he had his rrespondents with whom he communicated with reasonable regularity, 1ing more in this way to mould and direct the policies of his party than uld have been done in any other way. Seldom has there lived a more eless and voluminous letter-writer. With all the powerful elements rayed against him, he appreciated the importance of the press as did w others. "I desired you in my last to send me the newspapers, not-thstanding the expense," he wrote a friend from Paris. Believing that e people, in possession of the facts, would reach reasonable conclusions, considered newspapers a necessary engine of democracy. "If left to e," he once wrote, "to decide whether we should have a government without newspapers, or newspapers without a government, I should n« hesitate for a moment to prefer the latter." There is not a scintilla « evidence to confute his stout contention that he never wrote for th papers anonymously, but the evidence piles mountain-high to prove th. he constantly inspired the tone of the party press.

In his personal contacts he was captivating—a master of diplomacy ar tact, born of intuitive knowledge of men. Perhaps no better illustratic of his cleverness in analyzing men can be found than in his letter Madison on De Moustier, a newly appointed French Minister to th United States. "De M. is remarkably communicative. With adroitness h may be pumped of anything. His openness is from character, not affect tion. An intimacy with him may, on this account, be politically valuable

In his leadership we find more of leading than of driving. He had genius for gently and imperceptibly insinuating his own views into th minds of others and leaving them with the impression that they h: conceived the ideas and had convinced Jefferson. To Madison this was source of keen delight. Jefferson was the original "Easy Boss." His ta was proverbial. He never sought to overshadow or overawe. Inferior m« were not embarrassed or depressed in his presence. He was amazin? thoughtful and considerate. In a company he instinctively went to th assistance of the neglected. Thus at a dinner party, a guest, long abse from the country, and unknown to the diners, was left out of the conver: tion and ignored. In a momentary silence, Jefferson turned to him. "To yc Mr. C., we are indebted for this benefit—" he said, "no one deserv more the gratitude of his country." The other guests were all attentio "Yes, sir, the upland rice which you sent from Algiers, and which th far succeeds, will, when generally adopted by the planters, prove an i estimable blessing to our Southern States." After that the neglect« guest became the lion of the dinner. Thoughtfulness in small things this entered not a little into Jefferson's hold on his followers.

It was at the dinner table that he planned many of his battles. He d not care for the stormy and contentious atmosphere of a caucus. He w not an orator. In the Continental Congress he was disgusted by the "ra for debate." Later he was to find his lot in the Cabinet intolerable k cause he and Hamilton were constantly pitted against each other "li cocks in a pit." He was not afraid of a fight, but the futility of an£ controversy repelled him. It was this which made him a delightful dinr host—all controversial subjects that might offend were taboo. If his pc tion were warmly controverted, he changed the subject tactfully. It v never the opposition that interested him, but the reason for it; and wi rare subtlety he would seek to obliterate the prejudice, if it were prejudi or to remove the misunderstanding if it were ignorance of facts. Thus won many victories through a seeming retreat.

Unescapable quarrels and separations were minor tragedies to him. He
ng sought to get along with Hamilton. He advised his daughters to be
lerant of disagreeable people and acted on his own advice. Fiske has
plained him in a sentence: "He was in no wise lacking in moral cour-
e, but his sympathies were so broad and tender that he could not breathe
eely in an atmosphere of strife." Thus considerate of his foes, he never
irt the sensibilities of his friends through offensive methods. He liked
gather his lieutenants about him at the table and "talk it out"—each
an free to give his views. Here he ironed out differences, dominating by
e superiority of his intellect and fascinating personality while appearing
gularly free from domination.

In his power of self-control Jefferson had another advantage over his
iding political opponents. There was something uncanny in his capacity
simulate ignorance of the hate that often encompassed him. To the
ost virulent of his foes he was the pink of courtesy. He mastered others
mastering himself. And because he was master of himself, he had
other advantage—he kept his judgment clear as to the capacity and
aracter of his opponents. One may search in vain through the letters
Hamilton for expressions other than those of contemptuous belittle-
ent of his political foes. Jefferson never made that mistake. He conceded
imilton's ability and admired it. Visitors at Monticello, manifesting sur-
ise at finding busts by Ceracchi of Hamilton and Jefferson, facing each
her across the hall, elicited the smiling comment—"opposite in death
in life." There never would have been a bust of Jefferson at "The
ange." Through the long years of estrangement with Adams, Jefferson
pt the way clear for the restoration of their old relations. Writing Madi-
1 of Adams's faults, he emphasized his virtues and lovable qualities.
hen the bitter battles of their administrations were in the past and a
itual friend wrote that the old man in Quincy had said, "I always loved
fferson and always shall," he said, "That is enough for me," and set to
rk to revive the old friendship. Thus the time came when in reply to
fferson's congratulations on the election of John Quincy Adams in
24, Adams wrote: "I call him our John because when you were at
Cul de Sac in Paris, he appeared to me to be almost as much your boy
mine." This capacity for keeping his judgment clear of the benumbing
nes of prejudice concerning the qualities of his enemies was one of
strong points of his leadership.

This does not mean that in practical politics Jefferson was a "Miss
ncy" or a "Sister Sue." This first consummate practical politician of
Republic did not consider it practical to underestimate the foe, nor
dissipate his energy and cloud his judgment by mere prejudices and
es. He was not an idealist in his methods, and this has given his
mies a peg on which to hang the charge that he was dishonest. He was

an opportunist, to be sure; he never refused the half loaf he could ge
because of the whole loaf he could not have. He trimmed his sails at time
to save his credit—and this was wisdom. He compromised at the ca
of necessity. He was hard-headed and looked clear-eyed at the realities abou
him. He was cunning, for without cunning he could not have overcome
foe so powerfully entrenched. He was as elusive as a shadow, and this ha
been called cowardice—but it was difficult to trap him in consequence
His antipathy to the frontal attack has often been referred to with co
tempt, but, leading a large but unorganized army against one of tremei
dous power, he preferred the methods of Washington in the field—whic
was to avoid the frontal attack with his ragged Continentals against th
trained and disciplined army. Because of these conditions he was given t
mining. When apparently quiescent, he was probably sowing discor
among his foes—his part concealed. This was hateful to the Federalists-
just as the tactics of Frederick were hateful to the exasperated superi
forces against him.

Jefferson was the most resourceful politician of his time. For eve
problem he had a solution. He teemed with ideas. These were h
shock troops. If he seemed motionless, it was because by a nod or a loc
he had put his forces on the march. Like the wiser of the mode
bosses, he knew the virtues of silence. When in doubt, he said nothing-
to his foes. It was impossible to smoke him out when he preferred
stay in. In the midst of abuse he was serene. And he was a stickler f
party regularity. He appreciated the possibilities of organization and d
cipline. When money was needed for party purposes, his friends wou
receive a note: "I have put you down for so much." When the par
paper languished, he circulated subscription lists among his neighbo
and instructed his friends to imitate his example. He was never too b
for the small essential things, and he was a master of detail—very rare
true of men of large views. His energy was dynamic and he was tireless. I
never rested on his arms or went into winter quarters. His fight was en
less. The real secret of his triumph, however, is found in the reason giv
by one of his biographers: "He enjoyed a political vision penetrating deep
down into the inevitable movement of popular government, and farth
forward into the future of free institutions than was possessed by a
other man in public life in his day."

* * *

No American of his time had such versatility or such diversified interes
He was asked to frame the Declaration of Independence because of
reputation as a writer. Adams has told the story: "He brought with hin
reputation for literary science and a happy talent for composition. W

gs of his were handed about remarkable for their peculiar felicity of
pression." It was the *Summary View* which elicited the admiration of
Imund Burke. A more ambitious effort, his *Notes on Virginia*, were
itten during the fatal illness of his wife, and while he was confined to
e house two or three weeks by a riding accident. It was a valuable con-
bution to the natural, social, economic, and political history of the
ate, with a number of eloquent passages and fascinating pages.

He had an artistic temperament, loved music, and at the beginning of
career we find him busy planning his garden at Monticello, and
acticing three hours a day on his loved violin, under the instructions of
Italian musician. His hospitality to the Hessian prisoners is partly
plained by a mutual love of music. Returning from an absence to find
adwell, his early home, in ashes, he inquired anxiously about his books.
)h, my young master," exclaimed the distressed slave, "they were all
rnt, but we saved your fiddle."

Loving art in all its forms, he was fond of the company of artists. It
s he who arranged in Paris for Houdon to go to America to make the
tue of Washington. He entertained Trumbull in the French capital,
companying him to Versailles to see the king's art collection, and
ged him to remain in Paris and study. He was delighted with architec-
ral beauty and lingered about the masterpieces. From Nimes, he wrote
thusiastically to a woman friend: "Here I am, Madame, gazing whole
urs at the Maison Carrée, like a lover at his mistress. This is the second
ie that I have been in love since I left Paris. The first was with a
ana at the Château de Laye-Epinaye in Beaujolais, a delicious morsel of
ilpture, by M. A. Soldtz. This you will say was in rule, to fall in love
th a female beauty; but with a house. No, Madame, it is not without
precedent in my own history. While in Paris I was violently smitten
th the Hôtel de Salm." When the capitol at Richmond was in con-
nplation, he urged the construction of the most beautiful edifice possible
a model to be emulated in other buildings; drew some plans himself;
imined those of Hallet, was captivated with those of Thornton, and
ged their acceptance. "Simple, noble, beautiful," he wrote home.

And yet, so many-sided was this man that he was a utilitarian and
entist as well as artist. In Europe he was thought a philosopher, and
imboldt came to America to pass many hours under his roof. A perusal
his letters discloses the intensity and range of his interests. He was
tranced with clocks, and we find him writing David Rittenhouse remind-
; him of "a kind of promise of making me an accurate clock," and
er to Madison of a watch he had made for himself and inquiring if
friend wished one. He summoned a Swiss clock-maker to Monticello
10 died on the mountain and is buried in the enclosure with his patron.

311

He put the noted Buffon to rout in Paris on points of natural histc
Admiring the red men, he spent years collecting their vocabularies. Wh
in Paris he heard that an Arabic translation of Livy had been found
Sicily, and importuned the *chargé d'affaires* of Naples to make inquir.
and was much excited to hear that such a translation had been fou
"and will restore to us seventeen of the lost books." In the midst of
political diversions and social distractions of Paris he found time
write at length on the "latest discoveries in astrology." As early as
summer of 1785, when Pilatre de Rozière made his fatal attempt to cr
the English Channel in a balloon, we find him eagerly discussing the p
sibilities of his aeronautical science. A newly invented lamp pleased h
and he sent one to a friend from Paris. The use of steam in the operati
of grist mills interested him and he found time to witness the test. Ev
the absorbing drama of the French Revolution in its early stages
not lessen his interest in Paine's iron bridge, and he attended its
hibition, and finding the inventor hesitating between "the catenary a
portions of a circle," he sent to Italy for a scientific work by the Al
Mascheroni. Fascinated by inventions, he was, himself, the inventor o
plow.

* * *

Interested as he was in art and inventions, his heart was with
country life and the farmer's lot. He was never happier than when, in
early morning, mounted on one of his beloved horses, he rode over
broad acres at Monticello, observing with a perennial zest the budding
the trees in spring, the unfolding of the flowers, the ripening of the harve
Wherever he was, throughout his life, he longed for the house he
made on the hill, the broad fields, the family circle and the servitors a
slaves. There he was lord of the domain. If he employed Italian garden
they conformed to his ideas. If he had a supervisor, it was he himself w
determined what should be planted and where—where the orcha
should be, what trees should be set and their location; and even the vi
and shrubs, the nuts and seeds, the roots and bulbs claimed his perso
attention. Even his hogs were named, and when one was to be killed,
designated it by name. There, too, he lived in an atmosphere of affecti
There he had taken his bride, a woman of exquisite beauty, grace, a
loveliness; there his children had been born, and there, all too soon, th
mother died. He was passionately devoted to her and there was no success
To the daughters who were left he became both a father and a moth
resulting in an intimacy seldom found between father and daughters.
Paris he would not permit even his trusted servant to do their shoppi
reserving that duty for himself. Always patient, never harsh, and e
sympathetic, he was the ideal parent.

Though he did not remarry, he was fond of the society of women and
ey of his. The few letters to women that have been preserved are mas-
·pieces of their kind, sprightly, playful, sometimes beautiful. His rela-
·ns with the women of the Adams family are shown in a note to John
lams's married daughter, written from Paris: "Mr. Jefferson has the
nor to present his compliments to Mrs. Smith and to send her the two
ir of corsets she desired. He wishes they may be suitable, as Mrs. Smith
itted to send her measure. Times are altered since Mademoiselle de
mson had the honor of knowing her; should they be too small, however,
e will be so good as to lay them by for a while. There are ebbs as well
flows in this world. When the Mountain refused to go to Mahomet, he
·nt to the Mountain." In Paris he formed a few cherished friendships
th women, notably with Mrs. Cosway, Italian wife of an English
inter, a woman of charm, beauty, and intellect, with whom he cor-
·ponded. One of his letters, the dialogue between the Head and the
·art on her departure for England, is unique and sparkling. He ap-
·ciated the exquisite Mrs. Bingham whom he met in Paris, and his
·ding letters to her after her return to America must have pleased that
ificial lady immensely. He was a friend of the Comtesse De Tesse whose
·nd he admired, and of Madame De Corney whose beauty attracted
·n. "The Bois de Boulogne invited you earnestly to retire to its umbrage
·m the heats of the sad season," he wrote her gallantly. "I was through
·today as I am every day. Every tree charged me with this invitation."
Such was Thomas Jefferson who took upon himself the organization of
· forces of democracy, when its enemies were in the saddle, booted and
·rred, and with a well-disciplined and powerful army at their back. None
·t an extraordinary character could have dared hope for victory, and he
·s that, and more. Democrat and aristocrat, and sometimes autocrat;
·ilosopher and politician; sentimentalist and utilitarian; artist, naturalist,
·d scientist; thinker, dreamer, and doer; inventor and scholar; writer and
·tesman, he enthralled his followers and fascinated while infuriating his
·s.

Treason Most Foul

JAMES THOMAS FLEXNER

1780. On September 25, George Washington left the village of Fishkill at da
and rode to Benedict Arnold's headquarters, where he expected to breakf
with the commander of the important fortress of West Point. This account
Washington's discovery of Arnold's treason is taken from the second volu
of the author's not yet completed biography. Although many biographies
Washington exist, Mr. Flexner's is the first which combines scrupulous schol
ship with notable literary skill.

It was not a long ride from Fishkill to Benedict Arnold's headquarte
and Washington set out as soon as the autumnal skies began to lighte
However, there were several redoubts along the river which he felt
ought to visit. As he turned off the highroad down lanes rutted by t
wheels of cannon, his companions—Lafayette, Knox, and a flock of aides
became impatient. Eventually, Lafayette (so it is reported) remind
Washington that Mrs. Arnold was waiting breakfast for them.

The commander replied genially, "Ah, I know you young men are
in love with Mrs. Arnold. . . . You may go and take your breakfast w
her, and tell her not to wait for me." Lafayette and most of the pa

cided to stay with His Excellency, but two aides, Major Samuel Shaw
d Major James McHenry, rode ahead with the message.

Inspection takes time and the morning was far advanced before Wash-
gton finally glimpsed through the trees the roof of Arnold's headquarters.
n the east bank of the Hudson, Robinson's House (as the building was
own) was across the river from West Point and two miles below it.
orrect eighteenth-century gentlemen considered that the location—"sur-
unded on two sides by hideous mountains and dreary forests, [and] not
house in view but one within a mile"—could only appeal to "a taste for
mantic singularity and novelty." But Washington looked forward to a
rm welcome: the firm handshake of his fellow veteran Benedict Arnold,
nning smiles warming the features of sweet, blonde, girlish Peggy.

He spurred his horse slightly and came around the edge of a barn to a
wn overlooking the river that was about a quarter of a mile off to the
ht. The rambling, capacious two-story mansion house, with its three
fferent roof lines that reflected successive enlargements, was now at
s left. Since he had sent four light horsemen to alert the Arnolds of
s immediate arrival, he expected that the opening door would reveal that
endly couple in greeting poses. He saw instead a foppish young man
nding alone, bowing a meticulously powdered head while embarrass-
ent marked his features. Washington probably recognized Arnold's aide,
vid Salisbury Franks. In voluble sentences punctuated with nervous
ggles, Franks stated that Mrs. Arnold had not yet arisen and that the
neral had gone by water for West Point. The general had told Franks
at he was on his way to prepare a suitable welcome for His Excellency.
ad His Excellency breakfasted? When Washington said he had not,
anks bustled off to get food on the table.

This reception was disappointing. However, Washington knew that it
s natural for belles to sleep late, and he could not have been displeased
at Arnold was preparing a reception for him, since he believed that cere-
onies of respect to high officers improved both the appearance and the
scipline of the army. He ate a leisurely breakfast. Then, leaving Hamil-
n behind to receive any dispatches, he rode to the river and walked with
small group down the steep bank to the landing where a barge and its
w of oarsmen were waiting to transport him to West Point.

The oarsmen created ripples and the fortress came ever more clearly
o view. It seemed to slant backward as it mounted the precipitous west
ore of the river. Not very far above the water, the main redoubt clung
a sheer crag like a monstrous crab. As the surrounding hills billowed
her, they revealed ramparts pierced for cannon, while near the sky three
aks were topped with independent forts. The mazelike interweaving
lls were sometimes built of wood, sometimes of turf, and sometimes of

stone. Scars on the hillsides spoke of quarrying too recent to be green
over, while piles of rocks and logs indicated construction still only planne
Washington knew that downstream, where the river seemed almost
disappear into the hills, the flow swung into a turn that would slow a
sailing vessels which tried to brazen their way by. On this spot the ma
cannon were trained, and there the river washed, from bank to bank, o
the links of a tremendous iron chain.

Washington could not help being moved as the fortress came clos
This was the great engineering feat of his command, the only true stro
point created by the Continental Army. Volunteer engineers from abroad
Kościuszko, Duportail—had designed it. During more than three years
hard labor, the soldiers had shaped the towering ramparts. Inflated dolla
anguishedly raised, had been spent by the millions. And there the fortr
stood, serene in the pellucid autumn air, while Benedict Arnold—
Washington believed—was preparing the garrison for a military greet
to their Commander in Chief.

When the advance of Washington's barge brought the beach a
landing wharf into clear view, these were surprisingly empty. No bustle
officers lining up men: only the usual sentries somnolently pacing. As t
intervening strip of water narrowed, Washington saw Colonel John Lam
the resident commander of the fortress, coming running down the st
way from the main redoubt. Still out of breath when Washington stepp
ashore, Lamb puffed out apologies for having prepared no suitable rec
tion. If only he had been notified!

To Washington's startled query, Lamb replied that he had not se
Arnold that day. This seemed strange—but there were various landi
places under the various redoubts. Perhaps Arnold had come anot
way.

The inspection began. As Washington climbed over the hillsides, duck
through blockhouse doors, visited gun emplacements, he asked everywh
for Arnold. "No one could give me any information where he was. T
impropriety of his conduct, when he knew I was to be there, struck
very forcibly." Washington became increasingly anxious. "My min
as he put it, "misgave me," but he felt only a vague fear. "I had not
least idea of the real cause."

Washington was later to insist that he had found the post in "
most critical condition." However, he probably was not particularly up
until after he had learned what he was about to discover. If some of
redoubts were weak, broken, or unfinished, if work seemed to be progress
slowly, he could hardly have been surprised. Perfection rarely hovered o
the Continental Army.

Dinner at the Arnolds' had been set at four. Washington completed
inspection in time to permit his rowers to get him back to Robinso

ouse by three-thirty. He strode anxiously up the steep bluff from the
erbank, but again the opening door revealed neither Arnold nor Peggy.
was Hamilton who greeted him. No, Hamilton had heard nothing of
nold. No, Peggy had not emerged from her bedroom; she had sent
rd that she was indisposed.

Washington walked along a hallway to the chamber that had been
igned to him, and began to freshen up for the meal. A knock on the door.
milton came in carrying a bundle of papers. Washington reached out
the packet, separated the papers, and began to read.

As Lafayette primped in another room, Hamilton burst open the door.
begged the Marquis to attend instantly on His Excellency. Lafayette
inted down the hall to find Washington trembling with extreme emo-
n. "Arnold," Washington cried out, "has betrayed us!" And then he
ed, "Whom can we trust now?"

The first task, as soon as the men had regained enough control to do
thing rational, was to determine by a careful examination of the many
ders exactly what the situation was. There must have been (although
s now lost) a covering letter from the outpost commander, Lieutenant
n Jameson, stating that three irregulars had been prowling in the British
minated territory beyond the Croton River when they stopped a lone
er in civilian clothes. The rider, who stated that his name was John
derson, had behaved so strangely that they had stripped him, finding
uments in his shoes. Jameson was holding the man and was herewith
varding the documents.

here was an official pass allowing "John Anderson" to move between
lines and made out by Benedict Arnold. Also in Arnold's handwriting
e a transcript of secret information Washington had given a Council
War, pages of material about West Point that would be useful to a
eger, and a rough accounting of the 3,086 patriots Arnold had slated
death or capture.

eemingly a later addition to the packet was a letter, meticulously
cuted in an elegant script. It proved to be from the prisoner: "What
ave as yet said concerning myself," Washington read, "was in the
ifiable attempt to be extricated; I am too little accustomed to duplicity
ave succeeded." He wished now "to rescue myself from an imputation
having assumed a mean character for treacherous purposes or self-
rest, a conduct incompatible with the principles that actuate me, as
l as with my condition in life. . . . The person in your possession is
or John André, adjutant general to the British army." The rest of the
tle was given over to an argument in which André attempts, as Wash-
on later put it, "to show that he did not come under the description
a spy."

he documents understood, the next question was what to do. A glance out the window would have shown that the wind, blowing uprive was ideal for carrying British ships from their anchorage in New Yo Harbor to West Point. Washington could not know to what extent oth officers were in Arnold's plot; he could not be sure that, even thoug André had been intercepted alternate advices had not got through to t British. However, overriding emotions kept Washington from decidin that his first duty was to take every possible step to protect the endanger fortress.

The most important consideration, so it seemed to Washington, w to capture and hang the traitor. Although McHenry, who had breakfast with Arnold, reported that the villain had disappeared immediately aft receiving a letter which had thrown him "into some degree of agitatior Washington refused to accept the conclusion that Arnold had been notifi of André's capture and had, in the intervening five hours, surely made escape. Perhaps he was lurking somewhere within the lines, still ignora of his danger. Under these circumstances, Washington concluded move should be made that would indicate to anyone—you could not t who would alert Arnold—that the treason had been discovered. Wh all else went on as usual, Hamilton and McHenry should gallop, fast as the swiftest horses could carry them, to King's Ferry, eight mi downriver, where there were forts and forces that could stop Arnol barge "if she had not passed."

No sooner had Hamilton and McHenry pounded off than Arnold's sen aide, Lieutenant Colonel Richard Varick, who had been in bed with fever, came into Washington's room, flushed, a little unsteady, a clearly in the grip of strong emotion. He said that Mrs. Arnold seemed have gone mad. She had run through the halls almost naked and, af he got her back in bed, she had exclaimed "there was a hot iron on head, and no one but General Washington could take it off." Wo His Excellency please go to the anguished lady?

Washington mounted the stairs to Peggy's room. In her disarrang bed, with her hair flying around her touching face and her nightcloth pulled awry, she exhibited (so Hamilton was told) "all the sweetness beauty, all the loveliness of innocence, all the tenderness of a wife, a all the fondness of a mother . . . One moment she raved, another melted into tears. Sometimes she pressed her infant to her bosom." S dandled her babe wide-eyed and seemed oblivious of her visitors. Fina Varick said, "There is General Washington."

As Washington leaned over her, his features working with pity, she sta him hard in the face. "No!" she cried, and denied that he was Washingt

He gently assured her that he was.

"No!" she cried again, gesturing with her bare, shapely arms to shi her infant. "No, that is not General Washington! That is the man was agoing to assist Colonel Varick in killing my child."

Washington labored to disabuse her, but when she finally admitted that he was who he pretended to be, it was only to upbraid him for "being in a plot to murder her child." Her husband, she cried out, could not protect her: "General Arnold will never return. He is gone. He is gone forever, *there, there, there*: the spirits have carried him up there." She pointed at the ceiling. "They have put hot irons in his head."

As the lovely lady raved and gestured, her clothes parted to reveal charms that should have been hidden. Then she would push her baby aside and turn downward on the bed to cling to the mattress in a transport of tears. At last, finding that he could not make her respond to his reassurances, Washington went sadly away, hating Arnold all the more for having caused such anguish to a beauty he never doubted was innocent.

Peggy had been warned by Arnold before he fled that the treason had been discovered. Her performance was majestic, but she had not needed to use such heavy artillery to convince the courtly commander that she was a greatly wronged angel. Washington always shied away from connecting the tender sex with the dark emotions of war. He left Peggy's bedroom determined to protect her from every implication raised by her husband's guilt.*

Washington joined an uneasy group of officers in the living room. "Mrs. Arnold is sick," he said, "and General Arnold is away. We must therefore take our dinner without them."

"I had a high fever," Varick wrote, "but officiated at the head of the table." Both he and Franks, who had taken no part in the plot, had by now inferred that Arnold had gone to the enemy. Unwilling to accuse their superior without real evidence and realizing that if treason had taken place they would be under suspicion, they covertly watched Washington for indications of what he knew and how he felt toward them. "Never," Lafayette is quoted as reminiscing, "was there a more melancholy dinner. The General was silent and reserved, and none of us spoke of what we were thinking about. . . . Gloom and distress seemed to pervade every mind, and I have never seen General Washington so affected by any circumstance." However, Washington's courtesy did not desert him. Varick noted that "His Excellency behaved with his usual affability and politeness to me."

The food, "plentiful" but hardly touched, was finally all served and

---

* Peggy's active complicity in the plot remained hidden until long after her lifetime. It was not established until Clinton's papers were acquired by the Clements Library in the 1930's.

cleared away. The party separated. After a while, Washington asked Varick to put on his hat. As they walked outside, Washington told him of Arnold's perfidy. Then (so Varick wrote), "with delicacy, tenderness, and civility," Washington stated that, although "he had not the least cause of suspicion of Major Franks or myself," the two aides must consider themselves under arrest. "I then told him the little all I knew."

The inhabitants of Robinson's House were now alerted. It would have been a poor spy network indeed that was not now pulsing out warnings. Any great hope of gain to be achieved through secrecy would seem to be over. The wind was still blowing upriver. If Arnold had placed at key positions officers who were his partners in the plot, they still held their commands. West Point had not been alerted. Yet Washington still took no active steps. The man who had admired and trusted Arnold and within whose own character treason was inconceivable was circling in the mazes of what Varick called "the most affecting and pungent anxiety and distress."

Between six and seven in the evening, Washington received a letter from Hamilton at King's Ferry stating that Arnold had escaped to a British warship anchored in the river. "Though I do not believe the project will go on," Hamilton continued, "it is possible Arnold has made such dispositions with the garrison as may tempt the enemy, in its present weakness, to make the stroke this night. . . . Without making a bustle," Hamilton was notifying the commander of the main army in New Jersey (Greene) "to be in readiness to march and even to detach a brigade this way." He hoped Washington would approve, "as there may be no time to be lost."

Hamilton enclosed two letters which had been sent from the British warship to King's Ferry. Both were in Arnold's familiar handwriting. The one addressed to Washington contended defiantly that, whatever the misguided might think, it was true patriotism which had carried Arnold to the British. The second letter was addressed to Peggy. Washington sent it upstairs unopened, accompanied by a message that, although it had been his duty to try to capture Arnold, he was happy to relieve her anxiety by telling her that her husband was safe.

Washington could hardly have helped recognizing that he had been derelict in not ordering Hamilton to do what the aide had done on his own: warning the command of the main army to be prepared. This realization, plus the news that Arnold had actually escaped, seem to have shaken him out of his lethargy. In dispatches, sometimes headed "seven o'clock," sometimes "seven and a half o'clock," and sometimes just "o'clock" he changed the commands at key posts where Arnold might have placed collaborators; he alerted West Point, ordering that it be reinforced and put in readiness for an attack. (It was not actually in readiness until 2 A.M.)

When, during the night, the wind changed, blowing strongly down-river, the possibility was erased that the British could gain direct military advantage from Arnold's treason. The moment-to-moment tension dropped, but Washington still had to handle his own emotions; and the human flotsam that the wreck had left afloat; and the question whether there were more traitors to be discovered; and the frightening problem of how the treason of so conspicuous an officer could be prevented from psychologically damaging the already dipping cause.

The human flotsam closest to Washington's emotions was twenty-year-old Peggy, "whose face and whose youthfulness [as Lafayette wrote] make her so interesting." In the morning, she admitted to no memory of her hysteria of the day before, and now spoke frankly, if tearfully, of her apprehension that "the resentment of her country will fall upon her who is only unfortunate." Washington was all sympathy and grave reassurance; he offered to send her either to her husband in New York or her father in Philadelphia. She chose to turn her back on the plot that had failed; Franks accompanied her to Philadelphia. "It would be exceedingly painful to General Washington," Lafayette wrote Luzerne, "if she were not treated with the greatest kindness."

On Robinson's House now converged by Washington's order the various individuals known to have been concerned in André's foray behind the American lines. Interviewing them himself, Washington decided that only Joshua Hett Smith was adequately implicated to be tried.* Smith was demonstrated to have been Arnold's dupe, a fool rather than a villain. The conclusion was reached that Arnold had operated altogether as a lone wolf. (This was, except for his wife, mean go-betweens, and spies independently in the British pay, entirely correct.)

After André had been brought to headquarters, Washington found him "a man of the first abilities," and treated him, so the Briton wrote Clinton, "with the greatest attention." André was, indeed, a prisoner to wring Washington's heart. Of French background, although born in London, he had marked temperamental resemblances to Washington's beloved Lafayette. He was also young enough to be Washington's son, quick, mercurial, brilliant, chivalrous, and much concerned with personal honor. In a situation of mortal danger, he was displaying—could Lafayette have done it as well?—almost superhuman control. He behaved in the presence of his captors with charm, grace, almost relaxation.

To Washington, as to all the other officers concerned, André's plight was given particular poignancy because his romantic impetuosity had placed the important officer in a predicament which the eighteenth century considered far below his station. Gentlemen could be spymasters, but they

---

* Varick and Franks requested a military inquiry to clear their names, which it amply did.

did not themselves wear disguises and rummage behind the enemy lines. André claimed that he had come ashore in his uniform in his high official capacity, meeting Arnold on what was neutral ground, but he had been tricked by Arnold into entering an American post: then he had no choice but to try to achieve an escape in those civilian clothes that made him falsely resemble a spy. Hatred for Arnold made this believable, yet the fact remained that he had been caught bearing incriminating papers, functioning as a spy. The established punishment for that was not a gentleman's death—being shot—but the death of a varlet—being dangled from a gallows.

The meanness of his situation spurred André into a high line of "candor." To the Board of General Officers who conducted his trial, he confessed so much that the verdict was inevitable. The board ruled that he "ought to be considered a spy from the enemy, and that, agreeable to the law and usage of nations, it is their opinion that he ought to suffer death."

From André, Washington received a letter which the condemned man signed with his proud title, Adjutant General of the British Army: "Buoyed above the terror of death by the consciousness of a life devoted to honorable pursuits and stained with no action that can give me remorse, I trust that the request I make to your Excellency at this serious period, which is to soften my last moments, will not be rejected.

"Sympathy toward a soldier will surely induce your Excellency and a military tribunal to adapt the mode of my death to the feelings of a man of honor.

"Let me hope, sir, that if aught in my character impresses you with esteem toward me, if aught in my misfortunes marks me as the victim of policy and not of resentment, I shall experience the operation of these feelings in your breast by being informed that I am not to die on the gibbet."

The consideration was one that Washington, as a gentleman, could not help finding affecting—and he was always unhappy about executions. To make matters worse, his brilliant young officers were almost aswoon with admiration and pity for André. Hamilton, to whom the prisoner had made a personal appeal, was particularly insistent, even rude, and went off in a rage when Washington would not agree that André be shot. "Some people," Hamilton growled, "are only sensible to motives of policy!" Yet Washington felt he had no choice. The British propaganda machine was already in high scream, and, if André were not executed in the manner of a spy, that would be pointed to as proof that he had not really been a spy but had been wantonly murdered.

André occupied the same position in Clinton's heart that Lafayette did in Washington's. Across the lines came letters in which Clinton insisted that his friend had gone on an official mission to Arnold, and had subsequently merely obeyed orders which Arnold, as commander in the area, had a right to give. This argument was both specious (a spy is not blameless because he obeys the orders of the traitor he is suborning) and also contradicted André's own contention that Arnold had carried him behind the American lines without his knowledge and against his will. However, Washington saw in Clinton's concern a chance of saving the young man whom he considered "more unfortunate than criminal" and who had "much in his character to interest."

Washington might "lament," but he recognized a "necessity of rigor": the army was in effect under trial in the eyes of the American people. To spare the British agent out of hand would be interpreted as softness about treason. But supposing Washington could substitute on the gallows for the unfortunate go-between the real, the heinous criminal?

Captain Aaron Ogden of the light infantry was ordered to appear at headquarters at the dot of eight o'clock on the morning after André had been sentenced. To his surprise, he found His Excellency waiting for him outside the tent. Washington handed him some letters to take under a flag of truce to the British lines, and then told him to go to Lafayette's tent for further instructions. Lafayette was also eagerly awaiting him. Suggesting what Washington could not because of his high rank suggest, Lafayette urged Ogden to whisper to the commander of the British post "that if Sir Henry Clinton would in any way whatever suffer General Washington to get within his power General Arnold, then Major André should be immediately released."

When Ogden did as he had been told, the British officer who had met his flag leapt on a horse and galloped away. In two hours he was back with a glum face and the verbal answer: "A deserter was never given up." He also brought written information that a high-level British delegation would came to the American lines to intercede for André.

At the resulting meeting, Greene and Hamilton represented the American cause. Hints flew that André would be exchanged for Arnold. The hints were not responded to. The British representatives had nothing more to offer than the specious arguments which had already been submitted to Washington in writing. Grieved and deeply disappointed, Washington set the execution for noon the next day, October 2.

The macabre procession from André's place of confinement to the gallows would pass close to the headquarters Washington now occupied at Tappan, New York: the death march would pound in, even through closed windows. To allow the sufferer hope, Washington had not notified him how he was to be executed: there would be the dreadful moment when the accomplished young British gentleman saw the gallows. It was not an agreeable moment to contemplate.

If Washington was able to persuade himself that it would not be commented on, he surely rode out from his headquarters. Otherwise, he certainly sat in gloom. And, wherever he was during the actual tragedy, after it was over, he was surrounded by men in tears. Never had witnesses to an execution been more moved by the noble bearing of the victim.

In Washington's headquarters, eyes still wept when a belated dispatch appeared from the British lines. It was a letter from Benedict Arnold threatening that if André were executed, he personally would "think myself bound by every tie of duty and honor to retaliate on such unhappy persons of your army as may fall within my power. . . . I call Heaven and earth to witness that your Excellency will be justly answerable for the torrent of blood that may be spilt in consequence!"

"There are no terms," Washington wrote of Arnold, "that can describe the baseness of his heart." He instigated an elaborate plot (which misfired) to kidnap the traitor from his lodgings in New York City, and bring him out alive for hanging to patriot cheers.

As the British propaganda machine ground out statements attributed to Arnold in which he described his treason as true patriotism and urged his former associates to imitate him, hatred for the traitor swept the nation. Washington, who was not without his enemies, had supported Arnold to the civilian authorities; he had personally put the traitor in command at West Point. And the whole conservative wing of the revolutionary leadership was liable to the charge of guilt by association, since they had backed Arnold against the Pennsylvania radicals. As the leader of those radicals, Reed did make gestures at demonstrating that Washington and the aristocratic Schuyler had shown gross favoritism to the traitor, but even Reed was halfhearted, glad, it seems, quickly to abandon his efforts. In the end, the Pennsylvania radicals contented themselves with banishing Peggy from her father's house in Philadelphia. She was forced against her will to join her partner in treason behind the British lines.

One trembles to think what a modern "super-patriot" rabble-rouser might have done with the issue. However, our forefathers resisted all temptation to shatter, by venting spite or prejudice, the precarious national unity.

Washington's own attitude was expressed in dismissing a rumor that the American general Robert Howe was in the pay of the British. He wrote the Board of War that they ought not "to neglect any clues that may lead to discoveries, but, on the other hand, we ought to be equally circumspect in admitting suspicions or proceeding upon them without sufficient evidence. It will be the policy of the enemy to distract us as much as possible by sowing jealousies, and, if we swallow the bait, no character will be safe. There will be nothing but mutual distrust."

Washington labored to turn the popular emotion to gratitude that the plot had been foiled. "In no instance since the commencement of the war," he stated, "has the interposition of Providence appeared more conspicuous than in the rescue of West Point from Arnold's villainous perfidy."

Maillard, the Consumptive

————··◦≪≫◦··————

ANDRÉ CASTELOT

1789. The march of the women of Paris to Versailles and their triumphant return with King Louis XVI, Queen Marie Antoinette, and the royal children is one of the most famous episodes of the French Revolution. Less well-known is the part played in it by a consumptive Parisian bookkeeper recounted here by a distinguished contemporary French historian, an authority on the revolutionary and Napoleonic periods.

————··◦≪≫◦··————

On that July 14 a man named Stanislas-Marie Maillard was seen brandishing a flag and being the first to enter the Bastille. He was seen again on June 20, and August 10, 1792, when he was to play his part in the attack on the Tuileries. On September 2, 1792, the day of the massacres, he was to preside over the improvised tribunal in the Abbaye prison.

When the affair was over he went back home, asking nothing more than to be able to take care of his lungs, for the fierce Maillard, the man whom some historians have depicted with a knife between his teeth, yelling, shouting, leading *sans-culottes* and *tricoteuses* in the assault, was actually a quiet, pale young bookkeeper to a bailiff, a young man who

326

spat blood and, undermined by consumption, was to die before the end of the Revolution.

Moreover, Maillard seems to have taken a hand in revolutionary events only in order to avoid the worst. He was to prove this on September 2 when by himself he saved two or three hundred royalists. It was perhaps owing to him that the imprisoned royalty had to leave Versailles on October 5, 1789, but it was certainly thanks to his initiative and coolness that the archives of the Hôtel de Ville were saved and the storm diverted from Paris.

On Sunday, October 4, 1789, the eve of the drama, he had shuddered with all Paris as he read in the *Courrier de Versailles* the distorted account of the previous Thursday's "orgy." In the presence of the King and Queen —that "jade," the Parisians called her—a banquet had been given by the garrison. The tricolor cockade, so the *Courrier* affirmed, had been trampled underfoot. The guests had refused to drink the health of the nation. A banquet! When Paris lacked bread! "Senseless people," wrote the pamphleteer, "open your eyes at last, rouse yourself from your lethargy!"

On this bright autumn Sunday the Parisians walked to the Palais Royal or on the boulevards, talking of nothing but "the insult to the nation."

The night of October 4-5 fell on Paris. Here and there the tocsin was rung, as though to prevent the town from sleeping. At six o'clock in the morning, in the Saint-Eustache district, a little girl was seen to snatch up a drum and begin to beat it, shouting the while. Gradually women collected, and the procession that formed set off for the Hôtel de Ville.

This was "the first squad," as an eyewitness tells us. They were "young, robed in white, hair dressed and powdered, with an engaging air that presaged no evil intent." As they marched gaily along they forced the women they met to follow them.

"Come along! We are going to Versailles!"

At the Port Saint-Antoine they carried off with them a young girl of seventeen, Louise Chabry, called Louison, a sculptor's apprentice, who with her parents was watching the ever-increasing groups pass by. And a little flower girl of twenty, Françoise Rolin, living in the Rue de la Poterie near the Halles, was seized as she left home "to go to market."

During the first part of the morning groups from all parts of the town were going in the direction of the Place de Grève. To the young girls with "hair dressed and powdered" were now joined an increasing number of unbrushed and disheveled viragoes and also men, mainly from the Saint-Antoine and Saint-Marceau faubourgs. Together with the most excited of the women the men rushed at one of the doors of the Hôtel de Ville, freed the prisoners and gave them money to buy clothes. Then the women broke open the armory, seized eight hundred rifles and the municipal cash box—one may fight for liberty and yet not despise a little profit. Real harpies, carrying torches, wanted to burn the town archives.

It was at this point that Maillard appeared.

"I rushed toward them," he said later, giving his evidence to the commission of inquiry. "I took away their torches, which incidentally nearly cost me my life."

The women had only one cry: "To Versailles! To Versailles!" "In order to forestall the evil these women might commit"—these are his own words—Maillard decided to put himself at their head.

"Detachments left for the different districts to recruit other women, who were told to meet them in the Place Louis XV."

Maillard remained with the chief body of the troop, which, preceded by a drummer, marched toward the Place Louis XV (now the Place de la Concorde). Again, as they went, the fishwives forced the women they met to march with them. Among these were two shop girls from the Rue Saint-Honoré, a second-hand clothes dealer from the Rue Saint-André-des-Arcs, a lace worker from the Rue Meslée, a charwoman from the Rue Froidmanteau, a nurse from the Bailleul, a dyer from the Rue de la Calande, who was harnessed to one of the four cannons taken from the Hôtel de Ville. They even carried off a marquise, whom the women forced out of her carriage by the Louvre gate. (Maillard intervened and managed to get *her* let off.)

A horse guard rode by the column.

"Are you going to Versailles?" cried one of the fishwives. "Tell the Queen we shall soon be there to cut her throat."

In the Place Louis XV and the Champs-Elysées six to seven thousand women were gathered. Some were armed with broomsticks, according to Maillard's account, other with pitchforks, swords, skewers and old pistols. Here and there a few muskets were to be seen, but they were carried by men disguised as women. Beards spread over lawn shawls, and boots emerged from striped skirts. This is not a royalist legend: there exist 392 depositions for these October days that are very precise on the point. The reason for the masquerade is given by a contemporary: "They were less likely to decide to repel women by armed force."

Not without difficulty Maillard succeeded in giving his "army" some appearance of order. By now six or seven drummers and two cannons headed the procession.

As the marchers entered Chaillot, along the river, shutters were heard closing. The inhabitants were barricading themselves at the approach of the mob. The women, who were hungry and thirsty, knocked at the doors and even wanted to break them down. Not succeeding, they avenged themselves by tearing down signboards. Maillard grew angry.

"I told them they would do themselves no credit by acting like this and that I would retire from their leadership if they behaved so, and that their actions might be looked on with disapproval, whereas, if they went on peacefully and honestly, all the citizens of the capital would be grateful to them. They finally yielded to my reproaches and advice."

Everything continued in a more or less orderly fashion until Sèvres, when the vanguard dispatched by Maillard into the town found no "refreshment for the ladies" except eight four-pound loaves, which were cut up "in little portions." The "ladies" thereupon scattered into the town, "took benches and other pieces of wood," as Maillard related, "and set about breaking down the doors and destroying the signs of all the shop-keepers."

But thanks to a few jugs of wine somehow procured the "army" continued on the march. Rain had begun to fall. Soon, muddy and soaked, the women shouted to passers-by: "See what a state we are in, but the jade will pay us dearly!"

Some of them sharpened enormous kitchen knives on the milestones.

"How glad I should be if I could open her belly with this knife and tear out her heart by thrusting my arm in up to the elbow!"

Maillard was appalled at having to make his entry into Versailles with such a crew. He was also disturbed by the presence of the cannons at the head of the procession.

"I made them form a circle and told them that the two cannons they had should not be dragged at the head. Although they had no ammunition, they might be suspected of evil intentions and they ought rather to display gaiety than cause a riot in Versailles. . . . They consented to do as I wished. As a result the cannons were placed in the rear and I proposed that they should sing 'Long Live Henri IV!' as they entered Versailles and shout, 'Long live the King!' They did not cease repeating this among the people of the town, who were waiting for them and cried, 'Long live our women of Paris!' "

On arriving in front of the Hôtel des Menus-Plaisirs, where the Assembly was in session, the army halted, and Maillard and a delegation of women received permission to enter the session chamber.

"The people lack bread," declared the women's leader to the Assembly. "They are in despair, their arms are raised and they will certainly be led into some excesses. We ask permission to search the houses suspected of hoarding flour. It is for the Assembly to avert the shedding of blood, but the Assembly contains enemies of the people, who are the cause of the famine. Wicked men are giving money and bonds to the millers to make sure that they do not grind."

From every corner of the hall cries broke out: "The names, the names! Name them, name them!"

After a few seconds' hesitation Maillard said absurdly: "The Archbishop of Paris has given two hundred livres to a miller to stop grinding."

While the deputies raised a shout of indignation a few "advanced" representatives approved, and yelled: "It is the Archbishop of Paris!"

The disorder grew, as gradually the women, who had managed to slip into the hall through a side door, began calling to the representatives, straddling the benches, taking off their stockings, and even their skirts to dry them, and crying out in cadence: "Bread! Bread! Bread!"

Some of them kissed the deputies, even the Bishop of Langres, while the Vicomte de Mirabeau "caressed the prettiest bosoms." It was finally decided, in the midst of indescribable disorder, to send the President of the Assembly, Monnier, to the castle to explain to the King the sad state of the capital, where one was obliged to queue for a whole day to buy a piece of terribly costly bread. A delegation composed of a few deputies and about ten women set off with the President. "We were on foot, in the mud, under a heavy rain," he later related. "A considerable crowd of Versailles inhabitants lined the avenue leading to the château. The women of Paris formed various groups, mixed with a certain number of men, mostly dressed in rags, their eyes wild, their gestures menacing, and uttering horrible yells. They were armed with a few muskets, old pikes, axes, iron-tipped sticks or long poles with sword or knife blades on the end." (These were the rearguard of Maillard's army.) "Small detachments of the bodyguards were on patrol and galloped by quickly, in the midst of cries and boos." Not far from the gate, in front of the rows of troops defending the approaches to the royal courtyard, two young women threw themselves at Monnier's feet. They were the sculptor's apprentice and the flower girl, Louison Chabry and Françoise Rolin. They wanted to "go to the King."

"You have only to follow me," Monnier replied.

Not without difficulty the little band passed the horsemen, entered the gates and were shown into the royal antechamber. The president, Louison and four other women were shown into the presence of the King, who was in the Council Room. The little sculptor's apprentice was appointed spokeswoman for her companions. She advanced toward Louis XVI, who was waiting for her surrounded by a few of his gentlemen, and fell fainting with emotion, having only the strength to murmur: "Bread! Bread!"

When she came to she saw the King bending over her and helping her to drink a little wine in a large gold goblet. Then he made her smell spirits.

"My poor woman," sighed the King. "I have no bread in my pocket, but you can go to the pantries, where you will find provisions, not as much as there used to be, but in any case you will take what is there."

From the courtyard could be heard insults to the Queen.

"We want her head to take to Paris on the end of a pike!"

The King turned to Louison and asked sadly: "Have you come to harm the Queen?"

The poor child denied it in a trembling voice.

"The Queen agrees to come to Paris with me," went on the King.

Louison fell on her knees, asking to kiss the royal hand.

"You deserve better than that," Louis declared, raising the girl and kissing her.

The delegation withdrew enchanted and appeared in the courtyard crying: "Long live the King! Tomorrow we shall have bread!"

Louison and Françoise—who had been received only by the minister Saint-Priest—were booed. It was felt without doubt that they had been bought. They had received money. They had brought no written promise. No paper from the King. The two girls were punched and kicked. Two women put garters round their necks and dragged them to a lantern. Luckily, other women and two guards intervened. The two unfortunate women were sent back to the château. Louis XVI agreed to show himself on the balcony with Louison and declare to the crowd that the little working girl had not received a single copper. The King then wrote in his own hand the order to send corn from Senlis and Lagny to Paris, and he handed a deputy a letter for the town of Paris. When Louison and Françoise reappeared in the courtyard they were acclaimed. People danced around them, crying, "Long live the King!" and it was a happy procession that returned to the Assembly, where the royal note was read. "I am deeply touched by the insufficiency of supplies for Paris. I shall continue to second the zeal and efforts of the municipality by all the means and all the resources in my power, and I have given the most positive orders for the free circulation of corn on all the roads and for the transport of that intended for my good city of Paris."

A copy of the letter was handed to Maillard, who immediately left for Paris in company with Louison, Françoise and two hundred women. With the King's permission the whole delegation was piled into court carriages provided by the Messageries du Roi.

Toward midnight, at the end of the Avenue de Versailles, the carriages crossed the Paris National Guard, "as wet as ducks, floundering and stumbling in the mud." The regular army of Parisians marched very slowly in ranks of six, drums beating, flags flapping in the wind and rain, but behind them was a mob: fifteen thousand "volunteers," brandishing blunderbusses, halberds and even whips. At the head of this invasion marched Lafayette, whom the Parisians had forced to take the lead. After resisting for a long time he mounted his famous white horse—in reality a broken-down old nag—and took the road to Versailles.

At two o'clock in the morning Maillard, convinced that the affair was over, arrived at the Hôtel de Ville in company with 150 women who had refused to leave him. When the King's letter was handed over, the Mayor invited everyone to supper and gave them meat, rice and "as much as they wanted to drink." Poor Louison had not ceased being threatened by her companions, who reproached her for letting herself be kissed by the King. "In the heat of wine" they once more wanted to hang the girl, and the municipality sent her home with an armed escort to protect her.

It was nearly six in the morning when Maillard, accompanied by about ten female admirers, went to bed in a furnished room in the Rue Grenelle-Saint-Honoré. He was dead beat and wanted only to rest. But two hours later ten or twelve women dragged him from his bed. He must put himself at their head to go and present a laurel wreath to M. de Lafayette, who would soon be returning to Paris. Maillard got up and started off bravely, but at the entrance to Paris the little group was met by a messenger. He brought grave news. At dawn the château had been invaded by the Parisians, and the royal family, prisoners of the capital, would sleep that night in the Tuileries. Nevertheless, Maillard went on, on foot. At Viroflay he met the procession. The heads of the two bodyguards killed that morning as they were defending the entrance to the Queen's apartment were carried first. A barber of Sèvres had been forced to powder and arrange them. "After this vanguard came an immense, hideous and grotesque crowd. . . a tragic masquerade of soldiers, bandits, drunken women holding on with difficulty astride the cannons."

Instead of the Hundred Swiss, with starched ruffs and striped doublets, who habitually preceded His Majesty when he entered his good city of Paris, instead of the bodyguards and mayoral guards prancing on their black horses, the carriage was surrounded by a nameless mob of disheveled viragoes, yelling and drunken, covered with tricolor rosettes from their heads to the bottoms of their skirts. Instead of the silver trumpets—four in front and four behind—sounding high and clear, there were cries of: "To the lantern! Down with the clergy!" At the back, between two rows of National Guards, marched the disarmed bodyguards and soldiers of the Flanders Regiment.

At the Chaillot barrier—it was then pitch dark—Mayor Bailly, correct and cold, presented the King with the keys of the city on a gold platter and declared without the least irony—of which he would have been quite incapable: "What a wonderful day, Sire, on which the Parisians hold Your Majesty and his family in their city."

A battalion of mendicant friars, Franciscans, Recollets, Capuchins and

Picpusians hastily armed, gave the salute. Louis XVI turned his head and "furtively wiped away a tear."

But the "wonderful day" was not yet finished. Before going to the Tuileries Lafayette took "his prisoners" to the Hôtel de Ville, where the crowd acclaimed the royal family. Here was not the drunken escort but the real people of Paris, delighted at being able to shout: "Long live the King! Long live the Queen! Long live the Dauphin! Long live us all!"

Maillard, the consumptive Maillard, could do no more. Since the previous day he had walked nearly forty-five miles. He returned quickly to his room while the crowd in the square wept with joy. Without doubt as he went to bed Maillard, like all the other Parisians that evening, must have thought that the Revolution was ended.

It had barely begun.

The Ohio Frontier

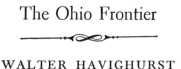

WALTER HAVIGHURST

1790–1820. The Ohio country stretched from Fort Pitt to the Mississippi, a vast area out of which five states would soon be carved: Ohio, Indiana, Illinois, Michigan, and Wisconsin. Most of it was unbroken forest, but much of Illinois consisted of prairies. Preceded by soldiers, traders, and land speculators, a tide of pioneer settlers flooded into this nearly empty territory and endured spectacular hardships. This glimpse of what their life was like was written by Walter Havighurst, a specialist in Middle Western history, in his Wilderness for Sale: The Story of the First Western Land Rush.

On a rutted, stump-filled street in a crude new settlement stood the little building that had lured settlers to the wilderness. The land office was a square, bare room with a rough table and an open ledger beside the surveyor's plots of the public lands. Steubenville, Marietta, Chillicothe, Cincinnati had the first offices; as new land districts were created, offices were opened at Zanesville, Vincennes, Shawneetown, Kaskaskia. By 1820 they had reached Detroit and St. Louis. In all these places a familiar ritual was repeated, day after day, season after season, year after year, till the public lands were private homesteads and the wilderness was gone. A woman sits with her children in the loaded wagon, peering through the doorway where her husband bends over the district maps. At last he counts out eighty dollars, signs his name in the ledger or makes his mark, and sees the decisive "A.P., *advance paid*," marked upon the general plan. When he comes out, squinting in broad sunlight, he has a certificate which he can exchange for a deed of entry when he has completed the three-hundred-twenty-dollar payment for his quarter section. Now the wagon leaves the straggling town. It creaks through the woods, rocking over roots and stumps, swaying past the blazed trees. At the end of the day a new family arrives on their land. The long journey is ended.

Out come ax and rifle, skillet, kettle and blankets. Smoke sifts up from a supper fire. The ax swings in underbrush and the slanting sunlight finds a tiny opening between big butts of oak and beech and walnut. That night the woman sleeps in the wagon bed while the man rolls up in a blanket on his land. It has been a silent land for three hundred centuries—ever since the great ice blanket, two miles deep, retreated northward, pulled a few wagon lengths a day by the relentless power of climate. But now the silence is ended. Thud, thud, thud, the ax is never still. With a swish of air and a cushioned thunder a big oak crashes down. Thud, thud, thud. The ax is gnawing at the forest.

If the season was late, with colored leaves falling and frost crisping them underfoot, the whole family turned to, making a pole-shed or "half-faced camp" for the first winter. It could be built quickly, since it had neither door, window, nor chimney. With two growing trees for corner posts, pole walls were raised on three sides and a roof of poles was covered with bark and branches. In the open side, faced south and away from the weather, a log fire would burn all winter. In the far corners blankets were spread on beds of rustling leaves. The rifle kept the pot full of game—squirrels, pigeons, turkeys, raccoon, deer meat. They lived like Indians that winter, but a woman kept her picture of a snug cabin with cupboard shelves, a warm stove chimney, and a clean-swept puncheon-floor.

Girdled trees made a deadening around the first rude cabin and spring sunlight struck through bare branches where a man chopped noiselessly through leaf mould and dropped Indian corn into the gashed ground. Then the ax thudded again at the base of trees. From the cabin doorway a man looked small against the forest. He stood there like the little men of that strange land of Lilliput, ticking away at a towering tulip tree. One great trunk and its lofty branches dwarfed him—a single tree. And the woods were beyond all numbering; they stretched on and on, dense, dark and dismaying, county after county cast in a timeless twilight. The forest was old, powerful and endless, and it was a man's folly to raise his tiny ax against it. Now for a moment the silence came back, the gloom and silence of the whole Black Forest, while a whetstone whispered on the ax-blade.

335

Then it swung again, white chips slowing on the dark ground. It was biting in.

The trees were a wary and stubborn enemy; beeches leafed out even after girdling and, from the roots of the thorny locust new shoots bristled overnight. Yet the woods were man's bounty, too. They gave walls for his dwelling, fire for his warmth, light in his darkness. They made his benches and tables, his wagon-spokes, his plow handles. They provided a fence to keep the deer out of his cornfield and his cattle from the woods. They even gave him an ax-helve for his naked blade; he used a piece of the forest to bring the forest down. *Thud, thud, thud.* It was the sound that a woman worked by, sifting wood ash to make soap, boiling oak bark to tan buckskins, while a man swung a four-inch blade on a hickory handle, hacking away at the endless woods.

Look at their place five years later. An open field smooth as a barn floor, flooded with sunlight, ribboned with young blades of corn. A fence of straight-split hackberry and black walnut, eight poles high, to keep the hogs and cattle out. A log house, solid and tightly-chinked, with wood-smoke feathering from a cat-and-clay chimney. Inside, a clean puncheon-floor, a bluestone hearth with the logs smoldering, a pantry shelf along the wall, spinning wheels beside the fire—a big wheel for wool and a little wheel for flax—clumps of herbs hanging from the rafters, boneset for fever, pennyroyal to purify the blood, ginseng for tonic, sassafras for supper tea. Around the room are beds, tables, benches, stools, all made from the vanished trees. Outside, at the edge of the field, soft smoke columns go up to the Ohio sky. Brush and branches burn with a crackling blaze, the big logs smolder night and day. Beyond the field rise the dark walls of the woods, but the wind brings the tang of other burnings. Other families are pushing back the wilderness. It was a deep, strong, dark country but now a woman is churning in the doorway while she rocks a cradle with her foot—

> "One in a bush, two in a log,
> One in a bush and two in a log,
> Run here, Sal, what a big groundhog"—

and across the clearing comes the *thud, thud, thud.* The ax would change it all.

In 1819 William Cobbett contrasted the neat farms of England with the tangled landscape of rural America. American farmers, he said, knew nothing about banking, hedging and other details of "miniature cultivation" which every English farmer understood. "They have no idea of the use of a *billhook*, which is so adroitly used in the coppices of Hampshire and Sussex. An *ax* is their tool, and with that tool, at *cutting down trees* or cutting *them up,* they will do *ten times* as much in a day as any other man that I saw. Set one of these men upon a wood of timber trees, and his slaughter will astonish you." Here was a true glimpse of western character and of a man's task in wild country.

A man worked in the woods and fields, he drove hogs to market and packed grain to the mill, he went hunting for bear, deer and turkey. But a woman's life was bounded by the clearing. She planted potatoes, pumpkins, squash, beans, beets and turnips in the garden; she made soap and candles in the dooryard; she spun flax and wool beside the hearth. She cooked and washed and sewed for a circle of children. Her task was endless. Wrote William Faux: "Soap, candles, sugar, cotton, leather and woolen clothes, of a good quality, are here all made from the land, but not without the most formidable, unremitting labor on the part of the females." A man could be lazy—"Armstrong, a hunter farmer, this day shot four deer, while he is still too idle to inclose his cornfield, which is devoured by cattle and horses, save when a boy watches to keep them off"— but his wife never got away from the spinning wheel and the cooking fire. The woman who picked up her knitting to do a few rounds while neighbors gathered for her husband's funeral was merely following the industrious habits of her life.

Many frontier settlers were satisfied when they had a roof, no matter how leaky, over their children's heads. Twenty miles from Princeton, Indiana, Faux found the Ferrel family, ten of them, crowded into a ten-by-fifteen-foot cabin floored with earth. On one side of the narrow room stood two beds, where all ten managed to sleep. On the other side a dining board rested on two blocks of wood. In wet weather a board was clapped over the chimney ("which I can reach with my hand") and the family huddled in smoke. Settler Ferrel had moved eight times on the frontier. Now he had this elegant house with a stump-filled field around it. Proudly he rubbed his rough hands together—"This is all I had to begin with."

Morris Birkbeck found frontier people fond of the word "elegant," observing that *"an elegant improvement* is a cabin of rude logs, and a few acres with trees cut down to the height of three feet, and surrounded by a worm-fence, or zig-zag railing. You hear of an *elegant* mill, an *elegant* orchard, an *elegant* tanyard, etc., and familiarly of *elegant* roads—meaning such as you may pass without extreme peril." On a trip through the Wabash bottoms, Birkbeck arrived one evening at a squatter's cabin in a ragged clearing. It was the third dwelling this man had built within twelve months ("To move," said another squatter, "all I hafen to do is put out the fire an' call the dog") and he might have a fourth before winter. His wife, surrounded by children, made the visitors welcome, clearing a place

337

for their blankets on the floor, which she assured them was "too damp for fleas." Birkbeck described the cabin—"formed of round logs, with apertures of three or four inches between: no chimney, but large intervals between the 'clapboards' for the escape of smoke. The roof was, however, a more effectual covering than we have generally experienced, as it protected us very tolerably from a drenching night. Two bedsteads of unhewn logs, and cleft boards laid across;—two chairs, one of them without a bottom, and a low stool, were all the furniture required by this numerous family. A string of buffalo hide, stretched across the hovel, was a wardrobe for their rags; and their utensils, consisting of a large iron pot, some baskets, the effective rifle and two that were superannuated, stood about in corners, and the fiddle, which was only silent when they were asleep, hung by them."

The literature of the western country shows many women left alone, or with their children, to deal with wolves, bears, Indians, or to endure cold and darkness, while the head of the household was off on some roving errand of fortune. "Oh, you had to be a stout body to be a woman way back here, for this was way up west in the Ohio wilderness," said Conrad Richter's Sayward Luckett—whose father had gone off with a rifle on his shoulder to see the Mississippi, whose brother strode off toward the Great Lakes, whose little sister wandered down the deer trail and was never seen again. There were many women like Sayward Luckett who faced the wilderness alone.

The first white household to winter in the Western Reserve, it is recorded, was the family of James Kingsbury, who, four years later, became the Reserve's first judge, in the wilderness near Conneaut Creek. But James Kingsbury left for New Hampshire before the winter winds swept over Lake Erie. Coming back in late December, he found New Connecticut buried in wastes of snow. When his horse died of exposure, after breaking through the ice on Elk Creek, Kingsbury struggled through drifts of snow with twenty pounds of flour on his back. He reached the cabin on Christmas Eve. He found his wife in bed, with a hungry child beside her and a new-born infant starving in her arms. The baby died soon after, and James Kingsbury hacked out a grave in the frozen woods. After weeks of fever and delirium his wife grew stronger. When the surveying crew arrived at the end of May, 1797, the Kingsburys went on to Cleveland with them.

In the backwoods above Marietta, Henry Howe heard the blithe story of a Yankee settler in Washington County who built himself a half-faced camp on sixty acres, two and a half miles from any house or road. "I soon (like Adam) saw the necessity of a helpmate, and persuaded a young woman to tie her destiny to mine. I built a log house twenty feet square —quite aristocratic in those days—and moved into it. I was fortunate enough to possess a jack-knife: with that I made a wooden knife and two wooden forks, which answered admirably for us to eat with. A bedstead was wanted; I took two round poles for the posts, inserted a pole in them for a side-rail, and two other poles were inserted for the end pieces, the ends of which were put in the logs of the house—some puncheons were then split and laid from the side-rail to the crevice between the logs of the house, which formed a substantial bed-cord—the only bed we had—on which we slept as soundly and woke as happy as Albert and Victoria.

"In process of time, a yard-and-a-half of calico was wanted; I started on foot through the woods ten miles to Marietta to procure it; but, alas! when I arrived there I found that, in the absence of both money and credit, the calico was not to be obtained. The dilemma was a serious one, and how to escape I could not devise; but I had no sooner informed my wife of my failure, than she suggested that I had a pair of thin pantaloons, which I could very well spare, that would make quite a decent frock; the pants were cut up, the frock made, and in due time the child was dressed.

"The long winter evenings were rather tedious, and in order to make them pass more smoothly, by great exertion I purchased a share in the Belpre library, six miles distant. From this I promised much entertainment, but another obstacle presented itself—I had no candles; however, the woods afforded plenty of pine knots—with these I made torches by which I could read, though I nearly spoiled my eyes. Many a night have I passed in this manner till twelve or one o'clock reading to my wife, while she was hatchelling, carding or spinning. Time rolled on, the payments for my land became due, and money, at that time in Ohio, was a cash article; however, I did not despair. I bought a few steers; some I bartered for, and others I got on credit—my credit having somewhat improved since the calico expedition—slung a knapsack and started alone with my cattle for Romney, on the Potomac, where I sold them, then travelled on to Litchfield, Connecticut, paid for my land and had just $1 left to bear my expenses home, six hundred miles distant. Before I returned I worked and procured fifty cents in cash; with this and my dollar I commenced my journey homeward. I laid out my dollar for cheap haircombs, and these, with a little Yankee pleasantry, kept me very comfortable at the private houses where I stopped till I got to Oswego, on the Susquehanna, where I had a power of attorney to collect some money for a neighbor in Ohio."

The records of the Ashtabula Historical Society contain the tale, considerably stranger than fiction, of Salmon Sweatland who went off before breakfast one windy morning in September, 1817, to hunt deer. It was his custom to let his dogs drive the game into Lake Erie and to take after them in a cottonwood canoe. On this morning he threw his rifle into the dugout, pushed into the water, and paddled after a swimming buck. A strong south wind carried him out of the cove and soon he was less concerned with hunting than with keeping afloat. A quarter of a mile out the wind shot him past the bobbing deer. When he tried to turn back his paddle was useless in the angry water. Soon mounting waves hid the land from sight.

From the shore his wife watched Salmon Sweatland disappear over the tossing lake. She roused a couple of neighbors who launched a light boat from the mouth of Conneaut Creek and pulled into the heaving water. They met an exhausted deer struggling toward the land, but they saw nothing else. Back ashore, leaning against the wind and drenched with spray, they watched for a sign of Salmon Sweatland or his canoe. They pushed out again, farther this time, until their boat tossed like a chip. It seemed impossible that a canoe could survive that sea. They fought their way back, giving up their neighbor for lost.

Out in Lake Erie, glimpsing a gray line of land when the canoe rose on a wave, Sweatland kept his craft afloat, waiting for the wind to change. If it swung to the north it would blow him back to Ohio, if it died he would paddle home—Lake Erie kicked up suddenly, and as quickly it could grow calm again. But now the wind howled on, a gray scud of clouds racing over the broken water. Twice he saw schooners, their sails close-hauled and topmasts pitching, but the wind tore his cry away and his waving paddle was not answered. A mounting wave gave him a last glimpse of shore; he saw his tiny cabin with the fields around it. Then a fury of wind all but swamped him. He pulled off a shoe and began bailing out water. When darkness came he fixed his hope on reaching the shore of Canada, fifty miles from home.

All night the craft rocked and rolled and pitched, and the blown spray lashed him. At last the sky cleared, giving him a course to follow; he kept his bow pointed toward the cold north star. The wind went down at daybreak and the morning light showed a long line of land over the heaving water. Two hours later he steered for the shelter of Long Point. A cross-sea nearly swamped him, but his tired arms kept the paddle thrusting. It was midday when he felt the beach grate under his canoe. He stumbled through knee-deep surf and sank down on the sand.

The Canada coast was lifeless, without a habitation for forty miles. It was a slow journey—a man ragged, hungry and exhausted dragging along the empty shore, finding some berries and shellfish, sleeping half buried in the sand. He came on the remains of a beached schooner, but there was no food in the wreckage. He kept on. A week after he had gone hunting from Conneaut Creek he stumbled into a Canadian settlement where he was given food and clothing.

With his Canadian friends he pulled back alongshore in a boat and salvaged the cargo of the wrecked schooner. There was money in his pocket when Salmon Sweatland tramped on to Buffalo. He bought a suit of clothes, ate a hearty dinner, and took passage on the Schooner *Traveler*. When the *Traveler* arrived at Conneaut Creek guns were fired from the deck and the crew cheered Sweatland's return from his hunting. "On landing," the account concludes, "he found his funeral services had been preached, and he had the rare privilege of seeing his own *widow* clothed in the habiliments of mourning."

A "settler" was often roving and restless, but once she had set up her spinning wheeel, churn, and cradle, a woman was there to stay. "At one of these lone dwellings,'" Birkbeck reports, "we found a neat, respectable-looking female spinning under the little piazza at one side of the cabin, which shaded her from the sun: her husband was absent on business, which would detain him some weeks: she had no family, and no companion but her husband's faithful dog, which usually attended him in his bear hunting in the winter: she was quite overcome with *lone* she said, and hoped we would tie our horses in the wood, and sit awhile with her, during the heat of the day. We did so, and she rewarded us with a basin of coffee. Her husband was kind and good to her, and never left her without necessity, but a true lover of bear hunting; which he pursued alone, taking only his dog with him, though it is common for hunters to go in parties to attack this dangerous animal. He had killed a great number last winter; five, I think, in one week. The cabin of this hunter was neatly arranged, and the garden well stocked."

The loneliness of their lives made frontier women welcome any visitor— a passing hunter, a neighbor on the way to the distant mill, the circuit rider with Bible and hymn book in his saddlebags, the peddler with his wagon full of wonders and his speech full of news of other places. It made them cherish neighbors, even the *idea* of neighbors who lived miles away and were seen only at an infrequent house-raising, log-rolling or camp meeting. In the Wabash communities Birkbeck found "such a genuine warmth of friendly feeling, a disposition to promote the happiness of each other, that the man who is lonely among them is not formed for society. . . . There is a great amount of social feeling, much real society in new countries, compared with the number of inhabitants. Their importance to each other . . . creates kind sentiments. They have fellow feeling in hope and fear, in difficulty and success, and they make tenfold more of each other than the crowded inhabitants of popular countries." Even the caustic William Faux observed: "humanity and hospitality seem national in the west."

Every cabin had a cradle, hollowed like a tiny dugout from a poplar or cottonwood log, and the cradle was seldom empty. Children came in the clearings almost as regularly as the seasons. "I cannot enumerate all the productions of this fine country," wrote Elias Fordham, Morris Birkbeck's colleague and friend. "Man is the only growth that's wanted here: and that want will soon be supplied. Every log cabin is swarming with half-naked children. Boys of eighteen build huts, marry, and raise hogs and children at about the same expense." Large families were an advantage in new lands; girls soon learned to help with primitive housekeeping and boys went to the woods and fields with their fathers. One day on his prairie farm beyond the Wabash, James Lemon was breaking a piece of stubble ground, his small son puffing beside him with a pitchfork—the boy's job was to rake accumulated stubble from the plowshare. At noon farmer Lemon pulled the harness off his sweating horse, hung it on the plow-handle, and went to the cabin for dinner. The boy, tired of raking stubble, hid the horse collar, thinking he would get a rest while his father plaited a new collar of corn husk and straw. But when the farmer came back there was no rest. He pulled off his buckskin breeches, stuffed the legs with straw, straddled them over the horse's neck and took up plowing—"as bare-legged as he came into the world." The boy puffed after him, stabbing a pitchfork at the matted plowshare.

Ten, twelve, fifteen children were common in frontier families, though not all of them survived. With the perils of cholera infantum, summer complaint, croupe, epidemic fevers, the mysterious milk sickness, many infants died in the first year, and many others did not live through the dreaded "second summer." It was a rare and fortunate family that did not have a little graveyard in the fence corner under a spreading oak or sycamore.

There were few widows in the western country, for in the clearings and on the prairie farms a woman's life was likely to be shorter than a man's. Many a settler buried a wife at the fence corner and looked for another woman to tend his fire. Some men married and buried two wives and stood a fair chance of outliving a third. The headstones in old cemeteries of the Ohio country tell of countless wives and mothers who did not live to their fortieth year. Mad Ann Bailey in her fence-pole cabin in the hills had outlasted two husbands and she would leave a legend of "Longevity." But the Madonna of the Trail is a young woman who will never see her grandchildren playing on the floor.

Women and General Bonaparte

J. CHRISTOPHER HEROLD

1797–1799. Compared with his campaigns in Europe, Napoleon's conquest of Egypt and Syria is little known. Nevertheless, although it was brief and achieved few permanent political results, that conquest was a gaudy and melodramatic affair. The French soldiers in the occupied city of Cairo behaved in the traditional manner of conquerors. And their twenty-nine-year-old commander's relations with women were as crudely and characteristically flamboyant as was every aspect of Napoleon's extraordinary career. J. Christopher Herold's account of them may be found in his Bonaparte in Egypt, *one of the best of the thousands of books written about Napoleon.*

On December 18, 1798, three days before his announcement that whatever he did was inspired by God, General Bonaparte issued an order to Citizen Fourès, lieutenant in the 22nd Regiment of *Chasseurs á Cheval,* to take the next diligence to Rosetta (the institution of a coach service was one among the many French innovations in Egypt) and thence to proceed to Malta and to Paris, taking certain dispatches with him. He was to remain in Paris for ten days, then to return "with all possible speed." The dispatches entrusted to him were, all four of them, utterly insignificant; yet there was more to his mission than meets the eye.

When King David took a liking to Bathsheba, he sent her husband

343

Uriah to the front lines, where he was slain; General Bonaparte sent Lieutenant Fourès to Paris, partly because he was too humane to want him dead, partly, perhaps, because his designs on Madame Fourès were not of so lasting a nature as to make her husband's permanent disappearance desirable.

If there is more than meets the eye in No. 3,775 in Napoleon's correspondence (his order to Fourès), there also was a great deal more in his sudden infatuation with Madame Fourès.

When Bonaparte was a very young man and still a lieutenant, he had literary ambitions. Among his manuscripts are two interesting dialogues—one a colloquy with a streetwalker whom he met in the gardens of the Palais-Royal and whom he took home for the mere purpose of lecturing her; the other, a dialogue on love in which he puts this statement in his own mouth: "I believe love to be harmful to society and to the individual happiness." Up to the time when he met Josephine de Beauharnais, in October 1795, his restraint in matters erotic, though not complete, was rather extraordinary for a young man of his era and profession. "It takes time to make oneself loved," he once remarked, "and even when I had nothing to do I always vaguely felt that I had no time to waste."

When he met Josephine, she was thirty-two, a widow, and the mistress, about to be discarded, of Barras. Judging from Barras' indiscreet memoirs, a close inspection of her face revealed even more than her years; yet her expression had a sweet, seductive quality, her movements had a feminine grace, her clothes, her house, her furnishings, had an aristocratic elegance, an exquisite sensuality which almost instantly subdued the rather raw young man, her junior by six years. After a few weeks, she yielded to him, and his passion was awakened. She was the only woman he ever really loved, and he loved her with an imperious sensuality which still vibrates in his letters to her. To him, she was *the* woman: her body, more youthful than her face, slim, long-limbed, lean, supple, drove him frenzied with desire. He knew her past; he was not jealous of it; yet he must marry her, to make her his complete possession. Josephine, concealing her pennilessness as well as her real age, soliciting the advice and help of her ex-lover Barras, and terrified of a future of poverty, made up her mind that General Bonaparte, uncouth and frightening though he might be, had a good career ahead of him. She pretended to reciprocate his passion. Shortly before his departure to take command of the Army of Italy, they married in a civil ceremony. On the certificate of marriage, he added two years to his age and she subtracted three from hers.

He expected her to follow him to Italy shortly; she found an inexhaustible variety of reasons for delaying her departure. While he won battle after battle, sending her proud bulletins of his victories, becoming the hero of Europe, Josephine went on her rounds of pleasure in the company of pretty young men. He cursed and worshipped her. "Take note of this: you have ruined me," he wrote her from Milan. "I knew it the moment my heart became yours, the moment you began to win, day by day, an unlimited power over me by enslaving all my senses." Yet, four days later, from Tortone: "I love you beyond anything imaginable; . . . every moment of my life is devoted to you; . . . I do not spend a single hour without thinking of you; it never entered my mind to think of another woman; . . . my strength, my arms, my mind are yours; . . . my soul is in your body; . . . the earth looks beautiful to me only because you inhabit it. . . . A thousand kisses on your eyes, on your lips, on your tongue, on your——." (The editor of this correspondence claims that the missing word is illegible.)

Still, she stayed on in Paris. There were rumors of a young lover. Bonaparte, who at that time was as moral as he was passionate, threatened to kill her if it was true. "He is a funny man, that Bonaparte," said Josephine, perhaps a little thrilled. At last, after he had threatened to resign his command in order to join her, Josephine arrived at Milan in July 1796. Among her escort, apart from the objectionable dog Fortuné, who once bit Napoleon in the leg while he was making love to her, was Citizen Hippolyte Charles, adjutant to General Leclerc. The reunion was volcanic in its amorous intensity. Unfortunately, there was a war to be fought. The hero shuttled back and forth from battlefield and victory to bed and ecstasy. In mid-November, he was at Verona making war and thinking of making love: "You know very well," he wrote to his wife, who was in Milan (or so he thought), "that I cannot forget our little visits; you know—the little black forest. I give it a thousand kisses and I am waiting impatiently until I can get there." One week later, having pushed the Austrians rather impetuously in his impatience, he was in Milan. He rushed into his *palazzo*: Josephine was off, in Genoa, with a maid, dog, and Citizen Charles. "I arrive in Milan," Bonaparte wrote to her, "I rush into your apartment, having left everything to see you, to press you in my arms. [More illegible matter follows.] You were gone. You are running after amusements. You go away when I come to you. You no longer care for your dear Napoleon. A caprice has made you love him; inconstancy has made you indifferent to him." There follows the classic threat of suicide: "Accustomed as I am to danger, I know the remedy to all the ills of life. The unhappiness I am experiencing is incalculable; I had a right not to count on it." In the frustrated lover, the chronic calculator was reborn.

He neither killed her nor sought death in battle. He even refused to admit the abundant evidence to the effect that Citizen Charles was his wife's lover—though he did have Charles discharged from the army. His family—mother, brothers, sisters—neglected nothing to acquaint him with the truth after his return to France, but who wants to see the truth when he is straying blissfully in enchanted forests? Besides, the interested motives of his informants were only too patent.

The thought of a possible divorce terrified Josephine, who was deep in debt. She accompanied her husband to Toulon, where he was to embark for Egypt. General Dumas, when he reported to his commander-in-chief one morning, found him in bed with his wife, who obviously was naked under the sheets. She was crying. "She wants to come with us to Egypt," said Bonaparte to the embarrassed black Hercules. "Are you taking your wife along, Dumas?" "No, by God," said that honest man, "she'd be a great embarrassment to me.'" Bonaparte made some consoling remarks about having soldiers' wives follow later, and gave his own a soldierly slap on her lean but shapely posterior. It is reasonable to suppose that Josephine's tears were sincere; perhaps she would rather have accompanied her conquering husband than returned to her pretty Monsieur Charles. But, however great Napoleon's passion may have been for Josephine, he budgeted his time for it. "Love," he remarked once, "is the idler's occupation, the warrior's relaxation, and the sovereign's ruination." If he had taken a different attitude toward love, there might have been no Monsieur Charles; of course there would have been no Emperor Napoleon either. As it was, he wanted no women to accompany his soldiers; he had integrity—or sense—enough to set an example.

The day after his entry into Cairo, it may be recalled, he wrote to his brother Joseph that "the veil had been completely lifted." How, and by whom it came to be lifted remains a mystery; but the event must have taken place some time between his departure from Toulon and his victory at the Pyramids. Somebody had convinced him at last that Monsieur Charles had been his wife's lover and was, at that moment, virtually living with her. What good is it to be General Bonaparte, or even Alexander the Great, if the person at whose feet one longs to place one's glory prefers the caresses of a young man who is on the board of directors of a business corporation?

According to the infuriatingly unreliable but indispensable memoirs of Bourrienne, it was Bonaparte's aide-de-camp Junot who furnished the proof of Josephine's infidelity. Junot's widow, the Duchess of Abrantès, indignantly denies this in her memoirs. Indeed, Bourrienne's account cannot be accurate, for he places the episode in February 1799, at El Arish, when Bonaparte was about to enter Syria. According to him, the General's rage was extreme, and the word "divorce" came to his lips about twenty times a minute. Now, this half a year after Bonaparte's letter to

Joseph, and at least two months after Bonaparte himself had decided that continued fidelity on his part would make him look silly. It is a fact that he firmly intended to divorce his wife after his return to France. No matter when, where, and by whom he was informed of the full extent of Josephine's treachery—and in all likelihood this took place before July 25, 1798—one thing is certain: the revelation produced some effect on him and his career. "There is nothing left for me but to become really and completely selfish," he wrote to his brother. Assuredly he had not lacked ruthless ambition before the revelation; quite likely he would have become a complete cynic even if Josephine had been as faithful as Penelope. Yet there was, in his life, a transformation: the lean-featured, romantic, idealistic hero rather suddenly turned into the bloated, cynical, materialistic tyrant. The change, though unnoticed for two or three years, took place in Egypt. Citizen Bonaparte turned into Sultan Kebir; the ambitious boy and ardent lover turned into the man whose procurers brought pretty women to his bed, to be crushed like an army when he had finished dictating his correspondence.

Shortly after his arrival in Cairo, Bonaparte was presented by his friends, the sheiks, with half a dozen Oriental beauties. He examined them, found them overweight and dismissed them, untouched. Josephine was lean. He did not like their scent either. He was very particular. Of a chance conquest he made in Vienna in 1805, he remarked, twelve years later, "She was one of the most agreeable women I've ever met: no smell." Tradition has it—though recorded evidence is lacking—that the sheik El-Bekri's daughter Zenab, who was only sixteen, appealed to him more. He was fond of beautiful bodies and delicate limbs, and when it comes to that, none can surpass a young Egyptian beauty. Why and to what extent her father condoned the liaison cannot be established; perhaps he was too preoccupied with the pursuit of his coveted slave boy, or with the consumption of his nightly bottles of brandy and burgundy, or with the fancy that he might become Sultan Kebir's father-in-law, to maintain very strict vigilance. When, in 1801, the French were obliged to evacuate Egypt, the more zealous among the faithful wished to punish the women who had consorted with the Infidels. Among their victims was Zenab, who in her better days had been known as "the General's Egyptian." Her liaison with Bonaparte must have been brief; so was her life. "On Tuesday the 24th Rabi el-Awwal 1216 (A.H.)," says El-Djabarti, "the daughter of the sheik El-Bekri was arrested. She had been debauched by the French. The pasha's emissaries presented themselves after sundown at her mother's house . . . and made her appear [before court] with her father. She was interrogated regarding her conduct, and made reply that she repented it. Her father's opinion was solicited. He answered that he disavowed his daughter's conduct. Then the unfortunate girl's head was cut off."

On December 1, 1798, perhaps already tired of the gentle Zenab, who lacked Josephine Beauharnais's experienced refinements, Bonaparte met Pauline Fourès. He was attending, with his staff, the unfortunate balloon ascent which so disappointed El-Djabarti. Two of his young aides-de-camp, one of them his step-son Eugène, noticed the beautiful Madame Fourès among the spectators and gave vent to their enthusiastic appreciation in tones loud enough to attract Bonaparte's attention. The General scrutinized the young woman; his interest was aroused. She was twenty, extremely pretty. Her blue eyes were set off by dark, long eyelashes, and her blond hair was magnificent. (According to General Paulin, who knew her well enough to be an authority, her hair, when let down, could serve her as a cloak, as if she were Lady Godiva.) The same evening, Bonaparte condescended to visit the newly opened Tivoli; sure enough Madame Fourès was there. He stared at her throughout his visit; his courting manners were never distinguished for their polish.

Pauline Fourès was the illegitimate daughter of an unknown father and of a cook named Bellisle; hence she was known to many under the rather charming nickname Bellilotte. Until her very recent marriage to Lieutenant Fourès, she had worked as a milliner, an occupation which, in eighteenth-century France, almost inevitably brought pretty girls into the arms of appreciative gentlemen. She had loved her husband well enough to put on the boots, trousers, vest, and tunic of his regiment, conceal her Lady Godiva hair under a cocked hat, and embark with him for parts unknown. On her transport, at Shubra Khit, she had had her baptism of fire. But it was easier to face the Mamelukes than to resist their conqueror. On December 17 Bonaparte issued orders to dispatch her husband to Malta and Paris—a journey almost everybody else in the army would have undertaken more gladly than did Lieutenant Fourès. No sooner had the husband taken the diligence to Rosetta than Bellilotte was invited, with several other European ladies, to a dinner party at Esbekiya Square. The host stared at her during the whole dinner. When coffee was served, the officer sitting at her side was very clumsy; he spilled a cup on her beautiful dress. No matter: he would take her upstairs to a room where she could repair the damage. She was still rubbing away at her dress when the commander-in-chief appeared. The guests waited for several hours before either of them returned. A few days later, Bellilotte, now known as Cleopatra, or Clioupâtre, occupied a mansion next to Bonaparte's on Esbekiya Square and rode about Cairo in his best carriage.

The trouble with idylls in wartime is that the enemy constantly keeps on the lookout. Lieutenant Fourès never reached Malta, let alone Paris. Having left Alexandria on December 18, the courier ship *Le Chasseur* was captured by H.M.S. *Lion* the next day. The English captain displayed extraordinary humanity toward Lieutenant Fourès. He would not condemn him, as he condemned the rest of the crew and passengers of *Le Chasseur*, to the horrors of a Turkish prison; he would not even keep him to be exchanged; he would send him right back to Alexandria, on parole. Lieutenant Fourès, rather bewildered, arrived in Alexandria; he was even more bewildered by General Marmont's attempts to keep him there, on grounds that seemed flimsy. If he could not accomplish his mission, at least he wanted to sleep with his Bellilotte. Nothing could keep him from returning to Cairo. When he returned, he did not find Bellilotte at home, but he heard a great deal of talk about her.

His illusions dispelled, Lieutenant Fourès made a show of gross temper, not to say mental cruelty. Bonaparte had made a fool of him; and, not unlikely, the British captain had made fools of all three. "To protect herself against his brutality," Bellilotte asked for a divorce, and obtained it with miraculous ease. Her lover, for his part, had promised to divorce his wife and marry her. Perhaps, unlike Josephine, she could even bear him a child. They both tried very hard, without success. "What is there to do?" Bonaparte expostulated with Bourrienne. "The stupid little ―― won't make a child for me." It was put to Bellilotte how rewarding it would be for her to become pregnant. "Good Lord!" she replied, "it isn't *my* fault!"

Once divorced, Mademoiselle Bellisle, as she now called herself, became Sultan Kebir's official mistress, presiding at his dinners and attended by his aides. Only Eugène Beauharnais was dispensed from the obligation of escorting the carriage of his stepfather's concubine—and this only after indignantly pointing out the anomaly of the situation to his stepfather.

The idyll did not last long. After about two months, Bonaparte set out on his Syrian campaign. Many of his generals and soldiers took their wives and mistresses along—a decision they were to regret bitterly. General Bonaparte was determined to be no Mark Antony to his Cleopatra; he left Bellilotte in Cairo, where he wrote to her presumably passionate letters which the editors of his correspondence did not see fit to print and which have vanished since. Throughout his career, he remained faithful to the principle never to take a woman with him on campaign.

349

Women and the Emperor Napoleon

DORMER CRESTON

1804–1813. After his coronation as the Emperor of the French, Napoleon continued to depend on the company and admiration of women. Prominent among those at his court were: Josephine, the empress, although Napoleon had several times considered divorcing her, as he eventually did; Laetitia, Napoleon's fierce Corsican mother; Hortense, Josephine's daughter and Napoleon's stepdaughter, who was also his sister-in-law because of her marriage to his brother Louis; Madame de Rémusat, a court lady admitted to Napoleon's intimate circle; and, of course, various mistresses.

With the coronation in view, in the December of 1804, every side-issue to do with the succession was brought to the fore. "It was," writes Hortense, "again a question of divorce: a council was called, and the animosity shown at it by the Emperor's brothers was so great that . . . the Emperor thought he discerned a special virulence on the part of his family directed against the Empress. Therefore, instead of agreeing with their advice, he formed the project, not only of having her crowned, but also of having her consecrated with him."

As an alternative to divorce an idea took form in Napoleon's mind. He asked Josephine if she would be willing to accept as her own another woman's child, and "to feign a pregnancy cleverly enough to deceive everyone." Josephine agreed. Napoleon then took his doctor, Corvisart, into his confidence, and asked him if he would be ready to act his part in the hoax. "If I succeed," he said to Corvisart, "in securing the birth of a boy who will be my own son I should want you, as witness of the feigned accouchement of the Empress, to do everything necessary to give this ruse all the appearance of being genuine." Corvisart refused. After Napoleon's second marriage, and the birth of the King of Rome, the doctor related the incident to Madame de Rémusat.

On the 2nd of December 1804, with every ecclesiastical pomp, the coronation of Napoleon and Josephine was solemnized. It was followed two or three days later by the distribution to the Army of the imperial standards with eagles. This took place on the Champ de Mars. This was succeeded by a plethora of fêtes and parties. "These fêtes," writes Hortense, "where the Emperor's presence was indispensable, had a little diverted him from his habitual business. At least he seemed to give himself up more to society and to take a pleasure in it. He had become gallant, speaking more than usual to the ladies"; but, she explains, the reason for all this display of civility was in reality to cover his attentions to one person in particular: young Madame Duchâtel, who the summer before had become one of the *Dames du Palais*. At the Tuileries his obsession with this blue-eyed, aquiline-nosed beauty was known to everyone.

For Josephine, it was the cause of many tears. "As for my mother," writes Hortense, "realizing quite well that someone was drawing her husband's tenderness away from herself, she became a prey to the saddest thoughts, and so unhappy that I could think of nothing to do to console her." Napoleon considered these tears made him ridiculous. "You must submit to all my whims . . ." he protested to his wife. "I have the right to reply to all your complaints by an eternal *moi*. I am a being apart. I accept conditions from no one." And another time he explained to her "so to speak mathematically," that to him everything was permissible. "I am not a man like other men and the laws of morality or custom cannot be applied to me." And when, after this clear demonstration of the position, Josephine still protested, there would follow, writes Clari de Rémusat, who often witnessed these scenes, "violences that went to such lengths that I would not dare enter into particulars." Madame de Rémusat and Hortense were each made at intervals the unwilling and embarrassed go-betweens; one moment witnessing Josephine's bitter weepings in her bedroom; the next being interviewed by Napoleon, who was inclined to blame them if Josephine was not as passive as he considered she ought to be. They would urge Napoleon to be more considerate, and Josephine to be more dignified, for, in her anxiety to find out all that was actually happening, she would go so far as to confide in shopkeepers. Then, quite suddenly, it would all be over: Napoleon, "moved by what she had suffered, would substitute for injuries caresses which were as unmeasured as his violences had been, and as she was sweet-natured and easily moved she again felt secure."

It is to Hortense's credit that, afraid as she always was of her step-father, she yet confronted him over the Duchâtel affair. He at first took an angry tone: "And you, too, Madame, then you are against me?" But she quietly, though determinedly, held her ground.

" 'You are right,' said the Emperor, suddenly becoming gentler, 'I see that if in big matters I am big, in small ones I am small,' and on this he walked off."

He knew of Hortense's sufferings at the hands of his brother, and would rate Louis for the impossible way he behaved to her. And, too, he admired Hortense's efforts to make the best of this disastrous marriage. "I assure you," he remarked to her one day, "you are not only one of the women, but one of the persons, for whom I have the most esteem." Hortense might be afraid of Napoleon, but she had an un-critical admiration for his opinions, and to have won this eulogy from her stepfather, who rarely praised anyone, was extraordinarily sweet to her.

As for Josephine, her great irritant to Napoleon was her habit of getting into debt. These debts were always enormous and, as Napoleon gave scrupulous attention to all domestic and Court expenses himself, a constant annoyance. Every fashionable jeweler, milliner, and dress-maker in Paris took advantage of Josephine's incapacity for saying No. Napoleon's intention had been that none of these shop-people should come to her at the Tuileries, but actually they swarmed like cockroaches. Through what back doors, along what little passages, whispering, tripping, scurrying, basket-box on arm, trepidation and hope in their heart, would the Paris *vendeuses* not come? "The little inside rooms were full of them." Full, too, of artists ready waiting with brush or crayon to catch an impression of the woman who was the center of all this atten-tion. Josephine, in consequence, would find herself in possession of a whole collection of portraits of herself which she would give away to anyone; to relations, friends, chamber-women, or even to the dressmakers and milliners themselves.

If lacking in cerebral intelligence, Josephine possessed a practical one. She went to the furthest of her capabilities, and there she had the sense to stop. The hours she spent at her dressing-table, the gauzy dresses, cachemire shawls, and butterfly fripperies that her women would daily hold out in front of her displayed in baskets for her to choose from, were all as much a necessary part of her virtuosity of living as is the wardrobe of a ballet dancer; they all helped to build up the enchanting figure whose presence relieved the taut atmosphere engendered by Napoleon's personality. It is he, and not her own capabilities, that has placed her in one of the rows of niches for women famous in history; but, once there, she knew how to adorn it. And if, putting aside this intuitive sense in the art of living, one has to admit she was to a great extent what is known as a silly woman, she was undeniably a kind one. No one dispossessed or despairing appealed to her in vain.

Once proclaimed Emperor, Napoleon began to bring his imperial Court to full bloom. Madame de Rémusat, having been some time in the country, returned to find herself caught up "in the whirlwind of our Court." At St. Cloud, where the Court was at the moment, everyone was excitedly trying to find out how everything had been done in the time of the Louis's. "The disease of etiquette seemed to have laid hold of all the inhabitants of the imperial Château of Saint-Cloud." Ponderous books of rules and regulations were dragged from the library shelves, and taken off to be studied. Madame Campan, who had been First Lady to Marie Antoinette, was sent for, and Madame de Rémusat filled a great copy-book with the precious syllables that fell from her lips. This was added by Napoleon to other note-books of further information gleaned from various sources. Applications, too, were being constantly made to Talleyrand's memory. Now that Napoleon was Emperor, it was obvious that he had to reconstruct Court life, but to read of his activities raises in the modern mind an inescapable comparison with those of a film director working at a period piece.

Madame de Rémusat's husband was appointed Grand Chamberlain, and he had to keep the ordinary Chamberlains within bounds when they showed signs of overstepping them, and in consequence the de Rémusats were forced to lead a life of continual petty warfare over "a cordon, a slight difference in a costume, precedence at a doorway, the entrée into such or such a *salon.*" The true function of ceremony, as of all the arts, is to put the mind in touch with reality; but for it to be effectual, it needs to be informed with the genuine spirit, and, above all, with dignity. The etiquette at Napoleon's Court all went with a rush: "carried out as if directed by the roll of a drum . . . and this kind of precipitation, the continual nervousness it gave rise to, joined to the slight knowledge of the formalities in a good half of the courtiers, gave his Court a more dejected than dignified appearance." Madame de Rémusat gives us a picture of an imperial procession: the group of Court ladies, long trains flung over arm so as not to hinder the general precipitancy, and perpetually urged to go faster by the chamberlains who, nearly treading on their heels, remorselessly repeated, "*Allons, allons, mesdames, avancez donc. Allons, allons, mesdames, avancez donc.*" ("They ought to call us the Palace *postilions*," protested Countess d'Arberg, scrambling along with the rest.) All this urgency was on account of Napoleon, who was all the time trying to accelerate the pace from behind. Talleyrand, when he in turn became Grand Chamberlain, had to walk immediately in front of him. Talleyrand, his feet injured from being dropped as a child, had difficulty in walking even slowly, and his efforts to hobble along quickly enough with the impatient Emperor pressing on immediately behind his back was a source of derisive amusement to the aides-de-camp.

The Court officials, with their silver-embroidered coats of violet, crimson, or amaranth, added to the variegated colors of the whole scene. Mixed with the Republican Court figures were now various members of the *ancien régime*, and Josephine was greatly gratified at having twelve Dames du Palais, among whom were "great ladies from all countries; people much surprised at finding themselves brought together in this way." Later, when, after Tilsit, Napoleon was at the summit of his power, the pressure of the members of the Faubourg St.-Germain at the gates of the Tuileries was so great that he would be seen to smile as his eye ran down a list of applicants who, at first, had jeered at the "royal displays" of the Corsican's Court. Now, the more exquisite the clothes worn at Court the more pleased was Napoleon, who, when he had not been able to afford it himself, had so condemned luxury. When he was back at the palace after the coronation he had walked, smiling, among all the bejeweled and bedecked Court ladies telling them how well finery becomes a woman, and saying, "It is to me, ladies, that you owe it that you are so charming."

Cards in the evening were part of the palace ceremonial. No one might play for money: whist or lotto was what the quartettes, dotted about at tables through several *salons*, occupied themselves with, or pretended to occupy themselves; for, in reality, they often sat merely holding the cards while they gossiped. At one table would be seen Josephine playing whist with the chief people of the evening, two of her Ladies and a Chamberlain in attendance. Her attention must have been a good deal deflected from her game by all the women in the room having to come and curtsey to her in turn. She could not either, but have been aware all the time that at another table in the same room sat the great Laetitia herself, who now bore with dubious grace the title of Madame Mère, bestowed on her by Napoleon. She had her own household, and Laure Junot had become one of her

Ladies. At times Napoleon would neglect his mother, irritated by her parsimonious ways, by her refusal to play up to his royal charade; while she, waiting grimly for the crash she foresaw might come any moment to her son's garish edifice, hoarded and saved for that moment. Exasperated, Napoleon would accost her with, "Well, Signora Laetitia, how do you like Court life? You are bored, aren't you? Look at your daughters, they seem born to it. I have given you a beautiful house, a beautiful property, and a million a year to enjoy it all, and you live like a bourgeois in the Rue Saint-Denis!" Another day he protested, "Madame Laetitia, I wish I could see you get through your million a year!" "I will spend it on condition that you give me two!" retorted Laetitia.

In the evenings at the Tuileries, a little knot of Chamberlains would at certain moments be seen advancing down the room, and behind them the small redoubtable figure in the dark-green and white uniform, with the indecisive step that was so strangely at variance with his character. On whatever part of the *salon* the little group of Emperor and Chamberlains were seen approaching, silence would fall. Those on the favored spot rose to their feet and remained rigid, waiting for the few brusque words that might or might not be shot at them. "There was not a woman who was not pleased to see him remove himself from her vicinity," writes an onlooker; for Napoleon had by now developed the hurtful rudeness of the newly-arrived man who will not trouble to make himself agreeable except where it is worth while; but when he wished to please, his roughness would glide into a delightfulness certain to seduce, the famous Bonaparte smile would soften every feature, only in its turn to be succeeded, if he saw his hearer becoming too basking, too reassured, by sudden severity or hinted threat, so that his victim would be left finally in a state of bewildered nervosity. For this was the condition that Napoleon deliberately fostered; it ensured his subjects' thoughts being directed continuously to their Emperor, wondering in what they had offended, or in what, if they were not careful, they would soon offend. In this state they were at their most malleable.

As for the actual men and women who formed his Court, Napoleon did not approve of their having any interests outside his. Personal interests had to be metamorphosed into Court ambitions. He had to be served with complete devotion, but he only called it "devotion," writes Clari de Rémusat, "when anyone surrendered his whole person, all his feelings and all his opinions," for the Emperor emphasized that "we must give up even the smallest of our old ways of living so as to have only one thought, that of his interests and his wishes. He would promise, in recompense, great elevation, much wealth, much satisfaction to one's pride."

A few days after the coronation, the de Rémusats happened to find themselves alone with Napoleon in one of the *salons* at the palace of St. Cloud. The de Rémusats, each in their own role, had now become egregious Court figures, but only a small part of their minds responded to Court life. Always reserving their judgment, they refused to have their intelligence distorted by the divagations of My Policy. Though for long now Napoleon, both in public and private, had cold-shouldered morality, he was still aware of that stern brow bent upon him from afar, and, when he found a moment's leisure in his urgent life, would endeavor to justify himself in the eyes of those whose opinions he valued.

Of this particular moment, "I feel," writes Clari de Rémusat, "as if I still saw him in the embrasure of one of the windows in one of the salons at Saint-Cloud, sitting astride a chair, chin propped on the back: Madame Bonaparte a few paces from him on a sofa: I sitting in front of him, and Monsieur de Rémusat standing behind my armchair." She tells how for some time no one had spoken, and so exactly has she described the scene that we, too, seem clearly to see the little group posed motionless in the window of this vast and tranquil French drawing-room.

Ever since the murder of the Duke d'Enghien, Napoleon had shown in his attitude to Clari de Rémusat "a kind of sustained indulgence." It is evident he did not like to fall in the opinion of that exceptionally attractive, intelligent, and firm-principled young woman. So now he broke the silence with, "*Eh bien*, you were displeased with me over the death of the Duke d'Enghien?"

"That is true, Sire, and I still am. . . ."

"But do you realize that he was waiting for me to be assassinated?"

"That is possible, Sire, but all the same he was not in France."

"Ah! it's not a bad thing from time to time to show that one is master in other countries."

"Say no more, Sire; don't let us talk of it any more or you will make me weep."

"Ah! tears! women have no other resource! . . . Isn't that so, Monsieur de Rémusat, that tears are women's strongest argument?"

"Sire," replied my husband, "there are some tears one can't blame them for."

"Ah! I see that you, too, take the affair seriously? However, it's quite simple: you people, you have your memories, you have seen other times. Myself, I only date from the time when I began to count for something. What is a Duc d'Enghien to me? One *émigré* who happens to be of more importance than another, that is all!"

Then he treated them to long dissertations on this central theme, but smilingly, with many neat twists and turns. It was a moment of *laisser aller*, of expansion, when he was deliberately putting forth all his powers to fascinate, to persuade; but, just as the Rémusats were feeling completely at ease, suddenly, says Clari de Rémusat, "his face became grave, that severe look returned which always seemed to heighten his short stature, and he gave Monsieur de Rémusat some unimportant order or other with all the sharpness of a man who is absolute master."

"You see," her husband said to her afterwards when they were alone, "he was afraid that this unbosoming of himself to us might diminish something of the fear he always wants to inspire."

The Last of the *Tonquin*

WASHINGTON IRVING

1811. In September of 1810, the ship Tonquin *sailed from New York bound for the Northwest Pacific coast via Cape Horn. John Jacob Astor, a shrewd German immigrant who had done well in the fur business, was sending out four of his partners and twelve clerks to establish a fur-trading post at the mouth of the Columbia River. The* Tonquin *carried a crew of twenty and was commanded by Jonathan Thorn, a U.S. naval lieutenant on leave of absence. Thorn was proud, courageous, hot-tempered, and stupid. After landing the traders at a site called Astoria, Thorn sailed north to buy furs from the coastal Indians. Washington Irving, the first American writer to win international popularity, was also the first distinguished American historian. This account is taken from his history of the Astor ventures into the Northwest,* Astoria.

The *Tonquin* set sail from the mouth of the river on the fifth of June. The whole number of persons aboard amounted to twenty-three. In one of the outer bays they picked up, from a fishing canoe, an Indian named Lamazee, who had already made two voyages along the coast and knew something of the language of the various tribes. He agreed to accompany them as interpreter.

Steering to the north, Captain Thorn arrived in a few days at Vancouver's Island, and anchored in the harbor of Neweetee, very much against the advice of his Indian interpreter, who warned him against the perfidious character of the natives of this part of the coast. Numbers of

358

canoes soon came off, bringing sea-otter skins to sell. It was too late in the day to commence a traffic, but Mr. M'Kay, accompanied by a few of the men, went on shore to a large village to visit the Wicananish, the chief of the surrounding territory, six of the natives remaining on board as hostages. He was received with great professions of friendship, entertained hospitably, and a couch of sea-otter skins was prepared for him in the dwelling of the chieftain, where he was prevailed upon to pass the night.

In the morning, before Mr. M'Kay had returned to the ship, great numbers of the natives came off in their canoes to trade, headed by two sons of Wicananish. As they brought an abundance of sea-otter skins, and there was every appearance of a brisk trade, Captain Thorn did not wait for the return of Mr. M'Kay, but spread his wares upon deck, making a tempting display of blankets, cloths, knives, beads, and fish-hooks, expecting a prompt and profitable sale. The Indians, however, were not so eager and simple as he had supposed, having learned the art of bargaining and the value of merchandise from the casual traders along the coast. They were guided, too, by a shrewd old chief named Nookamis, who had grown gray in traffic with New England skippers, and prided himself upon his acuteness. His opinion seemed to regulate the market. When Captain Thorn made what he considered a liberal offer for an otter skin, the wily old Indian treated it with scorn, and asked more than double. His comrades all took their cue from him, and not an otter skin was to be had at a reasonable rate.

The old fellow, however, overshot his mark, and mistook the character of the man he was treating with. Thorn was a plain, straight-forward sailor, who never had two minds nor two prices in his dealings, was deficient in patience and pliancy, and totally wanting in the chicanery of traffic. He had a vast deal of stern, but honest pride in his nature, and, moreover, held the whole savage race in sovereign contempt. Abandoning all further attempts, therefore, to bargain with his shuffling customers, he thrust his hands into his pockets, and paced up and down the deck in sullen silence. The cunning old Indian followed him to and fro, holding out a sea-otter skin to him at every turn, and pestering him to trade. Finding other means unavailing, he suddenly changed his tone, and began to jeer and banter him upon the mean prices he offered. This was too much for the patience of the captain, who was never remarkable for relishing a joke, especially when at his own expense. Turning suddenly upon his persecutor, he snatched the proffered otter skin from his hands, rubbed it in his face, and dismissed him over the side of the ship with no very complimentary application to accelerate his exit. He then kicked the peltries to the right and left about the deck, and broke up the market in the most ignominious manner. Old Nookamis made for shore in a furious passion, in which he was joined by Shewish, one of the sons of Wicananish, who went off breathing vengeance, and the ship was soon abandoned by the natives.

When Mr. M'Kay returned on board, the interpreter related what had passed, and begged him to prevail upon the captain to make sail, as, from his knowledge of the temper and pride of the people of the place, he was sure they would resent the indignity offered to one of their chiefs. Mr. M'Kay, who himself possessed some experience of Indian character, went to the captain, who was still pacing the deck in moody humor, represented the danger to which his hasty act had exposed the vessel, and urged him to weigh anchor. The captain made light of his counsels, and pointed to his cannon and firearms as sufficient safeguard against naked savages. Further remonstrances only provoked taunting replies and sharp altercations. The day passed away without any signs of hostility, and at night the captain retired as usual to his cabin, taking no more than the usual precautions.

On the following morning, at daybreak, while the captain and Mr. M'Kay were yet asleep, a canoe came alongside in which were twenty Indians, commanded by young Shewish. They were unarmed, their aspect and demeanor friendly, and they held up otter skins, and made signs indicative of a wish to trade. The caution enjoined by Mr. Astor, in respect to the admission of Indians on board of the ship, had been neglected for some time past; and the officer of the watch, perceiving those in the canoe to be without weapons, and having no orders to the contrary readily permitted them to mount the deck. Another canoe soon succeeded, the crew of which was likewise admitted. In a little while other canoes came off, and Indians were soon clambering into the vessel on all sides.

The officer of the watch now felt alarmed, and called to Captain Thorn and Mr. M'Kay. By the time they came on deck, it was thronged with Indians. The interpreter noticed to Mr. M'Kay that many of the natives wore short mantles of skins, and intimated a suspicion that they were secretly armed. Mr. M'Kay urged the captain to clear the ship and get under way. He again made light of the advice; but the augmented swarms of canoes about the ship, and the numbers still putting off from shore, at length awakened his distrust, and he ordered some of the crew to weigh anchor, while some were sent aloft to make sail.

The Indians now offered to trade with the captain on his own terms prompted, apparently, by the approaching departure of the ship. Accordingly, a hurried trade was commenced. The main articles sought by the savages in barter were knives; as fast as some were supplied they moved off, and others succeeded. By degrees they were thus distributed about the deck, and all with weapons.

The anchor was now nearly up, the sails were loose, and the captain, in a loud and peremptory tone, ordered the ship to be cleared. In an instant a signal yell was given: it was echoed on every side, knives and war-clubs were brandished in every direction, and the savages rushed upon their marked victims.

The first that fell was Mr. Lewis, the ship's clerk. He was leaning, with folded arms, over a bale of blankets, engaged in bargaining, when he received a deadly stab in the back, and fell down the companion-way.

Mr. M'Kay, who was seated on the taffrail, sprang on his feet, but was instantly knocked down with a war-club and flung backwards into the sea, where he was dispatched by the women in the canoes.

In the meantime Captain Thorn made desperate fight against fearful odds. He was a powerful as well as a resolute man, but he had come upon deck without weapons. Shewish, the young chief, singled him out as his peculiar prey, and rushed upon him at the first outbreak. The captain had barely time to draw a claspknife, with one blow of which he laid the young savage dead at his feet. Several of the stoutest followers of Shewish now set upon him. He defended himself vigorously, dealing crippling blows to right and left, and strewing the quarter-deck with the slain and wounded. His object was to fight his way to his cabin, where there were firearms; but he was hemmed in with foes, covered with wounds, and faint with loss of blood. For an instant he leaned upon the tiller wheel, when a blow from behind, with a war-club, felled him to the deck, where he was dispatched with knives and thrown overboard.

While this was transacting upon the quarter-deck, a chance-medley fight was going on throughout the ship. The crew fought desperately with knives, handspikes, and whatever weapon they could seize upon in the moment of surprise. They were soon, however, overpowered by numbers, and mercilessly butchered.

As to the seven who had been sent aloft to make sail, they contemplated with horror the carnage that was going on below. Being destitute of weapons, they let themselves down by the running rigging, in hopes of getting between decks. One fell in the attempt, and was instantly dispatched; another received a deathblow in the back as he was descending; a third, Stephen Weekes, the armorer, was mortally wounded as he was getting down the hatchway.

The remaining four made good their retreat into the cabin, where they found Mr. Lewis, still alive, though mortally wounded. Barricading the cabin door, they broke holes through the companion-way, and, with the muskets and ammunition which were at hand, opened a brisk fire that soon cleared the deck.

Thus far the Indian interpreter, from whom these particulars are derived, had been an eye-witness of the deadly conflict. He had taken no part in it, and had been spared by the natives as being of their race. In the confusion of the moment he took refuge with the rest, in the canoes. The survivors of the crew now sallied forth, and discharged some of the deck guns, which did great execution among the canoes, and drove all the savages to shore.

For the remainder of the day no one ventured to put off to the ship, deterred by the effects of the firearms. The night passed away without any further attempt on the part of the natives. When the day dawned, the *Tonquin* still lay at anchor in the bay, her sails all loose and flapping in the wind, and no one apparently on board her. After a time, some of the canoes ventured forth to reconnoitre, taking with them the interpreter. They paddled about her, keeping cautiously at a distance, but growing more and more emboldened at seeing her quiet and lifeless. One man at length made his appearance on the deck, and was recognized by the interpreter as Mr. Lewis. He made friendly signs, and invited them on board. It was long before they ventured to comply. Those who mounted the deck met with no opposition; no one was to be seen on board; for Mr. Lewis, after inviting them, had disappeared. Other canoes now pressed forward to board the prize; the decks were soon crowded, and the sides covered with clambering savages, all intent on plunder. In the midst of their eagerness and exultation, the ship blew up with a tremendous explosion. Arms, legs, and mutilated bodies were blown into the air, and dreadful havoc was made in the surrounding canoes. The interpreter was in the main-chains at the time of the explosion, and was thrown unhurt into the water, where he succeeded in getting into one of the canoes. According to his statement, the bay presented an awful spectacle after the catastrophe. The ship had disappeared, but the bay was covered with fragments of the wreck, with shattered canoes, and Indians swimming for their lives, or struggling in the agonies of death; while those who had escaped the danger remained aghast and stupefied, or made with frantic panic for the shore. Upwards of a hundred savages were destroyed by the explosion, many more were shockingly mutilated, and for days afterwards the limbs and bodies of the slain were thrown upon the beach.

The inhabitants of Neweetee were overwhelmed with consternation at this astounding calamity, which had burst upon them in the very moment of triumph. The warriors sat mute and mournful, while the women filled the air with loud lamentations. Their weeping and wailing, however, was suddenly changed into yells of fury at the sight of four unfortunate white men, brought captive into the village. They had been driven on shore in one of the ship's boats, and taken at some distance along the coast.

The interpreter was permitted to converse with them. They proved to be the four brave fellows who had made such desperate defence from the cabin. The interpreter gathered from them some of the particulars already related. They told him further, that, after they had beaten off the enemy, and cleared the ship, Lewis advised that they should slip the cable and endeavor to get to sea. They declined to take his advice, alleging that the wind set too strongly into the bay, and would drive them on shore. They resolved, as soon as it was dark, to put off quietly in the ship's boat, which they would be able to do unperceived, and to coast along back to Astoria. They put their resolution into effect; but Lewis refused to accompany them, being disabled by his wound, hopeless of escape, and determined on a terrible revenge. On the voyage out, he had repeatedly expressed a presentiment he should die by his own hands; thinking it highly probable that he should be engaged in some contest with the natives, and being resolved, in case of extremity, to commit suicide rather than be made a prisoner. He now declared his intention to remain on board of the ship until daylight, to decoy as many of the savages on board as possible, then to set fire to the powder magazine, and terminate his life by a signal act of vengeance. How well he succeeded has been shown. His companions bade him a melancholy adieu, and set off on their precarious expedition. They strove with might and main to get out of the bay, but found it impossible to weather a point of land, and were at length compelled to take shelter in a small cove, where they hoped to remain concealed until the wind should be more favorable. Exhausted by fatigue and watching, they fell into a sound sleep, and in that state were surprised by the savages. Better had it been for those unfortunate men had they remained with Lewis, and shared his heroic death: as it was, they perished in a more painful and protracted manner, being sacrificed by the natives to the manes of their friends with all the lingering tortures of savage cruelty. Some time after their death, the interpreter, who had remained a kind of prisoner at large, effected his escape, and brought the tragical tidings to Astoria.

Such is the melancholy story of the *Tonquin,* and such was the fate of her brave, but headstrong commander, and her adventurous crew. It is a catastrophe that shows the importance, in all enterprises of moment, to keep in mind the general instructions of the sagacious heads which devise them. Mr. Astor was well aware of the perils to which ships were exposed on this coast from quarrels with the natives, and from perfidious attempts of the latter to surprise and capture them in unguarded moments. He had repeatedly enjoined it upon Captain Thorn, in conversation, and at parting, in his letter of instructions, to be courteous and kind in his dealings with the savages, but by no means to confide in their apparent friendship, *nor to admit more than a few on board of his ship at a time.*

Had the deportment of Captain Thorn been properly regulated, the insult so wounding to savage pride would never have been given. Had he enforced the rule to admit but a few at a time, the savages would not have been able to get the mastery. He was too irritable, however, to practise the necessary self-command, and, having been nurtured in a proud contempt of danger, thought it beneath him to manifest any fear of a crew of unarmed savages.

With all his faults and foibles, we cannot but speak of him with esteem, and deplore his untimely fate; for we remember him well in early life, as a companion in pleasant scenes and joyous hours. When on shore, among his friends, he was a frank, manly, sound-hearted sailor. On board ship he evidently assumed the hardness of deportment and sternness of demeanor which many deem essential to naval service. Throughout the whole of the expedition, however, he showed himself loyal, single-minded, straight-forward, and fearless; and if the fate of his vessel may be charged to his harshness and imprudence, we should recollect that he paid for his error with his life.

The loss of the *Tonquin* was a grievous blow to the infant establishment of Astoria, and one that threatened to bring after it a train of disasters. The intelligence of it did not reach Mr. Astor until many months afterwards. He felt it in all its force, and was aware that it must cripple, if not entirely defeat, the great scheme of his ambition. In his letters, written at the time, he speaks of it as "a calamity, the length of which he could not foresee." He indulged, however, in no weak and vain lamentation, but sought to devise a prompt and efficient remedy. The very same evening he appeared at the theatre with his usual serenity of countenance. A friend, who knew the disastrous intelligence he had received, expressed his astonishment that he could have calmness of spirit sufficient for such a scene of light amusement. "What would you have me do?" was his characteristic reply; "would you have me stay at home and weep for what I cannot help?"

Waterloo

PHILIP GUEDALLA

1815. Probably none of the world's famous battles has been written about so often or at such length as Waterloo. Hugo, Stendhal, and Thackeray have all described it in great novels. Historians and biographers have analyzed Waterloo in tedious detail in countless works. This brief account of the battle as seen by Wellington himself is taken from what I consider the best-written biography of the Duke. Guedalla, an essayist, biographer, and historian, cultivated an ironic and artfully rhetorical style which, in the 1920s, was almost as widely admired as Lytton Strachey's.

The June days went by in Brussels. Late one Thursday carriages were clattering over the cobbles, and a sound of dance-music drifted into the summer night. The Duke was there. He had been working late with Müffling and the Staff; for he had news that afternoon that the French had passed the frontier opposite the Prussians, and orders had been sent to move the army in the direction of Quatre Bras. But it was just as well to reassure the doubters by shewing up at the ball; and when he made his bow, Mr. Creevey's girls found him looking as composed as ever; though one young lady, who shared a sofa with him, thought him quite preoccupied and noticed how he kept turning round and giving orders. More news arrived while they were all at supper; and he desired the senior officers to leave unobtrusively. He said something civil to his host and slipped off with him to look at a map, remarking when the door closed behind them that Napoleon had *humbugged* him, by God! and gained twenty-four hours' march upon him. Asked his intentions, he replied that he proposed to concentrate at Quatre Bras—"but we shall not stop him there, and if so, I must fight him"—his thumb nail traced a line on the map behind Hougoumont and La Haye Sainte—"*here.*" Then he went off to bed. It was a little after two; and Mr. Creevey, who had stayed at home that evening and heard a deal of hammering on doors along his street, was writing in his Journal:

June 16. Friday morning ½ past two.—The girls just returned from a ball at the Duke of Richmond's. . . .

The marching bayonets went down the empty streets, and in the summer dawn the pipes went by.

He followed them next morning (a gleeful English maid, who caught a glimpse of him as she was opening the shutters, cried, "O, my lady, get up quick; there he goes, God bless him, and he will not come back till he is King of France!"); and before noon he was staring at the woods beyond Quatre Bras. Then he rode over to the Prussians and had a word with Blücher. Their dispositions did not impress him, since they were rather recklessly aligned (in contrast with his own judicious practice) upon an exposed slope; and he said grimly that if they fought there, they would be damnably mauled. For his ally's benefit he translated this uncompromising view into the milder sentiment that every man, of course, knew his own troops, but that if his own were so disposed, he should expect them to be beaten. His expectation was not disappointed, since the Emperor shattered them that evening at Ligny. But Wellington employed the afternoon at Quatre Bras, where Ney flung four thousand men away in wild attacks. They heard the guns in Brussels; and the enquiring Creevey strolled on the ramparts, while sixteen miles away the Duke was steadying a line which was often far from steady. It was a wild affair of French lancers wheeling in the corn and redcoats hurrying up the long road from Brussels. Once Wellington was almost caught in a flurry of French cavalry far out beyond his firing-line. The ditch behind him was lined with Highlanders; and with a timely reminiscence of the hunting field he shouted to them to lie still, put his horse at the unusual obstacle, and cleared it, resuming a less exciting position of command. And once his deep voice was heard calling "Ninety-second, don't fire till I tell you." For he was everywhere as usual, while Ney, whose military talents were almost wholly pugilistic, raged up and down the line watching his cavalry surge vainly round the British squares. But the price paid was tolerably high, although a great lady in Brussels cooed consolingly to a friend that "poor Sir. D. Pack is severely wounded, and the poor Duke of Brunswick died of his wounds. . . . The Scotch were chiefly engaged, so there are no officers wounded that one knows."

But the reverse at Ligny served to nullify any advantage gained by the Duke at Quatre Bras; and he grimly observed that "old Blücher has had a damned good hiding, and has gone eighteen miles to the rear. We must do the same. I suppose they'll say in England that we have been licked; well, I can't help that." He took this unpalatable decision early the next morning; but (it was typical of him) the retreat was deferred until his men had cooked a meal. With that inside them they would, he felt, be more equal to the perils of a retirement with Napoleon at their heels. The red columns filed off towards Brussels; and as they went, the Duke remarked with obvious relief, "Well, there is the last of the infantry gone, and I don't care now." The cavalry, he knew, could look after themselves with a few guns to hold them. He watched the perilous retreat, occasionally sitting in a field and laughing over some old English newspapers or turning his glass on the immobile French. The morning opened brightly; but as the day wore on, there was a stillness, and a pile of leaden clouds climbed slowly up a sultry sky. The storm broke in floods of rain, as his cavalry was drawing off; and the thunder drowned the sharper note of guns, while the rockets (in fulfilment of the Duke's most skeptical anticipations) sputtered and fizzed and not infrequently exploded backwards. The rain drove down and the long *pavé* gleamed before them, as they struggled back towards the ridge in front of Waterloo, the French plodding after them across the sodden fields.

There was a night of damp discomfort; but food was waiting in the British bivouacs. They lit fires, and Peninsular veterans dispensed derisive consolations, observing cheerfully to newcomers, "Oho, my boy! this is but child's play to what *we* saw in Spain," and "Lord have mercy upon your poor tender carcass. What would such as you have done in the Pyrenees?" Uxbridge, his second-in-command, came to Wellington and asked what he proposed to do. The Duke countered with a question.

"Who will attack the first to-morrow—I or Buonaparte?"

"Buonaparte."

"Well," said the Duke, "Buonaparte has not given me any idea of his projects; and as my plans will depend upon his, how can you expect me to tell you what mine are?"

Then he rose, and laying a hand upon the other's shoulder, said kindly, "There is one thing certain, Uxbridge; that is, that whatever happens you and I will do our duty."

For his belief in plans was never strong. He once said pityingly of the Marshals that "they planned their campaigns just as you might make a splendid set of harness. It looks very well, and answers very well, until it gets broken; and then you are done for. Now, I made my campaigns of ropes. If anything went wrong, I tied a knot; and went on." Blücher had fallen back from Ligny; so Wellington had tied a knot, conforming with his ally's retreat by falling back to Waterloo. Now he was comfortably established on the ridge; but who could say what would happen next? If they attacked him in position, it might be Busaco all over again. Or they might know their business better and edge round his right. In that event they might give an opening—and then it would be Salamanca—or they might manoeuvre him from Waterloo without a battle. That would cost him Brussels and send the French royalties scampering from Ghent. It was too much to hope that Napoleon would choose a frontal attack, when the manoeuvre round his flank promised so richly; and Wellington inclined to think that he would choose the latter course. So he sat writing in the night—to warn the royalties at Ghent, to suggest that Lady Frances Webster would be wise to leave at once for Antwerp, and to beg some-one in authority in Brussels to "keep the English quiet if you can. Let them all prepare to move, but neither be in a hurry or a fright, as all will yet turn out well." And all night long the summer rain drove down on sodden fields; the trees dripped at Hougoumont; gleaming pools stood in the little farmyard at La Haye Sainte; somewhere across the darkness a square figure in a long grey coat was straining eager eyes into the night for a glimpse of Wellington's camp fires; and the two armies slept in the busy whisper of the rain.

A pale dawn broke over Belgium. The Emperor was breakfasting by eight o'clock. Soult was uneasy; Ney prophesied that Wellington would slip away again; but Napoleon swept away all objections.

"Il n'est plus temps. Wellington s'exposerait à une perte certaine. Il a jeté les dés, et ils sont pour nous."

When Soult pressed him to call up reinforcements, he snapped con-temptuously, "Parce que vous avez été battu par Wellington, vous le regardez comme un grand général. Et, moi je vous dis que Wellington est un mauvais général, que les Anglais sont de mauvaises troupes, et que ce sera l'affaire d'un déjeuner."

"Je le souhaite," replied the Marshal glumly.

The Emperor sailed before gusts of optimism that morning. Reille, who came in a little later, altogether failed to share his enthusiasm for a frontal attack on Wellington. But then Reille had served in Spain; even at Quatre Bras he shied nervously from an apparently unguarded position, because "ce pourrait être une bataille d'Espagne—les troupes Anglaises se *montreraient quand il en serait temps*"; and now the sight of a British line behind an easy slope made him uncomfortable—he had seen something of the kind before. But the Emperor was rarely a good listener.

Besides, he meant to have his victory. A victory would mean so much—the road to Brussels open, France reassured by a familiar bulletin, King Louis made ridiculous again by further flight, the British driven into the sea at last, and (who knows?) a change in Government in London, the enlightened Whigs in office, and a world at peace with his tricolour floating peacefully above the Tuileries. The sky was clearing now; a breeze sprang up; the ground would soon be dry enough for guns to move. He would have his victory; and June 18 should take its place among his anniversaries.

"*Nous coucherons ce soir,*" he said, "*à Bruxelles.*"

Across the little valley Wellington was waiting on that Sunday morning in his blue frock-coat and the low cocked-hat that bore the black cockade of England with the colours of Spain, Portugal, and the Netherlands. His mixed command was, if anything, more mixed than ever, since he had left some of his British troops to guard his right flank and the road to Ostend; and his foreigners outnumbered them by two to one. Still, he had got them in position on a ridge—one of his favourite ridges with an easy slope towards the enemy and shelter for his men behind its crest. The French outnumbered them; the Emperor had 70,000 men to the Duke's 63,000; and he had only 156 guns against 266 in the hands of that incomparable artillerist. But if Blücher was to be believed, some Prussians would be coming later. The old *sabreur* had been unhorsed and ridden over at Ligny; but he dosed himself with a deadly brew of gin and rhubarb (and apologised to a British officer whom he embraced, observing cheerfully, "*Ich stinke etwas*") and somewhere across the sodden fields his dark columns wound towards the Emperor's unguarded flank.

The Duke was waiting. As it was showery that morning, he kept putting on a cloak, "because I never get wet when I can help it." He waited for the French manoeuvre to begin; had not Marmont manoeuvred "in the usual French style" at Salamanca? But the Emperor made no attempt to manoeuvre. Then it was not to be another Salamanca. For they came plunging straight at the British lines in columns of attack, just as he had seen them when the French columns charged the heights above Vimeiro and Masséna's men struggled up the slope at Busaco. It was to be the old style of attack, to which he knew an answer that had never failed—the waiting line behind the crest, the volley long deferred, and then the bayonet. (As he wrote afterwards to Beresford, the Emperor "did not manoeuvre at all. He just moved forward in the old style, in columns, and was driven off in the old style.") But there were variations; for the fighting

369

surged around the outworks of his line at Hougoumont and La Haye Sainte. Then, the columns foiled, a stranger variation appeared, as the French cavalry came thundering uphill against his line. His infantry formed squares to meet them, and the delighted gunners blazed into the advancing target, until they scampered off to safety in the nearest square bowling a wheel from each dismantled gun before them, as the bewildered horsemen rode helplessly among the bristling squares of inhospitable bayonets. It was a picturesque, but scarcely an alarming, experience. "I had the infantry," as he wrote afterwards, "for some time in squares, and we had the French cavalry walking about us as if they had been our own. I never saw the British infantry behave so well."

The Duke, as usual, was everywhere, fighting his line along the ridge as a commander fights his ship in action. He rode Copenhagen; and all day long the chestnut carried him along the lanes of weary men. Each shift of the interminable battle elicited a gruff comment or an order scrawled on a scrap of parchment. He saw the Nassauers pressed out of Hougoumont and acidly observed to an Austrian General, "*Mais enfin, c'est avec ces Messieurs la qu'il faut que nous gagnions la bataille*," put in the Guards to retake the position with "There, my lads, in with you—let me see no more of you," and watched Mercer's guns dash into place between two squares with an appreciative "Ah! that's the way I like to see horse-artillery move." When the Life Guards charged, a deep voice was at hand to say, "Now, gentlemen, for the honour of the Household Troops"; and when they rode back, a low cocked-hat was raised with "Life Guards! I thank you." At one moment he formed a line of shaky infantry himself, like any company-commander, within twenty yards of the flash of an oncoming French column. And as the tide of cavalry was ebbing down the trampled slope, he asked the Rifles in his quiet manner to "drive those fellows away."

The light was failing now; and he rode down the line before the Guard was launched in the last charge of the Empire. The shadows lengthened from the west, as the tall bearskins came slowly on behind six generals and a Marshal walking (for it was Ney) with a drawn sword. They were still coming on "in the old style"; and the waiting line held back its fire in the Peninsular fashion until the Duke was heard calling, "Now, Maitland! Now's your time." The volley crashed; and as the smoke drifted into the sunset, the Guard broke—and with the Guard the memory of Austerlitz, of Eylau, Friedland, Jena, Wagram, and Borodino melted upon the air. Then the Duke galloped off with a single officer to order the advance. The smoke thinned for an instant; and a trim, bare-headed figure was seen pointing a cocked-hat towards the French. Someone enquired (a shade superfluously) which way to go; and the Duke's voice answered him, "Right ahead, to be sure."

Late that night Blücher met him in the road on horseback and clasped a weary Duke, exclaiming *"Mein lieber Kamerad"* and exhausted his entire stock of French by adding a trifle inadequately, *"Quelle affaire."* For the Emperor had shattered his last army in blind attacks upon the ridge and· then crushed it between Wellington and the Prussians. A lonely, white-faced man, he stood in the moonlight waiting in a little wood, waiting for troops that never came: his cheeks were wet with tears. Far to the south the Prussian cavalry were sabring the last remnant of the Grande Armée under the moon. . . . "No more firing was heard at Brussels—the pursuit rolled miles away. Darkness came down on the field and city; and Amelia was praying for George, who was lying on his face, dead, with a bullet through his heart."

The Duke rode slowly back to Waterloo. There was no feeling of ela-tion, and they were all exhausted. Besides, he had a solemn notion that, where so many had fallen close to him, he had somehow been preserved by Providence. "The finger of Providence was upon me," he wrote that night, "and I escaped unhurt"; and he repeated almost the same words in Paris later. Then they sat down to supper; the table had been laid for the usual number, but the Staff had suffered cruelly, and there were so many empty places. The Duke, who ate very little, kept looking at the door; and Álava knew that he was watching for the absent faces. When the meal was over, he left them. But as he rose, he lifted both hands saying, "The hand of God has been over me this day." Then he went out and began to write his despatch:

My Lord,
   Buonaparte having collected the 1st, 2nd, 3rd, 4th, and 6th corps of the French army, and the Imperial Guards . . ."

He asked them to bring in the casualty returns, and slept for a few hours. When he read them by the first morning light, he broke down. Picton, Ponsonby, De Lancey, Barnes, Gordon, Elley . . . it had been worse than Badajoz. Then he took his tea and toast, finished his despatch, and rode sadly into Brussels. He saw Creevey from his hotel window and waved a signal to come in. He was quite solemn still and said that it had been a damned serious business—a damned nice thing—the nearest run thing you ever saw in your life. His mind ran on the losses, and he added grimly that Blücher got so damnably licked on Friday night that he could not find him on Saturday morning and was obliged to fall back to keep in touch with him. Then he walked up and down the room and praised his men. Creevey enquired if the French had fought better than usual.

"No," said the Duke, "they have always fought the same since I first saw them at Vimeiro. By God! I don't think it would have been done if I had not been there."

Mountain Men

DALE VAN EVERY

1822–1838. The mountain men who spent years at a time in the Rocky Mountain wilderness, trapping beaver, fighting Indians, and living like Indians, were perhaps the most remarkable and picturesque of all American frontiersmen. Numerous accounts of their wild, violent life are available. This one is taken from The Final Challenge: The American Frontier, 1804–1845, *which is the fourth volume of Mr. Van Every's distinguished and fascinating history of the frontier from 1763 to 1845.*

Of all the memorable figures that have enlivened the American scene the mountain man was unquestionably the most colorful, the most striking, the widest departure from the behavior of his fellow countrymen. He had been able to achieve a personal fulfillment to which ordinary men must remain lifelong strangers. Never elsewhere in recorded history has the human male been afforded comparable scope to indulge his deepest, most instinctive, and most commonly frustrated yearnings. The mountain man's world was a kaleidoscope of horses, guns, and campfires, of startling and impromptu travels, of the closest comradeship with like-spirited companions, of perpetually novel scenes and situations, of a never-ceasing succession of amazing demands and adventures. His constant preoccupations were hunting, trapping, fishing, and fighting. The extraordinary hardships and dangers to which he was daily subjected reinforced his self-esteem with the comforting assurance that he was an equally extraordinary man. He could even feel that he was a material success for each year he amassed a fortune in furs even though almost as invariably he as soon lost or squandered it. Meanwhile his long isolation in the wilderness had not deprived him of the enjoyment of sex. His comparative wealth enabled him to select the Indian maiden who most suited his fancy upon whom to confer the privilege of becoming his devoted consort.

Washington Irving, who in his 1837 history of the period was enabled to draw upon personal acquaintance with contemporaries who had spent years in the mountains, captured the essence of the mountain man's temperament in his famous description of the free trapper's outward appearance:

It is a matter of vanity and ambition with them to discard everything that may bear the stamp of civilized life, and to adopt the manners, habits, dress, gesture and even walk of the Indian. . . . His hair, suffered to attain a great length, is carefully combed out, and either left to fall carelessly over his shoulders, or plaited neatly and tied up in otter skins, or parti-colored ribands. A hunting-shirt of ruffled calico of bright dyes, or of ornamented leather, falls to his knees; below which curiously fashioned leggins, ornamented with strings, fringes, and a profusion of hawks' bells, reach to a costly pair of moccasins of the finest Indian fabric, richly embroidered with beads. A blanket of scarlet, or some other bright color, hangs from his shoulders, and is girt around his waist with a red sash, in which he bestows his pistols, knife, and the stem of his Indian pipe; preparations either for peace or war. His gun is lavishly decorated with brass tacks or vermilion, and provided with a fringed cover, occasionally of buckskin, ornamented here and there with a feather. His horse . . . is selected for his speed and spirit, and prancing gait, and holds a place in his estimation second only to himself. . . . He is caparisoned in the most dashing and fantastic style; the bridles and crupper are wightily embossed with beads and cockades; and head, mane and tail, are interwoven with abundance of eagles' plumes, which flutter in the wind. To complete his grotesque equipment, the proud animal is bestreaked with vermilion, or with white clay, whichever presents the most glaring contrast to his real color. Such is the account given by Captain Bonneville of these rangers of the wilderness, and their appearance at the camp was strikingly characteristic. They came dashing forward at full speed, firing their fusees, and yelling in Indian style. Their dark, sunburned faces, and long flowing hair, their leggins, flaps, moccasins, and richly-dyed blankets, and their painted horses gaudily caparisoned, gave them so much the air and appearance of Indians, that it was difficult to persuade one's self that they were white men, and had been brought up in civilized life.

The great event of the mountain man's year was the annual rendezvous when the long months of hardship and loneliness were rewarded by weeks of roistering festivity. Irving's account caught the bizarre quality of the occasion:

The hunting season was over, all past tricks and manoeuvres forgotten, all feuds and bickerings buried in oblivion. From the middle of June to the middle of September, all trapping is suspended; for the beavers are then shedding their furs and their skins are of little value. This, then, is the trapper's holiday, when he is all for fun and frolic, and ready for a saturnalia among the mountains. . . . The leaders of the different companies . . . mingled on terms of perfect good fellowship; interchanging visits, and regaling each other in the best style their respective camps afforded . . . the "chivalry" of the various encampments engaged in contests of skill at running, jumping, wrestling, shooting with the rifle, and running horses. . . . They drank together, they sang, they laughed, they whooped; they tried to out-brag and out-lie each other in stories of their adventures and achievements. . . . The presence of the Shoshone tribe contributed occasionally to cause temporary jealousy and feuds. The Shoshone beauties became objects of rivalry among the more amorous mountaineers. . . . The caravans of supplies arrived at the valley just at this period of gallantry and good fellowship. Now commenced a scene of eager competition and wild prodigality at the different encampments. Bales were hastily ripped open, and their motley contents poured forth. A mania for purchasing spread itself throughout the several bands—munitions for war, for hunting, for gallantry, were seized upon with equal avidity—rifles, hunting knives, traps, scarlet cloth, red blankets, garish beads, and glittering trinkets, were bought at any price, and scores run up without any thought how they were ever to be rubbed off. . . . For a free mountaineer to pause at a paltry consideration of dollars and cents, in the attainment of any object which might strike his fancy, would stamp him with the mark of the beast in the estimation of his comrades. . . . Now succeeded another outbreak of rivalry and extravagance. The trappers were newly fitted out and arrayed, and dashed about with the horses caparisoned in Indian style. The Shoshone beauties also flaunted about in all the colors of the rainbow. Every freak of prodigality was indulged to its fullest extent, and in a little while most of the trappers, having squandered away all their wages . . . were ready for another hard campaign in the wilderness.

Finally, there was the unforgettable Indian maid, pictorialized by Irving with equal zest:

The free trapper, while a bachelor, has no greater pet than his horse; but the moment he takes a wife (a sort of brevet rank in matrimony occasionally bestowed upon some Indian fair one, like the heroes of ancient chivalry in the open field,) he discovers that he has a still more fanciful and capricious animal on which to lavish his expenses. No sooner does an Indian belle experience this promotion, than all her notions at once rise and expand to the dignity of her situation; and the purse of her lover, and his credit into the bargain, are taxed to the utmost to fit her out in becoming style. . . . In the first place, she must have a horse for her own riding; but no jaded, sorry, earth-spirited hack; such as is sometimes assigned by an Indian husband for the transportation of his squaw and papooses; the wife of a free trader must have the most beautiful animal she can lay her eyes on. And then, as to his decoration: headstall, breastbands, saddle and crupper, are lavishly embroidered with beads, and hung with thimbles, hawks' bells, and bunches of ribands. . . . As to her own person, she is even still more extravagant. Her hair, esteemed beautiful in proportion to its length, is carefully plaited, and made to fall with seeming negligence over either breast. Her riding hat is stuck full of parti-colored feathers; her robe, fashioned somewhat after that of the whites, is of red, green and sometimes grey cloth, but always of the finest texture that can be procured. Her leggins and moccasins are of the most beautiful and expensive workmanship . . . Then as to jewelry: in the way of finger-rings, earrings, necklaces, and other female glories, nothing within reach of the trapper's means is omitted, that can tend to impress the beholder with an idea of the lady's high estate.

Mountain men vanished from the far western scene as suddenly as they had appeared upon it. The period of their flourishing had lasted a short ten years before the profusion of beaver dwindled and a change in the style of men's hats produced an even more discouraging diminishment in the price. In none of those years did mountain men aggregate more than 500. The total number during the whole period who spent sufficient time in the mountains to consider themselves mountain men probably did not exceed 2,000. This compares roughly with the number of men who held the Kentucky and Cumberland perimeters during the Revolution. These two groups were in their separate fashions the heroes of the frontier's two greatest crises. Geography and climate imposed upon the later frontiersmen added hazards and demands from which even their hardy predecessors might well have recoiled. Behind the showy trappings of the midsummer festival loomed a year-round existence requiring incredible endurance. The environment which the mountain man had elected to make his own could scarcely have been more rigorous. His continual movements alternated between the forbidding vastness of glacial heights and the repellent expanses of burning deserts. He was constantly beset by blizzards and sandstorms, heat and cold, hunger and thirst. He never knew shelter and seldom knew rest. His chances of obtaining food could range within days from as many buffalo as he felt like shooting to such ants and crickets as he could manage to catch. However favorable his momentary luck with weather and game, he was under all circumstances condemned through two-thirds of the year to unrelieved physical misery by the very nature of his principal occupation—trapping beaver. Hiram Chittenden, the great chronicler of the fur trade, thus describes the basic process:

The universal mode of taking beaver was with the steel trap, in the use of which long experience had taught the hunters great skill. The trap is a strong one of about five pounds weight, and was valued in the fur trade period at twelve to sixteen dollars. The chain attached to the trap is about five feet long, with a swivel near the end to keep it from kinking. The trapper, in setting the trap, wades into the stream so that his tracks may not be apparent; plants his trap in three or four inches of water a little way from the bank, and fastens the chain to a strong stick, which he drives into the bed of the stream at the full chain length from the trap. Immediately over the trap a little twig is set so that one end shall be about four inches above the surface of the water. On this is put a peculiar bait, supplied by the animal itself, castor, castoreum or musk, the odor of which has a great attraction for the beaver. To reach the bait he raises his mouth toward it and in this act brings his feet directly under it. He thus treads on the trap, springs it and is caught. In his fright he seeks concealment by his usual method of diving into deep water, but finds himself held by the chain which he cannot gnaw in two, and after an ineffectual struggle, he sinks to the bottom and is drowned.

Beaver skins were only valuable when they had thickened during the colder months, and the trapper was as a result committed to spending every day of fall, winter, and spring floundering waist-deep in ice water, except for intervals when solid freezing made trapping totally impossible. Along with the bodily torment the necessary solitude of his trap-tending exposed him to more frequent attack by his two deadliest enemies, grizzlies and Blackfeet. The great bear, always quarrelsome and aggressive, was a monster of destruction when ineffectually wounded. The trapper's unavoidable relations with the Indians of the plains, mountains, and deserts represented a perpetual problem that ranged from exasperating to mortal. Friendlier Indians were insistent beggars who remained constantly alert to steal his horses or property, while throughout the mountain man's heyday hostile Indians, notably the far-ranging, implacable Blackfeet, sought every opportunity to kill him. Contemporary official reports list the deaths at the hands of Indians of some 500 trappers. Many others must have fallen, unrecorded. Considering the numbers involved this reflects a casualty rate comparable to that during the earlier Ohio Valley Indian wars.

Nothing so sharply distinguished the mountain man as his astounding capacity to withstand, and even to relish, hardships and dangers so extravagant. His stamina was literally inexhaustible. This inbred trait was most enlighteningly illustrated by the career of Hugh Glass. He was the mountain man's mountain man, the single figure who most completely represented his kind. Stories of his exploits and misadventures became the favorite saga most often dwelt upon around mountain campfires or in St. Louis and Taos barrooms. The tales varied in minor details but remained in agreement on all essentials and have been supported by a sufficient accumulation of contemporary evidence to permit an acceptable recapitulation of his remarkable experiences. Just about everything that could happen to a mountain man happened to Hugh Glass.

He first came to notice on the Missouri when he joined Ashley's 1823 expedition. All that was afterward recalled about his background was that he had come "from Pennsylvania." He may have been past his first youth inasmuch as in all stories circulated by his companions he was invariably referred to as "old Glass," though this is not conclusive since "old" was a frontier term commonly indicating exceptional respect or affection. His misadventures began promptly when he was wounded at Ashley's sandspit battle with the Aricara. He recuperated soon enough to start from Fort Kiowa with Andrew Henry's party making its September 1823 overland march to the mouth of the Yellowstone. This led to the most celebrated of all his exploits.

On the fifth day out he suffered the disaster most dreaded by mountain men. He was mangled by a wounded grizzly bear. His injuries were so frightful by the time rallying companions had completed the execution of the bear that it was obvious he could not be moved. It remained imperative, however, that the 80-man expedition proceed without delay if it was to accomplish its purpose of re-establishing the upper Missouri operation before winter had set in. In response to a reward offered by Henry, to which many members of the party contributed, two men volunteered to remain to attend the helpless and presumably expiring Glass. Most accounts agree that the two were John S. Fitzgerald and the 19-year-old James Bridger. The horribly injured invalid evinced no signs of improvement, and after 5 days' waiting his attendants concluded their vigil was useless. They took his rifle, knife, and other effects and upon rejoining Henry reported that Glass had died, as all had expected he would, and that they had buried him.

However, after they had departed, perhaps stimulated by the angry realization that he had been abandoned, Glass summoned the strength to crawl to a spring and to pick some wild cherries. On this meager fare he had sufficiently recovered after 10 days to contemplate the enormous effort of making his way the 100 miles back to Fort Kiowa. Before his stumbling progress had proceeded far, he sighted a pack of wolves dragging down a half-grown buffalo calf. Accounts differ on his response to this development. Some say that after he had waited until the wolves had satisfied their first hunger he was privileged to inherit the remains. Others say that his despoilers had overlooked his razor which he was able to use to strike sparks from a stone to ignite a grass fire which routed the wolves. In either event he lived off what was left of the calf while his wounds partially healed. He then resumed his struggle toward Fort Kiowa, depend-

377

ing on roots, berries, and decayed buffalo carcasses for food en route. At the end of 6 weeks he reached the post.

All accounts agree that he was possessed by a burning determination to rejoin Henry in order that he might confront his faithless nurses. Joseph Bazeau, in charge of the fur post, was sending a party of 6 upriver under Antoine Langevin to make the first attempt since the midsummer campaign to run the Aricara blockade. Toussaint Charbonneau, the aging Lewis and Clark interpreter, was a member of the crew of the dugout canoe. Glass, though still weak, stiff, and sore, eagerly joined them upon realizing that this represented the earliest possible opportunity to get back to Henry. During the journey upriver 3 men in a canoe bound downriver passed unobserved, the failure of either party to sight the other no doubt due to the care with which each was attempting to avoid being sighted by the Aricara. One of the men in the other canoe was Fitzgerald, the man Glass most desired to encounter.

The Langevin party found the charred Aricara towns still deserted. What they had no reason to surmise was that after their withdrawal to the plains the Aricara had elected to resettle on the southern outskirts of the Mandan towns. As the little party unsuspectingly approached the Mandan, Charbonneau, with the innate discretion that had kept him alive so long and was to enable him to live to past 80, disembarked to make his own cautious way overland. Glass went ashore to hunt. The vengeful Aricara cut off the party still afloat, killing all five. Glass, too, was perceived and attacked but saved at the last moment by the chance intervention of several mounted Mandan.

Though still lame from his recent wounds, he did not linger at the Mandan. He set off alone, on foot, in midwinter, for Fort Henry, 260 miles away at the mouth of the Yellowstone. When he found it abandoned, he kept on, trudging another 220 miles through the snow up the Yellowstone to the new Fort Henry at the mouth of the Bighorn. Here he received the astounded and tumultuous welcome due one returned from the dead, but along with it the most unwelcome news that Fitzgerald was no longer there. Glass was reported to have become soon reconciled with the abashed Bridger whom he forgave in view of his youth.

Only 6 months had passed since his so nearly fatal encounter with the grizzly and most of those months had been devoted to desperate and lonely travels. Nevertheless, when Henry proposed sending a dispatch to Ashley, Glass promptly volunteered for the mission, still intent on his pursuit of Fitzgerald, whom he considered primarily responsible for his abandonment. On February 28, 1824, in the fearful cold of a plains winter, he set out with four companions on the 750-mile overland journey to Fort Atkinson at the mouth of the Platte. They crossed the Tongue to the

Powder and from its headwaters to the still ice-encumbered North Platte. Here they built a bullboat and began their descent of the intractable river, the first and one of the few attempts to navigate a waterway soon to become upon better acquaintance generally execrated as "a mile wide and a foot deep." After reaching the open plains they sighted an Indian encampment which they heedlessly assumed to be friendly Pawnee, all Indians in their winter robes tending to look alike. Only after they had landed and been encompassed by their exultant hosts did they realize that the outstretched arms into which they had walked were Aricara. Glass managed to tear loose from his assailants, though without his rifle, and contrived to elude their pursuit among river bottom rocks and willows. Two of his companions were killed. The other two, with one rifle between them, also succeeded in escaping and made their way down the Platte to arrive eventually at Fort Atkinson in May.

Glass headed northeastward toward the somewhat nearer Fort Kiowa. Once more he was stranded on the plains alone and without firearms but, though this time he had more than 300 miles of precarious travel before him, he nevertheless felt easy and confident for he was possessed of the luxurious advantage of restored health plus a knife. The meat he required to sustain his 20 miles a day progress was everywhere available. It was the buffalo calving season. Recently born buffalo calves were so ill-advisedly curious and trusting that whenever they had strayed or had been otherwise separated from their mothers they were disposed to run to any moving creature, even a hungry man. As a consequence of these several advantages, Glass felt "right peart," according to his account of the episode published in the *Missouri Intelligencer,* and without special incident other than an encounter with friendly Sioux reached Fort Kiowa in 15 days. Joining a trader's party bound downriver, he resumed his search for Fitzgerald.

He ran his quarry to earth at Fort Atkinson but was again and finally denied whatever revenge he may have anticipated. Fitzgerald had in the meantime enlisted in the 6th Regiment and was safe in the sanctuary represented by the uniform of the United States Army. Glass did, however, recover his rifle and gain the entire garrison as an absorbed audience for the recital of his adventures. These, as always with a mountain man, were only beginning.

Reaching Franklin, he promptly joined the 1824 Santa Fe trading caravan and upon reaching Taos became one of that year's famous assembly of trappers fanning westward and northwestward across the southern Rockies. The one incident associated with his next three years that has come to light was reported in George C. Yount's account of Glass once having been obliged to travel 700 miles to have an arrowhead cut out of his back. He was at the 1828 Bear Lake rendezvous and there-

379

after became a figure of increasing standing and influence among his fellow mountain men during a period that competition was becoming so much sharper not only with the British but between American companies. In 1832 his luck, as had Jedediah Smith's, at last faltered. With two companions, he was killed while crossing the frozen Yellowstone by his old enemies, the Aricara.

Retribution came swiftly and was marked by mountain pungency. The wandering band of Aricara next encountered a trapping party led by Johnson Gardner, redoubtable challenger of the British at Ogden Hole, and stole some of his horses while professing friendship. Gardner seized three to hold as hostages for the restoration of his horses and when they were not returned he executed them, by burning, according to Beckworth. There was for Gardner, in his grim administration of mountain justice, the added satisfaction of realizing that he had punished the murderers of his old friend Glass, for from them he had recovered the by now celebrated Glass rifle.

The mountain man, whose eccentric and perpetually dangerous way of life was so well represented by the experiences of Hugh Glass, had little appreciation of the service that he was rendering his country. He was an utter hedonist, engrossed in his own self-indulgent and often fantastic impulses. But that service had been immense. His extemporaneous yet vigorous competition with the powerful Hudson's Bay Company denied at a critical last moment Great Britain's opportunity to establish what must otherwise have become an unassailable and permanent claim to the entire trans-mountain area. The sudden currency of stories of his adventures stirred in the American people a dawning interest in a distant and mysterious region that had until then seemed to most as far beyond the bounds of sensible American concern as were the Andes or the Mountains of the Moon. Above all, his restless and insatiable curiosity had made him within half a dozen years familiar with every most remote and inaccessible corner and recess of more than a million square miles of hitherto unknown plains, mountains, and deserts so that he was ready, when the time shortly came, to serve as sure and experienced guide not only to the wagon trains of the pioneers but to every government explorer. He had taken the next to the last stride, in the remarkable advance of the frontier people from the crest of the Appalachians to the Western Ocean.

The Young Disraeli: Social, Political, and Amorous

HESKETH PEARSON

1832–1836. In 1832, Benjamin Disraeli was twenty-nine, a fop, a social celebrity, and already the author of four novels, of which one, Vivian Grey, *was a huge success. Although his ambition was obvious, few suspected that he would become one of the great and most colorful Prime Ministers in English history. This excerpt is taken from* Dizzy, *by Hesketh Pearson, a witty biographer who specialized in books about men of wit.*

Disraeli was not by nature a party man. He had affinities and antipathies, like everyone else, but he was too individualistic to subscribe to any political program. For this reason he was distrusted by all the sheeplike members of parliament, both Whigs and Tories; and though he soon realized that he would achieve nothing without a label, the question of his sincerity remained an open one to the end of his days, the large majority of people being so made that they invariably suspect the integrity of those who have minds of their own. In many respects he was the most consistent and sincere politician of his age, though naturally his views expanded and were partly dictated by the changes and circumstances of the time. But this

381

must be said at the outset: he was, like every politician who comes to the front, a careerist. No one fights political battles for the sake of peace and quiet; no downright incorruptible idealist could endure the wire-pulling, charlatanry, humbug, chicanery, place-seeking, time-serving, and power-snatching which are the necessary ingredients of politics; and the spectacle of a successful and mainly disinterested statesman, whether right, left or center, is one that the world awaits in vain.

> *Get thee glass eyes*
> *And, like a scurvy politician, seem*
> *To see the things thou dost not . . .*

is Shakespeare's comment on that profession, and on the whole a true one. Only a saint could be quite honest in politics, and saints do not enter politics; but Disraeli was as honest as a man can be who is chiefly devoted to his own interests. He was less impressionable and less emotional than his great antagonist of later years, Gladstone, and consequently a better ruler of men, but he was just as sincere and quite as honest. Both of them played the power game for all it was worth, and neither was therefore primarily concerned with the welfare of mankind; but each believed that his own policy was for the good of the country, Gladstone passionately, Disraeli calmly.

Their personalities were as different as their achievements. Disraeli was perhaps the only figure in English political history who started public life as an object of ridicule and ended it as an object of reverence: it was as if Oscar Wilde, the aesthete of Gilbert's *Patience*, had closed his career in the atmosphere of sanctity that surrounded the last years of Tennyson. But behind the negligent figure and colored costume and long hair ringlets of "this miserable, circumcized, *soi-disant* Christian," as the actor Macready called him, were the determination, fortitude, prevision and persistence of Richelieu, with a patience that Richelieu might have envied, and a sense of humor that he lacked. Rebuff followed rebuff from the moment he entered the political scene.

Before the Reform Act came into operation he stood for High Wycombe as a Radical, declaring that he was neither a Whig nor a Tory and that his politics could be described in one word: England. He also made it clear that he was sprung from the people, that neither he nor his family had ever received a shilling from the public money, and that not a drop of Plantagenet blood flowed in his veins. After his opponent had paraded the town with a band and a hired mob, he "jumped up on the portico of the Red Lion and gave it to them for an hour and a half." He made a surprising appearance, with his profuse black hair, his rings and chains, his lace and cambric, his white face and elaborate waistcoat; and the people were amazed when this foppish figure let loose a stream of eloquence, with dramatic gestures to enforce his arguments, in a voice that could be heard far down the street. "When the poll is declared, I shall be there," he concluded, pointing at the head of the lion above the portico, "and my opponent will be there," indicating the lion's tail. "I made them all mad," he reported. "A great many absolutely *cried*. . . . All the women are on my side and wear my colors, pink and white." But however popular he was with the mob, the Corporation and burgesses who controlled the election placed him at the lion's tail, his opponent at the head; upon which he publicly asserted that "the Whigs have opposed me, not I them, and they shall repent it," and that the nearest thing to a Tory in disguise was a Whig in office.

This was in June, '32, and at the close of the same year he stood, again at High Wycombe, for the first reformed parliament. But again he antagonized the chief parties by saying in his election address: "Rid yourselves of all that political jargon and factious slang of Whig and Tory— two names with one meaning, used only to delude you—and unite in forming a great national party . . ." and he defined himself as a Conservative to preserve what was good in the constitution, a Radical to remove what was bad. The Tories were more friendly than the Whigs, who did their best to defeat him because, he said, he was not nobly born, and once more he was at the bottom of the poll. Without pausing, he put himself forward for the county of Buckinghamshire; but discovering that a second Tory candidate had just been nominated, he withdrew his own name and supported the other. The following year there was a chance of standing for Marylebone and he issued an address; but the vacancy did not occur, so he consoled himself by writing a pamphlet explaining his political faith and advising the Tories to merge with the Radicals. He disliked the Whigs, who had substituted a selfish oligarchy for a kingdom, and he thought the Tories, who had lost their traditions, could be purged of retrogression and reinstated in their historical position as leaders of the people and supporters of the monarchy. To bring this about was to be his own work for nearly half a century; but no one in the eighteen-thirties could have guessed that it was feasible, still less that the flashy young Jew would be the motive-force. Lord Melbourne, then Home Secretary, who met him at a dinner-party in '34, was attracted by his conversation and asked, "Well now, tell me, what do you want to be?" "I want to be Prime Minister," replied Disraeli with quiet gravity. Melbourne gave a weary sigh and then explained the utter impossibility of such an achievement, ending with, "You must put all these foolish notions out of your head; they won't do at all." But Melbourne lived to feel less confident, and when towards the close of '48, just before his death, he heard that Disraeli was to become Tory leader in the Commons, he exclaimed, "By God! the fellow will do it yet."

It certainly did not seem as if he would live to do it after his second defeat at High Wycombe, and for some years his activities were almost wholly social. We hear of him at Bath with Bulwer, smoking Latakia over their conversation and being mobbed at a public ball. Wherever he went his clothes aroused comment; at one dinner he appeared in a black velvet coat lined with satin, purple trousers with a gold band running down the outside seam, scarlet waistcoat, long lace ruffles reaching the tips of his fingers, white gloves with jeweled rings outside them, his well-oiled black ringlets touching his shoulders. His conversation, which ranged from the sarcastic to the eloquent, according to his mood, made him popular with hostesses who were not solely satisfied with the movement of their guests' jaws in mastication, and his table was covered with invitations, many from people he did not know. He could be extremely cutting when the occasion called for it. One of his hosts, after praising a certain wine, urged him to drink it. He agreed that it was very good. "Well," said the host, "I have got wine twenty times as good in my cellar." "No doubt, no doubt," said Disraeli, glancing round the table, "but, my dear fellow, this is quite good enough for such *canaille* as you have here today." He talked much about poetry and the East, and he told one girl that the great thing in life was repose, that nothing repaid exertion; but she noticed that his temperament was such that not even a glorious old age could compensate him for obscurity in youth. Naturally he thought a good deal about marriage, and in a letter to his sister asked, "Would you like Lady Z—— for a sister-in-law, very clever, £25,000, and domestic? As for 'love,' all my friends who married for love and beauty either beat their wives or live apart from them. This is literally the case. I may commit many follies in life, but I never intend to mary for 'love,' which I am sure is a guarantee of infelicity." All the same he was quick to notice physical blemishes in those women who engrossed his attention. "Handsome, brilliant, and young," he thought Lady Lincoln, "but with one great fault, a rabbit mouth."

In the autumn of '33 he began a diary, which however only engaged him intermittently while resting at Bradenham after the whirl of the social season. A few phrases in this document are revealing: "I have passed the whole of the year in uninterrupted lounging and pleasure. . . . My life has not been a happy one. Nature has given me an awful ambition and fiery passions. . . . My disposition is now indolent. I wish to be idle and enjoy myself. . . . Alas! I struggle from Pride. Yes! It is Pride that now prompts me, not Ambition. They shall not say I have failed. . . . All men of high imagination are indolent. . . . I have an unerring instinct—I can read characters at a glance. . . . I am only truly great in action. If ever I am placed in a truly eminent position I shall prove this. I could rule the House of Commons, although there would be a great prejudice against me at first. . . . Imagination governs mankind." On another occasion he wrote, "I am never well save in action, and then I feel immortal. . . . Dyspepsia always makes me wish for a civil war."

Except for his father and Bulwer, he now derived little pleasure from conversing with men: "As I never get anything in return, I do not think the exertion necessary." But he entered into their sports to prove that he was as tough as they: "I hunted the other day with Sir Henry Smythe's hounds and although not in scarlet was the best mounted man in the field, riding Lady Smythe's Arabian mare, which I nearly killed; a run of thirty miles, and I stopped at nothing. I gained great kudos. The only Londoner I met with was Henry Manners Sutton. . . . He asked me to return with him; but as Lady Manners was not there, I saw no fun and refused." His fellow-sportsmen would have been surprised to learn that he was then engaged on a long narrative poem. He had "an unconquerable desire of producing something great and lasting," and when wandering over the plains of Troy had conceived the idea of a revolutionary epic which would do for the Napoleonic saga what Homer had done for the ancient Greeks. He envisaged a work of some thirty thousand lines, and his intention was to read a canto to the Austens, if alone, when he dined with them in January, '34. But Mrs. Austen no doubt felt that a treat of this sort should not be confined to the family, and asked a number of people to dinner. The poet was undeterred, and the curious figure, dressed in a fantastic style that did not harmonize with Miltonic blank verse, stood with his back to the fire and declaimed pages of stuff that had nothing in common with the *Odyssey* except length. After he had left the room, a humorous member of the party recited an impromptu parody, guying the manner and matter of the epicist, and sent everyone into fits of laughter. But ridicule, even had he heard of it, was not enough to dishearten a poet who longed to be the Homer, Virgil, Dante or Milton of his age; and the first three parts were soon submitted to the indulgence of readers, with a preface implying that there was a good deal more to come, but that as "I am not one who finds consolation for the neglect of my contemporaries in the imaginary plaudits of a more sympathetic posterity" the decision of the public would be final, and, if unfriendly, his lyre would be hurled into limbo without a pang. Readers were as apathetic as posterity has been, and he stopped the manufacture of verse for three years, when he corrected what he had written and might have completed the work if, happily, politics had not intervened. He wished to dedicate the first volume to the Duke of Wellington, but the man who had faced Napoleon's bombardment without blenching quailed at the prospect of reading Disraeli's pentameters, and politely refused his permission.

While the second and third books of the heroic poem were going through the press he made the acquaintance of Lady Blessington and was soon a constant visitor at her house in Seamore Place, where all the male celebrities of the day were to be met. It was commonly supposed that she and Count D'Orsay were lovers, though he had married her step-daughter in order to benefit from her late husband's estate, and she was therefore outlawed by the other famous hostesses of the day, and married men called on her without their wives. Michael Sadleir has suggested that D'Orsay was probably impotent; on the other hand, Samuel Rogers told Henry Crabb Robinson that D'Orsay kept one of the dancers at the Opera but dared not look at her in Lady Blessington's presence. Anyhow there was quite enough uncertainty about the whole affair, as well as her own past, to make Lady Blessington a theme for scandal; and the fact that she was beautiful and witty made her imaginary transgressions all the more unendurable, jealousy being the strongest incitement to moral indignation. A good example of her stingless wit was her remark to Walter Savage Landor, who was violently attacking the Psalms to the discomfort of a Roman Catholic fellow-guest: "Do write something better, Mr. Landor." This silenced him without leaving him resentful.

D'Orsay was the great dandy of the time and led the fashion in men's clothes; but as he was able to give the whole of his leisure to the subject he dressed with exceptional distinction and never appeared over-dressed or ostentatious, like Bulwer, Ainsworth, Dickens, above all Disraeli. In addition D'Orsay was a tall handsome man, with an athletic figure and a personality of great charm; and both he and Lady Blessington evoked the admiration and affection in equal degree of many remarkable people, in particular Dickens, Disraeli and Bulwer, the second of whom gives a pleasant portrait of D'Orsay as "Count Mirabel" in the first novel he wrote after entering the Blessington circle, *Henrietta Temple*, wherein the Count is described as "the best-dressed man in London, fresh and gay as a bird, with not a care on his sparkling visage, and his eyes bright with bonhomie. . . . Care he knew nothing about; Time he defied Indisposition he could not comprehend. He had never been ill in his life, even for five minutes. . . . There was something in Count Mirabel's very presence which put everybody in good spirits. His light-heartedness was caught by all. Melancholy was a farce in the presence of his smile; and there was no possible combination of scrapes that could withstand his kind and brilliant raillery." D'Orsay takes the hero of the novel for a drive, and we may feel sure that this is a personal reminiscence: "The

Count Mirabel enjoyed the drive to Richmond as if he had never been to Richmond in his life. The warm sun, the western breeze, every object he passed and that passed him called for his praise or observation. He inoculated Ferdinand with his gaiety, as Ferdinand listened to his light, lively tales, and his flying remarks, so full of merriment and poignant truth and daring fancy." They arrive at their destination, and we learn that "Count Mirabel, who has the finest tact in the world, but whose secret spell, after all, was perhaps only that he was always natural, adapted himself in a moment to the characters, the scene, and the occasion." Several of D'Orsay's remarks are recorded:

"If a man be convinced that existence is the greatest pleasure, his happiness may be increased by good fortune, but it will be essentially independent of it."

"Feel slightly, think little, never plan, never brood. Everything depends upon the circulation; take care of it. Take the world as you find it; enjoy everything. Vive la bagatelle!"

"Men were made to listen as well as talk," says Lady Bellair.

"Without doubt," replies the Count, "for Nature has given us two ears, but only one mouth."

From the accounts of certain fellow-guests, it seems that Disraeli used his ears more than his mouth at the Blessington dinner-parties, where he was habitually silent and observant, though when his interest was aroused he would hold the table with a burst of eloquence, enlivened with satire and sarcasm, displaying such a grasp of his subject and command of language that people thought him the most wonderful talker they had ever heard. He was asked everywhere and got to know everyone of importance, being as popular with Lady Durham, a leading Whig, as with Lord Lyndhurst, a leading Tory. "I have had great success in society this year in every respect," he informed his sister. "I make my way easily in the highest set, where there is no envy, malice, etc., and where they like to admire and be amused," and he asserted that he was as popular with first-rate men as he was hated by the second-rate. Water-parties up the Thames to Greenwich, fêtes, picnics, supper-parties, receptions, balls: he enjoyed them all, and basked in an atmosphere of admiration.

Also he had found a mistress, whose Christian name was Henrietta and who was a member of the set he moved in. Their intimacy in 1833 made that year the happiest of his life; and in the autumn of '34 he wrote in his diary: "What a happy or rather amusing society Henrietta and myself commanded this year. What delicious little suppers after the Opera!" Her husband had a title, which no doubt added to her attraction, but Disraeli loved her with ardor and separation from her made him feel ill and sad. On reaching Bradenham in August, '34, he confided to Lady

Blessington that he was "very ill indeed from the pangs of parting. Indeed, I feel as desolate as a ghost, and I do not think that I ever shall be able to settle to anything again. It is a great shame, when people are happy together, that they should be ever separated; but it seems the great object of all human legislation that people never should be happy together." Ten days later he declared himself "Quite at a loss how to manage affairs in future as I find separation more irksome than ever my bitterest imagination predicted." And he told Bulwer that all the barriers of his life seemed to be failing simultaneously. He found relief in writing, and began a love story. But he only finished one volume, his attention over the next two years being fully engaged by the social round, by politics, and especially by Henrietta herself, whose extravagance seems to have increased his debts until, his ardor waning and his ambition waxing, he determined to break the liaison, noting in his diary for the autumn of '36 that he had parted from her for ever. Then, with his love affair behind him and his load of debts before him, he completed the story; and *Henrietta Temple*, dedicated to D'Orsay, repeated the success of *Vivian Grey*.

One does not expect a picture of real life from a born politician, and *Henrietta Temple*, because it deals mainly with the emotion of love, is further from reality than any of Disraeli's stories except *Alroy*. Having already depicted himself as a great conqueror, thinker, writer, leader, he now sees himself as a great lover, out-Romeoing Romeo, his intensity of feeling ending in delirium, prostration, and almost annihilation. The woman he loves is of course the most glorious creature in the universe, whose beauty out-vies art; while he is the most sensitive and imaginative of creatures, who loves at first sight, overwhelmingly and for ever. Sentimentality and rhetoric result from the suppression of what a writer really feels in favor of what he would like to feel, and the emotionalism in *Henrietta Temple* is heightened to absurdity. This is how Disraeli liked to imagine himself as a lover: "An immortal flame burns in the breast of that man who adores and is adored. . . . The cares of the world do not touch him; its most stirring events are to him but the dusty incidents of bygone annals. All the fortune of the world without his mistress is misery and with her all its mischances a transient dream. Revolutions, earthquakes, the change of governments, the fall of empires, are to him but childish games, distasteful to a manly spirit. . . . Nothing can subdue him. He laughs alike at loss of fortune, loss of friends, loss of character. . . ." Such elevation of feeling must have a worthy setting; and though we are informed that love can irradiate a hovel and lighten the fetter of a slave, nevertheless "fortunate the passion that is breathed in palaces, amid the ennobling creations of surrounding art, and greets the object of it fond solicitude amid perfumed gardens, and in the shade of green and silent woods!" Disraeli's isolation in aristocratic society is suggested by the hero being a Roman Catholic, unemancipated at the period of the story, and his romantic view of that society is rather more than suggested by such comments as: "The young marquis was an excellent specimen of a class inferior in talents, intelligence, and accomplishments, in public spirit and in private virtues, to none in the world, the English nobility."

But even in such an over-fervid and unnatural romance the author's worldly sense occasionally breaks through, and we are reminded that he was suffering from duns when we come across the sentence: "As men advance in life, all passions resolve themselves into money. Love, ambition, even poetry, end in this."

Profile of a President

―――――・⌾・―――――

BENJAMIN P. THOMAS

1861–1865. Although there are many hundreds of books about Abraham Lincoln, a number of them distinguished and famous, the best-written, most concise, and most useful to nonspecialist readers is Benjamin P. Thomas's one-volume biography first published in 1952. Instead of selecting some episode about Lincoln the politician or Lincoln the commander-in-chief, I have chosen Mr. Thomas's account of the informal aspects of Lincoln's life in the White House, an account which reminds us once again of the humane, wise, and humorous character of our greatest President.

―――――・⌾・―――――

A President's life is wearying and worrisome at best, but in Lincoln's case all the vast problems of the war were added to the normal tasks of office. Nicolay and Hay comprised his secretarial staff until William O. Stoddard was brought in to assist them midway of the war. Edward D. Neill succeeded Stoddard when the latter became ill, and in turn was succeeded by Charles Philbrick. These young men scrutinized and questioned visitors, prepared a daily digest of news and military information, read and sorted the mail, and took care of whatever other details happened to call for attention. They had rooms at the White House, but walked to Willard's for their meals.

Lincoln started his work day early, for he was a light and fitful sleeper, and sometimes walked alone across the White House lawn in the gray dawn to summon a newsboy. By eight o'clock, when breakfast was announced, he had already been at work for an hour or more. His morning meal consisted of an egg and a cup of coffee; he was so little concerned about eating that Mrs. Lincoln sometimes invited guests to breakfast to make sure he would come. After breakfast he put in another hour of work before his door opened to visitors.

Except for the hot summer months, when they lived at the Soldiers' Home, the Lincoln family occupied the west wing of the second floor of the White House. The east wing was devoted to business. Lincoln's office was a large room on the south, next to Nicolay's office in the southeast corner. Its furnishings were simple—a large oak table covered with cloth, around which the cabinet met; another table between the two long windows, at which Lincoln usually wrote, seated in a large arm-chair; a tall desk with pigeonholes for papers against the south wall; a few straight-back chairs, and two plain, hair-covered sofas. A marble mantel surmounted the fireplace with its high brass fender and brass andirons. Glass-globed gas jets hung from the ceiling. The only wall adornments were an old discolored engraving of President Jackson above the mantel, a photograph of John Bright, the English liberal leader, and numerous military maps in wooden frames. One door opened into Nicolay's office and another into the hall, where a messenger sat to bring in the cards of visitors. A bell cord hung near the President's desk.

At first Lincoln refused to limit the visiting hours. "They do not want much," he said of the throng waiting to see him, "and they get very little. . . . I know how I would feel in their place." So people began coming before breakfast, and some still remained late at night. Lincoln realized at last that something must be done to conserve his time, and agreed to restrict the visiting-period from ten o'clock in the morning till three in the afternoon. But his other work continued to pile up, and the hours were again shortened, from ten till one.

Priority was granted to cabinet members, senators, and representatives in that order; finally, if any time remained, ordinary citizens were admitted. Army officers, many of whom had made nuisances of themselves with requests for promotion or demands for redress from supposed injustices, were forbidden to come to Washington without special permission.

Notwithstanding Lincoln's wish to keep himself accessible, it was not easy to see him. His friend Dr. Anson G. Henry, who was a house guest at the White House in February 1863, noted that "nine times out of ten not half the Senators get in unless several go in together & this is very often done, and they can take in with them as many of their friends and constituents as they please. It is no uncommon thing for Senators to try for ten days before they get a private interview."

Many persons, after waiting unsuccessfully for several days, went home and made their wishes known by letter. Joseph Medill, of the Chicago *Tribune*, wrote to Lincoln: "Not having either time or inclination to hang around waiting rooms among a wolfish crowd seeking admission to your presence for office or contracts or personal favors, I prefer stating in writing the substance of what I would say verbally."

With only Edward Moran, a short, thin, humorous Irishman, who had served since President Taylor's time, stationed at the front door, and Louis Bargdorf, another White House veteran, posted in the upstairs corridor, the throng enjoyed access to all the public rooms and trooped about unhindered. Lamon warned Lincoln that eavesdroppers and traitors lurked among the crowd, and suggested that Allan Pinkerton or some other shrewd detective be employed to ferret them out. At least everyone should be kept downstairs until his name was called, he thought. But not until November 1864 were four District of Columbia policemen in plain clothes detailed to the White House. A secretary gave each visitor a final scrutiny, but even so, unworthy persons often managed to intrude upon the President.

Once a visitor had passed the outer barriers and entered Lincoln's office, he encountered no further formality. The President never effused: "I am delighted to see you," unless he meant it; he simply said: "How do you do?" or "What can I do for you?" with a pleasant nod and smile. Lincoln wore no outward signs of greatness. He inspired no awe or embarrassment. He had no pomp, no wish to impress. But along with his awkward angularity he had an innate poise and casual unaffected dignity. Meeting all sorts of people, he shaped his response to their approach. He was lowly to the meek, dignified to the pompous, flippant or stern with the presumptuous, and courteous to everyone, even to his foes, when they came to him in good faith. He respected the views of others and listened while they talked, for he knew that in some matters they might see truth more clearly than he, and that men arrive at truth by free discussion. His usual attitude while listening was to cross his long legs and lean forward, hands clasped around his knees, or with one elbow on his knee to support his arm while he stroked his chin.

Samuel R. Suddarth, Quartermaster General of Kentucky, observed after an interview: "His conversational powers are fine—and his custom of interspersing conversation with incidents, anecdotes and witticisms are well calculated to impress his hearers with the kindheartedness of the man. And they are so adroitly and delicately mingled in the thread of his discourse that one hardly notices the digression. His language is good though not select. . . . He is dignified in his manners without austerity." Suddarth was one of very few persons who heard Lincoln use profanity; "He is a damned rascal," the President said of a certain politician, and then added hastily, as though surprised: "God knows I do not know when I have sworn before."

Nicolay always rejoiced when Congress adjourned. The members presented countless trivial demands that kept the President vexed and anxious and troubled him no end. Many private citizens were scarcely less considerate of Lincoln's time. "Going into his room this morning to announce the Secretary of War," Nicolay confided to his fiancée, "I found a little party of Quakers holding a prayer-meeting around him, and he was compelled to bear the affliction until the 'spirit' moved them to stop. Isn't it strange that so many and such intelligent people often have so little common sense?"

Nicolay and Hay noted that through all the stirring days of war Lincoln almost invariably remained assured and steady on the surface no matter how afflicted he might be within. One caller observed the same fund of anecdote in Lincoln, but not the old free, lingering laugh. Another remarked about "the two-fold working of the two-fold nature of the man: Lincoln the Westerner, slightly humorous but thoroughly practical and sagacious. . . . Lincoln the President and statesman . . . seen in those abstract and serious eyes, which seemed withdrawn to an inner sanctuary of thought, sitting in judgment on the scene and feeling its far reach into the future."

It always gave Lincoln pleasure to be able to grant a request. But the glibbest talkers could not back him down. He seldom gave an outright "No." He was more likely to make the necessity of saying it so obvious that refusal became unnecessary. Or he would turn the conversation with a story or a jest; when petitioners found themselves back in the hall, they wondered how he had got rid of them. Men of the strongest personalities felt Lincoln's quiet dominance. Thurlow Weed went home after a talk with him and wrote: "I do not, when with you, say half I intend, partly because I do not like to 'crank,' and partly because you talk me out of my convictions and apprehensions. So bear with me, please, now, till I free my mind."

Lincoln gave way to annoyance at times. "Now go away!" he told one visitor. "Go away! I cannot attend to all these details. I could as easily bail out the Potomac with a teaspoon!" He replied sharply to a lady who sent him a long, demanding letter that "the bare reading of a letter of that length requires more than any person's share of my time."

Usually, however, he kept his temper under tight control, "If I do get up a little temper," he wrote, "I have not sufficient time to keep it up." He refused to quarrel himself, and tried to keep others from quarreling. He wrote to Senator Pomeroy about a senatorial dispute over an appointment: "I wish you and Lane would make an effort to get out of the mood you are in—it gives you the means of tormenting my life out of me, and nothing else."

One time it became the President's duty to administer a rebuke to a young captain, James Madison Cutts, a brother-in-law of Stephen A. Douglas, who became involved in quarrels with brother officers. Evidently Lincoln drew up a memorandum of what he wished to say, for among his papers is a document which reads: "Although what I am now to say is to be, in form, a reprimand, it is not intended to add a pang to what you have already suffered upon the subject to which it relates. You have too much of life yet before you, and have shown too much of promise as an officer, for your future to be lightly surrendered. . . . The advice of a father to his son, 'Beware of entrance to a quarrel, but being in, bear it that the opposed may beware of thee,' is good, and yet not the best. Quarrel not at all. No man resolved to make the most of himself, can spare time for personal contention. Still less can he afford to take all the consequences, including the vitiating of his temper, and the loss of self-control."

Lincoln had come a long way in charity and self-discipline from the satirical young politician of 1842, who goaded an opponent to challenge him to a duel, when he could say in November 1864: "So long as I have been here I have not willingly planted a thorn in any man's bosom."

He owed not a little of this self-mastery to the irrepressible sense of humor that enabled him to recognize the ridiculous and to hold things in true perspective. In addition to quarreling, Captain Cutts also faced the charge of taking a valise or portmanteau from his room at the Burnet House, in Cincinnati, and "placing himself thereon" in a corridor to look through a transom at a lady while she undressed. In reprimanding Cutts, Lincoln referred to this offense as "not of great enormity, and yet greatly to be avoided," and one which he felt sure that Cutts would not repeat. But as he remitted Cutts's sentence of dismissal from the army, he commented privately to Hay that the young man should be elevated to the "peerage" with the title of Count Peeper—a cognomen suggested to him by the name of the Swedish Minister, Edward Count Piper.

With government officials and men of influence so often turned away from Lincoln's office, it is remarkable that so many humble people managed to get in. But if he learned that some anxious old lady or worried wife, or a young soldier in a private's uniform had been waiting patiently from day to day to see him, he would arrange an appointment and if necessary overstay his time to hear his story. His secretaries estimated that he spent at least three quarters of his time in meeting people, despite their efforts to shield him from annoyance. It was as though he tried to make himself the nation's burden-bearer; and when his door swung shut at last, he was often near exhaustion.

While these daily sessions wore on him physically, they refreshed his mind and spirit. Through them he measured the pulse-beat of the people and learned to key his actions to its changing throb, using caution when it slowed, moving boldly when he felt it quicken. He called them his "public opinion baths," but they were more than that, for they also enabled him to curb the undue harshness of subordinates, and to override bureaucratic arrogance and indifference.

Time and again, after listening to someone's woes, the President would send him to Stanton, Welles, Seward, or some other person in authority with a brief but precious missive: "Mr. Secretary, please see and hear this man"; "Please give this matter your immediate attention"; "Can this man be accommodated?" "Has the Sec. of the Navy any knowledge of this case? and if any, what?" "There is a mistake somewhere in this case. . . . Will the Secretary of War please have the matter corrected? or explain to me wherein the hitch is?" "Mr. Defrees—Please see this girl who works in your office, and find out about her brother, and come and tell me." To Surgeon General William A. Hammond, Lincoln wrote: "A Baltimore committee called on me this morning, saying that city is full of straggling soldiers, half-sick, half-well, who profess to have been turned from the hospitals with no definite directions where to go. Is this true? Are men turned from the hospitals without knowing where to go?"

An "influence peddler," who gave his name as Captain Parker, claimed to know Judge Advocate General Joseph Holt, and promised a Mrs. Anna S. King that for three hundred dollars he would obtain a pardon for her husband. It was all the money the poor woman had; and John Hay, when he heard her story, took her to the President. After listening to her, Lincoln telegraphed to General Meade: "An intelligent woman in deep distress called this morning, saying her husband, a Lieutenant in the A.P., was to be shot next morning for desertion." She had left without giving her name or that of her husband, but the President made sure that Meade would delay all executions, ran down the man's identity, and commuted his sentence to imprisonment. The doors of military prisons opened for untold numbers of repentant Confederates at the behest of Lincoln's terse endorsement: "Let this man take the oath and be discharged."

Times almost innumerable the President sent petitioners joyfully on their way to a department head with a brief but authoritative note: "Let this woman have her son out of Old Capital Prison"; "Attorney-General, please make out and send me a pardon in this case"; "Injustice has probably been done in this case, Sec. of War please examine it"; or a brief statement of a request followed by: "Let it be done." It would be difficult to estimate how many tired, scared, or homesick boys in the Union army who fell asleep on picket duty, ran away in battle, or slipped off without leave to visit wives or parents were spared from the death sentence by a terse telegram from Lincoln: "Suspend sentence of execution and forward record of trial for examination," or "Let him fight instead of being shot."

Lincoln's orders to Stanton often display sly humor. The crabbed Secretary must have snorted with disgust when he read Lincoln's order: "Please have the Adjutant General ascertain whether second Lieutenant of Company D, 2nd infantry, Alexander E. Drake, is entitled to promotion. His wife thinks he is. Please have this looked into." Stanton had learned that he could oppose the President up to a point; but to go beyond that point might bring him a rebuff such as: "I personally wish Jacob R. Freese, of New Jersey, to be appointed a colonel of a colored regiment— and this regardless of whether he can tell the exact shade of Julius Caesar's hair." On August 23, 1862, Lincoln wrote, either to Stanton or as a memorandum for himself: "Today, Mrs. Major Paul of the Regular Army calls and urges the appointment of her husband as Brig-Genl. She is a saucy woman and I am afraid she will keep tormenting me till I have to do it." Less than two weeks later, Major Gabriel R. Paul was commissioned a brigadier general.

Many of Lincoln's instructions were subtly philosophical. "This man wants to work," he wrote, "so uncommon a want that I think it ought to be gratified." His most commonplace writings bear the stamp of individuality. "You request my autograph. Well here it is"—or "here 'tis. A. Lincoln," he scribbled many times.

This sort of work filled Lincoln's mornings. At one o'clock, or sometime afterward, he made his way to the living-quarters through the still-crowded corridor. His passage gave the more intrusive callers an opportunity to intercept him, for his informal habits made him prone to stop and talk. In 1864 a door cut from his office gave direct access to the family apartment.

The visiting time ended early on Tuesdays and Fridays, when the cabinet met regularly at noon. On Mondays, when the President held a reception from one to two, he usually missed his lunch. This was of small concern to him, however, for he normally ate only a biscuit, with perhaps some fruit in season, and drank a glass of milk.

After lunch Lincoln might sprawl in a big armchair by the window in the family sitting-room to read for a few minutes, one leg crossed over the other and bouncing up and down as though to music. Corns bothered him—he wrote a testimonial for a Jewish chiropodist who also performed confidential missions for him: "Dr. Zacharie has operated on my feet with good success, and considerable addition to my comfort"—so he often slipped off his shoes and sat in his stocking feet, until Mrs. Lincoln noticed it and sent a servant for his slippers. Some time during the day a servant shaved his upper lip and trimmed his beard, and had been seen to shake the towel out the White House window.

Early afternoon found Lincoln again at work. With the expansion of the army, thousands of commissions must be signed; later these became less numerous, but in their place came batches of court-martial sentences, amounting to thirty thousand in a year, for him to modify or approve. Those involving the death penalty received his closest attention, but none escaped his notice. John Hay told of six hours spent in such work on a humid July day and noted how eagerly Lincoln seized on any possible excuse to save a soldier's life. Only cases of meanness or cruelty failed to evoke his sympathy. He was especially averse to approving the death penalty for cowardice—"leg cases" he called those in which a soldier ran away in battle—and as he remitted sentence he said wryly: "It would frighten the poor fellows too terribly to kill them."

But while his impulse was always toward forgiveness, he could be hard when military discipline called for sternness. In the case of five bounty-jumpers sentenced to death for desertion, he wrote to General Meade: "I understand these are very flagrant cases and that you deem their punishment as being indispensable to the service. If I am not mistaken in this, please let them know at once that their appeal is denied."

Some time during the morning the secretaries had sorted the mail. Correspondence arrived in torrents: resolutions and petitions written in copperplate scroll, letters carefully composed, and almost illegible scrawls. Threatening or abusive letters were usually tossed into the wastebasket. Those of a routine nature went to various departments. Only a relatively small number reached the President's desk, usually with a secretarial notation—"Personal," "Political," or a brief summary of their contents written on the back.

Even after careful sifting they made a formidable pile. Lincoln snatched what time he could to read them, but many suffered the same fate as that of Dr. Henry P. Tappan, chancellor of the University of Michigan. The well-meaning educator sent Lincoln fifteen pages of advice, routing his letter by way of David Davis to make sure Lincoln would read it. Davis endorsed it: "This letter is an elaborate one, written in good temper & from the Christian character of the author entitled to be read." But even such a testimonial was not enough: "Mr. Nicolay, please run over this and tell me what is in it."

* * *

The wartime afflictions of friends and acquaintances never failed to touch Lincoln deeply. When Lieutenant Colonel William McCullough, of Bloomington, met death in the Vicksburg campaign, Lincoln learned that one of McCullough's daughters had become inconsolable. And just before Christmas in 1862 a letter came to young Fanny McCullough from a busy President: "It is with deep grief that I learn of the death of your kind and brave Father; and especially, that it is affecting your young heart beyond what is common in such cases. In this sad world of ours, sorrow comes to all; and, to the young, it comes with bitterest agony, because it takes them unawares. The older have learned to ever expect it. I am anxious to afford some alleviation of your present distress. Perfect relief is not possible, except with time. You can not now realize that you will ever feel better. Is not this so? And yet it is a mistake. You are sure to be happy again. . . . The memory of your dear Father, instead of an agony, will yet be a sad sweet feeling in your heart, of a purer, and holier sort than you have known before."

With his own son Willie not long dead, Lincoln understood the feelings of Congressman William Kellog when his son resigned from West Point under demerit that would have led to his dismissal. Lincoln defied the rules of the Academy and reappointed young Kellog. The case came upon him in the most painful manner, he explained: "Hon. William Kellog, the father, is not only a member of Congress from my state, but he is my personal friend of more than twenty years' standing, and of whom I had many personal kindnesses. This matter touches him very deeply— the feelings of a father for a child—as he thinks, all the future of his child. I can not be the instrument to crush his heart."

Lincoln's deep human sympathy reached beyond his acquaintances and made him kin to all. "I have been shown in the files of the war department," he wrote to Lydia Bixby, a Boston widow, "a statement of the Adjutant General of Massachusetts that you are the mother of five sons who have died gloriously on the field of battle. I feel how weak and fruitless must be any word of mine which should attempt to beguile you from the grief of a loss so overwhelming. But I cannot refrain from tendering to you the consolation that may be found in the thanks of the republic they died to save. I pray that our heavenly Father may assuage the anguish of your bereavement, and leave you only the cherished memory of the loved and lost, and the solemn pride that must be yours to have laid so costly a sacrifice upon the altar of freedom."

Lincoln had been misinformed: Mrs. Bixby had only two sons killed; of the other three, two deserted and one was honorably discharged. But that he wrote under a misconception detracts in no wise from the nobility of his motives, nor from the beauty of his tribute to democratic motherhood.

* * *

The Lincolns dined at six o'clock, unless a state function had been planned, and again the President ate sparingly of one or two courses. Military uniforms sometimes lent splendor to the White House dining-room. The artist Carpenter remembered a dinner attended by twelve officers; another time two generals and two colonels, captured at Bull Run and Seven Pines and recently exchanged, were honored guests. There was a splendid dinner for Prince Napoleon Jerome Bonaparte, when he visited the United States during the summer of 1861, and another for officers of the Russian navy in 1863. Grant, Meade, and other officers were dinner guests soon after Grant's appointment as commander in chief.

A memorandum furnished by the State Department for the President's social guidance decreed that state dinners should begin at seven thirty o'clock. Correct dress for gentlemen was a black dress coat or one of blue with bright buttons—one should never wear a frock coat. Protocol determined those officials who must be invited to various functions, and the proper seating arrangement. The Lincolns followed the custom of serving wine at official dinners.

Once a week, except in summer, the President held an evening reception or levee. People came by thousands to shake his hand and perhaps steal an opportunity to ask a favor of him. Mrs. Lincoln offered a striking contrast to her husband as she stood beside him elegantly gowned, with a sprig or wreath of flowers in her carefully dressed hair, and jewels at her wrists and throat; for while she saw to it that he wore good clothes and kept them brushed and pressed, they never seemed to hang right on his tall, stooped frame. The white gloves that were the fashion at receptions made his big hands look enormous; once when his glove burst with a loud pop under an especially strong handclasp, he held it up ruefully and laughed.

Carpenter thought these functions must be a torment to the careworn President. But whenever anyone tried to sympathize with Lincoln, he would parry with a jest, and remark that the tug at his hand was much easier to bear than the pull upon his heartstrings when people asked him for favors that were beyond his power to grant. As the artist bade him good-night, Lincoln asked in his homely way: "Well, Carpenter, you have seen one day's run—what is your opinion of it?"

Most evenings when no formal function had been planned, found

Lincoln back at his desk. Nicolay wrote that it was "impossible to portray by any adequate words, the labor, the thought, the responsibility, the strain of intellect and the anguish of soul" that he endured. Carpenter came into Lincoln's office at eleven o'clock one night and found him seated alone at his long table with a pile of military commissions before him. They were made of heavy, oily parchment, very hard to handle or sign, but he went about his labor with patient industry. "I do not, as you see, pretend to read over these documents," he said to Carpenter as the artist sat down beside him. "I see that Stanton has signed them so I conclude they are alright." He paused to read one. "John Williams is hereby appointed adjutant-general with the rank of captain, etc. E. M. Stanton, Secretary of War." "There," he said, adding his own signature, "That fixes him out." He went on chatting and writing till he reached the bottom of the stack. Then rising and stretching his long arms above his head, he remarked: "Well, I have that job *husked out*; now I guess I'll go over to the War Department before I go to bed and see if there is any news."

A visit to the War Department telegraph office was usually his last chore. The operators left copies of all military telegrams in a pile in a desk drawer for him, with the last dispatch on top. They noticed that as he read them he sat far forward on the edge of his chair with one knee almost touching the floor. When he had worked through the pile to the message he had read before, he put all of them back and said: "Well, I have got down to the raisins."

The curiosity of the young operators got the better of them at last, and one of them asked the President what he meant by that remark. He told them he had known a little girl back home who once gorged herself with a stupendous meal of soup, chicken, ham, salad, potatoes and sundry other vegetables, ice cream and cake, and at last a handful of raisins. Things began coming up; and after she had been busily occupied for some time, she looked at her mother and said reassuringly: "I am all right now. I have got down to the raisins."

Lincoln usually read a little before he went to bed. The telegraph operators noticed that he often carried a worn copy of *Macbeth* or *The Merry Wives of Windsor* under his arm when he made his last visit to their office. And John Hay told how at midnight, when he sat writing in his diary, the President came into the office laughing to read him and Nicolay a funny story by Thomas Hood, "seemingly utterly unconscious that he with his short shirt hanging about his long legs, and setting out behind like the tail feathers of an enormous ostrich, was infinitely funnier than anything in the book he was laughing at."

"What a man it is!" thought Hay. "Occupied all day with matters of vast moment, deeply anxious about the fate of the greatest army in the world, with his own plans and future hanging on the events of the passing hour, he yet has such a wealth of simple *bon hommie* and good fellowship that he gets out of bed and perambulates the house in his shirt to find us that we may share with him the fun of poor Hood's queer little conceits."

Mrs. Lincoln's days were busy, too. "I consider myself fortunate," she wrote to Mrs. James C. Conkling, "if at eleven o'clock, I once more find myself, in my pleasant room & very especially, if my tired & weary husband, is *there*, resting in the lounge to receive me—to chat over the occurrences of the day."

Occasionally in the evening Lincoln listened to music in the White House drawing-room. The massive Lamon had a deep, rich voice, and Lincoln loved to hear him sing. One of his special favorites was *The Blue-Tailed Fly*, and Lamon recalled how "he often called for that buzzing ballad when we were alone and he wanted to throw off the weight of public or private cares. . . . But while he had a great fondness for witty or mirth-provoking ballads, our grand old patriotic airs and songs of the tender and sentimental kind afforded him the deepest pleasure." The simple melodies of Stephen Foster never failed to move him deeply.

Lincoln enjoyed the Marine Band; it played twice weekly during the summer months on the south lawn of the White House. But the President was more of an attraction than the musicians, and Carpenter recalled how, when he appeared on the portico, the crowd loudly applauded and called for a speech. Lincoln bowed his thanks, stepped back into the parlor, and slumped down on a sofa. "I wish they would let me sit out there quietly, and enjoy the music," he said wistfully.

Henry C. Whitney, who had traveled the circuit with Lincoln, remembered how he often went alone to any sort of little show or concert and even slipped away one time to attend a magic-lantern show intended for children. Residence in Washington gave him his first chance to hear opera. He became very fond of it, as well as concert music, and as the war took a turn for the better, he attended the theatre, opera, or concerts whenever he could, usually with Mrs. Lincoln or a party of friends. Among the operas that he heard were Gounod's *Faust*, Verdi's *Ballo in Maschera* and Boïeldieu's *La Dame Blanche*. John W. Forney, of the Philadelphia *Press*, recalled an evening at the opera during which the President sat in a corner of his box the entire time, wrapped in a shawl, "either enjoying the music or communing with himself." A vicious battle was raging and Lincoln remarked afterward that he supposed some people would think it indiscreet of him to seek amusement at such a time. "But the truth is," he declared, "I must have a change of some sort or die."

Marshal Lamon never ceased worrying when Lincoln went to public functions without guards. On December 15, 1864, he wrote to Nicolay from New York that he had good reason to fear for the President's safety —"See that he don't go out alone either in the day or night time." Soon afterward, when Lamon made his customary inspection of the White House and found that the President had gone out, he left a note of warning on his desk: "Tonight, as you have done on several previous occasions, you went unattended to the theater. When I say unattended, I mean you went alone with Charles Sumner and a foreign minister, neither of whom could defend himself against an assault from any able-bodied woman in the city."

Valley of Dry Bones

BRUCE CATTON

1863. Gettysburg is the most famous battle in American history; but its immediate aftermath is much less well known than the events of the battle itself. What happened to the survivors, the wounded, and the dead, and the significance of the great slaughter, is described here by the most distinguished historian of the Civil War. No American writer has demonstrated better than Mr. Catton that history is a creative literary art as well as a scholarly discipline.

One day they would make a park there, with neat lawns and smooth black roadways, and there would be marble statues and bronze plaques to tell the story in bloodless prose. Silent cannon would rest behind grassy embankments, their wheels bolted down to concrete foundations, their malevolence wholly gone, and here and there birds would nest in their muzzles. In the museums and tourist-bait trinket shops old bullets and broken buckles and twisted bayonets would repose under glass, with a rusty musket or so on the wall and little illustrated booklets lying on top of the counter. There would be neat brick and timber cabins on the hillsides, and people would sleep soundly in houses built where the armies had stormed and cried at each other, as if to prove that men killed in battle send forth no restless ghosts to plague comfortable citizens at night. The town and the woods and the ridges and hills would become a national shrine, filled with romantic memories which are in themselves a kind of forgetting, and visitors would stand by the clump of trees and look off to the west and see nothing but the rolling fields and the quiet groves and the great blue bank of the mountains.

But first there would have to be a great deal of tidying up.

The day after the battle began muggy and cloudy, and there was a tremendous rainstorm. (There always seemed to be a great rain after a hard battle in that war, and men believed that something in the firing of many guns brought rain clouds and jarred the moisture out of them.) The long line of rebel cannon along the Emmitsburg road had been pulled back, and when Slocum and Howard sent scouting parties out to the north and east of town they found no rebels except wounded men and a few stragglers. On Seminary Ridge the Confederates were still in evidence, and for a time Meade appears to have been uncertain whether the battle was really over.

But the Confederate Army had had enough. It had lost 25,000 men, artillery ammunition was nearly exhausted, supplies were low, and Lee was holding his line on Seminary Ridge merely to let his trains and his advance guard get a decent start on the long roads back to Virginia. A wagon train seventeen miles long, loaded with wounded men, crawled over the mountain road toward Chambersburg. It was a nightmarish procession of pain. A great many of the wounded men had received no medical attention whatever, the almost springless wagons rolled and jolted over the uneven road, and no halts were permitted for any reason. The cavalry officer in charge of the train said that he learned more on that trip about the horrors of war than he had learned in all of his battles.

As the signs of a Confederate retreat multiplied, Meade worked the VI Corps forward to take up the pursuit, but he was in no hurry about it. If the rebels wanted to go back to Virginia, it seemed like a good idea to wish them Godspeed and let them go.

Meade was able to see some things very clearly. He knew that the victory had been brutally hard on his army, and above all things he was determined not to do anything that might create any risks. A quick checkup after the battle showed him that he had no more than 51,000 men armed and equipped and present for duty. This total was approximately 38,000 below the number he had had just before the battle. Casualties had been about 23,000, so it was evident that the impact of battle had jarred fully 15,000 uninjured men loose from the ranks. They would be back later, but for the moment they were lost, and the army was

not half as large as it had been when Hooker took it down to the Rappa-
hannock fords two months earlier. The I Corps was hardly as big as an
ordinary division, and the III Corps was not a great deal better off.
(Both of these famous corps were mortally hurt, as it turned out; in the
army reorganization of the following winter they were broken up and
their survivors were transferred to other units.) The II Corps had lost
more than a third of its men, and its best generals, Hancock and Gibbon,
would be out for months. The XI Corps had suffered nearly as much and
in addition had had another blow to its reputation and morale, with the
rest of the army making caustic remarks about its wild flight through
the town, the astounding number of prisoners it had lost, and its inability
to keep the rebels out of the guns on Cemetery Hill on the evening of
July 2. Some of the army's finest combat units had been all but destroyed—
the Iron Brigade, the 5th New Hampshire, the 1st Minnesota, the 2nd
Massachusetts, and the 16th Maine, among others—and artillery losses
had been so severe that Hunt had to consolidate some of his best batteries.
Three of the seven army corps were under temporary commanders.

Of all these things Meade was acutely aware. The old habit of caution
was strong at army headquarters, and another heritage from the Mc-
Clellan era was cropping out just now: Meade somehow had been
persuaded that the rebel army in this campaign was larger than his own.
So he waited where he was, ignoring the clear signs that he was in the
presence of a badly beaten enemy, and he moved his patrols forward
very carefully.

The soldiers themselves had no doubt about how the battle had come
out. On the afternoon of July 3 they had seen something they had never
seen before—the principal attacking column of the Army of Northern
Virginia running in desperate disordered fragments back to its lines after
a smashing repulse—and some of the men on Cemetery Ridge had stood
up exultantly and cried "Fredericksburg!" as they watched. As they went
forward through the town and down the Emmitsburg road they were
dazed by the human wreckage they saw. Toward the left, where for a
time nothing but artillery had beaten back the rebel attack, they found
bodies dreadfully broken and dismembered. An officer who went over
that part of the ground wrote that on no other field had he seen such
appalling numbers of dead. In places where the infantry fire had been
especially intense the dead men lay in great rows, and in the twilight it
seemed as if whole brigades had made their bivouac there and had gone
to sleep. On the ground covered by Pickett's charge one officer wrote that
"I saw men, horses, and material in some places piled up together, which
is something seldom seen unless in pictures of battles, and the appearance
of the field with these mounds of dead men and horses, and very many

bodies lying in every position singly, was terrible, especially as the night lent a somber hue to everything the eye rested on."

A fearful odor of decay lay over the field. A cavalry patrol went through Gettysburg to scout the Cashtown road to the west, and as it came out by the fields where dead bodies had been lying in the heat for four days the cavalrymen sickened and vomited as they rode. The country here was the ultimate abomination of desolation: "As far as the eye could reach on both sides of the Cashtown road you see blue-coated boys swollen up to look as giants, quite black in the face, but nearly all on their backs, looking into the clear blue with open eyes, with their clothes torn open. It is strange that dying men tear their clothes in this manner You see them lying in platoons of infantry with officers and arms exactly as they stood or ran—artillery men with caisson blown up and four horses, each in position, dead. You meet also limbs and fragments of men. The road is strewn with dead, whom the rebels have half buried and whom the heavy rain has uncovered."

Here and there by the road the cavalrymen met oddly embattled farmers, armed with pitchforks and flails, who had rounded up small batches of rebel stragglers and wanted to turn them over to the authorities. These farmers, it appeared, were moved not so much by patriotic fervor as by old-fashioned rage. In their retreat the Confederates had left the roads and had marched across the fields, trampling down the ripening wheat and rye in great swaths, and if the farmers could not have justice, they at least wanted to see the destroyers locked up.

The town of Gettysburg looked as if some universal moving day had been interrupted by catastrophe. Streets were barricaded up to window levels with everything that would serve—wagons, rocking chairs, bureaus, stoves, fence rails, old lumber, and piles of rocks—and there were scars from cannon balls and bullets. In row houses facing Cemetery Hill the rebel sharpshooters had found vantage points in second-floor rooms, and they had knocked out walls between houses to provide for communication along their line. One civilian had been killed—a girl named Jennie Wade, shot down by a stray bullet while she baked bread in her kitchen. When she died she had in her pocket a picture of her fiancé, Corporal Johnson Skelley of the 87th Pennsylvania, and she never knew that two weeks earlier Corporal Skelley had been mortally wounded in the fighting around Winchester, Virginia.

Details were at work all over the field, collecting the last of the helpless wounded and burying the dead. The last was an almost impossible job, since more than five thousand men had been killed in action. Federals who were buried by men of their own regiments were given little wooden markers, with the name and regimental identification carved with a jacknife or scrawled with pencil, but in hundreds and hundreds of cases no identification was possible and the men went into the ground as "unknown." Long wide trenches were dug and the men were laid in them side by side, and sometimes there was nothing more in the way of a gravestone than a little headboard at one end of the trench stating the number of bodies that were buried in it. In places the burial details just gave up and did not try to make graves, but simply shoveled earth over the bodies as they lay on the ground.

There was an immense harvest of discarded weapons to be picked up. As a first step the men attached bayonets to the rifles which lay on the field and stuck them in the ground for collection later, and along Cemetery Ridge there were whole acres of these, "standing as thick as trees in the nursery." Ordnance officers who took charge of these weapons noticed an oddity. Out of more than thirty-seven thousand muskets which had been left on the field, nearly a third were loaded with more than one cartridge. In the excitement of battle men forgot to fix percussion caps, sometimes even forgot to pull the trigger, and reloaded automatically without realizing that they had not fired. One man remarked briefly that "not all the forces attacking or attacked are fully conscious of what they are doing," and veterans were free to admit that in this as in all other battles there had been a great deal of wild, ineffective shooting. Whole regiments at times fired volleys with the line of muskets pointing vaguely toward the sky at an angle from the vertical no more than forty-five degrees, and men were often seen to fire with both eyes tightly shut. An Ohio soldier in the XII Corps reflected that in the Culp's Hill fighting on the morning of July 3 every man in the corps had fired 250 rounds, and he mused that "the mystery exists how any rebels escaped."

It was a rough war for wounded men. Immense field hospitals had been established in the low ground east of the Baltimore Pike, by Rock Creek, and the heavy rains of July 4 flooded this ground, and some of the helpless wounded men were drowned. An attempt was made to get some of the less seriously wounded over to the railroad, where they could be sent back to established hospitals in Baltimore, York, and Harrisburg, but Stuart's cavalry had broken the railroad and for a few days no trains were running. The wounded lay where they had been dropped, unsheltered on the bare ground, and the best that the army's medical inspector was able to report was that within a few days they were "made as comfortable as circumstances would permit," although it was admitted that things would have been better if the Medical Corps had been able to get straw for the men to lie on.

The wounded men were not much given to complaining. A man in the Corn Exchange Regiment saw an amputee sitting outside a hospital tent, perky enough, considering that he had but one leg, playing cards with a wounded comrade. An orderly passed by hauling a hideous load of amputated arms and legs from the operating tent, and the one-legged man looked up with interest, laid down his cards, and asked the orderly to stop and let him inspect the haul. He wanted to take one more look at his lost leg, he said, and he would be able to recognize it because of a certain bunion. The orderly had no intention whatever of shuffling through his ghastly cargo, and he rebuked the soldier and told him that if he believed in the resurrection of the body as a good Christian should, he could wait for the Last Day and take a good look at his missing limb then. The cardplayer agreed that that made sense and went on with his game.

Slowly, and with immense effort, this shot-to-pieces army pulled itself together and took to the road. The VI Corps was out in front, and it had suffered little in the battle and had rested from its prodigious twenty-four-hour hike, but Meade was still cautious and John Sedgwick was equally so, and the pursuit was not pressed. Pulling the army out of Gettysburg was like pulling a shod foot out of deep mud—something to be done slowly and carefully, with infinite pains—and the air of urgency was gone. Colonel Chamberlain of the battle-bruised 20th Maine looked back at his regiment's final bivouac and reported: "We returned to Little Round Top, where we buried our dead in the place where we had laid them during the fight, marking each grave by a headboard made of ammunition boxes, with each soldier's name cut upon it. We also buried fifty of the enemy's dead in front of our position of July 2. We then looked after our wounded, whom I had taken the responsibility of putting into the houses of citizens in the vicinity of Little Round Top, and on the morning of the fifth took up our march on the Emmitsburg road."

The Emmitsburg road had been the last long mile for many men— for handsome John Reynolds riding to meet an unknown Southern sharpshooter in a family barn, for the black-hatted Western regiments with their fife-and-drum corps playing them into battle for many unheard-of men who stepped off it into unmarked graves on slanting ricky fields—and for a few days it had been a famous military highway, pumping a stream of troops off to the unfathomable chances of war. Now it would be a quiet country road again, with a farmer's load of hay or drove of cattle as its most exciting wayfarers, the mountain wall to the west dropping long shadows across it in the blue summer evenings, the dust and the clamor and the rumbling guns gone forever. It was over at last, this enormous battle with its smoke and its grimness and its unheard-of violence, and here again was a simple road leading from one country town to another, with a commonplace little name that would ring and shine in the books forever.

Meade was on the road with his troops, an infinitely weary man with dust on his uniform and his gray beard, feeling responsibility as a paralyzing weight. He had been one of the few men who could have lost the war irretrievably in one day, and he had managed to avoid the mistakes that would have lost it. He would continue to avoid mistakes, even if he had to miss opportunity. Lee's army was at bay on the northern bank of the Potomac, the river too high for fording and all bridges gone, and there might still be a chance to sweep down on him, to force him to battle again and to destroy him and his army and the star-crossed, legendary cause which they represented in one last, blazing, triumphant assault. But it was a chance and no more than that. Meade could see all the things that might go wrong with it: could see the Potomac, moreover, as a border between two countries, so that the important thing just now might be to get the Southern army across that border back into the land where it belonged. Meade brought his army up to the river very slowly. Nevertheless, when he found that the rebels were still there, well dug in on a great crescent of rising ground not many miles from the old Antietam battlefield, he put his own men into line of battle and took them carefully forward.

It was more than a week after Gettysburg by now, and some of the army's temporary losses had been made good. The army rolled forward on a front six miles wide, battle flags snapping in the wind, sunlight glittering from thousands of bright muskets, guns clanking along ready to go into battery on command. A soldier who marched with it was struck with the picture: "Throughout the miles of deep lines it presented a beautiful sight as with the swinging cadenced step of veterans they moved over cultivated fields of grain, over roads, orchards, and vineyards, on plain, valley, and hill. Obstructions were leveled by the pioneers in advance, and regardless of damage the army of blue swept over the ground with heavy tread, leaving in their rear destruction and desolation."

The long blue line halted and skirmishers were sent out in front to guard against rebel surprises, and that night there was a heavy rain and the army entrenched, while Meade summoned his corps commanders to determine whether the army should attack or not. The corps commanders were decidedly against it, and the army waited for a day. On July 14 Meade put it in motion again, having quietly concluded that he would try to do what his lieutenants had advised him not to do. But now it was too late. The Army of Northern Virginia had gone south of the river at last, leaving a small rear guard for a delaying action. Meade's cavalry and infantry picked up some rebel wounded and stragglers, killed the General Pettigrew who had commanded the left wing of Pickett's great assault, and captured a gun or two. That was all. If the war was ever to be won, it would have to be won later—and somewhere else.

All of which was to the infinite displeasure of Abraham Lincoln.

The President had learned a great deal about the military art since those early amateurish days when he had decreed that all Union armies should advance willy-nilly on Washington's birthday and had juggled troops frantically back and forth from McClellan's army to the Shenandoah Valley in a vain effort to catch Stonewall Jackson by telegraphic order. It could even be argued now that he was as canny a strategist as the North possessed, and he had followed the army's slow progress down from Gettysburg in an agony of impatience. He still saw things as he had seen them three weeks earlier, when the governor of New Jersey had asked him to reinstate McClellan: Lee's advance into Pennsylvania had been an opportunity for the Federals, not for the Confederates; if the affair were handled right neither Lee nor his army should ever get back to Virginia; and all of this talk about "driving the enemy from our soil" struck him as deplorable blindness. Vicksburg had fallen and the back door to the Confederacy lay open; one more blow and it would all be over. The war could be won, once and forever, between Pennsylvania and the Potomac River, in this month of July 1863, if someone really set out to win it.

The flaming driving spirit of war, which could find no congenial home anywhere among the top commanders of the Army of the Potomac, had actually found its place at last in the mysterious heart of that melancholy, quizzical civilian, the President of the United States, the man who had confessed that he could not so much as kill a chicken for Sunday dinner without wincing at the sight of bloodshed. Lincoln wrote a harsh letter to Meade, crying in effect: *Why* couldn't you, just this once, go in and smash things and let me worry about picking up the pieces? He wrote it, and then characteristically he did not send it, letting it gather dust in a White House pigeonhole.

Halleck warned Meade that the President was dissatisfied, and Meade, worn to a frazzle, with a temper that was never stable, flared back that in that case, since he had done his level best, he would like to be relieved of his command. Halleck soothed him with a friendly, appreciative letter, and Lincoln in turn swallowed his vexation and decided to be grateful for what had been won. And the army crossed the river, marched south, and made a stab at trying to pen Lee's army up in the Shenandoah Valley. The III Corps had the advance, and the corps was now commanded by bumbling, red-faced General H. W. French, who mishandled his troops so flagrantly that Hooker's and Kearny's veterans sardonically referred to their outfit as "the III Corps as we understand it." The chance was missed and the Confederates got away and the Army of the Potomac went down to the Rapidan country and went into camp, to rest and refit before taking up the fight again.

So there would be a new campaign, with other campaigns to follow, and in due time the great gloomy Wilderness around Chancellorsville would know gunfire again, and the wild tumult of battle, and the screams of wounded men trapped in burning thickets. It would be the hard fate of this army to fight dreadful battles without glory and without triumph, using itself up so that the victory might be won by other armies on other fields. The army would be ready for it, but it would be a different army henceforth. The ranks were thinner and there was a new name on the regimental flags, and the men were wiser than they had been before. They were beginning to realize that while a great thing had been done they had really done it themselves. Meade was "old Four-Eyes," a general who had won his battle chiefly because his men were incomparably good soldiers. They had fought at Gettysburg with the highest pitch of inspiration, but the inspiration had come from within themselves and had not been fired by anyone at the top, and the staff officers who had felt obliged to hearten the men by spreading the McClellan rumor had simply shown that they themselves did not know what the men were really like. The army was a military instrument at last, and it could be used to the last measure of its own inexpressible devotion, but from now on it would display enthusiasm for no generals.

A few days after Gettysburg Meade issued a general order congratulating his troops on their victory, and the order was read in all the regiments at evening parade. The men were very matter-of-fact as they listened. In one regiment the colonel waved his hat and called for three cheers for General Meade, but the cheers were not forthcoming—not, as one of the men explained, because the men disliked Meade, but simply because they did not feel like cheering any more. These soldiers, he pointed out, "with their lights and experiences, could not see the wisdom or the occasion for any such manifestations of enthusiasm"; the army had matured, "its business sense increased with age," and hereafter it would wait and see before it tossed its caps in the air.

It would wait and see, and there would still be a great deal to look at, for half the price had not yet been paid. Yet the biggest test had been passed. Meade might draw no cheers, but in his own way he had not done badly. At Gettysburg, for the first time, the Army of the Potomac had not been crippled by the mistakes of its commanding general. It had been given a chance, and the chance had been enough. At that crisis of the war everything had come down to the naked fury of the fighting men, and the fighting men had stood up under it—along Willoughby Run and Seminary Ridge, amid the rocks and bushes of Little Round Top, on the slopes back of the peach orchard and the wheat field, in the smoky twilight around Culp's Hill and the cemetery, and in the dust of the terrible pounding near the little clump of trees. They had won a victory.

It might be less of a victory than Mr. Lincoln had hoped for, but it was nevertheless a victory—and, because of it, it was no longer possible for the Confederacy to win the war. The North might still lose it, to be sure, if the soldiers or the people should lose heart, but outright defeat was no longer in the cards. Both the army and the country were in shape to win at last, and from now on it would be a question of courage and endurance.

If the army was not especially enthusiastic, no more was Meade. He was crabbed and dyspeptic, a regular-army officer who had never cared much for the volunteer system, and less than a year ago he had remarked that most of the men in the army had not the faintest idea of what soldiering really meant. But he paid his tribute, just the same, in one sentence of a letter which he wrote to Mrs. Meade two days after the battle: "The men behaved splendidly; I really think they are becoming soldiers."